The Chatto Book of
CATS

The Chatto Book of
CATS

Edited, with an Introduction, by
FRANCIS WHEEN

Illustrated by
JOHN O'CONNOR

Chatto & Windus
LONDON

First published 1993

1 3 5 7 9 10 8 6 4 2

Introduction and selection © Francis Wheen 1993

Francis Wheen has asserted his right under
the Copyright, Designs and Patents Act, 1988
to be identified as the editor of this work

First published in the United Kingdom in 1993 by
Chatto & Windus Ltd
Random House, 20 Vauxhall Bridge Road,
London SW1V 2SA

Random House Australia (Pty) Limited
20 Alfred Street, Milsons Point, Sydney,
New South Wales 2061, Australia

Random House New Zealand Limited
18 Poland Road, Glenfield,
Auckland 10, New Zealand

Random House South Africa (Pty) Limited
PO Box 337, Bergvlei, South Africa

Random House UK Limited Reg. No. 954009

A CIP catalogue record for this book
is available from the British Library

ISBN 0 7011 4005 4

Typography by Humphrey Stone
Photoset by SX Composing Ltd, Rayleigh, Essex
Printed in Great Britain by Clays Ltd, St. Ives plc

Contents

Introduction

Look at the constellations in the night sky: the Swan, the Eagle, the Ram, the Crow, the Fox, the Bull, the Hare, the Lizard, the Great and Little Bear, the Great and Little Dog, the Whale, the Crab, the Giraffe; but, unless you count Leo, no Cat. Why, Voltaire once asked, should we interest ourselves in an animal which does not have a sign of the zodiac named after it?

Yet the household cat is more magical than any giraffe or eagle. No other animal inspires such reverence and dread. Worshipped as a god, persecuted as an agent of the devil, it has preserved its mystery even after centuries of domestication. Superstitions about cats could fill a book on their own.

Nor has any other pet so tenaciously guarded its independence. The tabby asleep on an armchair by the fire will also stalk mice and birds as if its life depended on the kill. The purring creature which leaps companionably into one's lap may, moments later, retreat into aloofness – which is why, I like to think, dictators fear and dislike cats. Napoleon and Hitler certainly did; and, as a passage in this book reveals, so did the late Nicolae Ceauşescu. There are exceptions, of course (Mussolini was sound on the subject, as most Italians are), but one can see why the cat has been represented as an emblem of freedom ever since Tiberius Gracchus built his temple to the Goddess of Liberty in the second century BC. Even the humblest suburban moggy is unbiddable.

There are, God knows, plenty of cat anthologies already. Most, however, are one-dimensional collections of stories or poems proclaiming the message that we all love dear little pussy. If only that were true; the existence of the Cats' Protection League suggests otherwise. My approach has been different. While paying homage to the dignity and beauty of cats, I have also sought to reflect the suffering they have endured from those who hate them. My sources are various – essays and novels, poems and press cuttings, ancient and modern. There are surprising juxtapositions and eerie echoes.

As with the art form known as *découpage*, this patchwork should, taken as a whole, reveal a picture that is greater than the sum of its parts. Hence the brevity of this introduction: my own feelings about cats will, I hope, be implicitly apparent from the order and selection of the passages that follow.

I am grateful to everyone who has proposed items for inclusion in this anthology, particularly Joan Smith, Christopher Hawtree, Neil Philip, Emma Bradford, Ian Irvine, Katherine Duncan-Jones, Robert Posner, Marta Molnar, Lee Chester, Christopher Silvester, Susan Campbell, Craig Brown, John Naughton and Julia Thorogood. I have had much useful help from my agent, Pat Kavanagh, and from Jenny Uglow, Carmen Callil and Jonathan Burnham of Chatto & Windus. I must also thank the staff of two unimprovable institutions, the London Library and the Bodleian Library. But my greatest debt of gratitude is to the three beloved cats who were with me for most of the time while I was working on the book – Sidney, Bertie and Lettice.

One

KITTENHOOD

'The Kitten'

Wanton droll, whose harmless play
Beguiles the rustic's closing day,
When, drawn the evening fire about,
Sit aged crone and thoughtless lout,
And child upon his three-foot stool,
Waiting until his supper cool,
And maid, whose cheek outblooms the rose,
As bright the blazing fagot glows,
Who, bending to the friendly light,
Plies her task with busy sleight;
Come, show thy tricks and sportive graces,
Thus circled round with merry faces!

   Backward coil'd and crouching low,
With glaring eyeballs watch thy foe,
The housewife's spindle whirling round,
Or thread or straw that on the ground
Its shadow throws, by urchin sly
Held out to lure thy roving eye;
Then stealing onward, fiercely spring
Upon the tempting faithless thing.
Now, wheeling round with bootless skill,
Thy bo-peep tail provokes thee still,
As still beyond thy curving side
Its jetty tip is seen to glide;
Till from thy centre starting far,
Thou sidelong veerst with rump in air
Erected stiff, and gait awry,
Like madam in her tantrums high;
Though ne'er a madam of them all,
Whose silken kirtle sweeps the hall,
More varied trick and whim displays
To catch the admiring stranger's gaze.

   Doth power in measured verses dwell,
All thy vagaries wild to tell?

Ah no! the start, the jet, the bound,
The giddy scamper round and round,
With leap and toss and high curvet,
And many a whirling somerset,
(Permitted by the modern muse
Expression technical to use)
These mock the deftest rhymester's skill,
But poor in art, though rich in will.

The featest tumbler, stage bedight,
To thee is but a clumsy wight,
Who every limb and sinew strains
To do what costs thee little pains;
For which, I trow, the gaping crowd
Requite him oft with plaudits loud.

But, stopp'd the while thy wanton play,
Applauses too thy pains repay:
For then, beneath some urchin's hand
With modest pride thou tak'st thy stand,
While many a stroke of kindness glides
Along thy back and tabby sides.
Dilated swells thy glossy fur,
And loudly croons thy busy purr,
As, timing well the equal sound,
Thy clutching feet bepat the ground,
And all their harmless claws disclose
Like prickles of an early rose,
While softly from thy whisker'd cheek
Thy half-closed eyes peer, mild and meek.

But not alone by cottage fire
Do rustics rude thy feats admire.
The learned sage, whose thoughts explore
The widest range of human lore,
Or with unfetter'd fancy fly
Through airy heights of poesy,
Pausing smiles with alter'd air

To see thee climb his elbow-chair,
Or, struggling on the mat below,
Hold warfare with his slipper'd toe.
The widow'd dame or lonely maid,
Who, in the still but cheerless shade
Of home unsocial, spends her age,
And rarely turns a letter'd page,
Upon her hearth for thee lets fall
The rounded cork or paper ball,
Nor chides thee on thy wicked watch,
The ends of ravell'd skein to catch,
But lets thee have thy wayward will,
Perplexing oft her better skill.

E'en he, whose mind of gloomy bent,
In lonely tower or prison pent,
Reviews the coil of former days,
And loathes the world and all its ways.
What time the lamp's unsteady gleam
Hath roused him from his moody dream,
Feels, as thou gambol'st round his seat,
His heart of pride less fiercely beat,
And smiles, a link in thee to find,
That joins it still to living kind.

Whence hast thou then, thou witless puss!
The magic power to charm us thus?
Is it that in thy glaring eye
And rapid movements, we descry –
Whilst we at ease, secure from ill,
The chimney corner snugly fill –
A lion darting on his prey,
A tiger at his ruthless play?
Or is it that in thee we trace,
With all thy varied wanton grace,
An emblem, view'd with kindred eye,
Of tricky, restless infancy?

Ah! many a lightly sportive child,
Who hath like thee our wits beguiled,
To dull and sober manhood grown,
With strange recoil our hearts disown.

    And so, poor kit! must thou endure,
When thou becom'st a cat demure,
Full many a cuff and angry word,
Chased roughly from the tempting board.
But yet, for that thou hast, I ween,
So oft our favour'd play-mate been,
Soft be the change which thou shalt prove!
When time hath spoil'd thee of our love,
Still be thou deem'd by housewife fat
A comely, careful, mousing cat,
Whose dish is, for the public good,
Replenish'd oft with savoury food,
Nor, when thy span of life is past,
Be thou to pond or dung-hill cast,
But, gently borne on goodman's spade,
Beneath the decent sod be laid;
And children show with glistening eyes
The place where poor old pussy lies.

From *Dramatic and Poetical Works* by Joanna Baillie, 1851

A Fresh Bellyful

Pauline, a 14-year-old girl in Zola's novel Joie de Vivre,
*tries to discover the facts of life from textbooks
on human anatomy and physiology.*

She could have learnt from the few animals in the house, if she had
never opened a book. Minouche in particular interested her. Four
times a year, the rakish creature would go on a wild spree. She who
was normally so fastidious, constantly preening herself, so scared
of getting dirty that she never set a paw outside without a shudder,

[7]

would vanish for two or three days at a time. She could be heard cursing and fighting, and the eyes of all the toms in Bonneville could be seen gleaming in the dark like candles. Then she would come home in a shocking state, all bedraggled, her fur so torn and dirty that she had to spend a whole week licking herself clean. After that she would resume her supercilious airs, rubbing herself against people's faces without seeming to notice that her belly was growing rounder. And one fine morning, she would be found with a litter of kittens. Véronique used to carry them all off in a corner of her apron to drown them. And Minouche, a shocking mother, did not even miss them; she was used to being rid of them in this fashion, and thought that she had fulfilled all her maternal duties. She would go on licking herself, purring, giving herself airs, until one evening she went off again shamelessly to collect a fresh bellyful, to the accompaniment of mewing and scratching. Mathieu [the dog] was a far better father to these children that were not his own, for he would walk whining after Véronique's apron; he loved licking helpless little creatures clean.

'Oh, auntie, do let's leave her one this time,' Pauline would say on each occasion, shocked and delighted by the cat's amorous airs and graces. But Véronique snapped: 'No, indeed! she'd only drag it about all over the place. And besides she doesn't care about them; she has all the fun and none of the burden.'

From *Zest for Life* by Emile Zola, 1884, translated from the French by Jean Stewart

'Cat-Goddesses'

A perverse habit of cat-goddesses –
Even the blackest of them, black as coals
Save for a new moon blazing on each breast,
With coral tongues and beryl eyes like lamps,
Long-legged, pacing three by three in nines –
This obstinate habit is to yield themselves,
In ver-similar love-ecstasies,
To tatter-eared and slinking alley-toms

No less below the common run of cats
Than they above it; which they do for spite,
To provoke jealousy – not the least abashed
By such gross-headed, rabbit-coloured litters
As soon they shall be happy to desert.

From *Collected Poems* by Robert Graves, 1975

'A Cat and Her Kittens'

Sir,

I have often read with interest your stories of animals. Perhaps the following may find favour with your cat-loving readers: – We have two cats – the mother, Betsy, and her daughter Lina, two years old. When the kittens came, we had always kept one of each family, but we decided that the next that came should all be destroyed. Accordingly, when Lina's four kittens arrived, they were all drowned. Three days later, Betsy had six kittens. On the cellar being opened in the morning where their bed was, Lina immediately took up the six kittens one by one to the attic, a distance of seventy stairs, doing it as quickly as possible, the last twelve being so steep that she had to hold her head very high to prevent her knocking the kitten she held in her mouth. Having deposited them all in a box, she tried to take the mother too to the supposed place of safety. After four were drowned, she repeated this with the remaining two several times, nursing them as though they were her own in the box, not allowing the mother to keep them downstairs at all. By what method of reasoning did she arrive at the intended destiny of these kittens? or did she think they were her own given back to her?

I am, Sir, &c.,

F.B.

From *The Spectator*, 14 July 1894

A Little Drunken Wretch

A letter from Samuel Butler to his sister, dated 21 October 1885,
describes his method of feline recruitment.

No, I will not have any Persian cat; it is undertaking too much responsibility. I must have a cat whom I find homeless, wandering
about the court, and to whom, therefore, I am under no obligation.
There is a Clifford's Inn euphemism about cats which the laun-
dresses use quite gravely: they say people come to this place 'to
lose their cats.' They mean that, when they have a cat they don't
want to kill and don't know how to get rid of, they bring it here,
drop it inside the railings of our grass-plot, and go away under the
impression that they have been 'losing' their cat. Well, this happens
very frequently and I have already selected a dirty little drunken
wretch of a kitten to be successor to my poor old cat. I don't suppose it drinks anything stronger than milk and water but then, you
know, so much milk and water must be bad for a kitten that age – at
any rate it looks as if it drank; but it gives me the impression of
being affectionate, intelligent, and fond of mice, and I believe, if it
had a home, it would become more respectable; at any rate I will
see how it works.

From *Samuel Butler, Author of Erewhon (1835-1902): A Memoir* (Vol II)
by Henry Festing Jones, 1919

A Presidential Rescue

White House, June 24 1906

Darling Ethel,
    To-day as I was marching to church, with Sloane some 25 yards
behind, I suddenly saw two terriers racing to attack a kitten which
was walking down the sidewalk. I bounced forward with my
umbrella, and after some active work put to flight the dogs while
Sloane captured the kitten, which was a friendly, helpless little
thing, evidently too well accustomed to being taken care of to know
how to shift for itself. I inquired of all the bystanders and of people
on the neighboring porches to know if they knew who owned it;

but as they all disclaimed, with many grins, any knowledge of it, I marched ahead with it in my arms for about half a block. Then I saw a very nice colored woman and little colored girl looking out of the window of a small house with on the door a dressmaker's advertisement, and I turned and walked up the steps and asked if they did not want the kitten. They said they did, and the little girl welcomed it lovingly; so I felt I had gotten it a home and continued toward church.

From *Theodore Roosevelt's Letters to His Children* edited by
Joseph Bucklin Bishop, 1919

A Gory Parcel

Daniel wrapped himself in his bed quilt, pushed his feet into his training shoes and tip-toed into the living room. The baby sitter had dropped off in the chair. The knitting dangled near the floor, and her beret had pushed itself askew on her head in sleep. Daniel struggled with the key to the back door. It turned with a startling, tell-tale squeak which caused a moment's irregularity in the sleeping black woman's breathing. Then all was well. A cricket shrilling in the hedge fell silent as he touched the grass. Above him Daniel saw that the stars were marvellously, giddily bright. The soldiers lay illumined in a square of light which fell from the kitchen window on to the grass. Beside them lay the box, throwing its shadow before it in a dark, elongated parallelogram. Daniel ran to them over the grass with a beating heart and knelt to gather them up. It was then he saw and heard the cat.

The cat was a stray. Unusually for a female, it was ginger. It was very small and thin, but for its great swollen belly which swung like panniers on either side of its rib-cage. It ran to Daniel eagerly for comfort, emitting occasional jerky little cries. Under its tail the animal's small, distended vulva was edged with blood. Though Daniel had no idea of it, the cat was experiencing a modest feline version of that discomfort accompanying the birth of a footling breach. Daniel stroked its head between the ears. He let the bed-quilt drop and he followed its lead to a narrow chink at the back of a small brick shed alongside the swimming pool which the animal

[11]

had chosen for its nest. Daniel crouched at the chink between wall and hedge for a good twenty minutes, his childish, predatory stalking having taught him unusual patience. It was too dark for him to see anything. He could hear that the cat, after one squeak louder than all the rest, had begun to purr. There was a wetness about it and a funny smell.

Daniel remembered that in his hand-luggage his mother had allowed him to pack, from his jungle survival kit, a much-favoured item which, under the influence of his father's transatlantic idiom, he still knew as 'a flash light'. He ran back across the grass, passing the abandoned soldiers on his way. Inside the house the black woman slept on. The only danger, with his brief scuffle in the sports bag, lay in the possibility that Hattie would wake, who shared the room with him, but that danger seemed happily to pass. He returned to the shed by the swimming pool where to his amazement he saw that the cat was already suckling two dampish, rat-like babies with flattened ears and hairless paws. She appeared at the same time to be chewing up a dark, gory little parcel attached to an equally gory rope between her hind legs. Daniel squatted beside the chink, keeping a respectful distance. He felt a sense of wonder and privilege – as one of the Magi – to witness such a birth under the vivid southern stars. He had no urge to interfere; only to watch. He was glad that Hattie was not there, who would have been making a lot of noise and itching to dress the kittens in Sacha doll clothes like the cats in Beatrix Potter. He knew that the mother cat was hungry because she was so thin and he knew that she would be thirsty. She needed milk.

He returned to the house where he found that, while all the crockery had been put away in high-up cupboards which he could not reach, there was an open shelf of funny things within his grasp. The explanation for this shelf was that Mummy's friend Julie Horowitz was so rich that she could afford to waste her money on china that she didn't like. Daniel liked all of it. There was a tea-pot shaped like a camel designed to spew tea out of its mouth, and several rather lecherous looking toby jugs. A couple of mugs said things in pointy gold writing that Daniel could not read, but the nicest thing of all was the jam pot house which Mummy had fallen upon earlier in the day with recognition and delight. It was just like one the Zulu maid had had when she was a child, she said, and she'd always wanted one the same. It looked like a thatched English cottage with its lid made into the roof. Daniel took off the roof to use as a saucer. Then he took from the fridge a litre bottle of milk and went back with his equipment to the cat. There were now three suckling kittens and the gory parcel had vanished. Daniel filled the roof of the jam pot house with milk and held it out to the mother cat. She lapped greedily, stippling his hand with cold, white droplets of milk from her tongue.

Then suddenly Hattie was there, coming up behind him.

'What are you doing?' she said. 'I've been watching you for ages from the window.' Daniel gasped. In haste he switched off the torch.

'Nothing,' he said, realizing suddenly how cold it was. 'It's nothing.' He stood up and faced her, holding his arms guiltily across the narrow corridor to bar her vision.

'Show me!' Hattie said. 'Show me or I'll tell about you being near the swimming pool.' Daniel began to cry.

'Show me!' Hattie said. She shouldered him from the access and took the torch from his hand. In the scuffle, Daniel knocked over the milk which ran eagerly into the dry, red earth below the hedge.

'It's kittens!' Hattie said with real delight. 'Oh, Dan, aren't they lovely!' The kittens by now had dried out into a presentable, striated fluffiness, one orange and two grey.

'It's a secret,' Daniel said. 'Please don't tell the grown-ups.'

'No,' Hattie said. 'Of course not. The ginger one can be mine. Yours can be the two grey ones.'

'But they don't belong to us,' Daniel said, 'They just sort of belong to themselves, Hattie.'

'The ginger one is a girl one,' Hattie said, reaching out to lift it from the nipple. 'Yours can both be boys. I don't mind if you have two.'

'But they don't belong to us Hattie,' Daniel said again. 'You shouldn't pick them up. They're too new.'

'Mine is called Susan,' Hattie said. 'She *wants* me to pick her up.'

From *Noah's Ark* by Barbara Trapido, 1984

'Our Office Cat'

Our Office cat is a happy cat
She has had two hundred kittens
And every one has been adopted into happy homes
By our cat-loving Britons.

From *The Collected Poems of Stevie Smith*, 1975

The Provoking Kitten

'And as for *you*,' she went on, turning fiercely upon the Red Queen, whom she considered as the cause of all the mischief – but the Queen was no longer at her side – she suddenly dwindled down to the size of a little doll, and was now on the table, merrily running round and round after her own shawl, which was trailing behind her.

At any other time, Alice would have felt surprised at this, but she was far too much excited to be surprised at anything *now*. 'As for *you*,' she repeated, catching hold of the little creature in the very act of jumping over a bottle which had just lighted upon the table. 'I'll shake you into a kitten, that I will!'

CHAPTER 10

Shaking

She took her off the table as she spoke and shook her backwards and forwards with all her might.

The Red Queen made no resistance whatever: only her face grew very small, and her eyes got large and green: and still, as Alice went on shaking her, she kept on growing shorter – and fatter – and softer – and rounder – and –

CHAPTER 11

Waking

– and it really *was* a kitten, after all.

CHAPTER 12

Which Dreamed It?

'Your Red Majesty shouldn't purr so loud,' Alice said, rubbing her eyes, and addressing the kitten, respectfully, yet with some severity. 'You woke me out of oh! such a nice dream; and you've been along with me, Kitty – all through the Looking-Glass world. Did you know it, dear?'

It is a very inconvenient habit of kittens (Alice had once made the remark) that, whatever you say to them, they *always* purr. 'If they would only purr for "yes," and mew for "no," or any rule of that sort,' she had said, 'so that one could keep up a conversation! But how *can* you talk with a person if they *always* say the same thing?'

On this occasion the kitten only purred: and it was impossible to guess whether it meant 'yes' or 'no.'

So Alice hunted among the chessmen on the table till she had found the Red Queen: then she went down on her knees on the hearth-rug, and put the kitten and the Queen to look at each other. 'Now, Kitty!' she cried, clapping her hands triumphantly. 'Confess that was what you turned into!'

('But it wouldn't look at it,' she said, when she was explaining the thing afterwards to her sister: 'it turned away its head, and pretended not to see it: but it looked a *little* ashamed of itself, so I think it *must* have been the Red Queen.')

'Sit up a little more stiffly, dear!' Alice cried with a merry laugh. 'And curtsey while you're thinking what to – what to purr. It saves time, remember!' And she caught it up and gave it one little kiss, 'just in honour of its having been a Red Queen.'

'Snowdrop, my pet!' she went on, looking over her shoulder at the White Kitten, which was still patiently undergoing its toilet, 'when *will* Dinah have finished with your White Majesty, I wonder? That must be the reason you were so untidy in my dream. – Dinah! Do you know that you're scrubbing a White Queen? Really, it's most disrespectful of you!

'And what did *Dinah* turn to, I wonder?' she prattled on, as she settled comfortably down, with one elbow on the rug, and her chin in her hand, to watch the kittens. 'Tell me, Dinah, did you turn to Humpty Dumpty? I *think* you did – however, you'd better not mention it to your friends just yet, for I'm not sure.

[15]

'By the way, Kitty, if only you'd been really with me in my dream, there was one thing you *would* have enjoyed – I had such a quantity of poetry said to me, all about fishes! To-morrow morning you shall have a real treat. All the time you're eating your breakfast, I'll repeat "The Walrus and the Carpenter" to you; and then you can make believe it's oysters, dear!

'Now, Kitty, let's consider who it was that dreamed it all. This is a serious question, my dear, and you should *not* go on licking your paw like that – as if Dinah hadn't washed you this morning! You see, Kitty, it *must* have been either me or the Red King. He was part of my dream, of course – but then I was part of his dream, too! *Was* it the red King, Kitty? You were his wife, my dear, so you ought to know – Oh, Kitty, do help to settle it! I'm sure your paw can wait!' But the provoking kitten only began on the other paw, and pretended it hadn't heard the question.

From *Through The Looking Glass* by Lewis Carroll, 1871

Bringing Up Baby

Of all Nature's lovely shows, and they are not a few, surely that of a cat playing with her kittens or educating them is the prettiest. Though a doting parent, she agrees with Solomon; – she spoils not the child for lack of due correction. Everything that it is right for a young cat to know she instills into their guileless breasts as if she foresaw their whole career. When she unbends so far as to give them her tail to play with she does not allow liberty to be carried into excess – nor will she let familiarity breed contempt of her authority. She points a moral by boxing the ears of that degenerate child who sets at naught her maxims. Professor Romanes cites a cat whose dormant sense of duty towards her kittens, relative to bringing them up in the paths of propriety, was roused by punishing her whenever her kittens misbehaved. Very soon this had the desired effect of causing the cat to train up her kittens in the way they should go, for whenever they did wrong she 'swore at them and boxed their ears,' till she brought them to habits of cleanliness.

Pussy has more sense than some human mothers, for she seldom spoils her children, though she will cheerfully lay down her life for theirs. She regulates their diet and will not let them have what she thinks bad for them whether they cry for it or not. There used to be a cat at a house I visited who always jumped up into the window seat every morning at a fixed hour to watch for the butcher's boy, whose advent she knew to be connected with that of something to eat. Her eldest hope, a plucky boy-kitten, thought he should like to watch for the butcher, too. Fired with the ambition of sharing both vigil and meat he jumped up to sit beside her one day. But considering this taste for flesh to be a very fast one in a cat as yet unable to lap, she administered a smart cuff which sent him rolling down the carpet. She did it again in a truly Spartan fashion every time that he picked himself up and remounted the post of observation.

The care which the mother cat takes to provide for her little ones ceases the moment it becomes unnecessary and undesirable for her charges. She pushes them away when they ought to be weaned and keeps them at arms' length as soon as it is time for them to become independent.

Young kittens are easy to rear by hand, but they seldom make fine cats if taken too early from the mother. For want of a 'licking' both literal and metaphorical, kittens, when artificially nurtured, are sufferers. They are often sickly because their toilets are not attended to, and are unclean in other ways for want of the maternal precept and example. Their human nurse must teach them manners; gently but firmly insisting on methods, or when they are old they will be a nuisance. A damp sponge is the best substitute for the mother's tongue. It is unjust to punish these little creatures for what they cannot help, and undue severity ruins a cat for life if practised in kittenhood, because they are already by nature far too nervous. If a shallow pan of earth is kept at hand kittens soon learn to use it, for the hereditary instinct to be clean is strong in them, but a little guidance will be required at first, with frequent attention.

Kittens ought never to be given to children as toys. Indeed no animal whatever ought to be handed over to little lads and lasses without supervision – we lead our children to do great wrong by loading them with responsibilities for which they are unfit. Without meaning to be cruel, children often worry and torment kittens to the uttermost. Dogs and cats will put up with much from the little ones, seeming to comprehend their ignorance of pain and to appreciate the privilege of standing on a nearer level with them than with their elders. I have seen a dog gravely sit up and pretend to eat the hay which a little crowing baby held out to him with her fat chubby arms, entering into the fun like any human big brother, and privately spitting out the grass afterwards. Cats are equally considerate to children, and will often guard a baby's cradle like a watch dog. For her very love's sake, if for no other, Pussy's gentleness ought not to be taken advantage of till she is forced in spite of herself to poke out her nails through those soft velvet mittens which she draws over them on her small friends' account. She will not scratch till at the last gasp, when half strangled by misplaced hugging – even then the action is more mechanical than voluntary. It is easy to play a kitten into fits, they need rest and sleep as much as babies do, and at intervals as brief, or briefer.

I once took from some children a poor infant puss which was but half alive after its overdose of romps. The poor weary little thing went to sleep clinging to my cloak the moment I took it up, it was completely worn out, and before night it was dead. As its little comrades had loved their pet and would not wilfully have hurt a hair of its whiskers, I buried it darkly, and its sepulchre remains a secret. Among the working classes it is common to hear a mother say 'I want a kitten for the baby,' as if they were talking about a rattle or an india-rubber ring. The fate of these living toys is indeed pitiful, it is high time that we taught the children to discriminate between *playthings* and *playmates*; – and till they are able to do so their toys should be made of something that cannot feel.

From *The Cat: Her Place in Society and Treatment* by Edith Carrington, 1896

'Lost Kitten'

Two men I saw reel from a bar
And stumble down the street;
Coarse and uncouth as workmen are,
They walked with wobbly feet.
I watched them, thinking sadly as
I heard their hobnails clink,
The only joy a toiler has
Is to get drowned in drink.

A kitten cowered on a wall,
A skinny, starving stray;
It looked so pitifully small,
A fluff of silver grey.
One of the men came to a stand,
A kindly chap was he,
For with a huge and horny hand
He stroked it tenderly.

With wistful hope it gazed at him
And arched a spine of fur;
It licked his hand so grimy grim
And feebly tried to purr.
And then it climbed upon his chest,
And to his drunken glee,
Upon his shoulder came to rest,
Contented as could be.

The other fellow with a jeer
Made feint to dash it down,
But as it shrank with sudden fear
I saw the first one frown;
And then I heard him coarsely cry:
'Have care for what you do;
Just harm a hair of it and I
Will twist my knife in you.'

So there they stood like brutes at bay,
Their blood at fighting heat;
And snarling at each other they
Went weaving down the street,
Leaving the kitten all alone
Upon its stoney shelf . . .
And as I haven't heart of stone
I took it home myself.

From *More Collected Verse* by Robert W. Service, 1955

'Babies in Rhinestones'

The Alfred Ellis School of Fine Art and the Araidne Elliot School of Dance and Drama stood semi-detached from one another behind a small tearful shrubbery of mahonia and hypericum, snowberries, bitter blue currants, spotted laurel and pink watery globes of berberis spiked on their own thorns. A crooked hedge of yellow-berried holly divided the two gardens. The artist's was distinguished by a rusting iron sculpture, while Miss Elliot's, or Madame as she was addressed by her pupils, held a grey polystyrene cupidon bearing a shell of muddy water.

In the green gloom of his hall Alfred Ellis held up a letter to the light to see if it contained any money. It was in fact addressed to Araidne Elliot and had come through the wrong door. As he crumpled it into his pocket he wondered again if she knew that her name should be Ariadne. He fancied, as he passed the half open door of his front room, or atelier, that something moved, but when he went in all the easels were posing woodenly in their places. In the kitchen he poured boiling water on to an old teabag and was sitting down to read the paper when a round striped ginger face appeared at the window.

'Good morning, Ginger,' he said as he let in the cat.

'I suppose you want your breakfast. I was about to read the Deaths, to see if I had died recently. Now I shall never know.' He brushed at the bouquets of smudgy paw marks on the black words and poured out a bowl of milk.

Dead or alive, half an hour later he set off for the shops. Ginger ran down the path before him. At the same time his neighbour emerged from her gate, struggling with a green umbrella. Araidne Elliot seemed more at the mercy of the elements than other people; the mild late autumn rain had, on her walk down the garden path, reduced her piled-up hair to a spangled ruin sliding from its combs. A scarlet mahonia leaf was slicked to the toe of her boot. A cluster of red glass berries dangled from each ear.

'Miss Elliot, you look the very spirit of autumn . . .'

She did not reply, being unsure, as so often, if he was being unpleasant, and looked down at Ginger who was rolling on his back on the pavement at their feet, displaying his belly where the stripes dissolved into a pool of milky fur.

'Home, Rufus!' she said sharply. 'You can't come to the library with me.'

'Rufus?'

She blushed. 'I call him that. I don't know his real name – he's not really mine, I'm afraid. He just walked in one day and made himself at home. He always comes for his breakfast and sometimes he stays the night. He sleeps on my bed.' She blushed again. 'I wish I could keep him, but he's obviously got a home . . .'

'His breakfast?' repeated Alfred Ellis. 'That's impossible!'

'Oh yes, every day, but the funny thing is, he won't touch milk!'

'You little tart, Ginger,' he said softly, inserting a not very gentle toe into the cat's wanton chest. Ginger gathered up his legs and departed, tail worn low, between two branches of spiraea.

'What a very unpleasant shrub that is,' said Alfred Ellis.

'How can you say that,' she cried. 'All flowers are lovely.'

Her doubts about him as an artist tumbled through her head; a rat's skull on the windowsill, a drain blocked with dead leaves, his profile like a battered boxer's, the sculpture like a rusting vegetable rack in his garden. They walked on.

'This is yours, I think.' He fished in the pocket of his stained corduroy trousers and handed her the letter.

'Not bad news, I trust?' he capered at her side, squinting over her shoulder.

'Not at all. Just a bill,' she said coldly, putting it in her bag.

'Manage to spell your name right, did they?'

'I don't know, I didn't look. Why?'

He could hardly tell her that every time he saw the board outside her house he had to suppress an urge to seize a paintbrush and alter it.

'Those grey trousers with bald knees make him look like an old elephant who has been in the zoo too long,' she was thinking as they crossed the railway tracks at the level crossing. Alfred Ellis suddenly stopped and waved an arm at a large bronze ballerina pirouetting in the wind.

'Ah, Dame Margot!' he cried. 'An inspiration to us all, eh Miss Elliot? Born plain Alice Marks in this very borough and still dancing away in all weathers . . .'

She strode away, her feet almost at right angles, a dancer in dudgeon. He laughed. He was often bored and it amused him to

[21]

provoke his neighbour. He was often lonely too, and was disproportionately hurt by the news that his friend Ginger was so free with his favours.

He crossed the road and forced to return his greeting an ex-pupil who was obviously about to cut him.

'I thought of you on Saturday,' she admitted. 'Yes, I was helping with the school Autumn Fayre and one of your pictures turned up on the bric-à-brac stall. I almost bought it, but the frame was in such poor condition . . .'

The artist turned away with what might have been a laugh.

He thought about her as he walked; one of too many ladies striding about the town with shopping trolleys, whose skin from years of smiling at the antics of dogs and children and husbands creased into fans of angst at the eyes, whose arms were muscled from turning over the pages of *Which?* and cookery books borrowed from the library; they never had time to read fiction; whose faces were still faintly tanned from their camping holiday in France where they had sat in the passenger seat of the car with maps and Blue Guides and Red Guides on their laps, reflecting that if they had gone to Cornwall they would not be boiling along between endless fields of sweetcorn and poplars; who had once suggested that they might stop and look at a cathedral, but had been hooted down by the rest of the family – and anyway the 'O' Level results hung in a thundercloud on the horizon; who sometimes came to his art classes to draw dead grasses and bunches of dried honesty.

He was struck by a house garlanded with a green climbing plant and stood watching the wind lifting the leaves so that the house looked airy and insubstantial, as if it might take wing, and remembered a birthday cake that his grandmother had sent him when he was a boy, white icing and green maidenhair fern, and marvelled that someone should once have thought him worth such a cake. A twist of smoke from his thin cigarette burned his eye. The pure white icing attacked his stained teeth as he went into the greengrocer's to buy the still life of his morning class. He was crossing the car park on his way home when he passed a stall selling fresh fish, cockles and mussels. He retraced his steps. So, banging his shin on the metal rim of a bucket of briny shells, he began his campaign of seduction.

'Oysters,' he said, his teeth glistening in his beard.

'We haven't any.'

He looked over white fluted shells holding tremulous raw eggs.

'Give me a mackerel. The bluest you have.'

In his mind's eye he saw the mackerel with a lemon on a plate.

He was painting it that afternoon, the blue fish curved on the white oval plate, the lemon with the faintest blush of green, beside the darkening window when he saw a figure slinking through the black grass under the holly hedge. He flung open the window and, wrecking his still life, waved the fish at the cat. Ginger stopped, sniffed, laid back his ears, lifted a loyal paw in the direction of Araidne's house, then leaped through the window.

'Gotcha!' Alfred slammed it shut. Soon heavy swirls of fishy steam mingled with the smell of linseed oil and paint and Ginger was arching his back, walking up and down the kitchen table, purring in anticipation. Half an hour later he lay replete and Alfred Ellis smirked and wiped his greasy fingers on his trousers as the sound of 'Puss, Puss, Puss' came through the rain. Ginger raised an ear, shook his head and stuck out a hind leg to wash. A cloudy eye watched from the draining board.

In the morning Araidne Elliot had to plug in the electric fire to take the chill off the air before the Tinies' Tap Class.

'Bit chilly in here, isn't it?' said a mother, pulling her fur coat around herself.

'We'll soon warm up,' replied Araidne listlessly. Rufus. She supposed he was the only person who loved her.

'Yes, well. Tara's only just got over a shocking cough. I was in two minds whether to bring her. She was barking all night.'

Araidne's ears, on either side of her hairnet, strained to hear a miaow. She looked in despair at her class. The cold was marbling the Tinies' thighs pink and blue to match their leotards and headbands. They seemed to troop incessantly to the toilet, returning with their leotards hiked up over their knickers. She feared that most of them had not washed their hands.

'I'm putting on my top hat . . .'

If she was to fit a lock on the bathroom door, she thought as she danced, that took two-pence pieces . . . her cane flashed dangerously.

' . . . polishing my nails.'

In a dusty corner lay an unperformed revue: 'Babies in Rhinestones,' written and choreographed by Araidne Elliot, in which strings of sparkling babes, shimmering in precision, crisscrossed a vast stage under a spinning prismatic globe, scattered like broken jewellery, and grouped and regrouped in endless stars, rings, necklaces, bangles, tiaras of rainbow glass.

On the other side of the wall Alfred Ellis elicited some disapproval from his students as he executed a bit of inelegant hoofing through the easels to the tap, tap, tap of forty little shoes and one clacking big pair.

'Really, Mr Ellis, that music is most distracting!'

'Lovely chiaroscuro on that teasel, Mrs Wyndham Lewis,' he attempted to placate her, 'If I might suggest . . . the onions . . .'

He added a few strokes of charcoal.

'I think I preferred it as it was,' she said, recoiling from his fishy breath.

'What I object to,' murmured one to another, 'is the fact that one can never finish anything. One embarks on a *nature morte* one lesson, only to find that he's eaten it by the next . . . most unprofessional.'

Araidne could hardly close the front door quickly enough; it clipped the heels of the last mummy, and forced herself to wait until the last car had pulled away before rushing out to check the gutters for a furry body.

She wondered if she would be able to pick it up. Her hair escaped like a catch of eels from its net as she stooped.

'Looking for something, Miss Elliot?'

The loathsome artist was grinning over his gate. She strode on, blushing. Rufus could be presumed alive so far, at least. She thought of his white-tipped paws, his meticulously striped tail, its white tip. She told herself that she was being absurd; he had simply been kept indoors; the people he lived, or condescended to lodge, with, showing some sense of responsibility at last. Nevertheless she scanned every garden that she passed and encountered some striped and tabby persons, but not the face of the beloved. She wandered for some time and at just after one o'clock arrived, or found herself, in a little road near the station. The few small shops were shut. There was nobody about; the little terraced houses looked empty. She heard her heels on the pavement and suddenly felt dispossessed, as if she was in a Tennessee Williams movie, *The Fugitive Kind*. She hesitated in front of a phone box; there was no one to call. It was a relief to arrive in the High Street. She purchased a bottle of pallid rosé and a stiff slice of Camembert to take to the end of term party of her French class, an event to which she looked forward with some gloom. Experience had taught her to avoid the Evening Institute on the first evening of the spring term, when, new aftershave failing to mask the scent of loneliness, people would be required to give details of their sad Christmases in French.

'On m'a donné beaucoup de cadeaux – er – le smoker's candle, le déodorant, le très petit pudding de Noel de Madame Peek . . .'

It was as she came out of the delicatessen that she saw, slouching along with a baby buggy, cigarette in hand, her one-time star pupil, the one for whom she had had the highest hopes. Could it be three years ago that she had brought down the house with her rendition of 'Bring on the Clowns'?

'Karen!'

'Madame!' She dropped her cigarette.

'What's his name?' She peered into the buggy.

'Neil.'

'I suppose we'll be seeing Neil in the Tinies' Class soon?' She chucked him awkwardly under the wet chin. 'I could do with a nice boy . . .'

'Couldn't we all?' replied her ex-pupil.

Araidne's eyes filled with tears. She couldn't resist calling after her in a slightly wavery voice,

'Shoulders back, Karen, and do tuck your tail in!'

While the riches of the sea, sardines painted in silver leaf, shrimps like pink corals, saucy pilchards, fins and tails, poured out in the artist's kitchen and Ginger waxed fat and indolent, his whiskers standing out from his round head in glossy quills, Araidne Elliot grew as boney and twitchy as a hooked hake. Alfred Ellis expected her daily to ask if he had seen the cat, but she did not come.

One morning, while picking a branch of snowberries from the front garden, he saw, further up the road, on the opposite side, a yellow removal van. He went to investigate and saw carried into the van a wicker basket whose lid was pushed open by a ginger face; it flapped shut, and then a striped tail flicked out in farewell.

'Mr Ellis!' Araidne was at her open window with a letter in her hand. 'I'm afraid the postman has muddled our mail again.'

He took it, and seeing the postmark almost ran to his own house, without a word of thanks or a word about Ginger's departure. It was from a man who owned a small gallery in Gravesend, who had seen some of Ellis's paintings in the Salon de Refusés of the South Surrey Arts Society exhibition and proposed to visit him with a view to mounting a one-man show of his work. He gobbled gleefully at what would have been Ginger's supper as he read and re-read the letter until it was creased and oily.

That evening he took down a large prepared canvas which had stood empty for months and would now receive his masterwork, the heart of his exhibition, the flowering of his genius; but his brush kept dancing to a faint beat coming through the wall – 'From the top again, please Mrs Taylor' – and the image of Araidne's old accompanist's resigned shoulders at the keyboard superimposed itself on the canvas, so eventually he had to admit defeat and switch on 'Dallas'. Later he went for a walk. It had rained, but now the air was frosty, the ivy all diamanté, the hedges cold and hard like marcasite.

'Rufus . . . Rufus,' came palely through the starlight.

The Muse was still recalcitrant the next morning, so he thought that he might seduce her with a pint or two in convivial company. He saw Araidne in the High Street; she saw him too and turned, but too late; he was performing a grotesque dance at her on the pavement, and whistling.

'I'm sorry if my music disturbed you,' she said stiffly. 'I do have a living to make . . .'

'Please don't apologise. The clog dance from "La Fille Mal Gardée" just happens to be my very, very, all-time favourite – especially when I'm trying to work.'

'Excuse me.'

He followed her at a distance and entered a shop behind her. She placed her basket on the counter and took out a packet.

'These tights aren't at all what I wanted.'

'What do you want then?'

She burst into tears, grabbed her basket, and ran out of the shop.

Alfred Ellis winked at the astonished assistant, but he could have wept too. Before she had fled he had looked into her basket: a packet of Fishy Treats, two frozen cod steaks and a library book, *Some Tame Gazelle* by Barbara Pym.

In the pub he muttered into his beer, attracting a fishy glance from the landlord who knew him of old. The shop assistant had asked her what she wanted and the book had replied for her: 'Something to love, oh, something to love.'

'Some tame gazelle, or some gentle dove ... give me a whisky, George. Better make it a double.'

The seduction of Ginger seemed less amusing now.

'Something to love, oh, something to love,' he murmured to the fruit machine as it turned up two lemons and a raspberry. He put a coin in the juke box to drown the rusty voice of shame, but he had to go and look for her.

'Miss Elliot, please. Will you come and have a drink with me. Don't run away. I've got something to tell you. It's most important. It's about Rufus.'

He saw her turn as white as the snowberries in his garden, as red as their twigs, and blanch again.

Two hours later two slightly tear-stained dishevelled people with foolish smiles, clutching a cardboard cat-carrier, a wicker basket, a sack of cat litter, a plastic tray and a carrier bag of tins, struggled down the High Street.

'I think Beulah for the little black one, what do you think?' Alfred Ellis was saying.

Araidne caught sight of their reflection in a shop window.

'Goodness, we almost look like a couple,' she thought. She said, 'We want to give them nice names, sensible names, that won't embarrass them when they go to school – grow up, I mean. Names are so important, don't you think?'

'I hated mine when I was a boy. Did you like yours?'

'I chose it.' She admitted. 'My real name's Gwen. I saw the name Araidne in a book and I thought it was so beautiful and romantic. So when I opened the dancing school I changed it to Araidne.'

'Ah,' he said.

'What about Tom for the boy? Can we put these down for a minute? My arms are breaking. Oh, I can hear a little voice! Oh, we'll soon be home, darlings.'

Outside their houses he turned to go into his, she into hers. The cat carrier was almost torn in two. Instant sobriety, hangover, realisation of what they had done. They stood on the pavement staring at one another. A cold wind blew up; the miaows from the box grew wilder.

'Whose dumb idea was this anyway?'

'Yours, I think. But don't worry, I'm taking them.'

'Oh no, you don't!'

'I refuse to stand here brawling in the street. Give me those kittens!'

She tried to snatch them, but he broke free and bolted down his path with them and she grabbed the rest of the stuff and hurried after him lest she be locked out and lose them altogether.

In his kitchen he set the box on the floor and opened it and they knelt on either side gazing at the two tiny faces, one black, one marked like a pansy, looking up, pink and black mouths opening on teeth as sharp as pins. Then, gently, with his big stained fingers, he lifted the kittens out, and on little ricketty-looking legs they entered into their kingdom. Alfred Ellis capitalised on Araidne's softened look by opening a bottle of wine; she opened a tin of evaporated milk.

'Let's go into the other room, where it's more comfortable,' he said, 'and try to think of some solution. Perhaps they should stay here tonight, anyway, as they seem to be making themselves at home . . .'

Some hours later two empty bottles and a pile of dirty plates stood on the table. Blue cigarette smoke lay flat across the air like branches of a cedar tree. Araidne lay heavy-eyed on the sofa with the kittens asleep in her lap. A gentle purring could be heard.

'Perhaps you should all stay the night,' said Alfred Ellis, putting a ballon of brandy to his lips. 'It would be upsetting for the kittens if you should go now . . .'

Araidne slunk up her path in the morning, feeling very ill, just in time to pre-empt her morning class.

'From the top, Mrs Taylor. But pianissimo, please.'

She was obviously not in a good mood when she returned.

'Switch that thing off! I've got the most appalling headache in the history of the world. What on earth are you doing?' She shouted, wrenching the plug of his Black and Decker from the socket.

'It's the perfect solution,' he said, his hair white with plaster dust. 'I'm drilling a passage from my house to yours so that the kittens can come and go as they please. There's half a Disprin left, if you want it,' he added.

As he spoke a crack zig-zagged through the plaster, then another. 'Oh dear. Perhaps we'd better take the whole wall down?'

The man from the gallery at Gravesend rang and rang the doorbell, and at last walked round the side of the house and looked through the window. The hindquarters of a man, covered in plaster and brick dust, were wriggling through a hole in the wall, while a woman, with a savage look on her face, stood in a lumpy sea of broken plaster, with two kittens running about her shoulders and biting her distracted hair, gulping a glass of water and grasping an electric drill as if she might plunge it into her companion's disappearing leg. He was a timid man, and he crept away.

The kittens proved to be bad wild infants who tore up canvases and danced away with the ribbons of ballet shoes in their mouths. Araidne lost a pair of twins from her beginner's ballet class due to alleged cat-scratch fever; a major disaster as they had three younger sisters. She started to choreograph a ballet based on the kittens, but when Alfred opined that the adult human impersonating a cat was the most embarrassing sight in the universe, and the infant human doing so was only marginally better, she lost heart. Alfred received a deep scratch on his thumb while disentangling Tom from a curtain, infected it with paint, and had to wear a clumsy bandage, which made painting impossible. They hardly spoke, addressing most of their remarks to the kittens.

Then one grey day, while the taped carols of the Rotarians pierced the woolly hat he had pulled down over his ears to muffle them, sidestepping a plastic-suited Santa shaking a tin, Alfred Ellis entered the Craft Market, a portfolio in his good hand, shame-facedly and without hope, and found himself appreciated as an artist at last.

He sold several rough studies, executed sinisterly, of the kittens; posing under an umbrella, gazing up expectantly from a pair of old boots, entangled in a ball of knitting wool and needles, Tom asleep with his arms flung out behind his head and Beulah curled into him with her paws crossed, and was commissioned by a local gift shop to supply it with more, and was approached by three golden retrievers who wanted portraits of their owners, or vice versa.

*

It was almost midnight. The kittens lay in one another's arms; their new jewelled collars sending reflections of firelight and the broken baubles they had torn from the tree, which stood in a huge jagged hole in the wall, sparkling round the room as the last bong of Big Ben rang in the future; babies in rhinestones. And the parents? They stayed together for the sake of the children.

From *Babies In Rhinestones* by Shena Mackay, 1983

'The Kittens and the Kid'

Indeed, I am sorry for the Three Little Kittens. Fame has come to them, and fame is not such wholesome stuff as milk in a saucer. They have found their way into the news, and this is a perilous adventure, even for kittens at that age when kittens are always adventurously finding their way to some place where kittens ought not to be.

I first saw them among the pictures on the back page, where they made the prettiest picture, sitting with their three tabby heads together, looking curiously about them. They were sitting upon a gramophone, but that I did not remark at the time; I do not love gramophones, and I think that my eyes are gaining a trick of missing things that I do not want to see. But afterwards, in the columns of print, I read the sad story of the Three Little Kittens, and knew that the gramophone had a part in it.

'They were born in a room where a gramophone is played almost daily.' Such rooms there are; in my neighbourhood I know of three basements from which the strains of the gramophone are for ever welling by day and by night. There must be people who are ill at ease in quiet, who will have daily noise as they will have daily bread; among them were born the Three Little Kittens.

'They have grown up in an atmosphere of musical comedy, of Liszt and Chopin.' In a world whose braying noises never cease they have lived for many weeks. Nature, that shall slay us all in the end, is eager that babies and kittens should live. A week in that house of the gramophone and I should be distraught and gibbering. But the Three Little Kittens had the will to live and they live yet.

More than this, they are become what men of science would call creatures of their environment, content in that unpeaceful place. 'When about six weeks old the kittens began to show a distinct interest in what was being played.' Also 'when the gramophone was silent they sometimes climbed to the top and looked into the doors'; yet that is no wise remarkable; kittens climb to all tops, look in at all doors. But of these Three Little Kittens it is said that they 'make obvious efforts to keep in time' to 'tunes with strong rhythm'; some tunes they love so well that 'they will climb up to the instrument and sit as near as possible to it.' For a last word, the correspondent asks if it be possible 'to train animals further in musical education'?

Alas, I do not doubt that it is possible. The trainers of animals have secret arts; they are mighty to train cats and dogs to all manner of undoggish and uncatty tricks. Woe to the Three Little Kittens should those cruel magicians read that question and answer it by offering them an engagement. In a little while I shall hear again of the Three Little Kittens; their innocent paws shall be plucking at strings or beating upon keys, making those noises which are called Chopin and Liszt. I should like to have a word with them, to tell them the sort of men that trainers are and of what the ruthless musician makes his violin strings.

Yet I hope for the best. The picture shows me that these are no long-haired aliens, but honest English kittens of the Tabby kind. I could believe anything of a Persian, of an Angora; but do not tell me that these Three Little Kittens are growing up as unhappy little prodigies. When they make music it shall be their own song, the profuse strains of unpremeditated art inspired by pussy's own wild muse, not by Liszt, not by Chopin. 'Our fat cat,' says the wise Spelling Book, 'is on the mat,' and that is the best place for her. Kittens who lose their mittens are happier than kittens who discover fugues. Let the Three Little Kittens be warned by the fate of the one poor little Kid, who, in the kittenish years of childhood, having won success in the Films, having signed contracts for three hundred and fifty thousand dollars worth of performances, is nigh to death, worn out and famous, with the reporters waiting at his door. From such dreadful fame may the kind Heaven keep all other babies and kittens.

From *Day In and Day Out* by 'The Londoner' [Arthur O. Barron] of the
Evening News, 1924

[31]

'Why does a kitten sometimes throw a toy
into the air when playing?'

The scene is familiar enough. A kitten tires of stalking and chasing a ball. It suddenly and without warning flips one of its paws under the ball, flinging it up into the air and backwards over its head. As the ball flies through the air, the kitten swings round and follows it, pouncing on it and 'killing' it yet again. As a slight variation, faced with a larger ball, it will perform the backward flip using both front feet at the same time.

The usual interpretation of this playful behaviour is that the kitten is being inventive and cunningly intelligent. Because its toy will not fly up into the air like a living bird, the kitten 'puts life into it' by flinging the ball over its shoulder, so that it can then enjoy pursuing the more excitingly 'lively' prey-substitute. This credits the kitten with a remarkable capacity for creative play – for inventing a bird in flight. In support of this idea is the fact that no adult cat hunting a real bird would use the 'flip-up' action of the front paws. This action, it is argued, is the truly inventive movement, reflecting the kitten's advanced intelligence.

Unfortunately this interpretation is wrong. It is based on an ignorance of the instinctive hunting actions of the cat. In the wild state, cats have three different patterns of attack, depending on whether they are hunting mice, birds or fish. With mice, they stalk, pounce, trap with the front feet and then bite. With birds they stalk, pounce and then, if the bird flies up into the air, they leap up after it, swiping at it with both front feet at once. If they are quick enough and trap the bird's body in the pincer movements of their front legs, they pull it *down* to the ground for the killing-bite. Less familiar is the way in which cats hunt for fish. They do this by lying in wait at the water's edge and then, when an unwary fish swims near, they dip a paw swiftly into the water and slide it rapidly under the fish's body, flipping the fish up out of the water. The direction of the flip is back and over the cat's shoulders, and it flings the fish clear of the water. As the startled fish lands on the grass behind the cat, the hunter swings round and pounces. If the fish is too large to be flipped with the claws of just one front foot, then the cat may risk plunging both front feet into the water at once, grabbing the fish from underneath with its extended claws and then flinging the prey bodily backwards over its head.

It is these instinctive fishing actions that the kittens are performing with their 'flip-up' of the toy ball, not some new action they have learned or invented. The reason why this has been overlooked in the past is because few people have watched cats fishing successfully in the wild, whereas many people have seen their pets leaping up at birds on the garden lawn.

A Dutch research project was able to reveal that the scooping up of fish from the water, using the 'flip-up' action, matures surprisingly early and without the benefit of maternal instruction. Kittens allowed to hunt fish regularly from their fifth week of life onwards, but in the absence of their mother, became successful anglers by the age of seven weeks. So the playful kitten throwing a ball over its shoulder is really doing no more than it would do for real, if it were growing up in the wild, near a pond or river.

From *Catwatching* by Desmond Morris, 1986

'The Kitten and Falling Leaves'

That way look, my Infant, lo!
What a pretty baby-show!
See the Kitten on the wall,
Sporting with the leaves that fall,
Withered leaves – one – two – and three –
From the lofty elder-tree!
Through the calm and frosty air
Of this morning bright and fair,
Eddying round and round they sink
Softly, slowly: one might think,
From the motions that are made,
Every little leaf conveyed
Sylph or Faery hither tending, –
To this lower world descending,
Each invisible and mute,
In his wavering parachute.
– But the Kitten, how she starts,
Crouches, stretches, paws, and darts!
First at one, and then its fellow
Just as light and just as yellow;

There are many now – now one –
Now they stop and there are none:
What intenseness of desire
In her upward eye of fire!
With a tiger-leap half way
Now she meets the coming prey,
Lets it go as fast, and then
Has it in her power again:
Now she works with three or four
Like an Indian conjurer;
Quick as he in feats of art,
Far beyond in joy of heart.
Were her antics played in the eye
Of a thousand standers-by,
Clapping hands with shout and stare,
What would little Tabby care
For the plaudits of the crowd!
Over happy to be proud,
Over wealthy in the treasure
Of her own exceeding pleasure!

   'Tis a pretty baby-treat;
Nor, I deem, for me unmeet;
Here, for neither Babe nor me,
Other play-mate can I see.
Of the countless living things,
That with stir of feet and wings
(In the sun or under shade,
Upon bough or grassy blade)
And with busy revellings,
Chirp and song, and murmurings,
Made this orchard's narrow space,
And this vale so blithe a place;
Multitudes are swept away
Never more to breathe the day:
Some are sleeping; some in bands
Travelled into distant lands;
Others slunk to moor and wood,
Far from human neighbourhood;
And, among the Kinds that keep

With us closer fellowship,
With us openly abide,
All have laid their mirth aside.

Where is he that giddy Sprite,
Blue-cap, with his colours bright,
Who was blest as bird could be,
Feeding in the apple-tree;
Made such wanton spoil and rout,
Turning blossoms inside out;
Hung – head pointing towards the ground –
Fluttered, perched, into a round
Bound himself, and then unbound;
Lithest, gaudiest Harlequin!
Prettiest Tumbler ever seen!
Light of heart and light of limb;
What is won become of Him?
Lambs, that through the mountains went
Frisking, bleating merriment,
When the year was in its prime,
They are sobered by this time.
If you look to vale or hill,
If you listen, all is still,
Save a little neighbouring rill,
That from out the rocky ground
Strikes a solitary sound.
Vainly glitter hill and plain,
And the air is calm in vain;
Vainly Morning spreads the lure
Of a sky serene and pure;
Creature none can she decoy
Into open sign of joy:
Is it that they have a fear
Of the dreary season near?
Or that other pleasures be
Sweeter even than gaiety?

Yet, whate'er enjoyments dwell
In the impenetrable cell
Of the silent heart which Nature

Furnishes to every creature;
Whatso'er we feel and know
Too sedate for outward show,
Such a light of gladness breaks,
Pretty Kitten! from thy freaks, –
Spreads with such a living grace
O'er my little Laura's face;
Yes, the sight so stirs and charms
Thee, Baby, laughing in my arms,
That almost I could repine
That your transports are not mine,
That I do not wholly fare
Even as ye do, thoughtless pair!
And I will have my careless season
Spite of melancholy reason,
Will walk through life in such a way
That, when time brings on decay,
Now and then I may possess
Hours of perfect gladsomeness.
– Pleased by any random toy;
By a kitten's busy joy,
Or an infant's laughing eye
Sharing in the ecstasy;
I would fare like that or this,
Find my wisdom in my bliss;
Keep the sprightly soul awake,
And have faculties to take,
Even from things by sorrow wrought,
Matter for a jocund thought,
Spite of care, and spite of grief,
To gambol with Life's falling Leaf.

William Wordsworth, 1804

Two

NAMES

'The Naming of Cats'

The Naming of Cats is a difficult matter,
　　It isn't just one of your holiday games;
You may think at first I'm as mad as a hatter
When I tell you, a cat must have THREE DIFFERENT NAMES.
First of all, there's the name that the family use daily
　　Such as Peter, Augustus, Alonzo or James,
Such as Victor or Jonathan, George or Bill Bailey –
　　All of them sensible everyday names.
There are fancier names if you think they sound sweeter,
　　Some for the gentlemen, some for the dames:
Such as Plato, Admetus, Electra, Demeter –
　　But all of them sensible everyday names.
But I tell you, a cat needs a name that's particular,
　　A name that's peculiar, and more dignified,
Else how can he keep up his tail perpendicular,
　　Or spread out his whiskers, or cherish his pride?
Of names of this kind, I can give you a quorum,
　　Such as Munkustrap, Quaxo, or Coricopat,
Such as Bombalurina, or else Jellylorum –
　　Names that never belong to more than one cat.
But above and beyond there's still one name left over,
　　And that is the name that you never will guess;
The name that no human research can discover –
　　But THE CAT HIMSELF KNOWS, and will never confess.
When you notice a cat in profound meditation,
　　The reason, I tell you, is always the same:
His mind is engaged in a rapt contemplation
　　Of the thought, of the thought, of the thought of his name:
　　　His ineffable effable
　　　Effanineffable
Deep and inscrutable singular Name.

From *Old Possum's Book of Practical Cats* by T. S. Eliot, 1940

Sir John Langborn's Titles

[Jeremy] Bentham was very fond of animals, particularly '*pussies*,' as he called them, 'when they had domestic virtues;' but he had no particular affection for the common race of *cats*. He had one, however, of which he used to boast that he had 'made a man of him,' and whom he was wont to invite to eat maccaroni at his own table. This puss got knighted, and rejoiced in the name of Sir John Langborn. In his early days he was a frisky, inconsiderate, and, to say the truth, somewhat profligate gentleman; and had, according to the report of his patron, the habit of seducing light and giddy young ladies, of his own race, into the garden of Queen's Square Place: but tired at last, like Solomon, of pleasures and vanities, he became sedate and thoughtful – took to the church, laid down his knightly title, and was installed as the Reverend John Langborn. He gradually obtained a great reputation for sanctity and learning, and a Doctor's degree was conferred upon him. When I knew him, in his declining days, he bore no other name than the Reverend Doctor John Lanborn; and he was alike conspicuous for his gravity and philosophy. Great respect was invariably shown his reverence: and it was supposed he was not far off from a mitre, when old age interfered with his hopes and honours. He departed amidst the regrets of his many friends, and was gathered to his fathers, and to eternal rest, in a cemetery in Milton's garden.

From *The Works of Jeremy Bentham* by John Bowring, 1843

The Importance of Sibilants

With the summer's crop of kittens flourishing, we held baptismal ceremonies. Thrusty, Martha's favorite cat, as a first-time mother had produced two spirited sons, black with white markings like their grandfather, Boise. Thrusty wasn't much of a cat or a mother, I felt, being too egocentric and careless in her manners, despite the teachings of Princesa, her noble and elegant mother. But the children showed promise and Ernest suggested we name them after poets. We agreed that cats like to have *s*'s in their names and decided that one of the boys should be Stephen Spender, which we switched to Spendthrift and Ernest promptly shortened to Spendy, who soon became my shadow and loving companion. Shakespeare, we felt, would be too great a burden for any Cuban cat to carry as a name. So we named Spendy's brother Barbershop, abbreviated to Shopsky, and beneath garlands of red bougainvillaea on the sunny front terrace we anointed them with catnip I'd brought from Miami and taught them their names.

In spite of his devotion to Ernest, Boise had developed a crush on me and before I had journeyed north had turned so possessive that he disapproved of Ernest's attentions to my person, and expressed his feelings with his claws on Ernest's most vulnerable parts. When I returned to the Finca, Boise's jealousy flared again so forcefully that after applying unguents we decided that we must attempt a cure. We were both distressed that Boise should be unhappy. 'Let's just explain things to him,' Ernest said, and that evening in the sitting room with Boise curled in his lap and I squatting beside his chair, touching Boise's head, he explained.

'I understand why you love her, Boy,' he said, 'and why you'd like her all for yourself. She loves you too. But wommies can't live on fruit rats. They can't truly.' (For months Boise had been bringing half-dead rats to my bedroom windows in the night, his most precious tribute.) 'She would like it so much if we could all be friends, and you not jealous and unhappy. You see, Boy, I can give her the things she needs to eat, things she likes better than fruit rats.'

'It's darling of you to bring them, Boise,' I said. 'Please don't think I'm unappreciative. It's just unfortunate that I like other things more. You mustn't be offended, Boy.' We went on in that vein, trying to dissolve the enmity.

Boise was mollified. He made no further attacks on Ernest, resumed his role as benign head of his family and a loving third of our triangle.

From *How It Was* by Mary Welsh Hemingway, 1977

Sour Mash, Apollinaris, Zoroaster and Blatherskite

Probably no man ever loved animals better than Mark Twain, and – as everybody knows – his favorite animal was the cat. He began to love cats as a boy, though, as the painkiller incident in *Tom Sawyer* shows, there were times when his sense of mischief got the better of his affections, and he liked to recall how, one Sunday morning, he had seen a cat walk into some flypapers placed close to the pulpit, 'saw her struggle and fall down, more and more unreconciled, more and more mutely profane.' He ate with cats, and slept with cats. 'Next to a wife whom I idolise, give me a cat.' When Jean is born, Susy and Clara could not worship her more if she were a cat. His own opinion as to the merits of the Tiger in the House, he summed up categorically: 'They are the cleanest, cunningest, and most intelligent things I know, outside the girl you love, of course.' Or, as Susy puts it, in her own charming way, 'The difference between papa and mama is, that mama loves morals and papa loves cats.'

It might be expected that such a man as Mark Twain would invent ingenious names for his cats. He does not disappoint us. Four kittens at Quarry Farm were named Sour Mash, Apollinaris, Zoroaster, and Blatherskite. He chose the names, he said, to give the children practice in pronunciation, and when all four animals died young, he was sure their names had killed them. When he came to spend a summer at Dublin, New Hampshire, he simply could not consider getting along without a cat, but he could not disregard the question of what would happen to the animal when he was no longer there to care for it. He solved the problem triumphantly by renting a cat instead of adopting one, renting two, in fact – Sackcloth and Ashes – and paying enough to insure their care after he should have returned home in the autumn. In a man as absent-minded, as careless in matters of detail, as Mark Twain was, one could hardly ask for more than this. 'Once,' writes Paine, 'as he was about to enter the screen-door that led to the hall, two of the kittens ran up in front of him and stood waiting. With grave politeness he opened the door, made a low bow, and stepped back and said: "Walk in, gentlemen. I always gives precedence to royalty." And the kittens marched in, tails in air.'

Danbury and Tammany were the great favorites in Stormfield days. 'Mark Twain might be preoccupied and indifferent to the comings and goings of other members of the household; but no matter what he was doing, let Danbury appear in the offing and he was observed and greeted with due deference, and complimented and made comfortable. Clemens would arise from the table and carry certain choice food out on the terrace to Tammany, and be satisfied with almost no acknowledgment by way of appreciation. And how fine and tender is his own story of the kitten on the billiard table.'

If I can find a photograph of my 'Tammany' and her kittens, I will enclose it in this. One of them likes to be crammed into a corner-pocket of the billiard-table – which he fits as snugly as does a finger in a glove and then he watches the game (and obstructs it) by the hour, and spoils many a shot by putting out his paw and changing the direction of a passing ball. Whenever a ball is in his arms, or so close to him that it cannot be played upon without risk of hurting him, the player is privileged to remove it to anyone of the 3 spots that chances to be vacant.

After Tammany's death, he lauded her to Louise Paine as 'the most beautiful cat on this western bulge of the globe, and perhaps the most gifted. She leaves behind her,' he added, 'inconsolable, two children by her first marriage – Billiards and Babylon; and three grandchildren by her second – Amanda, Annanci and Sindbad.' He requested that each M.A. (Member of the Aquarium) 'wear black head ribbons during one hour on the 30th of this month – Tammany's birthday.'

Sometimes the family cunningly played on Mark Twain's love of cats, as when they rented an apartment in an undesirable neighborhood in Berlin without consulting him. 'The women took that apartment in Slumland over my head, and lured me to approve of their choice by having two purring cats on the hearth when I first saw the place.' Mrs Samossoud tells us that if, as a child, she had occasion to disturb him at work, and had any reason to feel doubtful concerning her reception, she always took a kitten with her in her arms.

Dogs were quite another story. His great sensitiveness to sound made their barking very unpleasant to him, and he sometimes declared he wished he could exterminate them all.

From *Mark Twain: The Man and His Work* by Edward Wagenknecht, 1961

Hinse of Hinsfeldt

Part of a letter from Sir Walter Scott to Joanna Baillie dated 12 April 1816. The 'favourite cat' he mentions is Hinse, also known as Hinzie, Henze, 'Mr Hinse the brindled cat' and 'Hinse of Hinsfeldt (so called from one of the German Kinder-märchen, *a venerable tom-cat, fat and sleek).'*

I have added a most romantic inmate to my family a large blood-hound allowd to be the finest dog of the kind in Scotland perfectly gentle affectionate and good-natured and the darling of all the children. I had him in a present from Glengarry who has refused the breed to people of the very first rank. He is between the deer grey-hound and mastiff with a shaggy mane like a lion and always sits beside me at dinner – his head as high as the back of my chair. Yet it will gratify you to know that a favourite cat keeps him in the greatest possible order insists upon all rights of precedence and scratches with impunity the nose of an animal who would make no bones of a wolf and pulls down a red-deer without fear or difficulty. I heard my friend set up some most piteous howls and I assure you the noise was no joke – all occasioned by his fear of passing puss who had stationed himself on the stairs.

From *Letters of Sir Walter Scott 1815-1817*

Hinse's taunting of bloodhounds eventually did for him, as Scott recorded in a letter to his son Charles, dated 11 April 1827

The young bloodhound Nimrod has dispatched poor old Hinzie the stoutness of whose heart led him always to attack the mighty huntsman before the Lord till at last he paid the kain as we say.

Scott also mentioned the cat's demise in a letter the same day to his daughter-in-law, Mrs Walter Scott

From a hermit you can expect little news. The worst is that the new bloodhound has killed Walters friend old Hinzie the cat. I must say Hinzie had been the aggressor in former encounters but I was vexed to lose my old friend.

From *Letters of Sir Walter Scott 1826-1828*

*The ghost of Hinse reappears more than a year later, on 6 December
1828, in a letter to John Richardson*

I . . . was rather amused with Mrs Baillie's cat who worried the dog.
It is just like her Mrs who beats the male race of authors out of the
pitt in describing the higher passions that are more proper to their
sex than hers. Alack a day my poor cat Hinze my acquaintance and
in some sort my friend of fifteen years was snaped at once by the
paynim Nimrod. What could I say to him but what Brantome said
to some *fouilleur* who had been too successful in a duel 'Ah mon
grand ami vous avez tué mon autre grand ami.' It is a good thing to
have read queer books they always furnish you with a parallel case
in your afflictions.

From *Letters of Sir Walter Scott 1828-1831*

'My Cat Major'

Major is a fine cat
What is he at?
He hunts birds in the hydrangea
And in the tree
Major was ever a ranger
He ranges where no one can see.

Sometimes he goes up to the attic
With a hooped back
His paws hit the iron rungs
Of the ladder in a quick kick
How can this be done?
It is a knack.

Oh Major is a fine cat
He walks cleverly
And what is he at, my fine cat?
No one can see.

From *The Collected Poems of Stevie Smith*, 1975

Poor Moricaud

*The nineteenth-century politician and journalist Henri Rochefort endured
several terms of imprisonment and exile because of his outspoken attacks on
the French government. In this passage from his memoirs, he recalls an
occasion when he eluded his enemies by fleeing to Belgium.*

I reached Mons without trouble, but I was only just in time to slip
between the fingers of the police, for at daybreak the following
morning a commissary of police, armed with a search-warrant and
an order for my arrest, entered my house, accompanied by two
detectives, who turned everything upside down in the cage the
moment they found that the bird had flown.

In the same way as in 1871, everything movable was carried
away, and the governmental housebreakers placed under seals the
furniture which happened to be too heavy to be conveyed in the
official removal vans. The men with the search-warrant, hoping
perhaps to discover proofs of the conspiracy beneath the ground,
even put seals on my cellar door.

Frightened at the irruption of Constans' police, the cats which
then comprised my menagerie took refuge in the coal-store, and,
the seals having been affixed to the door, they remained prisoners.
After fasting for several hours, the unfortunate victims of this display of ministerial rancour began to make desperate calls for their
food, and I received an anxious telegram from my servant, informing me that the two captives were dying of starvation, and asking
my opinion as to the possibility of nourishing them by the aid of a
tube pushed through the key-hole of the cellar door. I found an excellent subject for an article in this pitiable appeal, and wrote the
following story, which put all the scoffers on our side. It took the
form of an open letter to the president of the Society for the Prevention of Cruelty to Animals, and was entitled, *Les tueurs de chats.*

I have just learned through the Havas agency that my cats have
been placed under seals, accused of conspiracy and other grave
offences against the person of M. Carnot. In the absence of any sort
of justice, it is to you, Monsieur le président, that I address myself. I
swear to you that my cats are innocent; they have never committed
any outrages except upon pieces of cat's meat. They have in no way
mixed themselves up with politics.

It is unnecessary for me to depict to you the horror of their situation, deprived as they are of all means of communication with the servant who has hitherto supplied them with food, and who cannot now give them nourishment without rendering herself liable to six months' imprisonment for breaking the seals affixed by the commissary of police. To leave them with no food until the Haute Cour pronounces a 'no bill' in their favour, or transforms them into a rabbit-stew, means exposing them to the danger of becoming mad, and constitutes a risk of a serious character for the public. These inoffensive animals probably do not appreciate the gravity of the terrible accusation that is hanging over them. I do not believe they have been attacked with the fever of Boulangism. Nevertheless, I must admit that the larger of the two, a beautiful black cat which I called Moricaud, often jumped on to my shoulders while I was writing my articles. Possibly the fact of putting his foot too frequently in my ink-bottle has given rise to an aversion to parliamentarians in his nature. There is a Grammont law which punishes cruelty to animals. I beg you, Monsieur le président, to see that it is applied against the assassins of my poor Moricaud. Save him from the guillotine that awaits him! I confide his fate into your hands. I admit that Moricaud has his faults; he is a gormandizer, and spends much of the time at night on the tiles. But the excesses of youth will pass. It pains me to think that he may be condemned to perpetual transportation in a fortified place, and that a war-vessel may be especially employed to transport him to New Caledonia.

This is my request: what I certainly would not do for myself I beg of you to do for Moricaud. Go and see Constans, tell him that you believe him to be an honourable man. One can very well tell a lie to save the life of a victim of the opportunists.

The most amazing part of the story is, that on the appearance of this fantastic article, the Society for the Prevention of Cruelty to Animals, regarding it as serious, sent a delegate to my residence with instructions to consult with my servant as to the means to be employed for saving Moricaud from starving to death. This is the plan of action that was adopted. By the aid of a strong kitchen knife, a sufficiently large hole was cut in the bottom of the cellar door to admit of the insertion of the three sous' worth of cat's meat to which my animals had been accustomed. They were thus kept alive artificially until the authorities appeared on the following day and removed the seals from the cellar door.

Two eagles that General Boulanger had given to a young social-ist named Michel Morphy were found when a search-warrant was executed at his lodgings, and all Count Dillon's dogs and cattle were sequestrated. This led even the governmental *Paris* to say –

'They are finding too many animals in this affair, and not enough documents.'

From The Adventures of My Life by Henri Rochefort, 1896

A Correspondence on Tiddles

Sir,

Would you allow me to apologise collectively and in individual to readers who quite rightly wrote in to me (Low Life, 10 November) to tell me that I am an idiot? Of course Prince Rupert's dog was killed at Marston Moor and not Naseby and his name was Boy. It seems that I now only open my mouth to change foot. Sorry about that. It could be brain damage. Next week I shall probably claim that Nelson took his cat, if he had one, to Trafalgar.

Jeffrey Bernard

Sir,

Jeffrey Bernard in his letter (Letters, 1 December) refers to Nelson's cat Tiddles, who was present at the battle of Trafalgar. The subject, which is of some interest, has been unjustly neglected by naval historians.

Discovered as an abandoned kitten in the courtyard of the Palazzo Sessa, the British Embassy in Naples, in March 1797, Tiddles was taken in and adopted by the kind-hearted Emma Hamilton. He frequently participated in her celebrated 'Attitudes' in the role of the Nemean Lion, and soon became a firm favourite not only of the ambassadress but also of the scheming Queen of Naples, Maria Carolina, whilst his mouse-hunting talents received the grudging admiration of King Ferdinand, thereby facilitating the aims of British diplomacy.

Returning with the Hamiltons and Nelson to England in 1800, his hopes of retirement from a diplomatic career were dashed when, in an emotional scene in May 1803, Tiddles was entrusted by Lady Hamilton to Nelson, and entered in the crew list of HMS Victory as Admiral's Servant. His second career, at sea, was even more brilliant than his previous diplomatic success. Tiddles's sang-froid during the battle of Trafalgar merited the approbation of all his shipmates, and although initially disconsolate at the death of his patron, his spirits were revived by the kindness of Captain Hardy, who arranged for his transfer to HMS Amphion, whose gallant captain, William Hoste, was the one officer in the fleet who could guarantee an adequate supply of his favourite Norfolk dumplings.

Promoted to Boatswain's Mate, Tiddles sailed with Hoste on both his successful Adriatic cruises; displaying his now legendary coolness under fire at the battle of Lissa, only to fall victim to a stray shot at the siege of Trieste in 1813. A handsome monument to his memory was erected in the Protestant cemetery of that city, which survived until 1924, when it was destroyed by Mussolini, a noted ailurophobe.

Guy Evans

Sir,

Apropos Nelson's cat Tiddles (Letters, 22/29 December), Churchill in his wartime underground headquarters had a cat called Nelson that lacked the battle courage of Tiddles. During an air raid, Jock Colville went to wake Churchill from his afternoon nap. He found the Prime Minister in his long-johns, on all fours, trying to entice the terrified cat from under a Queen Anne bureau. 'Come out,' Churchill was saying unaware of being overheard, 'come out, you should be ashamed, cowering there, you, the bearer of so proud a name.'

Quentin Crewe

From *The Spectator*, December 1990 – January 1991

Black, Castlerosse and Frou-frou

In 1938 the author Marguerite Steen and her husband, the artist William Nicholson, lived for some months in the French port of La Rochelle.

We had decided, when we returned in October, that we would spend at least six months in La Rochelle. Jean and Suzanne had kept their word; we found ourselves in possession of a delightful *appartement* on the port; William was enchanted to discover that he could identify the very spot – he declared, the very house – on the Callot map. All day long the sails went past under our windows, the dramas of the waterfront were ours just for the turn of a head. To make it even more homelike, we acquired Black.

Suzanne was responsible for Black. Having rashly mentioned in her hearing how much I wanted a cat, it was only to be expected that the door should open one day, and a tall, temperamental, round-eyed black kitten walk on tiptoe into the room.

The history of our cats would fill a volume by itself, but Black was, of them all, the most original, the fiercest, wildest, most loving and most humorous; he was a born clown of a cat. He not only joined in any game we cared to start with him – he invented games of his own, and, as William pointed out, Black's games, which he varied from day to day, were always the best. There was one game, however, to which he was obstinately faithful, and, if we did not begin it, he would stand by the door and scream with rage until we joined in.

The *appartement* was so arranged that the four rooms communicated with one another, and, having passed from kitchen to salon, from salon to dressing-room, from dressing-room to bedroom, you could complete the round tour by returning to the kitchen along a passage. It was Black's delight to be chased, and, in his turn, to chase, round this circle; but it was no simple chase, for every now and then he would cheat, would stop and crouch inside a doorway, then, when one reached it, he would leap up the door jamb, shoulder-high, and slide down again, gripping with his paws, before tearing on to the next doorway. This was his regular morning game, with which he coaxed or bullied us out of bed every morning; it was no use pretending to be asleep, or spreading out the newspaper to read; you cannot read with a very angry cat

[49]

bouncing up and down on the foot of the bed, bawling to be played with.

At night, like many cats, he had mad steeplechases from room to room; but Black's steeplechases differed from the average in that they seemed always to have some savage purpose. He leapt like a stag, and with ruthless disregard for all but his own enjoyment. William, dozing on the divan after a day spent in working, would rouse with a yelp and an oath as Black took off from the tenderest portion of his anatomy for some incredible bound, and the current paragraph of *The Sun is My Undoing* broke up in confusion as Black tore across the keyboard of the typewriter. 'Damn that cat!' said William, but he adored Black, for whom he had invented a game of his own.

He had brought out with him a beautiful irregular bowl of elm-wood, nearly two feet across at its widest part, which he intended to use for a Still Life; this became Black's favourite toy. Climbing into it, he would lie on his side while William spun it. Round and round went Black in the bowl, prone with rapture, until William's energy gave out, when Black would gather himself up and stagger with a very uncertain movement to the chair or windowsill which he favoured for the moment, his eyes glassy and squinting with bliss.

He was the idol of the household; Léonie, the *bonne-à-tout-faire*, called him '*Mon fils*,' and only occasionally forgot and addressed him as '*Mini*,' which he detested; his resentment of the common-place name was as obvious as it was ludicrous; he would get up and walk straight out of the room, when Léonie called him '*Mini*.' Once he was lost, and La Rochelle was practically shaken to its founda-tions; our landlady brought her dog to try and sniff Black out – Black who never stirred, tucked blissfully under the *couvrepied* and eiderdown on my bed.

Alas, when we left La Rochelle, the problem arose of how to dis-pose of Black, as our landlady could not keep him with her dog. We knew we could not take him back to England, but got Madame Gar-rigue's word to look after him, and try to find him a home while we were in St Jean de Luz. Our feelings can be imagined when a wire arrived – '*Petit chat ne mange pas ne dort pas*.' At first we were for taking the next train back to La Rochelle; then William, his face agonised, pointed out that this was only to prolong the agony – that

Black could not come home with us, and that, failing a good home, there was only one thing to be done. . . . We sent a telegram.

To try and put it out of our minds we went to Biarritz – a town we both loathe – and had a marvellous lunch, which neither of us tasted, as the tears were rolling quite openly down both our faces. We could talk and think of nothing but Black.

When we got back to our hotel there was another wire: '*Petit chat bien placé très content.*' We went back to Biarritz and had a marvellous dinner.

It was the first time we had succumbed to acquiring a cat abroad, and we swore it should never happen again; it meant too much heartache. The pity was, we both loved animals, and we could never keep any because of our frequent absences. There was a tortoiseshell kitten at Malaga which William lost his heart to, and some basket-makers in Sevilla had done their utmost to press upon us a furious, rust-coloured kitten which William christened El Moro on sight. Apart from our rabbit, Postlethwaite, whom William bought to amuse me when I was ill, we never had an animal of our own until we knew there would be no escape from England, perhaps for years.

Cats are enchanting models, and William made many drawings of Black, lying in his bowl, or rolling on his side to pat the goldfish tank which, with its inmates, was another of his favourite toys. Other cats he has drawn are Winston Churchill's marmalade tom, of which he made a sheet of sketches which he gave to Mrs Churchill, and our beautiful black neuter, Castlerosse, one of our two 'Blitz babies,' who accompanied us into our two years' exile from London. From Frou-frou onwards, he has owned many cats, among them a splendid Russian smooth, but his favourite, after Black, is his 'little black girl,' Castlerosse's twin sister, whose sheer plebeian commonness is only equalled by her charm, and whose welcoming purr is guaranteed to penetrate stone walls. One always knows if 'The Girl' is around, even if invisible, for the slightest movement on one's part is enough to call out that rich, metallic purr. She is as completely William's cat as Castlerosse is mine, and, although very pleasant to me, never mistakes her real ownership.

From *William Nicholson* by Marguerite Steen, 1943

Minty and Sooty

*An account of the ménage maintained by the novelist Paul Scott
and his wife Penny at their house in Hampstead Garden
Suburb during the 1950s.*

The main division was the one between the study, where Paul sat
immured at his desk, and the kitchen, which was Penny's domain. It
had yellow-painted walls and a coal-burning range with a cheerful
fire to heat the water, a work table, a sink below the window over-
looking the garden, and a big, solidly-built, wooden dresser with
capacious, crowded shelves and cupboards. There were pots of
geraniums on the windowsill, and cardboard boxes on the dresser
for the cats. Two senior cats had moved with the family into Addi-
son Way, where numbers quickly rose to eight: two black (Minty
and Sooty who belonged to the girls), three tortoiseshell, a neu-
tered ginger tom called Rota (after the antiquarian bookseller in
Covent Garden, who had been a neighbour in Palmers Green), and
a handsome pedigree Russian Blue brother and sister, called Baron
and Beauty. The kitchen was always warm and welcoming with the
radio playing and cats everywhere.

From *Paul Scott: A Life* by Hilary Spurling, 1990

Teabag

My overview of politics comes from my early interest in classical
antiquity and the ancient Near East, particularly Egypt. My understanding of motivation and behavior comes from my reading of
Nietzsche and Freud, as well as Homer, Shakespeare, and the nineteenth-century novel. The will-to-power must be contained, but is
not generated, by society. In my apartment building in New Haven
lived an affectionate calico she-cat named Teabag who ferociously
patrolled the sidewalk and fire escape, spontaneously attacking
other cats and large dogs and driving all before her. The passion for
dominance emanating from this scrawny little fluff, hurling herself
hissing and snarling at window panes, was obviously acculturated,
a prehistoric triumph of the will. My theory of nature follows Sade

rather than Rousseau: aggression and violence are primarily not learned but instinctual, nature's promptings, bursts of primitive energy from the animal realm that man has never left. Civilization is an ethical stronghold, the Apollonian place that reason has built.

From *Sex, Art, and American Culture* by Camille Paglia, 1993

The Crimes of Felony

They found it significant that I called my cat Felony. I argued that I had chosen her name for its euphonious qualities. She used to sink her incisors into the heel of my hand and pause a fraction of a milli-metre from breaking the skin, staring at me until her eyes were reduced to sadistic yellow semibreves. She murdered without a qualm. She toyed with her victims, smiling broadly at their squeaks and death throes.

'Why isn't *she* a criminal?' I asked. 'Here I am, so criminal that I must be hanged by the neck until I am dead, and yet *I* have never shown such cruelty.'

'The difference is,' said Mr Pringle, 'that we must assume your cat commits her crimes without mischievous discretion.'

From *Four Bare Legs in a Bed* by Helen Simpson, 1990

Rybolov and Dlinyeñki

The Russian composer Alyeksandr Borodin and his wife, Yekatyerina, lived in a state of constant domestic hurly-burly. It was vividly described by another Russian composer, Rimsky-Korsakoff.

Their whole home life was one unending disorder. Dinner time and other meal-times were most indefinite. Once I came to their house at 11 in the evening and found them at dinner. Leaving out of account the girls, their protegées, of whom their house had never any lack, their apartment was often used as shelter or a night's lodging by various poor (or 'visiting') relations, who picked that place to fall ill or even lose their minds. Borodin had his hands full of them, doctored them, took them to hospitals, and then visited them there. In the four rooms of his apartment there often slept several strange persons of this sort; sofas and floors were turned into beds. Frequently it proved impossible to play the piano, because some one lay asleep in the adjoining room. At dinner and at tea, too, great disorder prevailed. Several tom-cats that found a home in Borodin's apartment paraded across the dinner-table, sticking their noses into plates, unceremoniously leaping to the diners' backs. These tom-cats basked in Yekatyerina Sergeyevna's protection; various details of their biography were related. One tabby was called *Rybolov* ('Fisherman'), because, in the winter, he contrived to catch small fish with his paw through the ice-holes; the other was called *Dlinyeñki* ('Longy') and he was in the habit of fetching homeless kittens by the neck to Borodin's apartment; these the Borodins would harbour, later finding homes for them. Then there were other, and less remarkable specimens of the genus felis. You might sit at their tea-table, – and behold! Tommy marches along the board and makes for your plate; you shoo him off, but Yekatyerina Sergeyevna invariably takes his part and tells some incident from his biography. Meantime, zip! another cat has bounded at Alyeksandr Porfiryevich's neck and, twining himself about it, has fallen to warming that neck without pity. 'Listen, dear Sir, this is too much of a good thing!' says Borodin, but without stirring; and the cat lolls blissfully on.

From *My Musical Life* by N. A. Rimsky-Korsakoff, 1924

'Sheba and High Society'

As I've explained, this cat Sheba is not really my cat. Her name is not even Sheba. That is only what I call her. I do not know her square monicker. I intended to ask her true owner, Miss Gertrude Neisen, when I saw the lady a few weeks ago, but in Miss Neisen's presence trivial questions seem utterly trivial.

I hope the 'Nei' is correct, though it could be 'Nie'. Anyway, you pronounce it 'Nee-sen'. The spelling could be ambidextrous like that of Jerry Geisler, the famous Los Angeles lawyer, who lists himself in the telephone directory as 'Gie' and 'Gei' and responds with equal amiability to 'Gee' or 'Guy'.

Miss Neisen is the charming singing star who is my landlady. Now just a minute, gentlemen. She owns the house in Holmby Hills, West Los Angeles, California, where I temporarily set up a branch of my hermit business, but with the main office still on Hibiscus Island down in Dade County, Florida, of course. That is all, gentlemen. Miss Neisen is a landed proprietor of no mean proportions. Or should I say landed-lady? No, I guess I shouldn't.

She once made the front pages by bidding in for $26,000 one of those marble palaces at Newport built by some jillionaire and in spite of the fact that the water pipes burst and flooded the joint causing considerable damage she subsequently sold the place at a big profit. She owns at least one other house in Los Angeles besides that which I share with Sheba the cat and I think she recently bought one in New York City, so when everybody is running out of houses Miss Neisen will be all hunky-dory.

I have examined my agreement with the lady and I fail to find any clause relating to my upkeep of Sheba the cat, but I have willingly accepted this unexpected responsibility because I noticed that she seemed to have many high-toned callers, including a golden bobtailed Manx, a fawn-coloured Angora, the spittin' image of Sheba herself, a big blue Angora, and divers and sundry others I could not identify because I am not really a cat-man.

But I thought they were all Sheba's suitors and having heard that among my neighbours are Miss Claudette Colbert, Miss Irene Dunne, Miss Fanny Brice and others of the cinema elite I was highly flattered. Thinks I to myself, if Sheba can contract a really classy union with one of these feline dudes I might horn myself into the best social circles of Holmby Hills as her sponsor.

To show these swells, meaning the cats, that Sheba was no blower, I had set out for them such delicacies of the season as boiled fish heads, and sometimes raw liver and chicken giblets and presently Sheba had a veritable salmon. A Siamese joined the festive board one day and then I figured we were as good as in, socially. I figured this must be Miss Colbert's cat, at least.

But now I am commencing to have my doubts about the visitors. It is obvious that their intentions are not serious and probably not honourable. The blue Angora snitches the choicest portions of fish right from under Sheba's velvet nose. The bob-tailed Manx cops all the gizards on her and the fawn Angora drinks her milk. They are eating us out of house and home.

[55]

I have given up on Sheba as a social wedge. I think she must be a dope to tolerate these free-loaders, and so am I for not taking Al Ellum Club and passing among the pussys and knocking their ears down. But they are invariably so ravenous that I am disturbed by the thought that but for my bounty they might perforce go hungry to bed. Maybe I ought to take my tidbits around among the owners.

Up to the time of meeting Sheba I had no great passion for cats. I never owned but one and that was a big white cat that was given me when I was occupying the penthouse on the roof of the Forrest Hotel high over West Forty-ninth and boasted the only live cricket ever on Broadway.

I had a big box of growing flowers in a window box of the penthouse that I bought from a florist and presumably the cricket came in the box. Anyway, all one summer it chirped away like mad and Broadwayfarers flocked to my door in droves asking permission to sit and listen to the song of the cricket.

Well, suddenly the song ceased and was never heard again and since it seemed unreasonable that the cricket had taken it on the duffy out of there after all the kind treatment bestowed upon it, I was finally forced to the conclusion that that big old white cat had corralled my cricket.

I was pretty hot under the collar about the matter and dismissed the white cat from my life immediately but I was not as hot as a delegation of Broadway gents when they came to my place that evening and learned of the disappearance of the cricket. They had planned to use it as a gambling medium by wagering on how often it would chirp within a given space of time.

I was very cool toward all cats thereafter until as I say Sheba came along, although I always exchanged courteous greetings with the cat belonging to Jack Duffy the actor, which would ride on his shoulder into Lindy's and other shots.

From *Short Takes* by Damon Runyon, 1948

His Serene Highness

*A letter from the poet Robert Southey to his daughter, Edith,
dated 31 January 1825.*

My dear Daughter, –
Sorry am I to inform you of the illness of his Serene Highness the
Archduke Rumpelstilzchen, Marquis Macbum, Earl Tomlemagne,
Baron Raticide, Waouhler, and Skratsch. His Serene Highness is
afflicted with the mange. One of the ladies of the Kitchen first perceived that he was not in health; and as none of the king's
physicians were within reach, they consulted John Edmondson,
who, upon hearing the case, pronounced an unfavourable opinion,
saying it was a disorder from which few recovered. Acting, however, upon the maxim which, as you may remember, Grio
[Grierson, a druggist in Keswick] exhibited in golden letters opposite to his rival's door – *Dum vita spes*, the son of Edmonds
prescribed for his Serene Highness that he was to be rubbed with a
certain mixture, and take daily a certain quantity of brimstone; and
it was thought, after much consideration, that this brimstone could
best be taken in boluses, four at a time, each containing about as
much as twelve pills.

The physicians would think his Serene Highness an ugly patient,
for he has no faith in physic, and he gives no fees, to say nothing of
the risk which there is in feeling his pulse. The ladies of the
Kitchen, however, are so interested in his welfare, that they have
taken upon themselves the arduous task of administering the medicine; which is a matter of great difficulty and some danger, for his
Serene Highness rebels against it strongly. Madam Betty takes him
on her lap, and holds his head; Madam Mary holds his legs; and
Madam Hannah stands ready with a bolus, which is inserted when
he opens his mouth for a mournful mew. That painter who was
called the Raffaelle of cats would have found the scene a most
worthy subject for his pencil. I, who am historiographer to his
Serene Highness, feel but too sensibly that I cannot do justice to it
in words. But I rejoice to add that the treatment appears to be
attended with success, and that visible improvement is observed in
the patient.

From *Selections from the Letters of Robert Southey*, 1856

Dido the Heathen

Part of a letter from Robert Southey to his brother, Tom,
dated 16 August 1808.

We have got the prettiest kitten you ever saw, – a dark tabby, – and we have christened her by the heathenish name of Dido. You would be very much diverted to see her hunt Herbert all round the kitchen, playing with his little bare feet, which she just pricks at every pat, and the faster he moves back the more she paws them, at which he cries 'Naughty Dido!' and points to his feet and says, 'Hurt, hurt, naughty Dido.' Presently he feeds her with comfits, which Dido plays with awhile, but soon returns to her old game.

From *Selections from the Letters of Robert Southey*, 1856

'Mike'

The cat who assisted in keeping the main gate of the British Museum
from February 1909, to January 1929

In the days when that famous and learned man, Sir Richard Garnett, ruled over the Department of Printed Books in the British Museum, he was frequently visited by a cat who was generally known among the staff as 'Black Jack.'

He was a very handsome black creature, with a white shirt front and white paws, and whiskers of great length. He was fond of sitting on the desks in the Reading Room, and he never hesitated to ask a reader to hold open both folding doors when he wanted to go out into the corridor. Being shut in one of the newspaper rooms one Sunday, and being bored, he amused himself by sharpening his claws on the bindings of the volumes of newspapers, and it must be confessed did much damage. This brought down upon him the wrath of the officials, and he was banished from the library; the Clerk of the Works was ordered to get rid of him, and tried to do so, but failed, for Black Jack had disappeared mysteriously. The truth was that two of the members of the staff arranged for him to be kept in safety in a certain place, and provided him with food and milk. An official report was written to the effect that Black Jack had disappeared, and he was 'presumed dead'; the bindings of the volumes of newspapers were repaired, and the official mind was once more at peace. A few weeks later Black Jack reappeared, and everyone was delighted to see him again; and the chief officials asked no questions!

Early in the spring of 1908 the Keeper of the Egyptian cat mummies in the British Museum was going down the steps of his official residence, when he saw Black Jack coming towards the steps and carrying something rather large in his mouth. He came to the steps and deposited his burden on the steps at the Keeper's feet and then turned and walked solemnly away. The something which he deposited on the steps was a kitten, and that kitten was later known to fame as 'Mike.' The kitten was taken in and cared for and grew and flourished, and by great good luck was adopted as a pal by the two cats already in the house. So all was well.

When Mike was a little older he went and made friends with the kind-hearted gatekeeper at the main gate, and he began to frequent the lodge. By day and night he was always sure of a welcome, and thus he was the happy possessor of two homes. On Sunday mornings the house cat taught him to stalk pigeons in the colonnade. Mike was set to 'point' like a dog, and the house cat little by little drove the pigeons up into a corner. The pigeons became dazed, and fell down, and then each cat seized a bird and carried it into the house uninjured. The Housekeeper took the pigeons from the cats, and in return for them gave a slice of beef or mutton and milk to each cat. The pigeons were taken into a little side room, and after they had eaten some maize and drunk water, they flew out of the window none the worse for their handling by the cats. The fact was that neither cat liked to eat game with dirty, sooty, feathers on it; they preferred clean, cooked meat.

As time went on, Mike, wishing to keep his proceedings during the hours of night uncriticised by the household, preferred the lodge to the house, and finally he took up his abode there; the corner shelf out of the draughts was prepared for him to sleep on, and he could go out and come in at any time he pleased both by day and by night. The Keeper of the Mummied Cats took care to feed him during the lean years of the war, and whoever went short, Mike did not. During the last two years he was difficult to feed because of his decaying teeth, but a diet of tender meat and fish on alternate days kept him going. He preferred sole to whiting, and whiting to haddock, and sardines to herrings; for cod he had no use whatever. He owed much to the three kind-hearted gatekeepers who cooked his food for him, and treated him as a man and a brother.

From *Mike* by Sir Ernest A. Wallis Budge, 1934

Mademoiselle Selime

*Two letters from the poet Thomas Gray
to his friend Horace Walpole, February-March 1747.*

As one ought to be particularly careful to avoid blunders in a compliment of condolence, it would be a sensible satisfaction to me (before I testify my sorrow, and the sincere part I take in your misfortune) to know for certain, who it is I lament. I knew Zara and Selima, (Selima, was it? or Fatima) or rather I knew them both together, for I cannot justly say which was which. Then as to your handsome Cat, the name you distinguish her by, I am no less at a loss, as well knowing one's handsome cat is always the cat one likes best; or, if one be alive and the other dead, it is usually that latter that is the handsomest. Besides, if the point were never so clear, I hope you do not think me so ill-bred or so imprudent as to forfeit all my interest in the surviver: Oh no! I would rather seem to mistake, and imagine to be sure it must be the tabby one that had met with this sad accident.

*

Heigh ho! I feel (as you to be sure have done long since) that I have very little to say, at least in prose. Somebody will be the better for it; I do not mean you, but your Cat, feuë Mademoiselle Selime, whom I am about to immortalise for one week or fortnight, as follows.

On a favourite Cat, call'd Selima, that fell into a China Tub
with Gold-Fishes in it & was drown'd

'Twas on a lofty Vase's Side
Where China's gayest Art had dyed
The azure Flowers that blow:
Demurest of the Tabby Kind,
The pensive Selima reclined
Gazed on the Lake below.

Her conscious Tail her Joy declared.
The fair round Face, the snowy Beard,
The Velvet of her Paws,
Her Coat, that with the Tortoise vyes,
Her Ears of Jett, & Emerald Eyes
She saw, & purr'd Applause.

Still had she gazed, but 'midst the Tide
Two angel-Forms were seen to glide,
The Genii of the Stream:
Their scaly Armour's Tyrian Hue
Thro' richest Purple to the View
Betray'd a golden Gleam.

The hapless Nymph with Wonder saw.
A Whisker first, & then a Claw,
With many an ardent Wish,
She stretch'd in vain to reach the Prize.
What female Heart can Gold despise?
What Cat's averse to Fish?

Presumptuous Maid! with Eyes intent
Again she stretch'd, again she bent
Nor knew the Gulph between.
Malignant Fate sate by, & smiled.
The slippery Verge her Feet beguiled:
She tumbled headlong in.

Eight Times emergeing from the Flood
She mew'd to ev'ry watry God
Some speedy Aid to send
No Dolphin came, no Nereïd stirr'd,
Nor cruel Tom, nor Harry heard.
A Fav'rite has no Friend!

From hence, ye Beauties, undeceiv'd
Know, one false Step is ne'er retrieved,
And be with Caution bold.
Not all, that strikes your wand'rin Eyes,
And heedless Hearts is lawful Prize,
Nor all, that glisters, Gold.

There's a Poem for you, it is rather too long for an Epitaph.

From *Correspondence of Thomas Gray*, 1935

Three

EATING

'War Cat'

A poem by Dorothy L. Sayers

I am sorry, my little cat, I am sorry –
if I had it, you should have it;
but there is a war on.

No, there are no table-scraps;
there was only an omelette
made from dehydrated eggs,
and baked apples to follow, and we finished it all.
The butcher has no lights,
the fishmonger has no cod's heads –
there is nothing for you
but cat-biscuit
and those remnants of yesterday's ham;
you must do your best with it.

Round and pathetic eyes,
baby mouth opened in a reproachful cry,
how can I explain to you?
I know, I know:
'Mistress, it is not nice;
the ham is very salt
and the cat-biscuit very dull,
I sniffed at it, and the smell was not enticing.
Do you not love me any more?
Mistress, I do my best for the war-effort;
I killed four mice last week,
yesterday I caught a young stoat.
You stroked and praised me,
you called me a clever cat.
What have I done to offend you?
I am industrious, I earn my keep;
I am not like the parrot, who sits there
using bad language and devouring
parrot-seed at eight-and-sixpence a pound
without working for it.

If you will not pay me my wages
there is no justice;
if you have ceased to love me
there is no charity.

'See, now, I rub myself against your legs
to express my devotion,
which is not altered by any unkindness.
My little heart is contracted
because your goodwill is withdrawn from me;
my ribs are rubbing together
for lack of food,
but indeed I cannot eat this –
my soul revolts at the sight of it.
I have tried, believe me,
but it was like ashes in my mouth.
If your favour is departed
and your bowels of compassion are shut up,
then all that is left me
is to sit in a draught on the stone floor and look miserable
till I die of starvation
and a broken heart.'

Cat with the innocent face,
what can I say?
Everything is very hard on everybody.
If you were a little Greek cat,
or a little Polish cat,
there would be nothing for you at all,
not even cat-food:
indeed, you would be lucky
if you were not eaten yourself.
Think if you were a little Russian cat
prowling among the cinders of a deserted city!

Consider that pains and labour
and the valour of merchant-seamen and fishermen
have gone even to the making of this biscuit
which smells so unappetizing.
Alas! there is no language
in which I can tell you these things.

Well, well!
If you will not be comforted
we will put the contents of your saucer
into the chicken-bowl – there!
all gone! nasty old cat-food –
The hens, I dare say,
will be grateful for it.

Wait only a little
and I will go to the butcher
and see if by any chance
he can produce some fragments of the insides of something.
Only stop crying
and staring in that unbearable manner –
as soon as I have put on my hat
we will try to do something about it.
My hat is on,
I have put on my shoes,
I have taken my shopping basket –
What are you doing on the table?

The chicken-bowl is licked clean;
there is nothing left in it at all.
Cat,
hell-cat, Hitler-cat, human,
all-too-human cat,
cat corrupt, infected,
instinct with original sin,
cat of a fallen and perverse creation,
hypocrite with the innocent and limpid eyes –
is nothing desirable
till somebody else desires it?

Is anything and everything attractive
so long as it is got by stealing?
Furtive and squalid cat,
green glance, squinted over a cringing shoulder,
streaking hurriedly out of the back door
in expectation of judgment,
your manners and morals are perfectly abhorrent to me,
you dirty little thief and liar.

Nevertheless,
although you have made a fool of me,
yet, bearing in mind your pretty wheedling ways
(not to mention the four mice and the immature stoat),
and having put on my hat to go to the butcher's,
I may as well go.

From *Time and Tide*, 4 December 1943

Milk with the Prime Minister

On the morning of August 5 [1944] Churchill flew by Dakota from Northolt for France, to see Montgomery. After an hour and fifteen minutes the plane arrived over the Cherbourg peninsula, but was then recalled, as fog on the landing strip at which Churchill was expected had caused a preceding plane to crash, and all of its occupants had been killed.

Churchill's plane flew back to Britain, landing at Thorney Island, from where he was driven to Eisenhower's forward headquarters at Sharpener Camp. Churchill and Eisenhower then lunched together, 'the PM taking delight', as Eisenhower's Naval Aide-de-Camp, Captain Butcher, noted in his diary, 'in feeding milk to the General's black kitten, Shaef, from a saucer on the dinner table at his place'.

From *Winston S. Churchill: Road to Victory 1941-1945* by Martin Gilbert, 1986

Sleek Rotundity

His cellar was well stocked with a selection of the best vintages, under his own especial charge. In all its arrangements his house was a model of order and comfort; and the whole establishment partook of the genial physiognomy of the master. From the master and mistress to the cook, and from the cook to the tom cat, there was about the inhabitants of the vicarage a sleek and purring rotundity of face and figure that denoted community of feelings, habits, and diet; each in its kind, of course, for the Doctor had his port, the cook her ale, and the cat his milk, in sufficiently liberal allowance.

From *Gryll Grange* by Thomas Love Peacock, 1860

Down at Heel

As the dogs of shy neighbourhoods usually betray a slinking consciousness of being in poor circumstances — for the most part manifested in an aspect of anxiety, an awkwardness in their play, and a misgiving that somebody is going to harness them to something, to pick up a living — so the cats of shy neighbourhoods exhibit a strong tendency to relapse into barbarism. Not only are they made selfishly ferocious by ruminating on the surplus population around them, and on the densely crowded state of all the avenues to cat's meat; not only is there a moral and politico-economical haggardness in them, traceable to these reflections; but they evince a physical deterioration. Their linen is not clean, and is wretchedly got up; their black turns rusty, like old mourning; they wear very indifferent fur; and take to the shabbiest cotton velvet, instead of silk velvet. I am on terms of recognition with several small streets of cats, about the Obelisk in Saint George's Fields, and also in the vicinity of Clerkenwell-green, and also in the back settlements of Drury-lane. In appearance, they are very like the women among whom they live. They seem to turn out of their unwholesome beds into the street, without any preparation. They leave their young families to stagger about the gutters, unassisted, while they frouzily quarrel and swear and scratch and spit, at street corners. In particular, I remark that when they are about to increase their families (an event of frequent recurrence) the resemblance is strongly expressed in a certain dusty dowdiness, down-at-heel self-neglect, and general giving up of things. I cannot honestly report that I have ever seen a feline matron of this class washing her face when in an interesting condition.

From The Uncommercial Traveller by Charles Dickens, 1860

'The Stray Cat'

The grey cat stirs upon the ledge
Outside the glass doors just at dawn.
I open it; he tries to wedge
His nose indoors. It is withdrawn.
He sits back to assess my mood.
He sees me frown; he thinks of food.

I am familiar with his stunts.
His Grace, unfed, will not expire.
He may be hungry, but he hunts
When need compels him, or desire.
Just yesterday he caught a mouse
And yoyoed it outside the house.

But now he turns his topaz eyes
Upon my eyes, which must reveal
The private pressures of these days,
The numb anxieties I feel.
But no, his greyness settles back
And yawns, and lets his limbs go slack.

He ventures forth an easy paw
As if in bargain. Thus addressed,
I fetch a bowl, and watch him gnaw
The star-shaped nuggets he likes best.
He is permitted food, and I
The furred indulgence of a sigh.

From All You Who Sleep Tonight by Vikram Seth, 1990

Uninvited Guests

In 1897, Thomas Hardy began to write his epic The Dynasts

He worked upon it for several years, but we are given hardly a glimpse of him in this connection, quietly purposeful among his books and at his writing-table. In 1900, when Professor W. L. Phelps called on him, there was no invitation into the study, although kindness and hospitality shone. These qualities were enjoyed not only by human visitors. The place was a paradise of cats. 'Are all these your own cats?' 'Oh, dear, no, some of them are, and some are cats who come regularly to have tea, and some are still other cats, not invited by us, but who seem to find out about this time of day that tea will be going.'

From *Thomas Hardy* by Edmund Blunden, 1941

The Pussies' Tea-Party

Last winter I had a visit of a week or two from my youngest niece, of nine years old. Wishing to have some small jollification before she went home, I thought it would be nice to have a pussies' tea-party, and as the prospect delighted her, we set to work to talk it over in earnest. No time was to be lost, for it was to be the next afternoon. So we sat down and seriously considered the items of the bill of fare. After some consultation, we decided that the basis of it should be fish, so we sent for some fresh herrings, and they were boiled and held in readiness.

Meanwhile my little companion proposed to issue cards of invitation, and said that she would write them herself. I asked if she could do them in the proper way, and as she was sure she could, I offered no further suggestions, and waited to see what would appear. So she found some scraps of writing-paper and wrote the invitations, and we went round together and presented them to the pussies, who duly purred their acceptance. They were all indoors, as it was wintry weather.

Next day, early in the afternoon, we prepared the feast. The invited guests were four grown pussies and two kittens, so we got ready four large and two small saucers. First a thick strip of fish was laid right across each saucer; an equal strip of cold rice pudding met it transversely, forming a cross-shaped figure that left four spaces in the angles. Thick cream was poured into these spaces, and the solid portion was decorated with tiny balls of butter, one rather larger in the middle, and two smaller on each of the rays. A reserve of fish and cream was to be at hand to replenish the portions most quickly exhausted.

In the middle of the sitting-room we placed a small, rather low, round table; and four stools were ranged round for the bigger pussies. As the hour for the feast drew near, much was the wondering as to how the guests would behave. They were to sit on the stools with their fore-paws on the edge of the tablecloth. We decided not to have flowers, because it would have overcrowded the space, as the two kittens were to be allowed to sit on the table.

At last the hour came, and meanwhile the excitement had grown intense. Five grown-ups were present, all as keenly interested as the little girl. The pussies were brought and placed on their stools, and the kittens, Chloe and Brindle, were put up to their saucers upon the table. To our great delight they all took in the situation at once; there was only a little hesitation on Maggie's part; she thought it was not manners to put her paws on the tablecloth; but this was soon overcome, and they all set to work as if they were quite accustomed to tea-parties and knew that nice behaviour was expected.

It was good to watch the pleasure of my little niece. I had expected that she would rush about and scream with delight, but she stood perfectly silent and still, with hands half raised, mouth a little open, and big eager eyes drinking in the scene, as if she thought it would vanish if she made a movement. Meanwhile the small guests were steadily eating away at their portions. Pinkieboy, as became the oldest and heaviest, finished his first, and after licking his saucer quite clean, and then his own lips, he looked round and clearly said, 'That was very good, and please I should like a little more, especially fish and cream.'

When they had all done there was a grand purring and washing of paws and faces before they got off their stools, and as they dispersed to find cosy sleeping-places, as wise pussies do after a comfortable meal, we all thought that our little party had been brilliantly successful, and had even some thoughts of sending a report of it to the *Morning Post.*

From *Home and Garden* by Gertrude Jekyll, 1900

Webster Gets Squiffy

In P. G. Wodehouse's tale 'The Story of Webster', Lancelot Mulliner is, like so many Wodehouse heroes, torn between two women – Gladys Bingley, a vers libre *poet, and Brenda Carberry-Pirbright, a beauty. Worse still, he is tyrannised by his very large and very black cat, Webster, descendant of a long line of ecclesiastical ancestors, whose eyes 'seemed to pierce to the very roots of the young man's soul, filling him with a sense of guilt'. One day, after a particularly fraught encounter with Gladys and Brenda, Lancelot turns to the whisky bottle for solace.*

He uncorked it, and was pouring out a lavish stream, when a movement on the floor below him attracted his attention.

Webster was standing there, looking up at him. And in his eyes was that familiar expression of quiet rebuke.

'Scarcely what I have been accustomed to at the Deanery,' he seemed to be saying.

Lancelot stood paralysed. The feeling of being bound hand and foot, of being caught in a snare from which there was no escape, had become more poignant than ever. The bottle fell from his nerveless fingers and rolled across the floor, spilling its contents in an amber river, but he was too heavy in spirit to notice it. With a gesture such as Job might have made on discovering a new boil, he crossed to the window and stood looking moodily out.

Then, turning with a sigh, he looked at Webster again – and, looking, stood spellbound.

The spectacle which he beheld was of a kind to stun a stronger man than Lancelot Mulliner. At first, he shrank from believing his eyes. Then, slowly, came the realization that what he saw was no mere figment of a disordered imagination. This unbelievable thing was actually happening.

Webster sat crouched upon the floor beside the widening pool of whisky. But it was not horror and disgust that had caused him to crouch. He was crouched because, crouching, he could get nearer to the stuff and obtain crisper action. His tongue was moving in and out like a piston.

And then abruptly, for one fleeting instant, he stopped lapping and glanced up at Lancelot, and across his face there flitted a quick smile – so genial, so intimate, so full of jovial camaraderie, that the young man found himself automatically smiling back, and not only smiling but winking. And in answer to that wink Webster winked too – a whole-hearted, roguish wink that said as plainly as if he had spoken the words:

'How long has this been going on?'

Then with a slight hiccough he turned back to the task of getting his drink before it soaked into the floor.

Into the murky soul of Lancelot Mulliner there poured a sudden flood of sunshine. It was as if a great burden had been lifted from his shoulders. The intolerable obsession of the last two weeks had ceased to oppress him, and he felt a free man. At the eleventh hour the reprieve had come. Webster, that seeming pillar of austere virtue, was one of the boys, after all. Never again would Lancelot quail beneath his eye. He had the goods on him.

Webster, like the stag at eve, had now drunk his fill. He had left the pool of alcohol and was walking round in slow, meditative circles. From time to time he mewed tentatively, as if he were trying to say 'British Constitution'. His failure to articulate the syllables appeared to tickle him, for at the end of each attempt he would utter a slow, amused chuckle. It was about this moment that he suddenly broke into a rhythmic dance, not unlike the old Saraband.

It was an interesting spectacle, and at any other time Lancelot would have watched it raptly. But now he was busy at his desk, writing a brief note to Mrs Carberry-Pirbright, the burden of which was that if she thought he was coming within a mile of her foul house that night or any other night she had vastly underrated the dodging powers of Lancelot Mulliner.

And what of Webster? The Demon Rum now had him in an iron grip. A lifetime of abstinence had rendered him a ready victim to the fatal fluid. He had now reached the stage when geniality gives way to belligerence. The rather foolish smile had gone from his face, and in its stead there lowered a fighting frown. For a few moments he stood on his hind legs, looking about him for a suitable adversary: then, losing all vestiges of self-control, he ran five times round the room at a high rate of speed and, falling foul of a small footstool, attacked it with the utmost ferocity, sparing neither tooth nor claw.

From *Young Men in Spats* by P. G. Wodehouse, 1936

A Glass of Vodka

Styopa turned from the telephone and in the hallway mirror, which the lazy Grunya had not dusted for a long time, he clearly saw a most peculiar individual, lanky as a pole and in pince-nez (ah, if only Ivan Nikolayevich had been there! He would have recognized this character at once!). The individual was reflected for a moment and vanished. Styopa anxiously peered further into the hallway, and was jolted a second time, for a huge black tom passed through the mirror and also disappeared.

Styopa's heart dropped and he swayed.

'What is this?' he thought. 'Am I going mad? Where do these reflections come from?' He looked into the hallway and cried in alarm:

'Grunya! What is this cat slinking around here? Where does he come from? And who else is here?'

'Don't worry, Stepan Bogdanovich,' a voice replied from the bedroom, but it was not Grunya's voice. 'The tom is mine. Don't be nervous. And Grunya is not here, I sent her to Voronezh. She complained that you had cheated her out of her vacation.'

The words were so absurd and unexpected that Styopa decided he had not heard right. In total confusion he trotted back to the bedroom and froze on the threshold. His hair stirred on his head, and small drops of sweat broke out on his forehead.

His guest was no longer alone in the bedroom. The second chair was occupied by the character he had just glimpsed in the hallway. Now he was clearly visible: a tiny feather mustache, one lens glinting in the pince-nez, the other missing. But there were even worse things in the bedroom. A third visitor sprawled insolently on the padded ottoman that had once belonged to the jeweler's lady – namely, a black tom of terrifying proportions, with a glass of vodka in one paw and a fork in the other with which he had already managed to impale a pickled mushroom.

The dim light in the bedroom began to fade out altogether in Styopa's eyes. 'So that's how people lose their minds … ' he thought and caught at the doorpost.

'I see that you are a little surprised, my dearest Stepan Bogdanovich?' Woland inquired of Styopa who stared at the room with chattering teeth. 'But there is nothing to wonder at. This is my retinue.'

The tom emptied his glass of vodka, and Styopa's hand began to slide down the doorpost.

'And this retinue requires space,' continued Woland.

From The Master and Margarita by Mikhail Bulgakov, 1967

A Leetle Drop o'Brandy

Twice a day is often enough, but not too often, to feed your cat, and it is better to let her have her allowance put down to her at once, instead of feeding her with tid-bits. Nothing can be better for pussy's breakfast than oatmeal porridge and sweet milk. *Entre nous*, reader, nothing could be better for your own breakfast. Oatmeal is the food of both mind and matter, the food of the hero and the poet; it was the food of Wallace, Bruce, and Walter Scott, and has been the food of brave men and good since their day . . .

Bread-and-milk, soaked, is the next best thing for pussy; and at dinner you must let her have a wee bit of meat. Lights, boiled and cut in pieces, are best, but horseflesh isn't bad; but you mustn't give her too much of either, or you will induce diarrhoea. Give her fish, occasionally, as a treat. If pussy is a show cat, a little morsel of butter, given every day, after dinner, will make her dress her jacket with surprising regularity.

Now, as to what she drinks, a well-bred cat is always particular, and at times even fastidious; but two things they must have – water and milk. They will often prefer the former to the latter.

But do keep their dishes clean. Disease is often brought on from neglect of this precaution. Cats will drink tea or beer, and I have seen a Tom get as drunk as a duke on oatmeal and whisky. An old lady, an acquaintance of mine, has a fine red-and-white Tom, and whenever he is ailing she gives him 'just a leetle drop o' brandy, sir.' Tom, I think, must have had two little drops o' brandy yesterday, when he rode my fox-terrier, Princie, all round the paddock. Those naughty drops o'brandy!

From *The Domestic Cat* by Gordon Stables, 1876

Mulled Port and Rum Punch

Part of a letter to Samuel Butler from his faithful correspondent Miss Savage, dated 24 December 1879.

My cat has taken to mulled port and rum punch. Poor old dear! he is all the better for it. Dr W. B. Richardson says that the lower animals always refuse alcoholic drinks, and gives that as a reason why humans should do so too.

A very pretty reason, is it not?

From *Samuel Butler, Author of Erewhon (1835-1902):*
A Memoir by Henry Festing Jones, 1919

Cheese and Biscuits

The meal ended merrily. Lazare jokingly snatched the terrine from his father's hands; then, when dessert appeared – a Pont l'Évêque cheese and biscuits – to everybody's delight, Mathieu [the dog] emerged. He had been asleep up till then somewhere under the table. The arrival of the biscuits had woken him up – he seemed to smell them in his sleep; and every evening, exactly at this moment, he would shake himself and go prowling round the table, trying to read people's feelings on their faces. Lazare was usually the first to be moved to pity; only, this evening, Mathieu, on his second round, fixed his gentle, human eyes on Pauline; then, instinctively recognizing a lover of animals and human beings, he laid his huge head on the child's small knee, without taking his affectionate suppliant gaze from her.

'Oh, the greedy thing!' said Madame Chanteau. 'Gently, Mathieu, don't snatch at your food so wildly!'

The dog had swallowed at one gulp the piece of biscuit Pauline held out to him; and once more he laid his head on the child's knee, asking for another piece, still gazing up at his new friend. She was laughing and kissing him; she thought him very funny, with his dangling ears and the black patch on the left eye – the only mark on his long, curly white coat. Then came an interruption: Minouche, jealous, leapt lightly on to the table and purring, curving her back, she started butting the child's chin with her head, as daintily as a young kid. This was her way of caressing you, letting you feel her cold nose and the touch of her pointed teeth, while she pranced about on her hind legs like a baker's boy kneading dough. Pauline was delighted at this; she sat between the two animals, the cat on the left and the dog on the right, overrun by them and so shockingly exploited that she ended by sharing out all her dessert between them.

'Send them away,' said her aunt. 'They'll leave you nothing!'

'What does that matter?' she replied quite simply, happy in her self-despoilment.

Dinner ended and Véronique cleared the table. The two animals, seeing everything gone, went off without a thank you, giving themselves a final lick.

From *Zest For Life* by Emile Zola, 1899,
translated from the French by Jean Stewart

Melons and Chop Suey

*An entry in Mary Welsh Hemingway's diary
for 8 October 1952.*

Gay and healthy after his heart attack last year from which he nearly died, Boise has been lunching with us. He is probably one of the world's most sophisticated cats in his food preferences – no mere carnivore. Lately, joining us at the table he has eaten fresh mangoes, cantaloupe and honeydew melons, chop suey, Mexican tacos with burning hot sauce, potato salad including the raw onion, leeks, cole slaw, and today sauerkraut and potatoes and raw celery. He likes sunflower seeds, all pies and cakes, fresh apples although he prefers them in a pie, chili con carne and cucumbers raw with salad dressing. He still jumps like a feather in a breeze.

From *How It Was* by Mary Welsh Hemingway, 1977

Calf's Liver and Cod Pâté

The cats had been constantly on Gwen John's mind while she had been away. There was one in particular, Valentine, old and hideous beyond belief in the opinion of Louise Roche. Valentine had no teeth and Madame Roche had been requested to feed her 250 grammes of minced meat daily. 'I thought of writing to tell you to give her calf's liver but I didn't because I knew you wouldn't,' Gwen John told Madame Roche. '*Oh! Certainement non!*' Madame Roche commented in housewifely horror. Gwen John, who would not cook for herself, thought nothing of walking to the market to buy a cod's head for the cats which she would make into a delicate pâté.

From *Gwen John 1876-1939* by Susan Chitty, 1981

Fish and Bones

The nineteenth-century naturalist and taxidermist Charles Waterton, author of Essays on Natural History, *cared little for his dogs; to his cats, however, he was devoted.*

There was one cat nicknamed 'Whitty,' a 'very beautiful and enormously large' cat which eventually weighed fully sixteen pounds. This cat was a great favourite, and was allowed an unlimited licence to poach. In a letter dated 1846 the Squire mentions another favourite cat, 'Tommy Pussy,' which, he says, had just brought him in 'a half-grown rabbit.' The Squire knew that well-fed cats make the best mousers, and the daily feeding of the cats was an event which is differently described by different authors. According to the Rev J. G. Wood, they were fed on fish caught in the lake, especially pike, which were chopped up on a wooden block near the stables. Although not a cat might be visible when the chopping started, half a dozen blows brought them swarming round like 'alley cats round a cat's-meat man.' According to Dr Hobson, who may be writing of what happened in Lent, the Squire would carefully collect in an old newspaper 'scraps of fish and their bones' and take them to the saddle room. There he would pound the bones with a hammer, calling out, 'My pretty, my pretty!' With this call alone he could at any time assemble 'the whole feline retinue.'

From *The Strange Life of Charles Waterton 1782-1865* by Richard Aldington, 1949

Indigestible

Of course, your ladyship knows that such lace must never be starched or ironed. Some people wash it in sugar and water, and some in coffee, to make it the right yellow colour; but I myself have a very good receipt for washing it in milk, which stiffens it enough and gives it a very good creamy colour. Well, ma'am, I had tacked it together (and the beauty of this fine lace is that, when it is wet, it goes into a very little space), and put it to soak in milk, when, unfortunately, I left the room; on my return I found pussy on the table, looking very like a thief, but gulping very uncomfortably, as if she was half-choked with something she wanted to swallow and could not. And would you believe it? At first I pitied her, and said 'Poor pussy! Poor pussy!' till, all at once, I looked and saw the cup of milk empty – cleaned out! 'You naughty cat!' said I; and I believe I was provoked enough to give her a slap, which did no good, but only helped the lace down – just as one slaps a choking child on the back. I could have cried, I was so vexed; but I determined I would not give the lace up without a struggle for it. I hoped the lace might disagree with her, at any rate; but it would have been too much for Job, if he had seen, as I did, that cat come in, quite placid and purring, not a quarter of an hour after, and almost expecting to be stroked. 'No, pussy!' said I, 'if you have any conscience you ought not to expect that!' And then a thought struck me; and I rang the bell for my maid, and sent her to Mr Hoggins, with my compliments, and would he be kind enough to lend me one of his top-boots for an hour? I did not think there was anything odd in the message; but Jenny said the young men in the surgery laughed as if they would be ill at my wanting a top-boot. When it came, Jenny and I put pussy in, with her fore-feet straight down, so that they were fastened, and could not scratch, and we gave her a teaspoonful of currant-jelly in which (your ladyship must excuse me) I had mixed some tartar emetic. I shall never forget how anxious I was for the next half-hour. I took pussy to my own room, and spread a clean towel on the floor. I could have kissed her when she returned the lace to sight, very much as it had gone down. Jenny had boiling water ready, and we soaked it and soaked it, and spread it on a lavender-bush in the sun before I could touch it again, even to put it in milk. But now your ladyship would never guess that it had been in pussy's inside.

From *Cranford* by Mrs Gaskell, 1853

An Insatiable Appetite

There is a propensity belonging to common house-cats that is very remarkable; I mean their violent fondness for fish, which appears to be their most favourite food: and yet nature in this instance seems to have planted in them an appetite that, unassisted, they know not how to gratify: for of all quadrupeds cats are the least disposed towards water; and will not, when they can avoid it, deign to wet a foot, much less to plunge into that element.

From *The Natural History and Antiquities of Selborne* by the Revd Gilbert White, 1789

Turtle Meat

In 1947 the millionaire Tommy Shevlin and his new bride,
Durie, spent five days of their honeymoon aboard Ernest Hemingway's
fishing boat, the Pilar.

After Tommy's enthusiastic praise, Durie found Hemingway a
great disappointment. A man's man, he was not an attentive host
and did not seem at all interested in Durie. He had a scrubby beard,
wore a long visor cap with a sweaty handkerchief hanging behind
his neck, drank heavily and spoke in rapid pidgin English, with
'chickenshit' (an unfamiliar term to her) inserted after every few
words. When they saw two turtles mating on the beach, Durie said:
'Look, how sweet.' Hemingway immediately rowed ashore in a
dinghy, disturbed their congress, captured one for cat food and
carried it aboard. He turned the turtle on its back; and it became
pink, then purple, smelled horrible and died slowly. Tommy, who
adored Hemingway and was flattered by his friendship, was surprised that Durie did not find him sexually attractive.

From *Hemingway: A Biography* by Jeffrey Meyers, 1985

The Essential Ingredient

Digby Anderson, who writes a regular column in The Spectator *under*
the title 'Imperative Cooking', is a man of fierce and deliberately offensive
opinions, both culinary and political. But he is sound on cats, as the
following article proves.

To make a proper Spanish omelette, you need a cat. It does not
have to be a Spanish cat, though I have found that a young cat is
better.

The recipe books and the newspaper cookery columns never
mention the cat. What they go on about instead are ingredients,
mostly their quantity not their quality, and the method of cooking.
Neither takes one very far. Miss MacMiadhachain (*Spanish Regional
Cookery*) says '2 large potatoes, 2 large onions, olive oil, 4 eggs,
salt'. Miss Torres (*The Spanish Table*) says much the same but gives

precise quantities – 3.7ml salt, adds black pepper (2.5ml) and has slightly fewer eggs to potatoes; six eggs to 2lb. But it depends how large Miss M's 'large' potatoes are. Miss Manjon (*Gastronomy of Spain and Portugal*) has twice as many potatoes to eggs as Miss M, assuming they both mean the same thing by 'large', with six large spuds and six eggs. Colman Andrews (*Catalan Cuisine*, though here he is describing the 'ubiquitous' Spanish omelette) gives a pound of potatoes and six eggs – but no onion. The quantity of oil varies from 'a small cup' and 4 fl.oz to two cups and half a pint. All these numbers imply some sort of guidance, but it is largely an illusion.

Anyone who has tried to make a Spanish omelette knows that the crucial thing is too much or too little spud, oil or eggs but this lot, at least collectively, are not much help. Apart from the 'large' business, three don't give the size of egg. I find it odd none of them say what sort of eggs – hens', ducks', pullets', geese's, bantams', turkeys' or pheasants'. I suppose they mean hens', but might they not at least point out that an omelette made with the eggs of hens which have not roamed free and eaten well will be off-white and so tasteless as to be ruined? It is far more important that eggs should have the taste of grass or grain than that they should be fresh.

Even more important, what sort of potatoes? Do they mean the sort which when stewed in the oil go greeny-grey or the sort which disintegrate? It is not that they are short of space to discuss such crucial matters. They go on, for instance, about the man who invented the French omelette (he was a Spaniard; now fancy that) and about farmworkers eating omelettes for their midday meal, and about the possible effects of Pyrenean scenery.

The four are roughly agreed on method although not on the speed with which the potatoes are cooked: are we stewing or sautéing? Whichever, the spuds and any onions are cooked, taken out of the pan (one says non-stick; nonsense, iron), mixed in with the eggs of indeterminate size, origin and diet, the lot turned back into the pan and slowly cooked with a lid on, then turned over.

What they do not say is that it is actually quite difficult to do well. To do it right, as with getting the ingredients right, is not easy. And lots more instruction about ingredients and methods is not the answer. What they should mention is the cat.

For the way to cook a Spanish omelette is to read any old recipe, preferably three or four. Ignore the exact quantities and the guff about the Pyrenean air or the farmworkers. Instead lock yourself in the kitchen and practise with different ingredients and methods till you get it right. It will take two or three hours but once learned you have it always. While practising, you will have failures, maybe five or ten regardless of what recipe you start with. It doesn't matter much: even with six eggs it's only costing a pound a practice and in my experience, cats, especially young cats, love discarded omelettes, even ones with grey-green potatoes or where too speedy cooking has dried them out. When Louie II was getting over nursing Dornford, Arborio and their sisters, she would eat an omelette a day. The Yates boy, who was the smallest, caught up on eggs and is now a 12-pounder at 12 months.

The books rarely mention the practice, the failures and the cat, and never aggressively enough. Cookery columns are usually much worse than the books: they positively encourage the evil illusion that possession of recipes – having the right spell – can compensate for hard work and practice. Many even incite their readers to try out a new recipe this weekend on their guests.

Imperative cooks don't practise on guests. It is bad cooking and worse manners. If anyone does it to you, never return there. I always try and peer in the window first. What I am looking for is not shelves of cookery books but a pair of fat cats.

From *The Spectator*, 31 August 1991

Dressed as Mutton

'Weal pie,' said Mr Weller, soliloquising, as he arranged the eatables on the grass. 'Wery good thing is a weal pie, when you know the lady as made it, and is quite sure it an't kittens; and arter all, though, where's the odds, when they're so like weal that the wery piemen themselves don't know the difference?'

'Don't they, Sam?' said Mr Pickwick.

'Not they, sir,' replied Mr Weller, touching his hat. 'I lodged in the same house with a pieman once, sir, and a wery nice man he was – reg'lar clever chap, too – make pies out o' anything, he could. "What a number o' cats you keep, Mr Brooks," says I, when I'd got intimate with him. "Ah," says he, "I do – a good many," says he.

"You must be wery fond o' cats," says I. "Other people is," says he, a winkin' at me; "they an't in season till the winter, though," says he. "Not in season!" says I. "No," says he, "fruits is in, cats is out." "Why, what do you mean?" says I. "Mean?" says he. "That I'll never be a party to the combination o' the butchers, to keep up the prices o' meat," says he. "Mr Weller," says he, a squeezing my hand wery hard, and vispering in my ear – "don't mention this here agin – but it's the seasonin' as does it. They're all made o' them noble animals," says he, a pointing to a wery nice little tabby kitten, "and I seasons 'em for beef-steak, weal, or kidney, 'cordin to the demand. And more than that," says he, "I can make a weal a beef-steak, or a beef-steak a kidney, or any one on 'em a mutton, at a minute's notice, just as the market changes, and appetites wary!"'

'He must have been a very ingenious young man, that, Sam,' said Mr Pickwick with a slight shudder.

'Just was, sir,' replied Mr Weller, continuing his occupation of emptying the basket, 'and the pies was beautiful.'

From *The Posthumous Papers of the Pickwick Club* by Charles Dickens, 1837

Double Helpings of Gravy

You may be interested in hearing of the crafty trick of a black Persian. Prin is a magnificent animal, but withal a most dainty one, showing distinct disapproval of any meat not cooked in the especial way he likes, viz., roast. The cook, of whom he is very fond, determined to break this bad habit. Stewed or boiled meat was accordingly put ready for him, but, as he had often done before, he turned from it in disgust. However, this time no fish or roast was substituted. For three days the saucer of meat was untouched, and no other food given. But on the fourth morning the cook was much rejoiced at finding the saucer empty. Prin ran to meet her, and the good woman told her mistress how extra affectionate that repentant cat was that morning. He did enjoy his dinner of roast that day (no doubt served with a double amount of gravy). It was not till the potboard under the dresser was cleaned on Saturday that his artfulness was brought to light. There, in one of the stewpans back of the others, was the contents of the saucer of stewed meat. There was no other animal about the place, and the other two servants were as much astonished as the cook at the clever trick played on them by this terribly spoiled pet of the house. But the cook was mortified at the thought of that saucer of roast beef. I know this story to be true, and I have known the cat for the last nine or ten years. It lives at Clapham.

From My Literary Zoo by Kate Sanborn, 1896

The Problem With Flies

It may here be observed that the cat is even sometimes of a slightly insectivorous propensity. Young, sportive cats, more especially, have much amusement in playing with cockroaches, and sometimes eat them. But they appear to eat them more from accident or idleness than from desire; much the same as a schoolboy will eat acorns. Occasionally, pussy will be fortunate in catching such rare game as a cricket. Flies are not easily caught, except in a window; and they are said to make cats thin. Beetles, I think, do a cat no harm. Lions and other beasts of prey are known to feed largely upon locusts, which occur in such vast swarms in the great African continent.

From The Cat: Its Natural History, Domestic Varieties, Management and Treatment
by Philip M. Rule, 1887

'The Covetous Cat'

Because the common is remote
they walk along hand in hand.

On the path ahead of them
some bird-lover has scattered bread

and in the middle of it a plump cat crouches
chewing at the crusts.

Cats don't really like bread, the man remarks
he only wants it because it's someone else's.

Like you, she thinks,
withdrawing her hand slightly.

Connie Bensley, from *The Spectator,* 16 May 1992

Eat First, Wash Later

Do you know why Cats always wash themselves after a meal? A Cat caught a sparrow, and was about to devour it, but the sparrow said,
  'No gentleman eats till he has first washed his face.'
The Cat, struck with this remark, set the sparrow down, and began to wash his face with his paw, but the sparrow flew away. This vexed Pussy extremely, and he said,
  'As long as I live I will eat first and wash my face afterwards.'
Which all cats do, even to this day.

From *The Book of Cats: A Chit-Chat Chronicle* by Charles H. Ross, 1868

Four

VOICES

'The Singing Cat'

It was a little captive cat
  Upon a crowded train
His mistress takes him from his box
  To ease his fretful pain.

She holds him tight upon her knee
  The graceful animal
And all the people look at him
  He is so beautiful

But oh he pricks and oh he prods
  And turns upon her knee
Then lifteth up his innocent voice
  In plaintive melody.

He lifteth up his innocent voice
  He lifteth up, he singeth
And to each human countenance
  A smile of grace he bringeth.

He lifteth up his innocent paw
  Upon her breast he clingeth
And everybody cries, Behold
  The cat, the cat that singeth.

He lifteth up his innocent voice
  He lifteth up, he singeth
And all the people warm themselves
  In the love his beauty bringeth.

From *The Collected Poems of Stevie Smith*, 1975

A Dismal Howl

On the grateful impulse of the moment, Mr Sloppy kissed Mrs Boffin's hand, and then detaching himself from that good creature that he might have room enough for his feelings, threw back his head, opened his mouth wide, and uttered a dismal howl. It was creditable to his tenderness of heart, but suggested that he might on occasion give some offence to the neighbours: the rather as the footman looked in, and begged pardon, finding he was not wanted, but excused himself on the ground 'that he thought it was Cats.'

From *Our Mutual Friend* by Charles Dickens, 1865

The Grappling of the Words

Christopher Smart's Jubilate Agno, *written in about 1760 while the poet was confined in Bedlam, is best known for the verses about his cat Jeoffry. But it also includes this lovely rumination on feline linguistics.*

For languages work into one another by their bearings.
For the power of some animal is predominant in every language.
For the power and spirit of a C*A*T is in the Greek.
For the sound of a cat is in the most useful preposition κατ' ευχην.
For the pleasantry of a cat at pranks is in the language ten thousand times over.
For J*A*CK UPON PR*A*NCK is in the performance of περι together or separate.
For Clapperclaw is in the grappling of the words upon one another in all the modes of versification.
For the sleekness of a Cat is in his αγλαιηφι.
For the Greek is thrown from heaven and falls upon its feet.
For the Greek when distracted from the line is sooner restored to rank and rallied into some form than any other.
For the purring of a Cat is his τρυζει.
For his cry is in *ουαι*, which I am sorry for.

For the Mouse (*Mus*) prevails in the Latin.

For Edi-mus, bibi-mus, vivi-mus – ore-mus.

For the Mouse is a creature of great personal valour.

For – this is a true case – Cat takes female mouse from the company of male – male mouse will not depart, but stands threatening and daring.

For this is as much as to challenge, if you will let her go, I will engage you, as prodigious a creature as you are.

From *The Poetical Works of Christopher Smart*, (written c.1758-63) 1980

A Very Ludicrous Effect

Dr Turton says, 'The Cat has a more voluminous and expressive vocabulary than any other brute; the short twitter of complacency and affection, the purr of tranquillity and pleasure, the mew of distress, the growl of anger, and the horrible wailing of pain.' For myself, I seldom hear a caterwauling without thinking of that droll picture in *Punch* of the old lady sitting up in bed and pricking up her ears to the music of a mewing Cat.

'Oh, ah! yes, it's the waits,' says she, with a delighted chuckle; 'I love to listen to 'em. It may be fancy, but somehow they don't seem to play so sweetly as they did when I was a girl. Perhaps it is that I am getting old, and don't hear quite so well as I used to do.'

For, even among Pussy's most ardent admirers, who possess the faculty of hearing, and have heard the music of Cats, would desire the continuance of their 'sweet voices'; yet a concert was exhibited at Paris, wherein Cats were the performers. They were placed in rows, and a monkey beat time to them, as the Cats mewed; and the historian of the facts relates that the diversity of the tones which they emitted produced a very ludicrous effect. This exhibition was announced to the Parisian public by the title of 'Concert Miaulant.'

This would seem to prove that Cats may be taught tricks, which is not generally believed, but is nevertheless the case.

From *The Book of Cats: A Chit-Chat Chronicle* by Charles H. Ross, 1868

Good Vibrations

The most important ligaments . . . are those called the 'vocal cords,' of which there are two kinds on either side of the cavity of the larynx. The *superior* or *false vocal cords* – called also the *superior thyro-arytenoid ligaments* – are folds of membrane which pass (one on each side) from the anterior aspect of the arytenoid cartilages downwards and forwards to the mucous membrane of the middle of the posterior (dorsal) surface of the epiglottis and thyroid. These are very prominent folds of membrane, and it is by their vibrations that the sound of 'purring' is said to be produced.

The *inferior* or *true vocal cords* – called also the *inferior thyro-arytenoid ligaments* – have a similar but lower origin and insertion to the false vocal cords; they are less prominent and sharply edged. It is these true vocal cords which by their vibrations are said to produce the mewing and howling sounds.

From *The Cat: An Introduction to the Study of Backboned Animals Especially Mammals*
by St George Mivart, 1881

The Admiral Who Purred

Purring, in humans, is a rare accomplishment. Often a novelist will make one of his characters speak in a 'soft, purring voice', but the metaphor is inept; there may be a faint illusion of purring but it remains an illusion. Why? Because though the vast majority of humans can purr out, they cannot purr in. This is due to the inferior flexibility of the human tongue muscles. Try it for yourself. Take a deep breath and exhale, allowing the tongue to vibrate against the palate. You will achieve quite a passable imitation of a purr. Now try to do the same thing backwards, inhaling. You will achieve nothing but a distasteful sucking noise.

I once met a man with an almost perfect purr, in as well as out. He was an admiral of the fleet, and he was staying with the Governor of Gibraltar, with whom I was dining. How we began to talk about purring I cannot recollect, but you may imagine my delight when I discovered that so distinguished a man was gifted with so exceptional a talent. There he sat, in the candlelight, fingering the stem of his wine-glass, purring with supreme virtuosity. His uniform was ablaze with decorations, and I remember thinking how ironic it was that none of them had been awarded for purring.

When I was planning this little volume I wrote to the admiral asking if I might mention him by name. He replied, politely but firmly, that he would prefer to remain anonymous. He seemed to imagine that his gift, if widely known, might lead to adverse comment on the lower deck. I cannot believe that this was his true reason; I suspect that he really feared that it might make the other admirals jealous.

Hassan, my Indian bearer during the latter part of the war, was another man with an authentic two-way purr. This was by no means his only claim to originality; he had, for example, a remarkable flair for dress. Soon after I had engaged him, I was bidden to stay with the Viceroy at Delhi, and I told Hassan that he must smarten himself up if he wished to accompany me. The Viceroy's servants, I remembered, were very grand in scarlet and gold, and Hassan looked like a sort of pirate. So I gave him money to get a new outfit. For two days he disappeared, and I was about to give him up as a bad job, and engage another man, when suddenly he came back, looking more like a pirate than ever. His method of getting a new outfit had been to search the bazaars and the junk-shops for a mass of military decorations, badges, ribbons, cap-bands, stripes and symbols of every description, which he had proudly sewn on to his jacket. I pretended to be annoyed, though I was in fact enchanted, and to put me in a good humour – for he knew I loved cats – he suddenly lowered his head and began to purr, a deep, rich purr in and out, of impeccable felinity. He was a great success with the Viceroy, who informed me that nothing quite like him had ever entered the portals of Vice-regal Lodge before, which I can well believe.

Hassan eventually purred himself out of my life in Madras, accompanied by my cuff links, my cigarette case and a large wad of rupees which he had abstracted from my wallet in a fit of absent-mindedness. It was an expensive purr, but it was worth it.

The most exquisite purr I have known, a real prima donna of a purr, belongs to my own cat 'Four'. It has all the qualities which connoisseurs of purring esteem most highly ... a perfect *vibrato*, superb breath control, exquisite quality of tone and a quite exceptional range, which stretches from a rich contralto to a flawless E in alt. There is no role where purring is demanded which 'Four' could not play with the greatest distinction. Moreover, 'Four' needs no human encouragement to make him perform; like all great artists he purrs for the sake of purring. Often, when I have been sitting at my desk, without knowing that he was near me, I have been suddenly startled by the fluting sounds of 'Four's' purr, and I look down to see him gazing at me . . . rather in the manner of a prima donna who is waiting for her accompanist . . .

But nearly all will agree that the best purr of all, the purr that speaks most directly to the heart, is the first faint purr that comes from a frightened stray, that one has found in the rain and taken in one's arms and coaxed with confidence. This is the purr that is quite irresistible, the language that only a brute would fail to heed.

From *Cats' A-Z* by Beverley Nichols, 1977

Magical Whistling

Will anyone explain to me why a cat gets so strangely excited if you whistle to her very shrill and high? I have tried it with English, Italian, and German cats; there is no geographical distinction. When puss hears you whistling (especially if you whistle *Night of stars and night of love* as high as you can), she begins to rub herself against you fascinated, jumps on to your knee, sniffs at your lips in surprise, and finally, in rapturous excitement, she bites passionately at your mouth and nose with an expression disfigured by voluptuousness; on which you, of course, stop, and she begins to purr hoarsely and energetically like a small motor. I have thought about it time and again, and I don't know to this day from what ancient instinct cats adore whistling; I do not believe that at any time in the primeval era there was an age when male cats whistled shrilly instead of yowling in metallic and strident alto as they do to-day. Perhaps in distant and savage times there lived some cat-gods who used to speak to their cat-worshippers by means of magical whistling; but this is a mere hypothesis, and the fascination of music is one of the riddles of the cat soul.

From *Intimate Things* by Karel Čapek, translated by Dora Round, 1935

'The Young Cats' Club for Poetry-Music'

The philharmonic young cats' club
   Upon the roof was collected
Tonight, but not for sensual joys,
   No wrong could there be detected.

No summer night's wedding dream there
      was dreamt,
   No song of love did they utter
In the winter season, in frost and snow,
   For frozen was every gutter.

A newborn spirit hath recently
   Come over the whole cat-nation,
But chiefly the young, and the young cat feels
   More earnest with inspiration.

The frivolous generation of old
   Is extinct, and a newborn yearning,
A pussy-springtime of poetry
   In art and in life they're learning.

The philharmonic young cats' club
   Is now returning to artless
And primitive music, and naiveté,
   From modern fashions all heartless.

It seeks in music for poetry,
   Roulades with the quavers omitted;
It seeks for poetry, music-void,
   For voice and instrument fitted.

It seeks for genius's sovereign sway,
   Which often bungles truly,
Yet oft in art unconsciously
   Attains the highest stage duly.

It honors the genius which prefers
　　Dame Nature to keep at a distance,
And will not show off its learning, – in fact
　　Its learning not having existence.

This is the programme of our cat club,
　　And with these intentions elated,
It holds its first winter concert tonight
　　On the roof, as before I have stated.

Yet sad was the execution, alas,
　　Of this great idea so splendid;
I'm sorry, my dear friend Berlioz,
　　That by thee it wasn't attended.

It was a charivari, as though
　　With brandy elated greatly,
Three dozen pipers struck up the tune
　　That the poor cow died of lately.

It was an utter medley, as though
　　In Noah's ark were beginning
The whole of the beasts in unison
　　The Deluge to tell of in singing.

O what a croaking, snarling, and noise!
　　O what a mewing and yelling!
And even the chimneys all join'd in,
　　The wonderful chorus swelling.

And loudest of all was heard a voice
　　Which sounded languid and shrieking
As Sontag's voice became at the last,
　　When utterly broken and squeaking.

The whimsical concert! Methinks that they
　　A grand Te Deum were chanting,
To honour the triumph o'er reason obtain'd
　　By commonest frenzy and canting.

Perchance moreover the young cats' club
   The open grand were essaying
That the greatest pianist of Hungary*
   Composed for Charenton's playing.

It was not till the break of day
   That an end was put to the party;
A cook was in consequence brought to bed,
   Who before had seem'd well and hearty.

The lying-in woman lost her wits,
   Her memory, too, was affected,
And who was the father of her child
   No longer she recollected.

Say, was it Peter? Say, was it Paul?
   Say who is the father, Eliza!
'O Liszt, thou heavenly cat!' she said,
   And simper'd and look'd the wiser.

* Liszt.

From *The Poems of Heine*, translated by E. A. Bowring, 1861

A Siamese Fortissimo

He was ... a very conversational cat, especially when we were
alone together. He understood every inflection of my voice; and I
learned to know the meaning of at least some of his many cries. To
a stranger and even, I believe, to other people who knew him well,
his plaintive voice must have sounded the same note whenever he
used it. But anyone who has lived close to a Siamese cat knows that
he has a wide range of expression. I could always distinguish between Charles's cry for a door to be opened, his demands for food,
his requests for notice to be taken of him.

   He had his own peculiar and distinguishable utterances for
various occasions: as for instance when he had made use of his tray
and wanted to be sure that it would be made ready for him again.
He could be assertive without being clamorous: he could talk softly

and as he grew older he often did. He could even make himself understood silently when he chose.

Sometimes in the night he would be distressed – could it have been bad dreams? – and would awake me with a strident and insistent clamour, and that was something not to be borne patiently, for I defy anyone to sleep through a Siamese fortissimo. But although as I came to the surface from the depths of sleep I momentarily lost patience even with Charles, I could not be truly angry with him.

He liked to have his own way, and he had many different ways of getting it. There were times when his voice was pure honey, and the touch of his paw so gentle that it could scarcely be felt. If he sensed that I had other things on my mind he would approach me cautiously, so that I was almost unaware of his slow, ingratiating progress. When I petted one of the other cats he gave me a basilisk stare until I remembered my obligations and transferred my affection to him. If I took no notice of him, preferring to sit at the piano, he jumped past me and sat serenely on a level with my head as if he were taking part in the entertainment. He used me increasingly as a pillow, lying asleep on my knee and sometimes dreaming perhaps of unfought battles, his delicately formed mouth slightly open, revealing his white teeth bared in a harmless snarl, his long whiskers bristling. Sometimes he persuaded me to open a drawer for him, so that he could climb into it and settle down with deep satisfaction for a sleep.

From *Charles: The Story of a Friendship* by Michael Joseph, 1943

Discordant and horrid

At the Baron's feet was lying
Gracefully the worthy tom-cat,
Hiddigeigei, with the coal-black
Velvet fur and mighty tail.
'Twas an heirloom from his long-lost,
Much-beloved, and stately consort,
Leonore Monfort du Plessys.
Hiddigeigei's native country

Was Hungaria, and his mother,
Who was of the race Angora
Bore him to a Puszta tom-cat.
In his early youth to Paris
He was sent as a fond token
Of the love of an Hungarian,
Who, though far in Debreczin, still
With due reverence had remembered
The blue eyes of Leonora,
And the rats in her old palace.
With the stately Leonora
To the Rhine came Hiddigeigei.
A true house-pet, somewhat lonesome
Did he while away his life there;
For, he hated to consort with
Any of the German cat-tribe.
'They may have,' thus he was thinking
In his consequential cat-pride,
'Right good hearts, and may possess too
At the bottom some good feeling,
But 'tis polish that is wanting;
A fine culture and high breeding,
I miss sorely in these vulgar
Natives of this forest-city.
And a cat who won his knight spurs
In fair Paris, and who often
In the quarter of Montfaucon
Has enjoyed a racy rat-hunt,
Misses in this little town here
All that is to him congenial,
Any intercourse with equals.'
Isolated, therefore, but still
Ever dignified and solemn
Lived he in this lonely castle.
Graceful through the halls he glided,
Most melodious was his purring;
And in fits of passion even,
When he curved his back in anger,
And his hair stood bristling backward,

Never did he fail to mingle
Dignity with graceful bearing.
But when over roof and gable
Up he softly clambered, starting
On a hunting expedition,
Then mysteriously by moonlight
His green eyes like emeralds glistened;
Then, indeed, he looked imposing
This majestic Hiddigeigei . . .

So the maiden shyly entered,
Shyly she took up the trumpet,
To her rosy lips she pressed it;
But with fright she well-nigh trembled
At her breath to sound transforming
In the trumpet's golden calyx,
Which the air was bearing farther,
Farther – ah, who knoweth where?
But she cannot stop the fun now,
And with sounds discordant, horrid,
Fit to rend the ears to pieces
So disturbed the morning stillness,
That the poor cat Hiddigeigei's
Long black hair stood up like bristles,
Like the sharp quills of a hedgehog.
Raising then his paw to cover
His offended ear, he spoke thus:
'Suffer on, my valiant cat-heart,
Which so much has borne already,
Also bear this maiden's music!
We, we understand the laws well,
Which do regulate and govern
Sound, enigma of creation.
And we know the charm mysterious
Which invisibly through space floats,
And, intangible a phantom,
Penetrates our hearing organs,
And in beasts' as well as men's hearts
Wakes up love, delight and longing,
Raving madness and wild frenzy.

And yet, we must bear this insult,
That when nightly in sweet mewing
We our love-pangs are outpouring,
Men will only laugh and mock us,
And our finest compositions
Rudely brand as caterwauling.
And in spite of this we witness
That these same fault-finding beings
Can produce such horrid sounds as
Those which I have just now heard.
Are such tones not like a nosegay
Made of straw, and thorns, and nettles,
In the midst a prickly thistle?
And in presence of this maiden
Who the trumpet there is blowing,
Can a man then without blushing
E'er sneer at our caterwauling?
But, thou valiant heart, be patient!
Suffer now, the time will yet come
When this self-sufficient monster,
Man, will steal from us the true art
Of expressing all his feelings;
When the whole world in its struggle
For the highest form of culture
Will adopt our style of music.
For in history, there is justice,
She redresses every wrong.'

From *The Trumpeter of Säkkingen* by Joseph Victor von Scheffel, translated from
the German by Mrs Francis Brünnow, 1877

'The Safety-Valve'

Now baby-talk for babies is taboo,
And Baby must be Fotheringham to you,
Not muzzer's ickle precious any more –
The cats come in for it. It's not a bore
To them; in fact, the stuff is highly prized.
They hog it, but are not demoralised.

Even in households where a word of slang
Provokes the tyrant's frown, the scholar's fang,
No one demurs when bucketsful of gab
Are emptied in a sugared flood on Tab.

And personally I think it's no bad thing
For people who can't act, or swear, or sing,
To have old *F. Domesticus* for theme –
A grand excuse to let off psychic steam.

He is so pronkum, and his pitty nose
Is finished in such darling shades of rose;
His pads so tippitty, his peepy face
(Look, like a baby's, with this bit of lace)
So yumsome, and that mimsy mouth of his
So cupid, that we must go kiss, kiss, kiss.
(Our germs can't hurt him, nor his germs hurt us –
If it were Fotheringham, there'd be a fuss).
His bellikins, all set with little studs
(Mind where you comb) like tiny coral buds,
His pretty sit-upon and cherub thighs,
And most of all his love-love-lovely eyes,
Make all of us so feeble and so fain
That not an inhibition can remain.

Tab purrs in bliss, for he can use it all:
Hark! what was that? I think I hear a squall;
But it evokes only a careless Damn,
The distant howl of lonely Fotheringham.

From On Cats by Ruth Pitter, 1947

'Tobermory'

It was a chill, rain-washed afternoon of a late August day, that indefinite season when partridges are still in security or cold storage,
and there is nothing to hunt – unless one is bounded on the north
by the Bristol Channel, in which case one may lawfully gallop after

fat red stags. Lady Blemley's house-party was not bounded on the north by the Bristol Channel, hence there was a full gathering of her guests round the tea-table on this particular afternoon. And, in spite of the blankness of the season and the triteness of the occasion, there was no trace in the company of that fatigued restlessness which means a dread of the pianola and a subdued hankering for auction bridge. The undisguised open-mouthed attention of the entire party was fixed on the homely negative personality of Mr Cornelius Appin. Of all her guests, he was the one who had come to Lady Blemley with the vaguest reputation. Some one had said he was 'clever,' and he had got his invitation in the moderate expectation, on the part of his hostess, that some portion at least of his cleverness would be contributed to the general entertainment. Until tea-time that day she had been unable to discover in what direction, if any, his cleverness lay. He was neither a wit nor a croquet champion, a hypnotic force nor a begetter of amateur theatricals. Neither did his exterior suggest the sort of man in whom women are willing to pardon a generous measure of mental deficiency. He had subsided into mere Mr Appin, and the Cornelius seemed a piece of transparent baptismal bluff. And now he was claiming to have launched on the world a discovery beside which the invention of gunpowder, of the printing-press, and of steam locomotion were inconsiderable trifles. Science had made bewildering strides in many directions during recent decades, but this thing seemed to belong to the domain of miracle rather than to scientific achievement.

'And do you really ask us to believe,' Sir Wilfrid was saying, 'that you have discovered a means for instructing animals in the art of human speech, and that dear old Tobermory has proved your first successful pupil?'

'It is a problem at which I have worked for the last seventeen years,' said Mr Appin, 'but only during the last eight or nine months have I been rewarded with glimmerings of success. Of course I have experimented with thousands of animals, but latterly only with cats, those wonderful creatures which have assimilated themselves so marvellously with our civilization while retaining all their highly developed feral instincts. Here and there among cats one comes across an outstanding superior intellect, just as one does among the ruck of human beings, and when I made the acquaintance of Tobermory a week ago I saw at once that I was in contact with a "Beyond-cat" of extraordinary intelligence. I had gone far along the road to success in recent experiments; with Tobermory, as you call him, I have reached the goal.'

Mr Appin concluded his remarkable statement in a voice which he strove to divest of a triumphant inflection. No one said 'Rats,' though Clovis's lips moved in a monosyllabic contortion which probably invoked those rodents of disbelief.

'And do you mean to say,' asked Miss Resker, after a slight pause, 'that you have taught Tobermory to say and understand easy sentences of one syllable?'

'My dear Miss Resker,' said the wonder-worker patiently, 'one teaches little children and savages and backward adults in that piecemeal fashion; when one has once solved the problem of making a beginning with an animal of highly developed intelligence one has no need for those halting methods. Tobermory can speak our language with perfect correctness.'

This time Clovis very distinctly said, 'Beyond-rats!' Sir Wilfrid was more polite, but equally sceptical.

'Hadn't we better have the cat in and judge for ourselves?' suggested Lady Blemley.

Sir Wilfrid went in search of the animal, and the company settled themselves down to the languid expectation of witnessing some more or less adroit drawing-room ventriloquism.

In a minute Sir Wilfrid was back in the room, his face white beneath its tan and his eyes dilated with excitement.

'By Gad, it's true!'

His agitation was unmistakably genuine, and his hearers started forward in a thrill of awakened interest.

Collapsing into an armchair he continued breathlessly: 'I found him dozing in the smoking-room, and called out to him to come for his tea. He blinked at me in his usual way, and I said, "Come on, Toby; don't keep us waiting"; and, by Gad! he drawled out in a most horribly natural voice that he'd come when he dashed well pleased! I nearly jumped out of my skin!'

Appin had preached to absolutely incredulous hearers; Sir Wilfrid's statement carried instant conviction. A Babel-like chorus of startled exclamation arose, amid which the scientist sat mutely enjoying the first fruit of his stupendous discovery.

In the midst of the clamour Tobermory entered the room and made his way with velvet tread and studied unconcern across to the group seated round the tea-table.

A sudden hush of awkwardness and constraint fell on the company. Somehow there seemed an element of embarrassment in addressing on equal terms a domestic cat of acknowledged dental ability.

'Will you have some milk, Tobermory?' asked Lady Blemley in a rather strained voice.

'I don't mind if I do,' was the response, couched in a tone of even indifference. A shiver of suppressed excitement went through the listeners, and Lady Blemley might be excused for pouring out the saucerful of milk rather unsteadily.

'I'm afraid I've spilt a good deal of it,' she said apologetically.

'After all, it's not my Axminster,' was Tobermory's rejoinder.

Another silence fell on the group, and then Miss Resker, in her best district-visitor manner, asked if the human language had been difficult to learn. Tobermory looked squarely at her for a moment and then fixed his gaze serenely on the middle distance. It was obvious that boring questions lay outside his scheme of life.

'What do you think of human intelligence?' asked Mavis Pellington lamely.

'Of whose intelligence in particular?' asked Tobermory coldly.

'Oh, well, mine for instance,' said Mavis, with a feeble laugh.

'You put me in an embarrassing position,' said Tobermory, whose tone and attitude certainly did not suggest a shred of embarrassment. 'When your inclusion in this house-party was suggested Sir Wilfrid protested that you were the most brainless woman of his acquaintance, and that there was a wide distinction between hospitality and the care of the feeble-minded. Lady Blemley replied that your lack of brain-power was the precise quality which had earned you your invitation, as you were the only person she could think of who might be idiotic enough to buy their old car. You know, the one they call "The Envy of Sisyphus," because it goes quite nicely up-hill if you push it.'

Lady Blemley's protestations would have had greater effect if she had not casually suggested to Mavis only that morning that the car in question would be just the thing for her down at her Devonshire home.

Major Barfield plunged in heavily to effect a diversion.

'How about your carryings-on with the tortoiseshell puss up at the stables, eh?'

The moment he had said it every one realized the blunder.

'One does not usually discuss these matters in public,' said Tobermory frigidly. 'From a slight observation of your ways since you've been in this house I should imagine you'd find it inconvenient if I were to shift the conversation on to your own little affairs.'

The panic which ensued was not confined to the Major.

'Would you like to go and see if cook has got your dinner ready?' suggested Lady Blemley hurriedly, affecting to ignore the fact that it wanted at least two hours to Tobermory's dinner-time.

'Thanks,' said Tobermory, 'not quite so soon after my tea. 'I don't want to die of indigestion.'

'Cats have nine lives, you know,' said Sir Wilfrid heartily.

'Possibly,' answered Tobermory; 'but only one liver.'

'Adelaide!' said Mrs Cornett, 'do you mean to encourage that cat to go out and gossip about us in the servants' hall?'

The panic had indeed become general. A narrow ornamental balustrade ran in front of most of the bedroom windows at the Towers, and it was recalled with dismay that this had formed a favourite promenade for Tobermory at all hours, whence he could watch the pigeons – and heaven knew what else besides. If he intended to become reminiscent in his present outspoken strain the effect would be something more than disconcerting. Mrs Cornett, who spent much time at her toilet table, and whose complexion was reputed to be of a nomadic though punctual disposition, looked as ill at ease as the Major. Miss Scrawen, who wrote fiercely sensuous poetry and led a blameless life, merely displayed irritation; if you are methodical and virtuous in private you don't necessarily want every one to know it. Bertie van Tahn, who was so depraved at seventeen that he had long ago given up trying to be any worse, turned a dull shade of gardenia white, but he did not commit the error of dashing out of the room like Odo Finsberry, a young gentleman who was understood to be reading for the Church and who was possibly disturbed at the thought of scandals he might hear concerning other people. Clovis had the presence of mind to maintain a composed exterior; privately he was calculating how long it would take to procure a box of fancy mice through the agency of the *Exchange and Mart* as a species of hush-money.

Even in a delicate situation like the present, Agnes Resker could not endure to remain too long in the background.

'Why did I ever come down here?' she asked dramatically.

Tobermory immediately accepted the opening.

'Judging by what you said to Mrs Cornett on the croquet-lawn yesterday, you were out for food. You described the Blemleys as the dullest people to stay with that you knew, but said they were clever enough to employ a first-rate cook; otherwise they'd find it difficult to get anyone to come down a second time.'

'There's not a word of truth in it! I appeal to Mrs Cornett – ' exclaimed the discomfited Agnes.

'Mrs Cornett repeated your remark afterwards to Bertie van Tahn,' continued Tobermory, 'and said, "That woman is a regular Hunger Marcher, she'd go anywhere for four square meals a day," and Bertie van Tahn said – '

At this point the chronicle mercifully ceased. Tobermory had caught a glimpse of the big yellow Tom from the Rectory working his way through the shrubbery towards the stable wing. In a flash he had vanished through the open French window.

With the disappearance of his too brilliant pupil Cornelius Appin found himself beset by a hurricane of bitter upbraiding, anxious inquiry, and frightened entreaty. The responsibility for the situation lay with him, and he must prevent matters from becoming worse. Could Tobermory impart his dangerous gift to other cats? was the first question he had to answer. It was possible, he replied, that he might have initiated his intimate friend the stable puss into his new accomplishment, but it was unlikely that his teaching could have taken a wider range as yet.

'Then,' said Mrs Cornett, 'Tobermory may be a valuable cat and a great pet; but I'm sure you'll agree, Adelaide, that both he and the stable cat must be done away with without delay.'

'You don't suppose I've enjoyed the last quarter of an hour, do you?' said Lady Blemley bitterly. 'My husband and I are very fond of Tobermory – at least, we were before this horrible accomplishment was infused into him, but now, of course, the only thing is to have him destroyed as soon as possible.'

'We can put some strychnine in the scraps he always gets at dinner-time,' said Sir Wilfrid, 'and I will go and drown the stable cat myself. The coachman will be very sore at losing his pet, but I'll say a very catching form of mange has broken out in both cats and we're afraid of it spreading to the kennels.'

'But my great discovery!' expostulated Mr Appin; 'after all my years of research and experiment – '

'You can go and experiment on the shorthorns at the farm, who are under proper control,' said Mrs Cornett, 'or the elephants at the Zoological Gardens. They're said to be highly intelligent, and they have this recommendation, that they don't come creeping about our bedrooms and under chairs, and so forth.'

An archangel ecstatically proclaiming the Millennium, and then finding that it clashed unpardonably with Henley and would have to be indefinitely postponed, could hardly have felt more crestfallen than Cornelius Appin at the reception of his wonderful achievement. Public opinion, however, was against him – in fact, had the general voice been consulted on the subject it is probable that a strong minority vote would have been in favour of including him in the strychnine diet.

Defective train arrangements and a nervous desire to see matters brought to a finish prevented an immediate dispersal of the party, but dinner that evening was not a social success. Sir Wilfrid had had rather a trying time with the stable cat and subsequently with the coachman. Agnes Resker ostentatiously limited her repast to a morsel of dry toast, which she bit as though it were a personal enemy; while Mavis Pellington maintained a vindictive silence throughout the meal. Lady Blemley kept up a flow of what she hoped was conversation, but her attention was fixed on the doorway. A plateful of carefully dosed fish scraps was in readiness on the sideboard, but sweets and savoury and dessert went their way, and no Tobermory appeared either in the dining-room or kitchen.

The sepulchral dinner was cheerful compared with the subsequent vigil in the smoking-room. Eating and drinking had at least supplied a distraction and cloak to the prevailing embarrassment. Bridge was out of the question in the general tension of nerves and tempers, and after Odo Finsberry had given a lugubrious rendering of 'Melisande in the Wood' to a frigid audience, music was tacitly avoided. At eleven the servants went to bed, announcing that the small window in the pantry had been left open as usual for Tobermory's private use. The guests read steadily through the current batch of magazines, and fell back gradually on the 'Badminton

Library' and bound volumes of *Punch*. Lady Blemley made periodic visits to the pantry, returning each time with an expression of listless depression which forestalled questioning.

At two o'clock Clovis broke the dominating silence.

'He won't turn up to-night. He's probably in the local newspaper office at the present moment, dictating the first instalment of his reminiscences. Lady What's-her-name's book won't be in it. It will be the event of the day.'

Having made this contribution to the general cheerfulness, Clovis went to bed. At long intervals the various members of the house-party followed his example.

The servants taking round the early tea made a uniform announcement in reply to a uniform question. Tobermory had not returned.

Breakfast was, if anything, a more unpleasant function than dinner had been, but before its conclusion the situation was relieved. Tobermory's corpse was brought in from the shrubbery, where a gardener had just discovered it. From the bites on his throat and the yellow fur which coated his claws it was evident that he had fallen in unequal combat with the big Tom from the Rectory.

By midday most of the guests had quitted the Towers, and after lunch Lady Blemley had sufficiently recovered her spirits to write an extremely nasty letter to the Rectory about the loss of her valuable pet.

Tobermory had been Appin's one successful pupil, and he was destined to have no successor. A few weeks later an elephant in the Dresden Zoological Garden, which had shown no previous signs of irritability, broke loose and killed an Englishman who had apparently been teasing it. The victim's name was variously reported in the papers as Oppin and Eppelin, but his front name was faithfully rendered Cornelius.

'If he was trying German irregular verbs on the poor beast,' said Clovis, 'he deserved all he got.'

From *The Chronicles of Clovis* by Saki, 1911

A Kitten's Recollections

Like all our race I was born blind and it was some days before I opened my eyes. Even when I could see I did not make much of what I saw. I suppose that this is partly because I was so small and the world was so big. I could see my brothers and my sister, snuggling, as I was, next to our mother. And I could see my mother – then. Often since I grew up I have seen a female cat suckling her young and I have tried to remember my own mother. I know that she was tabby with white markings – as I am myself – but I cannot remember her features. I can only remember the feeling of warmth and security I enjoyed for those first few days and weeks of my life, when I was alone somewhere, in a room, with just my mother and my brothers and my sister and no intrusion from the human world.

My mother must have had decent human minders. They had let her give birth to us. They had not drowned us as so many people drown kittens; and, as I say, they left us in peace. Being born and coming to life was for me like waking up after a long, delightfully deep and lazy sleep. There was no hurry about waking up. As I have told you, little grandson, for the first few days I did not even open my eyes. And then for quite a few days more I simply lay there, squeaking and purring with my tiny voice, and with a constant supply of delicious warm milk always laid on by my mother. Although I cannot remember her appearance, how well I remember that feeling of well-being, when I was cuddled up beside her – I think we were in a large open drawer at the bottom of a bed or a wardrobe – the warmth of her fur, the tenderness with which she licked us and groomed us and taught us to be clean.

After I was about a fortnight old I became aware that the world was not entirely populated by cats. My mother had begun to tell us that there were *people* in the world. But what could that mean to me when I had no idea what they were like? Then gradually, over the next few days or weeks, my brothers and I got to know the human look and that human smell. The drawer where we were lying peacefully would be roughly shaken and one would hear a grown-up human voice say, 'Just peep at them, mind! Don't touch them, yet, or it will disturb them!' or 'Aren't they *gorgeous*.'

Of course I reconstruct what they said but this is the sort of thing

I have heard drooling, well-meaning two-footers say when staring at kittens. And who can blame them? There are no creatures in the world more endearing than young kittens with large eyes and large paws and soft, fluffy little coats. Yes, even I was a young kitten once, though you may find it impossible to believe. Young and frisky and as silly as you. The first thing which struck me about the human beings was not what they said but what they looked like. I remember, when we had been visited a number of times by them, trying to focus my eyes on the enormous red faces which peered so closely at our own. At that stage nothing had happened to make me dread or fear the human race; but I think I did fear them. They seemed so large and, by the refined standards of my own mother, so very coarse and ugly. I remember the extraordinary smells they gave off as they peered at us – you know the human stench already and how horrible it is to animal nostrils.

But, as I say, though I was in the house of human kind, they were reasonably good specimens. Gradually, as we grew older, the people fed us with eggs and boiled chicken until we were used to solid foods. And before long they were feeding us on tinned foods and minced offal, and playing with us. We left the room where we were born and were carried down some stairs in a basket; and there, in front of a big fire, we would scamper about, chase balls of wool, and amuse ourselves and the people in whose house we had been born. They were still happy days, I suppose, but for me the days of pure and true happiness will always be the days in that bedroom, when it was just cats and no human interruptions.

From *Stray* by A. N. Wilson, 1987

The Cheshire-Cat Speaks

The baby grunted again, and Alice looked very anxiously into its face to see what was the matter with it. There could be no doubt that it had a *very* turn-up nose, much more like a snout than a real nose: also its eyes were getting extremely small for a baby: altogether Alice did not like the look of the thing at all. 'But perhaps it was only sobbing,' she thought, and looked into its eyes again, to see if there were any tears.

No, there were no tears. 'If you're going to turn into a pig, my dear,' said Alice, seriously, 'I'll have nothing more to do with you. Mind now!' The poor little thing sobbed again (or grunted, it was impossible to say which), and they went on for some while in silence.

Alice was just beginning to think to herself, 'Now, what am I to do with this creature, when I get it home?' when it grunted again, so violently, that she looked down into its face in some alarm. This time there could be *no* mistake about it: it was neither more or less than a pig, and she felt that it would be quite absurd for her to carry it any further.

So she set the little creature down, and felt quite relieved to see it trot away quietly into the wood. 'If it had grown up,' she said to herself, 'it would have made a dreadfully ugly child: but it makes rather a handsome pig, I think.' And she began thinking over other children she knew, who might do very well as pigs, and was just saying to herself 'if one only knew the right way to change them – ' when she was a little startled by seeing the Cheshire-Cat sitting on a bough of a tree a few yards off.

The Cat only grinned when it saw Alice. It looked good-natured, she thought: still it had *very* long claws and a great many teeth, so she felt that it ought to be treated with respect.

'Cheshire-Puss,' she began rather timidly, as she did not at all know whether it would like the name: however, it only grinned a little wider. 'Come, it's pleased so far,' thought Alice, and she went on. 'Would you tell me, please, which way I ought to go from here?'

'That depends a good deal on where you want to get to,' said the Cat.

'I don't much care where – ' said Alice.

'Then it doesn't matter which way you go,' said the Cat.

' – so long as I get *somewhere*,' Alice added as an explanation.

'Oh, you're sure to do that,' said the Cat, 'if you only walk long enough.'

Alice felt that this could not be denied, so she tried another question. 'What sort of people live about here?'

'In *that* direction,' the Cat said, waving its right paw round, 'lives a Hatter: and in *that* direction,' waving the other paw, 'lives a March Hare. Visit either you like: they're both mad.'

'But I don't want to go among mad people,' Alice remarked.

'Oh, you ca'n't help that,' said the Cat: 'we're all mad here. I'm mad. You're mad.'

'How do you know I'm mad?' said Alice.

'You must be,' said the Cat, 'or you wouldn't have come here.'

Alice didn't think that proved it at all: however, she went on: 'And how do you know that you're mad?'

'To begin with,' said the Cat, 'a dog's not mad. You grant that?'

'I suppose so,' said Alice.

'Well, then,' the Cat went on, 'you see a dog growls when it's angry, and wags its tail when it's pleased. Now *I* growl when I'm pleased, and wag my tail when I'm angry. Therefore I'm mad.'

'*I* call it purring, not growling,' said Alice.

'Call it what you like,' said the Cat. 'Do you play croquet with the Queen to-day?'

'I should like it very much,' said Alice, 'but I haven't been invited yet.'

'You'll see me there,' said the Cat, and vanished.

Alice was not much surprised at this, she was getting so well used to queer things happening. While she was still looking at the place where it had been, it suddenly appeared again.

'By-the-bye, what became of the baby?' said the Cat. 'I'd nearly forgotten to ask.'

'It turned into a pig,' Alice answered very quietly, just as if the Cat had come back in a natural way.

'I thought it would,' said the Cat, and vanished again.

Alice waited a little, half expecting to see it again, but it did not appear, and after a minute or two she walked on in the direction in which the March Hare was said to live. 'I've seen hatters before,' she said to herself: 'the March Hare will be much the most interesting, and perhaps, as this is May, it wo'n't be raving mad – at least not so mad as it was in March.' As she said this, she looked up, and there was the Cat again, sitting on a branch of a tree.

'Did you say "pig", or "fig"?' said the Cat.

'I said "pig",' replied Alice; 'and I wish you wouldn't keep appearing and vanishing so suddenly: you make one quite giddy!'

'All right,' said the Cat; and this time it vanished quite slowly, beginning with the end of the tail, and ending with the grin, which remained some time after the rest of it had gone.

'Well! I've often seen a cat without a grin,' thought Alice; 'but a grin without a cat! It's the most curious thing I ever saw in all my life!'

From *Alice's Adventures in Wonderland* by Lewis Carroll, 1865

'From the Laws of the Cats'

This is my Man. I am not afraid of him.

He is very strong for he eats a great deal; he is an Eater of All Things. What are you eating? Give me some!

He is not beautiful, for he has no fur. Not having enough saliva, he has to wash himself with water. He miaows in a harsh voice and a great deal more than he need. Sometimes in his sleep he purrs.

Open the door for me!

I do not know why he has made himself Master; perhaps he has eaten something sublime.

He keeps my rooms clean for me.

In his paws he carries a sharp black claw and he scratches with it on white sheets of paper. That is the only game he plays. He sleeps at night instead of by day, he cannot see in the dark, he has no pleasures. He never thinks of blood, never dreams of hunting or fighting; he never sings songs of love.

Often at night when *I* can hear mysterious and magic voices, when I can see that the darkness is all alive, *he* sits at the table with bent head and goes on and on, scratching with his black claw on the white papers. Don't imagine that I am at all interested in you. I am only listening to the soft whispering of your claw. Sometimes the whispering is silent, the poor dull head does not know how to go on playing and then I am sorry for him and I miaow softly in sweet and sharp discord. Then my Man picks me up and buries his hot face in my fur. At those times he divines for an instant a glimpse of a higher life, and he sighs with happiness and purrs something which can almost be understood.

But don't think that I am at all interested in you. You have warmed me, and now I will go out again and listen to the dark voices.

From *Intimate Things* by Karel Čapek, translated by Dora Round, 1935

'Sad Memories'

They tell me I am beautiful: they praise my silken hair,
My little feet that silently slip on from stair to stair:
They praise my pretty trustful face and innocent grey eye;
Fond hands caress me oftentimes, yet would that I might die!

Why was I born to be abhorr'd of man and bird and beast?
The bulfinch marks me stealing by, and straight his song hath
ceased;
The shrewmouse eyes me shudderingly, then flees; and, worse
than that,
The housedog he flees after me – why was I born a cat?

Men prize the heartless hound who quits dry-eyed his native land;
Who wags a mercenary tail and licks a tyrant hand.
The leal true cat they prize not, that if e'er compell'd to roam
Still flies, when let out of the bag, precipitately home.

They call me cruel. Do I know if mouse or songbird feels?
I only know they make me light and salutary meals:
And if, as 'tis my nature to, ere I devour I tease 'em,
Why should a low-bred gardener's boy pursue me with a besom?

Should china fall or chandeliers, or anything but stocks –
Nay stocks, when they're in flowerpots – the cat expects hard
knocks:
Should ever anything be missed – milk, coals, umbrellas, brandy
The cat's pitch'd into with a boot or any thing that's handy.

'I remember, I remember,' how one night I 'fleeted by,'
And gain'd the blessed tiles and gazed into the cold clear sky.
'I remember, I remember, how my little lovers came;'
And there, beneath the crescent moon, play'd many a little game.

They fought – by good St Catharine, 'twas a fearsome sight to see
The coal-black crest, the glowering orbs, of one gigantic He.
Like bow by some tall bowman bent at Hastings or Poictiers,
His huge back curved, till none observed a vestige of his ears:

He stood, an ebon crescent, flouting that ivory moon;
Then raised the pibroch of his race, the Song without a Tune;

Gleam'd his white teeth, his mammoth tail waved darkly to and
fro,
As with one complex yell he burst, all claws, upon the foe.

It thrills me now, that final Miaow – that weird unearthly din:
Lone maidens heard it far away, and leap'd out of their skin.
A potboy from his den o'erhead peep'd with a scared wan face;
Then sent a random brickbat down, which knock'd me into space.

Nine days I fell, or thereabouts: and, had we not nine lives,
I wis I ne'er had seen again thy sausage-shop, St Ives!
Had I, as some cats have, nine tails, how gladly I would lick
The hand, and person generally, of him who heaved that brick!

For me they fill the milkbowl up, and cull the choice sardine:
But ah! I nevermore shall be the cat I once have been!
The memories of that fatal night they haunt me even now:
In dreams I see that rampant He, and tremble at that Miaow.

From *Fly Leaves* by C. S. Calverley, 1878

A Noise and a Wawling

An extract from what is sometimes referred to as 'the first English novel'.

I would counsel all men to bury or burn all executed bodies, and re-
frain from making such abhominable sacrifice as I have often seen,
with ravens or rather devils feeding upon them, in this foresaid
leads – in the which every night many cats assembled, and there
made such a noise that I could not sleep for them.

Wherefore, on a time as I was sitting by the fire with certain of
the house, I told them what a noise and what a wawling the cats
had made there the night before from ten o'clock till one, so that
neither I could sleep nor study for them; and by means of this introduction we fell in communication of cats. And some affirming, as
I do now (but I was against it then), that they had understanding,
for confirmation whereof one of the servants told this story.

'There was in my country,' quod he, 'a man' (the fellow was born
in Staffordshire) 'that had a young cat which he had brought up of a
kitling, and would nightly dally and play with it; and on a time as

he rode through Kankwood about certain business, a cat, as he thought, leaped out of a bush before him and called him twice or thrice by his name. But because he made none answer nor spake (for he was so afraid that he could not), she spake to him plainly twice or thrice these words following: "Commend me unto Titton Tatton and to Puss thy Catton, and tell her that Grimalkin is dead." This done she went her way, and the man went forward about his business. And after that he was returned home, in an evening sitting by the fire with his wife and his household, he told of his adventure in the wood. And when he had told them all the cat's message, his cat, which had harkened unto the tale, looked upon him sadly, and at the last said, "And is Grimalkin dead? Then farewell dame," and therewith went her way and was never seen after.'

From *Beware The Cat* by William Baldwin, 1570

Give Me Your Voice

Part of a letter from David Garnett to T. H. White, 18 October 1958

My Amaryllis daughter is 15 today. We gave her a gramophone & shall be either cheered or maddened by it in the years to come. My daughter Nerissa (11) wrote a poem about a cat.* Did I send it to you? I think it is magnificent. But alas you dont [sic] like cats – just as you disapprove of women! My dear Tim, I really love you & value you. So please be careful of yourself.

Yours ever BUNNY

Puss
A sleeping shape lies on the bed
A cat morose, at peace, well-fed.
Oh, Puss, you sleeping mass of fur,
Give me your voice, and let me purr.

Nerissa Stephen Garnett
(11 years old)

From *The White/Garnett Letters*, 1968

Five

WISDOM

The Remarkablest Cat

One of my comrades there [at a Californian mining camp] – another of those victims of eighteen years of unrequited toil and blighted hopes – was one of the gentlest spirits that ever bore its patient cross in a weary exile: grave and simple Dick Baker, pocket miner of Dead-House Gulch. He was forty-six, grey as a rat, earnest, thoughtful, slenderly educated, slouchily dressed and clay-soiled, but his heart was finer metal than any gold his shovel ever brought to light – than any, indeed, that ever was mined or minted.

Whenever he was out of luck and a little down-hearted, he would fall to mourning over the loss of a wonderful cat he used to own (for where women and children are not, men of kindly impulses take up with pets, for they must love something). And he always spoke of the strange sagacity of that cat with the air of a man who believed in his secret heart that there was something human about it – maybe even supernatural.

I heard him talking about this animal once. He said:

'Gentlemen, I used to have a cat here, by the name of Tom Quartz, which you'd a took an interest in, I reckon – most anybody would. I had him here eight year – and he was the remarkablest cat *I* ever see. He was a large grey one of the Tom specie, an' he had more hard, natchral sense than any man in this camp – 'n' a *power* of dignity – he wouldn't let the Guv'nor of Californy be familiar with him. He never ketched a rat in his life – 'peared to be above it. He never cared for nothing but mining. He knowed more about mining, that cat did, than any man *I* ever, ever see. You couldn't tell *him* noth'n' 'bout placer diggin's – 'n' as for pocket mining, why, he was just born for it. He would dig out after me an' Jim when we went over the hills propsect'n', and he would trot along behind us for as much as five mile, if we went so fur. An' he had the best judgment about mining ground – why, you never see anything like it. When we went to work, he'd scatter a glance around, 'n' if he didn't think much of the indications, he would give a look as much as to say, 'Well, I'll have to get you to excuse *me*'; 'n' without another word he'd hyste his nose into the air 'n' shove for home. But if the ground suited him, he would lay low 'n' keep dark till the first pan was washed, 'n' then he would sidle up 'n' take a look, an' if there was about six or seven grains of gold *he* was satisfied – he didn't want no better prospect 'n' that – 'n' then he would lay down on our coats and snore like a steamboat till we'd struck the pocket, an' then get up 'n' superintend. He was nearly lightnin' on superintending.

'Well, by-an'-bye, up comes this yer quartz excitement. Everybody was into it – everybody was pick'n' 'n' blast'n' instead of shovellin' dirt on the hill-side – everybody was put'n' down a shaft instead of scrapin' the surface. Noth'n' would do Jim but *we* must tackle the ledges, too, 'n' so we did. We commenced put'n' down a shaft, 'n' Tom Quartz he begin to wonder what in the Dickens it was all about. *He* hadn't ever seen any mining like that before, 'n' he was all upset, as you may say – he couldn't come to a right understanding of it no way – it was too many for *him*. He was down on it, too, you bet you – he was down on it powerful – 'n' always appeared to consider it the cussedest foolishness out. But that cat, you know, was *always* agin new-fangled arrangements – somehow he never could abide 'em. *You* know how it is with old habits. But by-an'-bye Tom Quartz begin to git sort of reconciled a little, though he never *could* altogether understand that eternal sinkin' of a shaft an' never pannin' out anything. At last he got to comin' down in the shaft, hisself, to try to cipher it out. An' when he'd git the blues, 'n' feel kind of scruffy, 'n' aggravated 'n' disgusted – knowin', as he did, that the bills was runnin' up all the time an' we warn't makin' a cent – he would curl up on a gunny-sack in the corner an' go to sleep. Well, one day when the shaft was down about eight foot, the rock got so hard that we had to put in a blast – the first blast'n' we'd ever done since Tom Quartz was born. An' then we lit the fuse, 'n' clumb out 'n' got off 'bout fifty yards – 'n' forgot 'n' left Tom Quartz sound asleep on the gunny-sack. In 'bout a minute we seen a puff of smoke bust up out of the hole, 'n' then everything let go with an awful crash, 'n' about four million ton of rocks 'n' dirt 'n' smoke 'n' splinters shot up 'bout a mile an' a half into the air, an' by George, right in the dead centre of it was old Tom Quartz a-goin' end over end, an' a snortin' an' a sneez'n', an' a clawin' an' a reachin' for things like all possessed. But it warn't no use, you know, it warn't no use. An' that was the last we see of *him* for about two minutes 'n' a half, an' then all of a sudden it begin to rain rocks and rubbage, an' directly he come down kerwhop about ten foot off f'm where we stood. Well, I reckon he was p'raps the orneriest-lookin' beast you ever see. One ear was sot back on his neck, 'n' his tail was stove up, 'n' his eye-winkers was swinged off, 'n' he was all blacked up with powder an' smoke, an' all sloppy with mud 'n' slush f'm one end to the other. Well, sir, it arn't no use to try to apologize – we couldn't say a word. He took a sort of a disgusted look at hisself, 'n' then he looked at us – an' it was just exactly the same as if he had said – "Gents, maybe *you* think it's smart to take advantage of a cat that 'ain't had no experience of quartz minin', but *I* think *different*" – an' then he turned on his heel 'n' marched off home without ever saying another word.

'That was jest his style. An' maybe you won't believe it, but after that you never see a cat so prejudiced agin quartz mining as what he was. An' by-an'-bye when he *did* get to goin' down in the shaft agin, you'd 'a been astonished at his sagacity. The minute we'd tetch off a blast 'n' the fuse'd begin to sizzle, he'd give a look as much as to say, "Well, I'll have to git you to excuse *me*," an' it was surpris'n' the way he'd shin out of that hole 'n' go f'r a tree. Sagacity? It ain't no name for it. 'Twas *inspiration!*'

I said, 'Well, Mr Baker, his prejudice against quartz mining *was* remarkable, considering how he came by it. Couldn't you ever cure him of it?'

'*Cure him!* No! When Tom Quartz was sot once, he was *always* sot – and you might a blowed him up as much as three million times 'n' you'd never a broken him of his cussed prejudice agin quartz mining.'

The affection and the pride that lit up Baker's face when he delivered this tribute to the firmness of his humble friend of other days will always be a vivid memory with me.

From *The Innocents At Home* by Mark Twain, 1882

The Cunningest Kitten

White House, Jan. 6, 1903

Dear Kermit,

We felt very melancholy after you and Ted left and the house seemed empty and lonely. But it was the greatest possible comfort to feel that you both really have enjoyed school and are both doing well there.

Tom Quartz is certainly the cunningest kitten I have ever seen. He is always playing pranks on Jack and I get very nervous lest Jack should grow too irritated. The other evening they were both in the library – Jack sleeping before the fire – Tom Quartz scampering about, an exceedingly playful little wild creature – which is about what he is. He would race across the floor, then jump upon the curtain or play with the tassel. Suddenly he spied Jack and galloped up to him. Jack, looking exceedingly sullen and shame-faced, jumped out of the way and got upon the sofa, where Tom Quartz instantly jumped upon him again. Jack suddenly shifted to the other sofa, where Tom Quartz again went after him. Then Jack started for the door, while Tom made a rapid turn under the sofa and around the table, and just as Jack reached the door leaped on his hind-quarters. Jack bounded forward and away and the two went tandem out of the room – Jack not reappearing at all; and after about five minutes Tom Quartz stalked solemnly back.

Another evening the next Speaker of the House, Mr Cannon, an exceedingly solemn, elderly gentleman with chin whiskers, who certainly does not look to be of playful nature, came to call upon me. He is a great friend of mine, and we sat talking over what our policies for the session should be until about eleven o'clock; and when he went away I accompanied him to the head of the stairs. He had gone about half-way down when Tom Quartz strolled by, his tail erect and very fluffy. He spied Mr Cannon going down the stairs, jumped to the conclusion that he was a playmate escaping, and raced after him, suddenly grasping him by the leg the way he does Archie and Quentin when they play hide and seek with him; then loosening his hold he tore downstairs ahead of Mr Cannon, who eyed him with iron calm and not one particle of surprise . . .

From *Theodore Roosevelt's Letters to His Children*, 1919

Summoned by Bells

A family were accustomed to feed their cat in the dining-room every day, while they were at dinner. Puss was so well acquainted with the sound of the bell, which announced that the meal was on the table, that she never failed to repair thither regularly with the family. By accident, one day, she was shut up in a room by herself, where she remained undiscovered till dinner was over. Some hours afterwards, however, she was emancipated from her confinement, when she hastened to the room, but found nothing reserved for her. Hungry and disappointed, she ran to the bell, and began tumbling it about with the intention of ringing it; but it proved too unwieldy for her.

From *Interesting Anecdotes of the Animal Kingdom* by Thomas Brown, 1834

The Sun Seekers

It is stated in a Japanese book that the tip of a Cat's nose is always cold, except on the day corresponding with our Midsummer-day. This is a question I cannot say I have gone into very deeply. I know, however, that Cats always have a warm nose when they awaken from sleep. All Cats are fond of warmth. I knew one which used to open an oven door after the kitchen fire was out, and creep into the oven. One day the servant shut the door, not noticing the cat was inside, and lighted the fire. For a long while she could not make out whence came the sounds of its crying and scratching, but fortunately made the discovery in time to save its life. A Cat's love of the sunshine is well known, and perhaps this story may not be unfamiliar to the reader:-

One broiling hot summer's day Charles James Fox and the Prince of Wales were lounging up St James's street, and Fox laid the Prince a wager that he would see more Cats than his Royal Highness during their promenade, although the Prince might choose which side of the street he thought fit. On reaching Piccadilly, it turned out that Fox had seen thirteen Cats and the Prince none. The Prince asked for an explanation of this apparent miracle.

'Your Royal Highness,' said Fox, 'chose, of course, the shady side of the way as most agreeable. I knew that the sunny side would be left for me, and that Cats prefer the sunshine.'

From *The Book of Cats: A Chit-Chat Chronicle* by Charles H. Ross, 1868

Beggars Can Be Choosers

Four cats, belonging to one of my friends, had taught themselves the art of begging like a dog. They had frequently seen the dog practise that accomplishment at the table, and had observed that he generally received a reward for so doing. By a process of inductive reasoning, they decided that if they possessed the same accomplishment, they would in all probability receive the same reward. Acting on this opinion, they waited until they saw the dog sit up in a begging posture, and immediately assumed the attitude with imperturbable gravity. Of course their ingenuity was not suffered to pass unrewarded and they always found that their newly-discovered accomplishment was an unfailing source of supplies for them.

From *Sketches and Anecdotes of Animal Life* by the Revd J. G. Wood, 1861

Quietly Rational

In the *Plymouth Journal* for the year 1827, a writer states, 'That there is now at the Battery in the Devil's Point, a cat which is an expert catcher of fish, being in the constant habit of diving into the sea and bringing up the fish alive in her mouth, and depositing them in the guard-room for the use of the sailors.' This remarkable cat was indirectly trained by her instructors to sport in this way, having long been accustomed to dive into the sea after water-rats. 'Her love for the water,' says the writer, 'was as great as that of any Newfoundland dog.' This anecdote proves how the nature of the beast may be changed by circumstances.

No doubt had she had kittens, and fish and water-rats being the only food they could obtain, they might have followed the mother's curious habit, and in course of time, the instinct becoming hereditary, there might have been a race of sea-diving cats! Cats can reason, or put two and two together, in a quiet way. Sam Slick tells a tale touching this faculty, which might not be believed were it not backed up by other unimpeachable evidence. A servant continually entering the master's library upon the summons of a bell, and as continually told that it had not been rung, persisting in saying that he had heard it, the domestics began to suspect that the house was haunted, and so it turned out to be – not by a ghost, however, but by a cat, who, wishing the company of her master, and not being able to obtain admission by reason of the closed door, must have noticed that when a certain bell within her reach rung, it was opened by the servant. Puss noticing cause and effect, used to ring the bell, and always ran to the door and entered when he did; the fact of their simultaneous entry leading to the discovery of her cunning trick. This, it will be said, was but a Sam Slickism; but here is a still cleverer trick, which is related of an Angora cat belonging to a Carthusian Monastery at Paris. This cat having observed that the cook always answered a certain bell just before the dinners, portioned out in plates, were served out to the monks, leaving them in consequence unprotected, had wit enough to take advantage of this fact, for she used to ring the bell outside the kitchen door, watch the cook off guard, spring through the window, help herself to a portion, and then return before he had time to come back!

We have shown the capabilities of a fish-catching cat, but a trap-setting puss is more curious still. A writer tells us that a tom-cat at Callendar, having been observed to carry off a piece of beef, as the servant supposed, for the vulgar purpose of eating it, the latter followed the animal, and observed that it went to the corner of a yard and laid the morsel down near where there was a rat-hole; having done so, the cat hid herself. Presently the rat came out, and was dragging away the meat, when the cat pounced upon him. No biped could have caught the animal with more skill. It is quite clear that rat flesh was a greater delicacy than the beef, unless we are to suppose a zest was added to it from the fact of its being made gamey by the trouble of sporting for it.

From Fruit Between the Leaves by Andrew Wynter, 1875

Higher Education

Cats, when young, can be taught a whole host of amusing tricks.

The most graceful of these is, perhaps, leaping heights. A cat that has had constant exercise at this sort of thing will spring almost incredible distances. The best plan to train her to this is to attach a hare's foot to the end of a rod and set it in motion for her. You can every day place it a little higher, and she will soon take to it naturally. Cats thus trained will climb the tallest trees, and leap from branch to branch like squirrels.

By holding your arms in front of pussy you will soon teach her to leap backwards and forwards over them. As she gets older, increase the distance of your arms from the ground, until at last you place them right over your head, and pussy will go over and through like any old steeple-chaser.

You may teach her to go through a hoop, or hoops, held at any elevation, and in all conceivable positions. Remember always to speak kindly to her when teaching her anything. Never chastise her; and when she has performed her little feat to your satisfaction, make much of her, and give her a morsel of fish, or any favourite food.

Cats are easily taught to fish in this manner: take them when young to a shallow stream, on a clear day, where the minnows are plentiful, and throw in a dead one or two, and encourage the cat to catch them. She will soon be after the living ones.

I had a cat that I taught to retrieve like a dog, and to fetch and carry. The same cat had for its constant companion my cheeky little starling, who used to hop about and on her, pick her teeth, and open her claws, but she never attempted to molest him.

You can teach your cat to follow you like a dog, and take long walks with you, and to come to you whenever you call her by whistling.

I have told you how to make your cat a good mouser, now I'll give you another wrinkle – how to make her a good trickster – *love her* and take an interest in all her little performances, and you will be surprised at the amount of tricks she will learn.

Without reference to the accomplishments of performing cats, who require a special education, I may here enumerate just a few of the many simple performances, which, with firmness, gentleness, and patience, you may easily teach any cat of ordinary brain calibre. A cat may be taught to beg like a dog; to embrace you; to pat your nose or your neighbour's nose when told – (N.B. It's just as well it should *always* be your neighbour's nose) – to down charge; to watch by a mouse's hold; to stand in a corner on her hindlegs; to move rhythmically to music; to mew when told; to shut her eyes when told; to leap six or eight feet through a hoop or over your head; to feign sleep; to feign death; to swim, and retrieve either in the water or on the land.

I have a cat who, if I hold her up in front of the map of London, will place her paw upon any principal building I like to name. The cat has been used to be carried round the room to catch flies on the wall. The principal buildings in the map are marked with square black spots, which she naturally mistakes for flies, so you have only to hold her in front of the map nearest to the spot you want her to touch, and slightly elevate your voice when you name the place, and the thing is done.

From The Domestic Cat by Gordon Stables, 1876

'Sonnet: Cat Logic'

Cat sentimentality is a human thing. Cats
are indifferent, their minds can't comprehend
the concept 'I shall die', they just go on living.
Death is more foreign to their thought than
to us the idea of a lime-green lobster. That's
why holding these warm containers of purring fur
is poignant, that they just don't *know*.
Life is in them, like the brandy in the bottle.

One morning a cat wakes up, and doesn't feel
disposed to eat or wash or walk. It doesn't panic
or scream: 'My last hour has come!' It
simply fades. Cats never go grey at the edges
like us, they don't even look old. Peter Pans,
insouciant. No wonder people identify with cats.

From The Collected Ewart 1933-1980 by Gavin Ewart, 1980

'What It Is about Cats'

There used to be, and probably still is, activity in the area called Comparative Psychology that consists of various attempts to work

[126]

out ways of studying and quantifying memory and intelligence across different species. There was sometimes a certain amount of difficulty in coming up with experimental designs that gave clear results. In one case that I remember something of, various animals were shown the location of hidden food and then brought back minutes, hours or days later and watched to see how well they did in finding the food again. Human beings did moderately well in some of these studies, dogs respectably, but it was the digger wasp that outperformed us all. The way I remember the conversations I used to hear about this, it was less obvious to the researchers than it ought to have been that the digger wasp had shown us that what we call 'intelligence' might be a complicated and even chimerical phenomenon. Beyond that it seemed to me as a tracking-dog trainer that not nearly enough had been done to rule out the effects on the tests of the animals' superior abilities, especially scent powers.

I cheered for the digger wasp, because the results in question did at least cause some pause in the machinery of behaviorist speculations. But the animal that defeated such speculations absolutely was the cat. I used to hear older experimenters advising younger ones about working with cats. It seems that under certain circumstances, if you give a cat or cats a problem to solve or a task to perform in order to find food, they work it out pretty quickly, and the graph of their comparative intelligence shows a sharply rising line. But, as I heard, 'the trouble is that as soon as they figure out that the researcher or technician *wants* them to push the lever, they stop doing it; some of them will *starve* to death rather than do it.' (This violently anti-behaviorist theory never, so far as I know, saw print.)

That result fascinated me – I would have dropped everything in order to find out what the cats were trying to do or say to the researchers. After all, when human beings behave that way, we come up with a pretty fancy catalogue of virtues in order to account for it. But, of course, I was stupidly supposing that the point of these efforts was to understand animals, and it wasn't at all. The point was simply to Do Science, or so I began to suspect when I heard one venerable professor tell a young researcher, 'Don't use cats, they'll screw up your data.'

What is it about cats? Among gentler and more tentative philosophers than the investigators I describe, cats are considered unobtrusively ubiquitous, and the philosophers are by and large grateful for this. At least, I hear the sound of gratitude in Montaigne when he says to himself that while our way of talking is to say that one plays with one's cat, there is no reason we shouldn't suppose that it is the other way about, that one's cat is playing with one. Montaigne's delicate alertness to such possibilities of grammatical reversal is sadly missing from most modern speculations about language and consciousness, but our cats are still here, which means that the most agreeable of philosophical expressions, the grateful one, is still possible.

The cats who starved to death in the laboratories were, no doubt about it, frustrated animals. The refusal of food is a signal made to the cosmos itself when one despairs of signaling one's chums that something deep in nature is being denied. Infants deprived of touch move in such ways through rage to despair, starvation and death. A mare on the point of foaling will not eat or drink if there is insufficient congruence between her sense of the event she anticipates and the attitudes of the creatures and landscape around her. Children refuse food when they are overloaded with various phoninesses disguised as love, even when they don't go so far as to die. And if you take a house cat and put it in a situation in which there is only one choice, that of responding in a linear way to human expectations, the cat won't eat if eating entails the performance of a kind of 'pleasing' that is a violation of the cat's nature, a distortion of the cat's duties on the planet.

This does not mean that cats are perverse, but rather that the pleasures and expectations of human beings are profoundly important to cats. In fact, it suggests that, contrary to popular wisdom, getting it right, accurate, just, about pleasing us is in some ways far more to the point of cat nature than it is to the point of dog nature. Dogs are by and large more like humans in being merely amused and relieved when their imitations and approximations of obedience are accepted by us, and their resemblance to us in that way may be one of the reasons it is easier to achieve general agreement on the interpretation of a given doggy action. But cats take the task of pleasing us far more seriously. Science has shown us this.

Of course, science has also shown us that merely having some lunkheaded expectation and presenting it to the cat doesn't satisfy the cat. The cat's job includes making us aware of the invented nature of our expectations, and cats can't do this when the bulldozer effect takes over our expectations, as it can do in science and in our erotic relationships.

I should interrupt myself and say what I mean by my simple-minded assault on science in general and behaviorism in particular. I don't mean that there is much point in simply discarding, for now at least, such notions as Conditioned Response or Operant Behavior. They are far too useful, philosophically and morally. For one thing, thinking about interactions between stimuli and behaviors without reference to internal events can make it turn out that most things are not our fault, thus relieving us of the 'bad conscience' Nietzsche so despised. But there are certain confusions that get into the discussions in practice, usually in the guise of genuine difficulties. The result tends to be that the behaviorist overtly denies the interpretive significance of internal events while covertly making appeal to them when the going gets philosophically rough. The opposite happens too, of course. Some animal trainers declare themselves the enemies of academic psychology without acknowledging the extent to which such things as the Stimulus-Response model has clarified their thinking and practice. All of this is well and good, but it still doesn't turn out that behaviorism in its pure form has come up with a better response to cats' refusals than 'Don't use cats, they'll screw up your data.'

From *Adam's Task* by Vicki Hearne, 1987

'Snow in Lambourn'

The 'snowy spell' mentioned in this anecdote by Julia Strachey occurred during January 1960.

During a snowy spell at Lambourn, I set out one Sunday morning to call upon the woman who supplies us with eggs.

The egg-woman, Miss Smith, lived on the far side of the village. Sunday was the only time to catch her, for on weekdays – although herself an old age pensioner – she 'took off' in her late father's plaid overcoat and old jockey-cap with the peak sticking far out over her nose, to work at the almshouses. She mended the old people's clothes and cleaned their rooms; did not return till after dark. Miss Smith as it happened had no roof to her mouth and was also deaf. I began to feel the lightly joking conversation I had planned, about the strange noises made by the local bell-ringers, might not go off too easily after all. But *some* pleasant and not too serious opening could surely be managed before I turned the talk around, to enquire casually why the whites of the eggs she had lately been sending to our house had all changed, when boiled, to a dark and stormy battleship grey? We could then discuss what could be done about it.

That January morning snow was everywhere. I put on my warmest outdoor clothes, piling on everything I found hanging on the pegs in the boot-room. Finally I pulled on my gum-boots, still wet from yesterday, and off I set, crunching my way along the road. The thought came to me that if I were to stick my head into the big refrigerator in my kitchen at home it would feel something like this. For there was no light out of doors this morning: an arctic fog hung in the air, hiding everything. It took a little time to recognise the silhouettes of the cottages looming through the turnip-soup fog. The new council house, for example, and the willow tree on the river bank, whose old arching trunk had died and tumbled over into the water – all were mere shadows. And there was the same acute numbness of my nose, forehead and cheeks as there would be were I being savaged by my large fridge at home.

Arrived at Miss Smith's gate, I found pinned to it a pencilled notice saying that she was up at the almshouses this Sunday morning. But I was much too cold to care where she was. I turned round and followed the path that circled the village, heading for home. Next door to the house of our daily help – the ancient and greatly beloved Mrs Rose – stood the cottage belonging to her greatest friend, ginger-haired Mrs MacDonald. And as I passed Mrs Mac-Donald's garden, now white and formless under a blanket of snow, I caught sight of a being in the garden whom I had heard much about from Mrs Rose, but had never yet met – Mrs MacDonald's Abyssinian cat. Here she was at long last!

She was standing alone in the middle of the snow-humped garden, facing in my direction and with her tail held upright and stiff as a ramrod. I halted on the path opposite Mrs MacDonald's garden. At once the cat came running towards me, total stranger that I was. There was an urgency in her manner that made plain she had something of great import to ask me. But she was suddenly brought up short by the wire fence at the end of the garden. She stood there nonplussed; then she tilted up her prim oriental face, with her eyes fixed urgently upon me in a round, electric goosegog stare. At the same time her mouth opened wide, but silently. Opened and shut once more, but with an emotion so violently passionate that, soundless though the phantom mewings were, each one shook the cat's body through and through. It was like watching a desperately-roaring tiger, caught behind soundproof glass.

What *did* that cat want?

She was plainly calling for help, felt herself in some disastrous predicament or extremity. The garden door was open into Mrs MacDonald's kitchen, so she had not been shut out. Just a step or two – and inside the cottage was warmth.

Strange!

It couldn't have been a protest then against icy, aching paws. So what could be the trouble? I waited a minute or so, but what could I possibly do? I walked off home.

Back in my house I went straight to the kitchen and recited the whole incident to Mrs Rose. 'Mrs MacDonald's cat looked *so* upset there in the snow!' I added.

The old lady, tiny as an elf but still very handsome, did not answer. She seldom did; she 'kept herself to herself', as was her habit. She pushed aside a colander full of sprouts on the kitchen table, evidently to make room for something else.

I chattered on: 'I don't blame her, I must say. Going by the pain in my own nose and ears, her paws must have felt excruciatingly cold.'

Mrs Rose bent down, opened the oven door behind her; in complete silence she took out the baking-tin with its half-roasted chicken and set it on the table. Then, 'It wasn't only *that*, you see,' she said unexpectedly. The old lady reached for the hollow glass rod resembling a thermometer, dipped it in the steaming gravy and began to baste the bird.

'You know, madam,' she continued after a moment, her handsome face grim as it looked down at the chicken: 'when a cat is accustomed to Doing its Business out on the grass or flower-beds, or among the green leaves and all – you understand what I'm talking about, madam?'

'I do. I do. A cat accustomed to "do it" on the grass? – '

'Yes. Well, when they are trained properly for *that*, they can't do it anywhere else. Must have the green to be right for it. But after this snow it's all white. And the *white* is *wrong* for it.'

'The white is wrong for it,' I repeated thoughtfully.

'Yes, madam. They don't know what to do with theirselves – every *blooming* thing is white! It's pitiful.'

'Pitiful,' I echoed. 'It is,' said Mrs Rose as she went on basting the chicken.

From *Julia: A Portrait by Herself and Frances Partridge*, 1983

'Niger sed Sapiens'

To dwell in peace as a welcome guest,
With ample house-room, fare of the best,
A corner for quiet, a pleasance for play,
Contents me well for the passing day.
Delights that pass, be they small or great,
In the final balance have little weight;
I take their good for its current worth,
And pity the folk of unlucky birth,
Wiseacres who little joys despise –
     Saith Simon the Wise.

Rule-breakers we, whom the herd defame,
No whit we reck of their praise or blame.
Worshipped in state at Pharaoh's court,
Or hunted to make a rabble sport,
From Thames to Nile, from gutter to throne,
Ever we hold our souls our own.
What ill hap mars, or better may mend,
Moves not the sage who sees the end;
Comfort and penury, hopes and fears,
Are toys of time and the wreck of years,
But freedom the gift of eternity –
     Saith Simon the Free.

Scorning the ways of the servile hound,
I greet my hosts in a seemly round:
Well-bred companions, we live at ease
In talk or silence as each may please
(Talk where better than words avail
The wag of an ear and the flick of a tail).
And, since to retain a friend's esteem
Of himself a man must nobly deem,
My tribe are sure that creation's plan
Meant US for the genuine super-man:
When you prate of your Nietzsches and Bernard Shaws,
With a dainty smile we lick our paws;
For thousands of years we've known all that –
      Saith Simon the Black, my cat.

From *Outside the Law: Diversions Partly Serious* by Sir Frederick Pollock, Bart., 1927

Mr Macmillan's Cat

No marvel I'm conversing with a cat.

The curious thing is it's Macmillan's pet.
(I'm sitting by the former Premier's fire.)
It tells me its master is ignoring it.

I say: 'Why don't you jump upon his knee?
I'm sure the action wouldn't be *de trop*.'
However, the cat replies that it prefers

To wait until the guests go then come up,
From bidding them farewell, alone with Mac.
I think before I wake

How wise the cat is in the ways of love.

From *New and Collected Poems, 1934-84* by Roy Fuller, 1985

Without Benefit of Education

Dec. 12, 1856

Wonderful, wonderful is our life, and that of our companions! That there should be such a thing as a brute animal, not human! that it should attain to a sort of society with our race! Think of cats, for instance; they are neither Chinese nor Tartars, they neither go to school, nor read the Testament. Yet how near they come to doing so, how much they are like us who do so. At length without having solved any of these problems, we fatten and kill and eat some of our cousins!

Where is the great natural historian? Is he a butcher? or the patron of butchers? As well look for a great anthropologist among cannibals or New Zealanders.

From *Autumn* by Henry David Thoreau, 1884

Conscious Automatons

Sir,

Some time ago, a machine of the cat species was received into our house under distressing circumstances, and adopted by our household. We have all rendered ourselves ridiculous in scientific eyes by becoming much attached to this rescued foundling, and he has assumed, under the name of Bruin, a position of importance which becomes his size, intelligence, and estimate of his own merits. Under the second of these heads, I could furnish you with several interesting particulars; I content myself, however, with one, which relates to our machine of the cat species, and to another machine called a gas-stove. We had one of the latter articles put up in a study beyond the dining-room at the beginning of winter, and Bruin speedily selected it as his own particular fireplace, in preference to the dining-room grate, no doubt because it was less frequented and the heat was more uniform. When the severe cold set in, it struck Bruin's master that it would be comfortable for him to have the stove to sleep by, and might tend to modify his erratic habits. Accordingly the stove was left alight (at half-strength), and Bruin signified his approbation by curling himself up in front of it early in the evening, and sleeping soundly until he was roused, under protest, and yawning widely, to a late breakfast, during all the nights and mornings which have since elapsed. On Thursday night – Christmas Eve – his master left home, and it occurred to me to test Bruin's intelligence concerning that event. I left the stove unlighted, and watched his proceedings when the hour at which he usually retires to rest arrived. He marched into the room with the air of important business to be immediately attended to which strongly characterises him, looked at the blank coppery space, uttered an angry cry, and ran out of the room to the coat-and-umbrella stand in the hall. He sniffed at a couple of waterproofs and an interloping *en tout cas*, but detected the absence of the familiar great-coat and the sturdy umbrella which he associates with his master. Then he rushed upstairs, evidently with a strong sense of injury upon him, and I followed, to find him crying at the door of his master's bedroom, which I opened for him. He jumped on the bed, sniffed about the pillow, jumped down again, once more cried angrily, and ran downstairs. I followed, and took my seat in the dining-room, pretending not to notice him. He sat for two or three minutes in front of the stove, then came into the dining-room and put his paws upon my knees, and gazed into my face with a gasp – not a cry, but a mode of speech which this machine has made us understand. I pretended to be puzzled; he scratched my gown and gasped again. 'You are not thirsty, Bruin,' I remarked; 'what do you want? I am to get up, am I, and you will show me?' I suited the action to the word, and he preceded me into the study, stepped inside the fender, put up his paws on the front of the stove, and turned his head towards me over his shoulder with a look of content that I had been clever enough to interpret his meaning, which gave me very sincere satisfaction. As I know that you, Sir, are an advocate for the study of animals otherwise than by the torture of them, I venture to send you this anecdote of an automaton who really seems, to my ignorant mind, to have something like what we fancy we mean by 'consciousness.'

I am, Sir, &c.,
A CONSTANT READER AND DISCIPLE.

From *The Spectator*, January 1875

'No, I never thought a cat would get acclimatized so quickly.'

'A cat's merely a cat. But Saha's Saha.'

Alain was proudly doing the honours of Saha. He himself had never kept her so close at hand, imprisoned in twenty-five square metres and visible at all hours. For her feline meditation, for her craving for solitude and shadow, she was reduced to withdrawing under the giant armchairs scattered about the studio or into the miniature hall or into one of the built-in wardrobes camouflaged with mirrors.

But Saha was determined to triumph over all obstacles. She accepted the uncertain times of meals and of getting up and going to bed. She chose the bathroom with its cork-topped stool to sleep in and she explored the Wedge with no affectation of wildness or disgust. In the kitchen, she condescended to listen to the lazy voice of Mme Buque summoning 'the pussy' to raw liver. When Alain and Camille went out, she installed herself on the giddy parapet and gazed into the abysses of air, following the flying backs of swallows and sparrows below her with a calm, untroubled eye. Her impassiveness on the edge of a sheer drop of nine storeys and the habit she had of washing herself at length on the parapet, terrified Camille.

'Stop her,' she yelled to Alain. 'She makes my heart turn over and gives me cramp in my calves.'

Alain gave an unperturbed smile and admired his cat who had recovered her taste for food and life.

It was not that she was blooming or particularly gay. She did not recover the iridescence of her fur that had gleamed like a pigeon's mauve plumage. But she was more alive; she waited for the dull 'poum' of the lift which brought up Alain and accepted extra attentions from Camille, such as a tiny saucer of milk at five o'clock or a small chicken bone offered high up, as if to a dog who was expected to jump for it.

'Not like that! Not like that!' scolded Alain.

And he would lay the bone on a bathmat or simply on the thick-piled beige carpet.

'Really . . . on Patrick's carpet!' Camille scolded in turn.

'But a cat can't eat a bone or any solid food on a polished surface.

When a cat takes a bone off a plate and puts it down on the carpet before eating it, she's told she's dirty. But the cat needs to hold it down with her paw while she crunches and tears it and she can only do it on bare earth or on a carpet. People don't know that.'

Amazed, Camille broke in: 'And how do *you* know?'

He had never asked himself that and got out of it by a joke: 'Hush! It's because I'm extremely intelligent. Don't tell a soul. M. Veuillet hasn't a notion of it.'

He taught her all the ways and habits of the cat, like a foreign language over-rich in subtle shades of meaning. In spite of himself, he spoke with emphatic authority as he taught. Camille observed him narrowly and asked him any number of questions which he answered unreservedly.

'Why does the cat play with a piece of string when she's frightened of the big ship's rope?'

'Because the ship's rope is a snake. It's the thickness of a snake. She's afraid of snakes.'

'Has she ever seen a snake?'

Alain looked at his wife with the grey-green, black-lashed eyes she found so beautiful . . . 'So treacherous' she said.

'No . . . certainly not. Where could she have seen one?'

'Well, then?'

'Well, then she invents one. She creates one. You'd be frightened of snakes too, even if you'd never seen one.'

'Yes, but I've been told about them. I've seen them in pictures. I know they exist.'

'So does Saha.'

'But how?'

He gave her a haughty smile.

'How? But by her birth, like persons of quality.'

From *The Cat* by Colette, translated by Antonia White, 1953

A Very Strange Power

Cats can so associate sensations and the images of objects in various relations as to draw practical inferences. My friend, Mr J. J. Weir, tells me of a cat which, having been chased by boys, ran towards a door, jumped up, put one paw through the handle, and with the other raised the latch, thus causing the door to open and enable it to escape. This action he saw several times repeated. Mr Harrison Weir has also assured me that he has seen a cat unfasten a latch and then open the door it fastened, by pressing its feet against the door-post. He has also had a cat that knocked at a door with the knocker – these acts being untaught, and due only to the cat's spontaneous acts of cognition. I have also heard of a cat which habitually jumped down from a staircase in such a way as in its descent to press with its paws obliquely on the handle of a door and so open it. My friend Captain Noble, of Maresfield, informs me that he has himself known a cat which was in the habit of catching starlings by getting on to a cow's back and waiting till the cow happened to approach the birds, which little suspected what the approaching inoffensive beast bore crouching upon it. He assures me he has himself witnessed this elaborate trick, by means of which the cat managed to catch starlings which otherwise it could never have got near. Many cats will readily learn the signification of certain words, and will answer to their names and come when called. Very strange is the power which cats may show of finding their way home by routes which they have never before traversed. We cannot explain this (as it has been sought to explain the like power in dogs), by the power of smell being the predominate sense, so that a passed succession of smells can be retraversed in reverse order, as a number of places seen in succession on a journey may be retraversed in reverse order by ourselves. On the whole, it seems probable that the power in question may be due to a highly developed 'sense of direction,' like that which enables some men so much to excel others in finding their way about cities, or that which enables the inhabitants of Siberia to find their way through woods or over hummocky ice, and who, though constantly changing the direction they immediately pursue, yet keep their main direction unchanged.

From *The Cat: An Introduction to the Study of Backboned Animals Especially Mammals* by St George Mivart, 1881

Six

MAGIC

'Cats'

No-one but indefatigable lovers and old
Chilly philosophers can understand the true
Charm of these animals serene and potent, who
Likewise are sedentary and suffer from the cold.

They are the friends of learning and of sexual bliss;
Silence they love, and darkness where temptation breeds.
Erebus would have made them his funereal steeds,
Save that their proud free nature would not stoop to this.

Like those great sphinxes lounging through eternity
In noble attitudes upon the desert sand,
They gaze incuriously at nothing, calm and wise.

Their fecund loins give forth electric flashes, and
Thousands of golden particles drift ceaselessly,
Like galaxies of stars, in their mysterious eyes.

From *Flowers of Evil* by Charles Baudelaire, 1857, translated by George Dillon

Cat-Gods of Egypt

In contrast with representations of the dog [in ancient Egyptian art], which always portray the living animal, those of the cat frequently convey a religious or symbolic meaning. Stelae depicting cats actually refer to the sun god or to a female deity. In the arch of a stela in the Ashmolean Museum, Oxford, there are two felines, designated 'the Great Lady Cat' and 'the beautiful Lady Cat', and it is inscribed with a hymn to Re, 'the Great Tomcat'. Another stela, likewise from Deir el-Medina, bears the usual offering formula for 'the beautiful and gracious cat'. Exactly which goddess is described remains uncertain since several, such as Bastet, Sekhmet, Mut or Neith, were connected with felines. Bastet in particular was so frequently represented in this guise that most of the famous Late and Graeco-Roman Period cat bronzes in museum collections do not indicate the animal itself.

Moreover, depictions of cats below the chairs of their mistresses (they seem never to sit under the seat of a man) possess an additional erotic implication, their presence pointing to female sexuality. Several such scenes are entitled 'making a feast day' and others picture banquets with nude dancing girls. A famous painting from the Theban tomb of Anen, the Second Priest of Amun and brother of Amenophis III's wife Tiye, shows a striped cat embracing a goose with its forepaw whilst a monkey leaps in ecstasy over them. The purpose of this unnatural combination is to assert that worldly chaos is curbed and transformed into an idyllic peace. Perhaps there is also a political implication, with the cat representing the queen, and the goose Amen-Re. The embrace is then reminiscent of the ritual scenes in the Luxor Temple when Amenophis III is shown as the divine issue of a union between the god and the queen-mother.

This does not signify, however, that the animal under the chair is not also an actual pet. Symbol and reality coincide, as confirmed, for instance, by a scene in the tomb of Ipuy at Deir el-Medina where the cat proudly wears a silver earring, whilst her kitten is on its master's lap playing with his flapping sleeves. The figure of a young servant cradling a kitten in her arm likewise reflects real life.

A further, very exclusive manner of portraying cats in some tomb paintings is to show them sitting in or beside the semi-circular window above the front door of the house. They are sunning themselves in one of the warmest spots, yet are sheltered from the glaring sunlight. Later on this scene from daily life was no longer understood and the cat became an emblematic sphinx.

Cats comprised part of the original Egyptian fauna and those occurring in art were descendants of the African wild cat, *Felis libyca* although some interbreeding with the swamp cat is not impossible. Like their wild ancestors, the Egyptian cats were mostly lithely built tabbies, with a patchy grey coat and black, tawny or light-coloured spots and stripes. Intentional breeding was not practised, so modern breeds, such as the Persian or Manx, did not occur. The *Mau* of modern Egypt, descending from the ancient Egyptian cat, is now, however, a recognised championship breed.

The cat was first represented during the Middle Kingdom, although 'Pussy-cat' as a female name is attested prior to this date. Moreover, cat skeletons are known from Predynastic cemeteries, indicating that they were already tamed, fed and kept, particularly as hunters of vermin in the granaries. The earliest proof for their full domestication is the Eleventh Dynasty stela in the Petrie Museum at University College London, showing a fat tom crouched under the chair of his owners and, as has been suggested, defecating behind the feet of his mistress. It is more likely to be the clumsy artistic style of the period which creates this impression.

From *Egyptian Household Animals* by Rosalind and Jack Janssen, 1989

The Dance of Burning Cats

In the French department of the Ardennes the whole village used to dance and sing round the bonfires which were lighted on the first Sunday in Lent. Here, too, it was the person last married, some-times a man and sometimes a woman, who put the match to the fire. The custom is still kept up very commonly in the district. Cats used to be burnt in the fire or roasted to death by being held over it; and while they were burning the shepherds drove their flocks through the smoke and flames as a sure means of guarding them against sickness and witchcraft. In some communes it was believed that the livelier the dance round the fire, the better would be the crops that year . . .

In the midsummer fires formerly kindled on the Place de Grève at Paris it was the custom to burn a basket, barrel, or sack full of live cats, which was hung from a tall mast in the midst of the bonfire; sometimes a fox was burned. The people collected the embers and ashes of the fire and took them home, believing that they brought good luck. The French kings often witnessed these spectacles and even lit the bonfires with their own hands. In 1648 Louis the Four-teenth, crowned with a wreath of roses and carrying a bunch of roses in his hand, kindled the fire, danced at it and partook of the banquet afterwards in the town hall. But this was the last occasion when a monarch presided at the midsummer bonfire in Paris. At Metz midsummer fires were lighted with great pomp on the espla-nade, and a dozen cats, enclosed in wicker-cages, were burned alive in them, to the amusement of the people. Similarly at Gap, in the department of the High Alps, cats used to be roasted over the mid-summer bonfire.

From *Balder the Beautiful: The Fire-Festivals of Europe and the Doctrine of the External Soul* by J. G. Frazer, 1914

Cats in the Corn

The corn-spirit sometimes takes the form of a cat. Near Kiel children are warned not to go into the corn-fields because 'the Cat sits there.' In the Eisenach Oberland they are told 'the Corn-cat will come and fetch you,' 'the Corn-cat goes in the corn.' In some parts of Silesia at mowing the last corn they say, 'The Cat is caught'; and at threshing, the man who gives the last stroke is called the Cat. In the neighbourhood of Lyons the last sheaf and the harvest-supper are both called the Cat. About Vesoul when they cut the last corn they say, 'We have the Cat by the tail.' At Briançon, in Dauphiné, at the beginning of reaping, a cat is decked out with ribbons, flowers, and ears of corn. It is called the Cat of the ball-skin (*le chat de peau de balle*). If a reaper is wounded at his work, they make the cat lick the wound. At the close of the reaping the cat is again decked out with ribbons and ears of corn; then they dance and make merry. When the dance is over the girls solemnly strip the cat of its finery. At Grüneberg, in Silesia, the reaper who cuts the last corn goes by the name of the Tom-cat. He is enveloped in rye-stalks and green withes, and is furnished with a long plaited tail. Sometimes as a companion he has a man similarly dressed, who is called the (female) Cat. Their duty is to run after people whom they see and to beat them with a long stick. Near Amiens the expression for finishing the harvest is, 'They are going to kill the Cat'; and when the last corn is cut they kill a cat in the farmyard. At threshing, in some parts of France, a live cat is placed under the last bundle of corn to be threshed, and is struck dead with the flails. Then on Sunday it is roasted and eaten as a holiday dish. In the Vosges Mountains the close of haymaking or harvest is called 'catching the cat,' 'killing the dog,' or more rarely 'catching the hare.' The cat, the dog, or the hare is said to be fat or lean according as the crop is good or bad. The man who cuts the last handful of hay or of wheat

[143]

is said to catch the cat or the hare or to kill the dog. He is congratulated by his comrades and has the honour of carrying the nosegay or rather the small fir-tree decked with ribbons which marks the end of the haymaking or of the harvest. In Franche-Comté also the close of harvest is called 'catching or killing the cat.'

From *Spirits of the Corn and of the Wild* by J. G. Frazer, 1920

In Sickness and in Health

The following represent some common beliefs about cats: Illness in a family can be cured by washing the patient and throwing the water over a cat. When the cat is driven out-of-doors, it will take the illness with it. A sailor's superstition holds that, should a cat be frolicsome on board a ship, such presages wind, gales, and rain; should a cat be thrown overboard, a storm will arise at sea. Yet another seamen's practice was to place a cat under a pot on the deck should a ship need wind to rise.

It is generally thought unlucky to let a cat die in one's house. Should a cat sneeze, rain is on the way. Should a cat sneeze three times, colds will run through the family. Should a cat scratch the leg of a table, a change in the weather is predicted. A cat sitting with its back to the fire is a sign that a storm is on its way, and a great deal of rain is predicted when a cat washes her face over her ears.

A cat in the presence of a bride indicates good luck for her in matrimonial affairs, but should a cat pass over a coffin, it indicates disaster, unless the cat is caught and killed.

Cats that are purchased are said to be useless for catching mice. In Devon and Wiltshire it is believed that cats born in the month of May never catch rats or mice, but rather snakes and glowworms.

Never drown cats for this tempts Satan to take your soul. Never kick a cat or you will get rheumatism.

In New England, tradition holds that one can tell time and the tides by looking into the pupils of a cat's eyes. Should a cat meow on board a ship, a dangerous voyage is portended according to a Welsh tradition. In Wisconsin, if a cat washed itself while seated in a doorway, it was believed that a clergyman would soon visit the house. In Ireland, it is considered bad luck to take a cat when one moves from one house to another.

Some West Africans believe that the human soul passes into the body of a cat at death. An Italian legend told of a cat that gave birth to kittens beneath the manger in which Christ was born.

In some parts of Europe, a cat was often personified with the spirit of the harvest of corn. At Briançon, France, for instance, a cat is ceremonially dressed in ribbons, flowers, and corn ears, and in Amiens, a cat was ritually killed when the last sheaves of corn were cut.

On Shrove Tuesday and on Easter, in some European communities, cats were roasted alive in the belief that this would drive away evil spirits. One tradition held that sacrificing a cat would protect a building against fire.

The belief that cats are able to see in the dark is widespread. Likewise, common is the belief that a cat has nine lives. Popular, too, is the myth that cats should never be left alone in the house with a baby; some country folk believe it will jump up on the infant and suck out his breath.

Legend has it that drawing the tail of a cat downwards over one's eye will cure a sty. Likewise, the 'tail cure' was said to be effective in the treatment of warts, whitlows, and general itching. Toothaches could be relieved by applying properly dried cat skin to one's face. At one time, a whole cat boiled in olive oil was thought to make an excellent dressing for wounds.

From *Zolar's Encyclopaedia of Omens, Signs and Superstitions*, 1989

Stage Fright

The very fact that the success or failure of a play depends on how the actors perform and how the audience reacts to them makes the theatre a rich breeding ground for all manner of omens and superstitions. Theatres themselves are often considered lucky or unlucky, and it is not unusual for one that has had a string of failures or suffered accidents on or off stage to have its name changed. A black cat has always been a lucky animal in any theatre (the Haymarket Theatre in London used to keep one there permanently), but it is a bad sign if it runs across the stage during a performance.

From *Superstitions* by Peter Haining, 1979

How to Clean a House

There was an old belief that when bridges were erected the work was accompanied by human sacrifice. It is perhaps from Wales that folklore has preserved the bridge-sacrifice tradition most clearly. There is a bridge called 'Devil's Bridge' near Beddgelert. Many of the people in that neighbourhood used to believe that this structure was formed by supernatural agency. It is said that the devil proposed to the neighbouring inhabitants that he would build them a bridge across the pass, on condition that, for his trouble, he should have the first to cross it. The bargain was made, and the bridge appeared in its place, but an old woman cheated the devil by whipping a dog in front of her. Here, of course, we have a substituted animal sacrifice for the original human sacrifice. Even in our time the laying of the foundation-stone of a famous building is often attended with ceremony; even though the sacrifice is no longer offered, the form remains. We are not even now completely free from the lingering remains of pagan superstition. When leaving one house for another, it was thought to be unlucky to move into a house which was too clean. Superstition claimed that all its good fortune got swept out with the dirt and was supplanted by evil. Thus grew up the custom of throwing a cat into a new house before its human occupants went in. Any evil spirit in the dwelling would take possession of the cat, which would soon sicken and die.

From *Religious Superstition Through the Ages* by Don Lewis, 1975

Omens on the Way to School

When a child steps out of his home to go to school, whether he lives in a remote hamlet or in one of the backstreets of a great city, he is on his own, and looking after himself. The day ahead looms large and endless in front of him, and his eyes are wide open for the prognostics which will tell him his fortune . . .

It is considered good luck if one meets a black cat and says 'black cat bring me luck', or if one strokes it three times from head to tail, and then makes a wish. But a black cat does not necessarily bring luck: much depends on the creature's behaviour. The consensus of opinion seems to be that if the cat sits in front of one, or walks ahead in one's path, all is well. But if it runs away, turns back, or walks round one, or if it crosses one's path, and in particular if it crosses one's path from left to right, it is very bad luck. A Golspie boy says, 'You must spit to avoid a terrible accident which is bound to happen'. A Welsh girl says one must make the sign of the cross and turn completely round. A Shropshire girl says one must turn round three times. And a boy in Manchester says that if a black cat crosses in front of a car from left to right, it means a puncture. To see a white cat on the way to school is taken to be a sign of trouble ahead.

From *The Lore and Language of Schoolchildren* by Iona and Peter Opie, 1959

Boiled Alive

The room underneath the story-tellers was lit by a single candle and by the saffron light of its peat fire. It was a poor room for a royal one, but at least it had a bed in it – the great four-poster which was used as a throne during the daytime. An iron cauldron with three legs was boiling over the fire. The candle stood in front of a sheet of polished brass, which served as a mirror. There were two living beings in the chamber, a Queen and a cat. Both of them had black hair and blue eyes.

The black cat lay on its side in the firelight as if it were dead. This was because its legs were tied together, like the legs of a roe-deer

which is to be carried home from the hunt. It had given up struggling and now lay gazing into the fire with slit eyes and heaving
sides, curiously resigned. Or else it was exhausted – for animals
know when they have come to the end. Most of them have a dignity
about dying, denied to human beings. This cat, with the small
flames dancing in its oblique eyes, was perhaps seeing the pageant
of its past eight lives, reviewing them with an animal's stoicism,
beyond hope or fear.

The Queen picked up the cat. She was trying a well-known
piseog to amuse herself, or at any rate to pass the time while the
men were away at the war. It was a method of becoming invisible.
She was not a serious witch like her sister Morgan le Fay – for her
head was too empty to take any great art seriously, even if it were
the Black one. She was doing it because the little magics ran in her
blood – as they did with all the women of her race.

In the boiling water, the cat gave some horrible convulsions and
a dreadful cry. Its wet fur bobbed in the steam, gleaming like the
side of a speared whale, as it tried to leap or to swim with its bound
feet. Its mouth opened hideously, showing the whole of its pink
gullet, and the sharp, white cat-teeth, like thorns. After the first
shriek it was not able to articulate, but only to stretch its paws.
Later it was dead.

Queen Morgause of Lothian and Orkney sat beside the cauldron
and waited. Occasionally she stirred the cat with a wooden spoon.
The stench of boiling fur began to fill the room. A watcher would
have seen, in the flattering peat light, what an exquisite creature she
was tonight: her deep, big eyes, her hair glinting with dark lustre,
her full body, and her faint air of watchfulness as she listened for
the whispering in the room above . . .

The cat had come to pieces. The long boiling had shredded its meat
away until there was nothing in the cauldron except a deep scum of
hair and grease and gobbets. Underneath, the white bones revolved
in the eddies of the water, the heavy ones lying still and the airy
membranes lifting gracefully, like leaves in an autumn wind. The
Queen, wrinkling her nose slightly in the thick stench of unsalted
broth, strained the liquid into a second pot. On top of the flannel
strainer there was left a sediment of cat, a sodden mass of matted
hair and meat shreds and the delicate bones. She blew on the sediment and began turning it over with the handle of the spoon,

[148]

prodding it to let the heat out. Later, she was able to sort it with her fingers.

The Queen knew that every pure black cat had a certain bone in it, which, if it were held in the mouth after boiling the cat alive, was able to make you invisible. But nobody knew precisely, even in those days, which the bone was. This was why magic had to be done in front of a mirror, so that the right one could be found by practice.

It was not that Morgause courted invisibility – indeed, she would have detested it, because she was beautiful. But the men were away. It was something to do, an easy and well-known charm. Besides, it was an excuse for lingering with the mirror.

The Queen scraped the remains of her cat into two heaps, one of them a neat pile of warm bones, the other a miscellaneous lump which softly steamed. Then she chose one of the bones and lifted it to her red lips, cocking the little finger. She held it between her teeth and stood in front of the polished brass, looking at herself with sleepy pleasure. She threw the bone into the fire and fetched another.

There was nobody to see her. It was strange, in these circumstances, the way in which she turned and turned, from mirror to bone-pile, always putting a bone in her mouth, and looking at herself to see if she had vanished, and throwing the bone away. She moved so gracefully, as if she were dancing, as if there really was somebody to see her, or as if it were enough that she should see herself.

Finally, but before she had tested all the bones, she lost interest. She threw the last ones down impatiently and tipped the mess out of the window, not caring where it fell. Then she smoored the fire, stretched herself on the big bed with a strange motion, and lay there in the darkness for a long time without sleeping – her body moving discontentedly.

From *The Once and Future King* by T. H. White, 1958

An Insanely Immoral Superstition

The black magician Aleister Crowley was known as 'the wickedest man in the world' or, more concisely, 'the Great Beast'. The following passage from his memoirs reveals that he was pretty beastly even as a child.

There is one amazing incident; at the age of fourteen as near as I can remember. I must premise that I have always been exceptionally tender-hearted except to tyrants, for whom I think no tortures bad enough. In particular, I am uniformly kind to animals; no question of cruelty or sadism arises in the incident which I am about to narrate.

I had been told 'A cat has nine lives.' I deduced that it must be practically impossible to kill a cat. As usual, I became full of ambition to perform the feat. (Observe that I took my information unquestioningly *au pied de la lettre*.) Perhaps through some analogy with the story of Hercules and the hydra, I got it into my head that the nine lives of the cat must be taken more or less simultaneously. I therefore caught a cat, and having administered a large dose of arsenic I chloroformed it, hanged it above the gas jet, stabbed it, cut its throat, smashed its skull and, when it had been pretty thoroughly burnt, drowned it and threw it out of the window that the fall might remove the ninth life. In fact, the operation was successful; I had killed the cat. I remember that all the time I was genuinely sorry for the animal; I simply forced myself to carry out the experiment in the interest of pure science.

The combination of innocence, ignorance, knowledge, ingenuity and high moral principle seems extraordinary. It is evident that the insanely immoral superstition in which I had been brought up is responsible for so atrocious an absurdity. Again and again we shall see how the imposition of the anti-natural theory and principles of Christianity upon a peculiarly sane, matter-of-fact, reality-facing genius created a conflict whose solution was expressed on the material plane by some extravagant action. My mind is severely logical; or, rather, it was so until mystic experience enabled it to shake off its fetters. Logic is responsible for most of the absurd and abominable deeds which have disgraced history. Given Christian premises, the Inquisition was acting in accordance with the highest humanitarian principles in destroying a man's body to save his soul. The followers of Descartes were right to torture animals, believing them to be automata. Genuine determinists would be justified in committing any crime, since the fact of its occurrence would prove that it was unavoidable. Huxley, in *Evolution and Ethics*, makes out a very poor case against infanticide and race suicide. We are constantly using our judgment to preserve one section of humanity as against another; we are in fact constantly compelled to do so. As for the future of humanity, the certainty of final extermination when the planet becomes uninhabitable makes all human endeavour a colossal fatuity.

From *The Confessions of Aleister Crowley: An Autohagiography*, 1969

'The Repairer of Reputations'

The narrator of this bizarre short story by Robert Chambers, a man named Castaigne, is detained in an Asylum for the Criminal Insane, from where he recounts the horrors that toppled him over the edge. These horrors include the inevitable cat.

I climbed the three dilapidated flights of stairs, which I had so often climbed before, and knocked at a small door at the end of the corridor. Mr Wilde opened the door and I walked in.

When he had double-locked the door and pushed a heavy chest against it, he came and sat down beside me, peering up into my face with his little light-colored eyes. Half a dozen new scratches covered his nose and cheeks, and the silver wires which supported his artificial ears had become displaced. I thought I had never seen him so hideously fascinating. He had no ears. The artificial ones, which now stood out at an angle from the fine wire, were his one weakness. They were made of wax and painted a shell pink, but the rest of his face was yellow. He might better have revelled in the luxury of some artificial fingers for his left hand, which was absolutely fingerless, but it seemed to cause him no inconvenience, and he was satisfied with his wax ears. He was very small, scarcely higher than a child of ten, but his arms were magnificently developed, and his thighs as thick as any athlete's. Still, the most remarkable thing about Mr Wilde was that a man of his marvellous intelligence and knowledge should have such a head. It was flat and pointed, like the heads of many of those unfortunates whom people

[151]

imprison in asylums for the weak-minded. Many called him insane but I knew him to be as sane as I was.

I do not deny that he was eccentric; the mania he had for keeping that cat and teasing her until she flew at his face like a demon, was certainly eccentric. I never could understand why he kept the creature, nor what pleasure he found in shutting himself up in his room with the surly, vicious beast. I remember once, glancing up from the manuscript I was studying by the light of some tallow dips, and seeing Mr Wilde squatting motionless on his high chair, his eyes fairly blazing with excitement, while the cat, which had risen from her place before the stove, came creeping across the floor right at him. Before I could move she flattened her belly to the ground, crouched, trembled, and sprang into his face. Howling and foaming they rolled over and over on the floor, scratching and clawing, until the cat screamed and fled under the cabinet, and Mr Wilde turned over on his back, his limbs contracting and curling up like the legs of a dying spider. He *was* eccentric.

Mr Wilde earns his living as a 'repairer of reputations'. On Castaigne's next encounter with him, we learn a little more of what the job entails.

I knocked, and entered without ceremony. Mr Wilde lay groaning on the floor, his face covered with blood, his clothes torn to shreds. Drops of blood were scattered about over the carpet, which had also been ripped and frayed in the evidently recent struggle.

'It's that cursed cat,' he said, ceasing his groans, and turning his colorless eyes to me; 'she attacked me while I was asleep. I believe she will kill me yet.'

This was too much, so I went into the kitchen and seizing a hatchet from the pantry, started to find the infernal beast and settle her then and there. My search was fruitless, and after a while I gave it up and came back to find Mr Wilde squatting on his high chair by the table. He had washed his face and changed his clothes. The great furrows which the cat's claws had ploughed up in his face he had filled with collodion, and a rag hid the wound in his throat. I told him I should kill the cat when I came across her, but he only shook his head and turned to the open ledger before him. He read name after name of the people who had come to him in regard to their reputation, and the sums he had amassed were startling.

'I put on the screws now and then,' he explained.

'One day or other some of these people will assassinate you,' I insisted.

'Do you think so?' he said, rubbing his mutilated ears.

On Castaigne's final visit to the apartment, the door is open but there is no sign of Mr Wilde. Suddenly a groan is heard from the dark corridor outside . . .

I seized the tallow dip and sprang to the door. The cat passed me like a demon, and the tallow dip went out, but my long knife flew swifter than she, and I heard her screech, and I knew that my knife had found her. For a moment I listened to her tumbling and thumping about in the darkness, and then when her frenzy ceased, I lighted a lamp and raised it over my head. Mr Wilde lay on the floor with his throat torn open. At first I thought he was dead, but as I looked, a green sparkle came into his sunken eyes, his mutilated hand trembled, and then a spasm stretched his mouth from ear to ear. For a moment my terror and despair gave place to hope, but as I bent over him his eyeballs rolled clean around in his head, and he died.

From *The King in Yellow* by Robert W. Chambers, 1895

A Compact with the Devil

As she spoke, she felt something move by her foot. She glanced down and saw a small kitten. It crouched by her foot, biting her shoe-lace, and lashing its tail from side to side. Laura did not like cats; but this creature, so small, so intent, and so ferocious, amused her into kindly feelings. 'How did you come here? Did you come in through the keyhole?' she asked, and bent down to stroke it. Scarcely had she touched its hard little head when it writhed itself round her hand, noiselessly clawing and biting, and kicking with its hind legs. She felt frightened by an attack so fierce and irrational, and her fears increased as she tried to shake off the tiny weight. At last she freed her hand, and looked at it. It was covered with fast-reddening scratches, and as she looked she saw a bright round drop of blood ooze out from one of them. Her heart gave a violent leap, and seemed to drop dead in her bosom. She gripped the back of a chair to steady herself and stared at the kitten. Abruptly pacified, it had curled itself into a ball and fallen asleep. Its lean ribs heaved with a rhythmic tide of sleep. As she stared she saw its pink tongue flicker for one moment over its lips. It slept like a suckling.

Not for one moment did she doubt . . . She, Laura Willowes, in England, in the year 1922, had entered into a compact with the Devil. The compact was made, and affirmed, and sealed with the round red seal of her blood.

From Lolly Willowes by Sylvia Townsend Warner, 1926

'Of the Witch's Powers of Transformation'

One of the most ordinary disguises of *'Ban-Buchichd'* [a witch] is the similitude of a hare. This transformation she finds exceedingly convenient while performing her cantrips in the field – bewitching farming implements – destroying corn and grass – holding communion with the sisterhood, and similar pieces of business . . .

A second is the likeness of a cat – by personating which, she procures admission to the inmost recesses of a house, to deposit her infernal machinery, without exciting the least suspicions of her real character and intentions.

From The Popular Superstitions and Festive Amusements of the Highlanders of Scotland
by William Grant Stewart, 1851

The Goodwife's Metamorphosis

John Garve Macgillichallum of Razay was an ancient hero of great celebrity. Distinguished in the age in which he lived for the gallantry of his exploits, he has often been selected by the bard as the theme of his poems and songs. Alongst with a constitution of body naturally vigorous and powerful, Razay was gifted with all those noble qualities of the mind which a true hero is supposed to possess. And what reflected additional lustre on his character, was that he never failed to apply his talents and powers to the best uses. He was the active and inexorable enemy of the weird sisterhood, many of whom he was the auspicious instrument of sending to their 'black inheritance' much sooner than they either expected or desired. It was not therefore to be supposed, that, while those amiable actions endeared Razay to all good people, they were at all calculated to win him the regard of those infernal hags to whom he was so deadly a foe. As might be naturally expected, they cherished towards him the most implacable thirst of revenge, and sought, with unremitting vigilance, for an opportunity of quenching it. That such an opportunity did unhappily occur, and that the meditated revenge of these hags was too well accomplished, will speedily appear from this melancholy story.

It happened upon a time that Razay and a number of friends planned an expedition to the island of Lewes, for the purpose of hunting the deer of that place. They accordingly embarked on board the chieftain's yacht, manned by the flower of the young men of Razay, and in a few hours they chased the fleet-bounding hart on the mountains of Lewes. Their sport proved excellent. Hart after hart, and hind after hind, were soon levelled to the ground by the unerring hand of Razay; and when night terminated the chase, they retired to their shooting quarters, where they spent the night with joviality and mirth, little dreaming of their melancholy fate in the morning.

In the morning of next day, the chief of Razay and his followers rose with the sun, with the view of returning to Razay. The day was squally and occasionally boisterous, and the billows raged with great violence. But Razay was determined to cross the channel to his residence, and ordered his yacht to prepare for the voyage. The more cautious and less courageous of his suite, however, urged on him to defer the expedition till the weather should somewhat settle – an advice which Razay, with a courage which knew no fear, rejected, and expressed his firm determination to proceed without delay. Probably with a view to inspire his company with the necessary degree of courage to induce them all to concur in the undertaking, he adjourned with them to the ferry-house, where they had recourse to that supporter of spirits under every trial, the usquebaugh, a few bottles of which added vastly to the resolution of the company. Just as the party were disputing the practicability of the proposed adventure, an old woman, with wrinkled front, bending on a crutch, entered the ferry-house; and Razay, in the heat of argument, appealed to the old woman, whether the passage of the channel on such a day was not perfectly practicable and free from danger. The woman, without hesitation, replied in the affirmative, adding such observations, reflecting on their courage, as immediately silenced every opposition to the voyage; and accordingly the whole party embarked in the yacht for Razay. But, alas! what were the consequences? No sooner were they abandoned to the mercy of the waves than the elements seemed to conspire to their destruction. All attempts to put back the vessel proved unavailing, and she was speedily driven out before the wind in the direction of Razay. The heroic chieftain laboured hard to animate his company, and to dispel the despair which began to seize them, by the most exemplary courage and resolution. He took charge of the helm, and, in spite of the combined efforts of the sea, wind, and lightning, he kept the vessel steadily on her course towards the lofty point of Aird in Skye. The drooping spirits of his crew began to revive, and hope began to smile upon them – when lo! to their great astonishment, a large cat was seen to climb the rigging. This cat was soon followed by another of equal size, and the last by a successor, until at length the shrouds, masts, and whole tackle, were actually covered with them. Nor did the sight of all those cats, although he knew well enough their real character, intimidate the resolute Razay, until a large black cat, larger than any of the rest, appeared on the mast-head, as commander-in-chief of the whole legion. Razay, on observing him, instantly foresaw the result; he, however, determined to sell his life as dearly as possible, and immediately commanded an attack upon the cats – but, alas! it soon proved abortive. With a simultaneous effort the cats overturned the vessel on her leeward wale, and every soul on board was precipitated into a watery grave. Thus ended the glorious life of *Jan Garbh Macgillichallum* of Razay, to the lasting regret of the brave clan Leod and all good people, and to the great satisfaction of the abominable witches who thus accomplished his lamentable doom.

The same day, another hero, celebrated for his hatred of witchcraft, was warming himself in his hunting hut, in the forest of Gaick in Badenoch. His faithful hounds, fatigued with the morning chase, lay stretched on the turf by his side, – his gun, that would not miss, reclined in the neuk of the boothy, – the *skian dhu* of the sharp edge hung by his side, and these alone constituted his company. As the hunter sat listening to the howling storm as it whistled by, there entered at the door an apparently poor weather-beaten cat, shivering with cold, and drenched to the skin. On observing her, the hairs of the dogs became erected bristles, and they immediately rose to attack the pitiable cat, which stood trembling at the door. 'Great hunter of the hills,' exclaims the poor-looking trembling cat, 'I claim your protection. I know your hatred to my craft, and perhaps it is just. Still spare, oh spare a poor jaded wretch, who thus flies to you for protection from the cruelty and oppression of her sisterhood.' Moved to compassion by her eloquent address, and disdaining to take advantage of his greatest enemy in such a seemingly forlorn situation, he pacified his infuriated dogs, and desired her to come forward to the fire and warm herself. 'Nay,' says she, 'in the first place, you will please bind with this long hair those two furious hounds of yours, for I am afraid they will tear my poor hams to pieces. I pray you, therefore, my dear sir, that you would have the goodness to bind them together by the necks with this long hair.' But the curious nature of the hair induced the hunter to dissemble a little. Instead of having bound his dogs with it, as he pretended, he threw it across a beam of wood which connected the couple of the boothy. The witch then supposing the dogs securely bound, approached the fire, and squatted heself down as if to dry herself. She had not sitten many minutes, when the hunter could easily discover a striking increase in her size, which he could not forbear remarking in a jocular manner to herself. 'A bad death to you, you nasty beast,' says the hunter; 'you are getting very large.' – 'Aye, aye,' replied the cat, equally jocosely, 'as my hairs imbibe the heat, they naturally expand.' These jokes, however, were but a prelude to a more serious conversation. The cat still continuing her growth, had at length attained a most extraordinary size, – when, in the twinkling of an eye, she transformed herself into her proper likeness of the Goodwife of Laggan, and thus addressed him: 'Hunter of the Hills, your hour of reckoning is arrived. Behold me before you, the avowed champion of my devoted sisterhood, of whom Macgillichallum of Razay and you were always the most relentless enemies. But Razay is no more. His last breath is fled. He lies a lifeless corpse on the bottom of the main; and now, Hunter of the Hills, it is your turn.' With these words, assuming a most hideous and terrific appearance, she made a spring at the hunter. The two dogs, which she supposed securely bound by the infernal hair, sprung at her in her turn, and a most furious conflict ensued. The witch, thus unexpectedly attacked by the dogs, now began to repent of her temerity. 'Fasten, hair, fasten,' she perpetually exclaimed, supposing the dogs to have been bound by the hair; and so effectually did the hair *fasten*, according to her order, that it at last snapt the beam in twain. At length, finding herself completely over-powered, she attempted a retreat, but so closely were the hounds fastened in her breasts, that it was with no small difficulty she could get herself disengaged from them. Screaming and shrieking, the Wife of Laggan dragged herself out of the house, trailing after the dogs, which were fastened in her so closely, that they never loosed their hold until she demolished every tooth in their heads. Then metamorphosing herself into the likeness of a raven, she fled over the mountains in the direction of her home. The two faithful dogs, bleeding and exhausted, returned to their master, and, in the act of caressing his hand, both fell down and expired at his feet. Re-gretting their loss with a sorrow only known to the parent who weeps over the remains of departed children, he buried his devoted dogs, and returned to his family. His wife was not in the house when he arrived, but she soon made her appearance. 'Where hae you been, my love?' inquired the husband. – 'Indeed,' replies she, 'I have been seeing the Goodwife of Laggan, who has been just seized with so severe an illness, that she is not expected to live for any time.' – 'Aye! aye!' says he, 'what is the matter with the worthy woman?' – 'She was all day absent in the moss at her peats,' replies the wife, 'and was seized with a sudden colic, in consequence of getting wet feet, and now all her friends and neighbours are ex-pecting her demision.' – 'Poor woman,' says the husband, 'I am sorry for her. Get me some dinner, it will be right that I should go and see her also.' Dinner being provided and dispatched, the hunter immediately proceeded to the house of Laggan, where he found a great assemblage of neighbours mourning, with great sincerity, the approaching decease of a woman whom they all had hitherto esteemed virtuous. The hunter, walking up to the sick woman's bed in a rage, proportioned to the greatness of its cause, stripped the sick woman of all her coverings. A shriek from the now exposed witch brought all the company around her. 'Behold,' says he, 'the object of your solicitude, who is nothing less than an infernal witch. To-day, she informs me, she was present at the death of the Laird of Razay, and only a few hours have elapsed since she attempted to make me share his fate. This night, however, she shall expiate her crime, by the forfeiture of her horrid life.'

From *The Popular Superstitions and Festive Amusements of the Highlanders of Scotland* by William Grant Stewart, 1851

The Devil Kissed Them

Part of the confession of Marie Lamont, an eighteen-year-old Scotswoman who was tried for witchcraft in March 1662.

She confesses that she was at a meitting in the Bridylinne, with Jean King, Kettie Scot, Margrat M'Kenzie, and several others, where the devill was with with them in the likeness of a brown dog. The end of their meitting was to raise stormie weather to hinder boats from the killing fishing; and shee confessed that shee, Kettie Scot, and Margrat Holm, cam to Allan Orr's house in the likeness of kats, and followed his wif into the chalmer, where they took a herring owt of a barrell, and having taken a byt off it, they left it behind them; the qlk herring the said Allan his wif did eat, and yairefter taking heavy disease, died. The quarrel was, because the said Allan had put Margrat Holm out of the houss wher shee was dwelling, whereupon shee threitened in wrath, that he and his wif sould not be long together. This agrees with the tent article of Kettie Scot's confession . . .

She confessed, that shee knew some witches carried meikle ill will at Blackhall, younger, and Mr John Hamilton, and would fain give them ane ill cast if they could; therefor, about five weeks sine, Jean King, Kettie Scot, Jonet Holm, herself, and severall others, met together in the night, at the back gate of Ardgowand, where the devill was with them in the likeness of a black man, with cloven featt, and directed some of them to fetch wyt sand from the shore, and cast it about the gates of Ardgowand, and about the minister's house; but

[159]

shee sayes, when they war about that business, the devil turned them in likeness of kats, by shaking his hands above their heads . . .

Shee confessed alsoe, that shee was with Katie Scot, Margrat M'Kenzie, and others, at a meitting at Kempoch, where they intendit to cast the longston into the sea, thereby to destroy boats and shipes, wher they danced, and the devil kissed them when they went away. These artickles were confessed by the said Marie Lamont, at Innerkip, before us, undersubscribers Archibald Stewart, fiare of Blackhall; J. Hamilton, minister at Innerkip.

From A Historical Account of the Belief in Witchcraft in Scotland
by Charles Kirkpatrick Sharpe, 1884

An Imp

In *A Dialogue Concerning Witches and Witchcrafts*, by George Giffard, minister of God's word at Maldon, 1603, is a story of a witch who employed an imp in the shape of a cat to destroy three hogs and a cow belonging to a farmer whom she hated. – 'The man suspecting, burnt a pig alive, and, as she say'd, her cat would never go thither any more.'

From A Historical Account of the Belief in Witchcraft in Scotland
by Charles Kirkpatrick Sharpe, 1884

A Regimental Superstition

My staff duties at Poona brought me into contact with two regimental commanding officers who laboured hard to make mountains out of molehills, and to bring into ridicule the institution of trial by court-martial. They were both martinets of a severe type, and had no sense of the sympathetic or amusing side of things. One of them commanded a regiment of British infantry, and on returning from leave of absence to England, he decreed the cessation of wearing beards, a custom which had been permitted during and after the Mutiny campaign.

In the other case the officer commanded a regiment of native infantry, and it had been discovered that for twenty-five years past an oral addition to the written standing orders of the native guard at Government House, near Poona, had been communicated regularly from one guard to another, on relief, to the effect that any cat passing out of the front door after dark was to be regarded as His Excellency the Governor, and to be saluted accordingly. The meaning of this was that Sir Robert Grant, Governor of Bombay, had died there in 1838, and on the evening of the day of his death a cat was seen to leave the house by the front door and walk up and down a particular path, as had been the Governor's habit to do, after sunset. A Hindu sentry had observed this, and he mentioned it to others of his faith, who made it a subject of superstitious conjecture, the result being that one of the priestly class explained the mystery of the dogma of the transmigration of the soul from one body to another, and interpreted the circumstances to mean that the spirit of the deceased Governor had entered into one of the house pets. It was difficult to fix on a particular one, and it was therefore decided that every cat passing out of the main entrance after dark was to be regarded as the tabernacle of Governor Grant's soul, and to be treated with due respect and the proper honours. This decision was accepted without question by all the native attendants and others belonging to Government House. The whole guard, from sepoy to subadar, fully acquiesced in it, and an oral addition was made to the standing orders that the sentry at the front door would 'present arms' to any cat passing out there after dark. The notion was essentially Hindu, yet the Mahomedans and native Christians and Jews (native Jews are to be found in the Bombay army) devoutly assented to it. Dread of the supernatural overcame all religious objections, and every one scrupulously bowed to the heathen decree.

This sepoy guard was a weekly one, furnished alternately by the two native infantry regiments of the garrison. The respective commanding officers at that time were of diametrically different dispositions. The one was of sympathetic temperament and calm judgment; the other impetuous and arbitrary, a rigid disciplinarian, and a severe commander. I and others were at pains to ascertain the truth of the story concerning military honours to the cat, and I mentioned it to both commanding officers, as an interesting subject of wonder at the long continuance of the oral order without it becoming known. The one said he would laugh his native officers out of the idea, the other said he would order them to discontinue the folly, and there would be an end of the absurdity. The latter had the fullest belief in his ability to influence his men to dare the demons of darkness rather than openly disobey them. He set his mind firmly on this, and he assembled the native officers and ordered them to refuse to take over, or countenance in any way, the unwritten order regarding the house cat, warning them of the severe court-martial consequences of disobedience. When the first guard furnished by his regiment after this warning returned from the week's duty at Government House, the subadar in command was questioned regarding the oral order. It then came out that his fear of the supernatural was greater than his fear of the stern, uncompromising colonel, and in his awful presence he meekly said, in a few words, that to act as ordered meant to him a life of terror and a death of horror, and having disobeyed, he was ready to lose his highly-prized commission, and the pension reward of his long and faithful service. The colonel insisted on treating the matter as 'subversive of good order and military discipline,' and placing the subadar in arrest, he prepared an application for his trial by court-martial. To me he said, 'I know you will laugh, but my authority must be vindicated.' The brigadier took a sympathetic view of the case, ordered the native officer to be released from arrest, and quietly advised the colonel to contend more gently and patiently with simple superstitions.

From *A Varied Life: A Record of Military and Civil Service,*
of Sport and of Travel in India, Central Asia and Persia, 1849-1902
by General Sir Thomas Edward Gordon, 1906

'The Sending of Dana Da'

When the Devil rides on your chest remember the low-caste man.
Native Proverb.

Once upon a time, some people in India made a new Heaven and a new Earth out of broken tea-cups, a missing brooch or two, and a hair-brush. These were hidden under bushes, or stuffed into holes in the hillside, and an entire Civil Service of Subordinate Gods used to find or mend them again; and every one said: – 'There are more things in Heaven and Earth than are dreamt of in our philosophy'. Several other things happened also, but the Religion never seemed to get much beyond its first manifestations; though it added an air-line post and orchestral effects, in order to keep abreast of the times and stall off competition.

This Religion was too elastic for ordinary use. It stretched itself and embraced pieces of everything that medicine-men of all ages have manufactured. It approved of and stole from Freemasonry; looted the Latterday Rosicrucians of half their pet words; took any fragments of Egyptian philosophy that it found in the Encyclopae-dia Britannica; annexed as many of the Vedas as had been translated into French or English, and talked of all the rest; built in the Ger-man versions of what is left of the Zend Avesta; encouraged White, Grey and Black Magic, including spiritualism, palmistry, fortune-telling by cards, hot chestnuts, double-kernelled nuts and tallow dropping: would have adopted Voodoo and Oboe had it known anything about them, and showed itself, in every way, one of the most accommodating arrangements that had ever been invented since the birth of the Sea.

When it was in thorough working order, with all the machinery down to the subscriptions complete, Dana Da came from nowhere, with nothing in his hands, and wrote a chapter in its history which has hitherto been unpublished. He said that his first name was Dana, and his second was Da. Now, setting aside Dana of the New York *Sun*, Dana is a Bhil name, and Da fits no native of India unless you accept the Bengali Dé as the original spelling. Da is Lap or Finnish; and Dana Da was neither Finn, Chin, Bhil, Bengali, Lap, Nair, Gond, Romaney, Magh, Bokhariot, Kurd, Armenian, Levan-tine, Jew, Persian, Punjabi, Madrasi, Parsee, nor anything else known to ethnologists. He was simply Dana Da, and declined to give further information. For the sake of brevity and as roughly in-dicating his origin, he was called 'The Native'. He might have been the original Old Man of the Mountains, who is said to be the only authorised head of the Tea-cup Creed. Some people said that he was; but Dana Da used to smile and deny any connection with the cult; explaining that he was an 'Independent Experimentor'.

As I have said, he came from nowhere, with his hands behind his back, and studied the Creed for three weeks; sitting at the feet of those best competent to explain its mysteries. Then he laughed aloud and went away, but the laugh might have been either of devotion or derision.

When he returned he was without money, but his pride was unabated. He declared that he knew more about the Things in Heaven and Earth than those who taught him, and for this contumacy was abandoned altogether.

His next appearance in public life was at a big cantonment in Upper India, and he was then telling fortunes with the help of three leaden dice, a very dirty old cloth, and a little tin box of opium pills. He told better fortunes when he was allowed half a bottle of whiskey; but the things which he invented on the opium were quite worth the money. He was in reduced circumstances. Among other people's he told the fortune of an Englishman who had once been interested in the Simla Creed, but who, later on, had married and forgotten all his old knowledge in the study of babies and Exchange. The Englishman allowed Dana Da to tell a fortune for charity's sake, and gave him five rupees, a dinner, and some old clothes. When he had eaten, Dana Da professed gratitude, and asked if there were anything that he could do for his host – in the esoteric line.

'Is there any one that you love?' said Dana Da. The Englishman loved his wife but had no desire to drag her name into the conversation. He therefore shook his head.

'Is there any one that you hate?' said Dana Da. The Englishman said that there were several men whom he hated deeply.

'Very good,' said Dana Da, upon whom the whiskey and the opium were beginning to tell. 'Only give me their names and I will despatch a Sending to them and kill them.'

Now a Sending is a horrible arrangement, first invented, they say, in Iceland. It is a Thing sent by a wizard, and may take any form, but, most generally, wanders about the land in the shape of a little purple cloud till it finds the Sendee, and him it kills by changing into the form of a horse, or a cat, or a man without a face. It is not strictly a native patent, though some low-caste men can, if irritated, despatch a Sending which sits on the breast of their enemy by night and nearly kills him. Very few natives care to irritate low-caste men for this reason.

'Let me despatch a Sending,' said Dana Da; 'I am nearly dead now with want, and drink, and opium; but I should like to kill a man before I die. I can send a Sending anywhere you choose, and in any form except in the shape of a man.'

The Englishman had no friends that he wished to kill, but partly to soothe Dana Da, whose eyes were rolling, and partly to see what would be done, he asked whether a modified Sending could not be arranged for – such a Sending as should make a man's life a burden to him, and yet do him no harm. If this were possible, he notified his willingness to give Dana Da ten rupees for the job.

'I am not what I was once,' said Dana Da, 'and I must take the money because I am poor. To what Englishman shall I send it?'

'Send a Sending to Lone *Sahib*,' said the Englishman, naming a man who had been most bitter in rebuking him for his apostasy from the Tea-cup Creed. Dana Da laughed and nodded.

'I could have chosen no better man myself,' said he. 'I will see that he finds the Sending about his path and about his bed.'

He lay down on the hearth-rug, turned up the whites of his eyes, shivered all over and began to snort. This was Magic, or Opium, or the Sending, or all three. When he opened his eyes he vowed that the Sending had started upon the warpath, and was at that moment flying up to the town where Lone *Sahib* lived.

'Give me my ten rupees,' said Dana Da wearily, 'and write a letter to Lone *Sahib*, telling him, and all who believe with him, that you and a friend are using a power greater than theirs. They will see that you are speaking the truth.'

He departed unsteadily, with the promise of some more rupees if anything came of the Sending.

The Englishman sent a letter to Lone *Sahib*, couched in what he remembered of the terminology of the Creed. He wrote:- 'I also, in the days of what you held to be my backsliding, have obtained Enlightenment, and with Englightenment has come Power.' Then he grew so deeply mysterious that the recipient of the letter could make neither head nor tail of it, and was proportionately impressed; for he fancied that his friend had become a 'fifth-rounder'. When a man is a 'fifth-rounder' he can do more than Slade and Houdin combined.

Lone *Sahib* read the letter in five different fashions, and was beginning a sixth interpretation when his bearer dashed in with the news that there was a cat on the bed. Now if there was one thing that Lone *Sahib* hated more than another it was a cat. He rated the bearer for not turning it out of the house. The bearer said that he was afraid. All the doors of the bedroom had been shut throughout the morning, and no cat could possibly have entered the room. He would prefer not to meddle with the creature.

Lone *Sahib* entered the room gingerly, and there, on the pillow of his bed, sprawled and whimpered a wee white kitten, not a jumpsome, frisky little beast, but a slug-like crawler with its eyes barely opened and its paws lacking strength or direction – a kitten that ought to have been in a basket with its mamma. Lone *Sahib* caught it by the scruff of its neck, handed it over to the sweeper to be drowned, and fined the bearer four annas.

That evening, as he was reading in his room, he fancied that he saw something moving about on the hearth-rug, outside the circle of light from his reading-lamp. When the thing began to myowl, he realised that it was a kitten – a wee white kitten, nearly blind and very miserable. He was seriously angry, and spoke bitterly to his bearer, who said that there was no kitten in the room when he brought in the lamp, and real kittens of tender age generally had mother-cats in attendance.

'If the Presence will go out into the verandah and listen,' said the bearer, 'he will hear no cats. How, therefore, can the kittens on the bed and the kitten on the hearth-rug be real kittens?'

Lone *Sahib* went out to listen, and the bearer followed him, but there was no sound of Rachel mewing for her children. He returned to his room, having hurled the kitten down the hillside, and wrote out the incidents of the day for the benefit of his co-religionists. Those people were so absolutely free from superstition that they ascribed anything a little out of the common to Agencies. As it was their business to know all about the Agencies, they were on terms of almost indecent familiarity with Manifestations of every kind. Their letters dropped from the ceiling – unstamped – and Spirits used to squatter up and down their staircases all night. But they had never come into contact with kittens. Lone *Sahib* wrote out the facts, noting the hour and the minute, as every Psychical Observer is bound to do, and appending the Englishman's letter because it was the most mysterious document, and might have had a bearing upon anything in this world or the next. An outsider would have translated all the tangle thus: – 'Look out! You laughed at me once, and now I am going to make you sit up'.

Lone *Sahib*'s co-religionists found that meaning in it; but their translation was refined and full of four-syllable words. They held a sederunt, and were filled with tremulous joy, for, in spite of their familiarity with all the other worlds and cycles, they had a very human awe of things sent from Ghostland. They met in Lone *Sahib*'s room in shrouded and sepulchral gloom, and their conclave was broken up by a clinking among the photo-frames on the mantelpiece. A wee white kitten, nearly blind, was looping and writhing itself between the clock and the candlesticks. That stopped all investigations or doubtings. Here was the Manifestation in the flesh. It was, so far as could be seen, devoid of purpose, but it was a Manifestation of undoubted authenticity.

They drafted a Round Robin to the Englishman, the backslider of old days, adjuring him in the interests of the Creed to explain whether there was any connection between the embodiment of some Egyptian God or other [I have forgotten the name] and his communication. They called the kitten Ra, or Toth, or Shem, or Noah, or something; and when Lone *Sahib* confessed that the first one had, at his most misguided instance, been drowned by the sweeper, they said consolingly that in his next life he would be a 'bounder' and not even a 'rounder' of the lowest grade. These words may not be quite correct, but they express the sense of the house accurately.

When the Englishman received the Round Robin – it came by post – he was startled and bewildered. He sent into the bazar for Dana Da, who read the letter and laughed. 'That is my Sending,' said he. 'I told you I would work well. Now give me another ten rupees.'

'But what in the world is this gibberish about Egyptian Gods?' asked the Englishman.

'Cats,' said Dana Da with a hiccough, for he had discovered the Englishman's whiskey bottle. 'Cats, and cats, and cats! Never was such a Sending. A hundred of cats. Now give me ten more rupees and write as I dictate.'

Dana Da's letter was a curiosity. It bore the Englishman's signature, and hinted at cats – at a Sending of Cats. The mere words on paper were creepy and uncanny to behold.

'What have you done, though?' said the Englishman, 'I am as much in the dark as ever. Do you mean to say that you can actually send this absurd Sending you talk about?'

'Judge for yourself,' said Dana Da. 'What does that letter mean? In a little time they will all be at my feet and yours, and I, O glory, will be drugged or drunk all day long.'

Dana Da knew his people.

When a man who hates cats wakes up in the morning and finds a little squirming kitten on his breast, or puts his hand into his ulster-pocket and finds a little half-dead kitten where his gloves should be, or opens his trunk and finds a vile kitten among his dress shirts, or goes for a long ride with his macintosh strapped on his saddle-bow and shakes a little squawling kitten from its folds when he opens it, or goes out to dinner and finds a little blind kitten under his chair, or stays at home and finds a writhing kitten under the quilt, or wriggling among his boots, or hanging head downwards in his tobacco jar, or being mangled by his terrier in the verandah, – when such a man finds one kitten, neither more nor less, once a day in a place where no kitten rightly could or should be, he is naturally upset. When he dare not murder his daily trove because he believes it to be a Manifestation, an Emissary, an Embodiment, and half-a-dozen other things all out of the regular course of nature, he is more than upset. He is actually distressed. Some of Lone *Sahib*'s co-religionists thought that he was a highly-favoured individual; but many said that if he had treated the first kitten with proper respect – as suited a Toth-Ra-Tum-Sennacherib Embodiment – all this trouble would have been averted. They compared him to the Ancient Mariner, but none the less they were proud of him and proud of the Englishman who had sent the Manifestation. They did not call it a Sending because Icelandic magic was not in their pro-gramme.

After sixteen kittens, that is to say after one fortnight, for there were three kittens on the first day to impress the fact of the Sending, the whole camp was uplifted by a letter – it came flying through a window – from the Old Man of the Mountains – the Head of all the Creed – explaining the Manifestation in the most beautiful language and soaking up all the credit of it for himself. The Englishman, said the letter, was not there at all. He was a back-slider without Power or Asceticism, who couldn't even raise a table by force of volition, much less project an army of kittens through space. The entire arrangement, said the letter, was strictly orthodox, worked and sanctioned by the highest Authorities within the pale of the Creed. There was great joy at this, for some of the weaker brethren seeing that an outsider who had been working on independent lines could create kittens, whereas their own rulers had never gone beyond crockery – and broken at that – were showing a desire to break line on their own trail. In fact, there was the promise of a schism. A second Round Robin was drafted to the Englishman, beginning: – 'O Scoffer,' and ending with a selection of curses from the Rites of Mizraim and Memphis and the Commination of Jugana who was a 'fifth-rounder,' upon whose name an upstart 'third-rounder' once traded. A Papal excommunication is a love-letter compared to the Commination of Jugana. The Englishman had been proved, under the hand and seal of the Old Man of the Mountains, to have appropriated Virtue and pretended to have Power which, in reality, belonged only to the Supreme Head. Naturally the Round Robin did not spare him.

He handed the letter to Dana Da to translate into decent English. The effect on Dana Da was curious. At first he was furiously angry, and then he laughed for five minutes.

'I had thought,' he said, 'that they would have come to me. In another week I would have shown that I sent the Sending, and they would have discrowned the Old Man of the Mountains who – has sent this Sending of mine. Do you do nothing. The time has come for me to act. Write as I dictate, and I will put them to shame. But give me ten more rupees.'

At Dana Da's dictation the Englishman wrote nothing less than a formal challenge to the Old Man of the Mountains. It wound up: – 'And if this Manifestation be from your hand, then let it go forward; but if it be from my hand, I will that the Sending shall cease in two days' time. On that day there shall be twelve kittens and thenceforward none at all. The people shall judge between us.' This was signed by Dana Da who added pentacles and pentagrams, and a crux ansata, and half-a-dozen swastikas, and a Triple Tau to his name, just to show that he was all he laid claim to be.

The challenge was read out to the gentlemen and ladies, and they remembered then that Dana Da had laughed at them some years ago. It was officially announced that the Old Man of the Mountains would treat the matter with contempt; Dana Da being an Independent Investigator without a single 'round' at the back of him. But this did not soothe his people. They wanted to see a fight. They were very human for all their spirituality. Lone *Sahib*, who was really being worn out with kittens, submitted meekly to his fate. He felt that he was being 'kittened to prove the power of Dana Da,' as the poet says.

When the stated day dawned, the shower of kittens began. Some were white and some were tabby, and all were about the same loathsome age. There on his hearth-rug, three in his bathroom, and the other six turned up at intervals among the visitors who came to see the prophecy break down. Never was a more satisfactory Sending. On the next day there were no kittens, and the next day and all the other days were kittenless and quiet. The people murmured and looked to the Old Man of the Mountains for an explanation. A letter, written on a palm-leaf, dropped from the ceiling, but everyone except Lone *Sahib* felt that letters were not what the occasion demanded. There should have been cats, there should have been cats, – full-grown ones. The letter proved conclusively that there had been a hitch in the Psychic Current which, colliding with a Dual Identity, had interfered with the Percipient Activity all along the main line. The kittens were still going on, but owing to some failure in the Developing Fluid, they were not materialized. The air was thick with letters for a few days afterwards. Unseen hands played Gluck and Beethoven on finger-bowls and clock-shades; but all men felt that Psychic Life was a mockery without Materialized kittens. Even Lone *Sahib* shouted with the majority on this head. Dana Da's letters were very insulting, and if he had then offered to lead a new departure, there is no knowing what might not have happened.

But Dana Da was dying of whiskey and opium in the Englishman's godown, and had small heart for new creeds.

'They have been put to shame,' said he. 'Never was such a Sending. It has killed me.'

'Nonsense,' said the Englishman, 'you are going to die, Dana Da, and that sort of stuff must be left behind. I'll admit that you have made some queer things come about. Tell me honestly, now, how was it done?'

'Give me ten more rupees,' said Dana Da faintly, 'and if I die before I spend them, bury them with me.' The silver was counted out while Dana Da was fighting with Death. His hand closed upon the money and he smiled a grim smile.

'Bend low,' he whispered. The Englishman bent.

'Mission-School – expelled – pedler – Ceylon pearl-merchant – all mine English education – out-casted, and made up name Dana Da – went to England with American thought-reading man and – and – you gave me ten rupees several times – I gave the *Sahib*'s bearer two rupees a month for cats – little, little cats. I wrote, and he put them about – very clever man. Very few kittens now in the bazar. Ask Lone *Sahib*'s sweeper's wife.'

So saying, Dana Da gasped and passed away into a land where, if all be true, there are no materializations and the making of new creeds is discouraged.

But consider the gorgeous simplicity of it all!

From *In Black and White* by Rudyard Kipling, 1888

'The Cat'

This poem, first published anonymously in a Cambridge anthology in 1905, was written by Lytton Strachey.

Dear creature by the fire a-purr,
　　Strange idol eminently bland,
Miraculous puss! As o'er your fur
　　I trail a negligible hand,

And gaze into your gazing eyes,
　　And wonder in a demi-dream
What mystery it is that lies
　　Behind those slits that glare and gleam,

An exquisite enchantment falls
　　About the portals of my sense;
Meandering through enormous halls
　　I breathe luxurious frankincense.

An ampler air, a warmer June
   Enfold me, and my wondering eye
Salutes a more imperial moon
   Throned in a more resplendent sky

Than ever knew this northern shore.
   O, strange! For you are with me too,
And I who am a cat once more
   Follow the woman that was you.

With tail erect and pompous march,
   The proudest puss that ever trod,
Through many a grove, 'neath many an arch,
   Impenetrable as a god,

Down many an alabaster flight
   Of broad and cedar-shaded stairs,
While over us the elaborate night
   Mysteriously gleams and glares!

From *Euphrosyne: A Collection of Verse,* 1905

The Zombi

A letter from the poet Robert Southey to his friend Grosvenor C. Bedford

April 3, 1821

My dear G. –
The King has desired Sir William Knighton to let me know that 'he
has read the *Vision of Judgement* twice, and that he is much gratified
by the dedication, and pleased with the poem'. . .

Now to a more important subject. You were duly apprised towards
the end of the year of Othello's death. Since that lamented event
this house was cat-less, till on Saturday, March 24, Mrs Calvert,
knowing how grievously we were annoyed by rats, offered me

what she described as a fine full-grown black cat, who was moreover a tom. She gave him an excellent character in all points but one, which was that he was a most expert pigeon-catcher; and as they had a pigeon-house, the propensity rendered it necessary to pass sentence upon him either of transportation or of death. Moved by compassion (his colour and his tomship also being taken into consideration), I consented to give him an asylum, and on the evening of that day here he came in a sack.

You, Grosvenor, who are a *philogalist*, and therefore understand more of cat nature than has been ever attained by the most profound naturalists, know how difficult it is to reconcile a cat to a new domicile. When the sack was opened, the kitchen door, which led into the passage, was open also, and the cat disappeared; not indeed like a flash of lightning, but as fast as one – that is to say, for all purposes of a simile. There was no chance of his making his way back to the pigeon-house. He might have done this had he been carried thrice the distance in any other direction; but in this there was either a river to cross, or a part of the town to pass, both of which were such obstacles to his travels that we were quite sure all on this side of them was to him *terra incognita*. Food, therefore, was placed where he would be likely to find it in the night; and at the unanimous desire of the children, I took upon myself the charge of providing him with a name, for it is not proper that a cat should remain without one. Taking into consideration his complexion, as well as his sex, my first thought was to call him Henrique Diaz, a name which poor Koster would have approved, had he been living to have heard it; but it presently occurred to me that the Zombi would be an appellation equally appropriate and more dignified. The Zombi, therefore, he was named.

It was soon ascertained that the Zombi had taken possession of poor Wilsey's cellar, which being filled with pea-sticks afforded him a secure hiding-place; the kitchen also of that part of the house being forsaken, he was in perfect quiet. Food was laid for him every day, and the children waited impatiently for the time when the Zombi would become acquainted with the house, and suffer them to become acquainted with him. Once or twice in the evening he was seen out of doors, and it was known that he reconnoitred the premises in the night; but in obstinate retirement he continued from Saturday till Saturday, seven days and nights, notwithstanding all

kind words were used to bring him out, as if he had been determined to live and die a hermit.

But between four and five o'clock on the Sunday morning, all
who had ears to hear were awakened by such screams as if the
Zombi had been caught in a rat-trap, or had met with some other
excruciating accident. You, Mr Bedford, understand cats, and know
very well that a cat-*solo* is a very different thing from a *duet*; and that
no person versed in their tongue can mistake their expression of
pain for anything else. The creature seemed to be in agonies. A
light was procured, that it might be relieved if that were possible.
Upon searching the house, the Zombi was seen at the top of Wilsey's stairs, from whence he disappeared, retreating to his
stronghold in the cellar; nor could any traces be discovered of any
hurt that could have befallen him, nor has it since appeared that he
had received any, so that the cause of this nocturnal disturbance remains an impenetrable mystery.

Various have been our attempts to explain it. Some of the women
who measure the power of rats by their own fears, would have it
that he was bitten by a rat, or by an association of rats; but to this I
indignantly replied that in that case the ground would have been
strewn with their bodies, and that it would have been the rats' cry,
not the Zombi's, that would have been heard. Dismissing, therefore, that impossible supposition, I submit to your consideration, in
the form of queries, the various possibilities which have occurred to
me – all unsatisfactory, I confess – requesting you to assist me in
my endeavour to find out the mystery of this wonderful history, as
it may truly be called. You will be pleased to bear in mind that the
Zombi was the only cat concerned in the transaction: of that I am
perfectly certain.

Now then, Grosvenor –
1. Had he seen the devil?
2. Was he making love to himself?
3. Was he engaged in single combat with himself?
4. Was he attempting to raise the devil by invocation?
5. Had he heard me sing, and was he attempting (vainly) to imitate it?

These queries, you will perceive, all proceed upon the supposition that it was the Zombi who made the noise. But I have further to
ask – 6. Was it the devil?

7. Was it Jeffery?

8. Were either of these personages tormenting the Zombi?

I have only to add that from that time to this he continues in the same obstinate retirement, and to assure you that

I remain, Mr Bedford. With the highest consideration,
Yours as ever,
Robert Southey

PS. One further query occurs while I am writing. Sunday having been the first of the month –

9. Was he making April fools of us? R.S.

From *Selections from the Letters of Robert Southey*, 1856

'Cat'

A poem written by the then Poet Laureate, C. Day-Lewis, as the prologue to a book of cat stories published in the 1960s.

Tearaway kitten or staid mother of fifty,
Persian, Chinchilla, Siamese
Or backstreet brawler – you all have a tiger in your blood
And eyes opaque as the sacred mysteries.

The hunter's instinct sends you pouncing, dallying,
Formal and wild as a temple dance.
You take from man what is your due – the fireside saucer,
And give him his – a purr of tolerance.

Like poets you wrap your solitude around you
And catch your meaning unawares:
With consequential trot or frantic tarantella
You follow up your top-secret affairs.

Simpkin, our pretty cat, assumes my lap
As a princess her rightful throne,
Pads round and drops asleep there. Each is a familiar
Warmth to the other, each no less alone.

From *The Best Cat Stories*, 1969

'Dark Forces'

'Why are you acting so funny?' Sunshine enquired politely.

'How do you mean, *funny?*'

'The past few days you've been behaving – well, sort of odd. If I may say so.' Almost as if were up to something. But surely he couldn't be up to it nowadays.

'Do you mean *mysterious?*'

'Perhaps I do,' said Sunshine amenably.

'I hope you do – I've been to considerable trouble to be it!'

'No, no, you be it very well . . . ' Whatever it might be.

Kuching explained in the equivalent of words of one syllable that cats were held to be mysterious; they were greatly esteemed for it in some circles. Cats sensed things, they were in touch with *dark forces* ('certainly not, dark horses are completely different!'), they could predict earthquakes ('that's true, but we haven't had any round here lately'), they could see the unseen and hear the unheard. All of which was safe enough these days, witches being more acceptable in the modern world. They had ESP. ('Extra-Special Perception') and PSI ('Pusses' Superior Intuition'); they went into trances ('trances are much like snoozing') and had visions. Cats were sfinks-like ('that's an important sort of cat in Egypt'). And also seraphic and subtle, so a foreign poet had written; there was something to be said for poets, as long as one said it quietly . . .

Moreover, they were keepers of time, for the Chinese used to tell the hour by peering into the eyes of a cat and observing the shape and size of the pupils.

'Ugh!' Sunshine squeaked. 'You mean – they hung us up on the wall?'

'In that case the clock would soon stop. If only you could control that overheated imagination of yours!'

Cats knew what was *going on*. Their tails were like airy-alls ('then look at the tee-vee and you'll see'), picking up miss-tick messages from The Beyond. Dogs never knew what was going on; they thumped their tails senselessly. And humans weren't much brighter, they didn't have tails at all, they were forever saying things like 'I don't know what this world is coming to'.

'We should keep this reputation alive,' Kuching said firmly. 'You never know when it might come in handy.'

'When I act like that, you tell me off.'

'That's because you look vacuous, as if you can't remember who you are and what you were going to do. You should study me, and then go away and practise.' He softened. 'Actually it's not awfully hard work, being mystic and inscrutable.'

From *The Way of the Cat* by D. J. Enright, 1992

A Shocking Parlour-Cat

The first week in December was very wet, with the barometer very low. On the 7th, with the barometer at 28-five-tenths, came on a vast snow, which continued all that day and the next, and most part of the following night; so that by the morning of the 9th the works of men were quite overwhelmed, the lanes filled so as to be impassable, and the ground covered twelve or fifteen inches without any drifting. In the evening of the 9th the air began to be so very sharp that we thought it would be curious to attend to the motions of a thermometer: we therefore hung out two; one made by Martin and one by Dollond, which soon began to show us what we were to expect; for, by ten o'clock, they fell to 21, and at eleven to 4, when we went to bed. On the 10th, in the morning, the quicksilver of Dollond's glass was down to half a degree below zero; and that of Martin's, which was absurdly graduated only to four degrees above zero, sunk quite into the brass guard of the ball; so that when the weather became most interesting this was useless. On the 10th, at eleven at night, though the air was perfectly still, Dollond's glass went down to one degree below zero! . . .

I must not omit to tell you that, during those two Siberian days, my parlour-cat was so electric, that had a person stroked her, and been properly insulated, the shock might have been given to a whole circle of people.

From *The Natural History and Antiquities of Selborne* by the Revd Gilbert White,
1789

'The Black Cat'

For the most wild, yet most homely narrative which I am about to pen, I neither expect nor solicit belief. Mad indeed would I be to expect it in a case where my very senses reject their own evidence. Yet mad am I not – and very surely do I not dream. But to-morrow I die, and to-day I would unburthen my soul. My immediate purpose is to place before the world plainly, succinctly, and without comment, a series of mere household events. In their consequences these events have terrified – have tortured – have destroyed me. Yet I will not attempt to expound them. To me they have presented little but Horror – to many they will seem less terrible than *barroques*. Hereafter, perhaps, some intellect may be found which will reduce my phantasm to the commonplace – some intellect more calm, more logical, and far less excitable than my own, which will perceive, in the circumstances I detail with awe, nothing more than an ordinary succession of very natural causes and effects.

From my infancy I was noted for the docility and humanity of my disposition. My tenderness of heart was even so conspicuous as to make me the jest of my companions. I was especially fond of animals, and was indulged by my parents with a great variety of pets. With these I spent most of my time, and never was so happy as when feeding and caressing them. This peculiarity of character grew with my growth, and in my manhood I derived from it one of my principal sources of pleasure. To those who have cherished an affection for a faithful and sagacious dog, I need hardly be at the trouble of explaining the nature of the intensity of the gratification thus derivable. There is something in the unselfish and self-sacrificing love of a brute which goes directly to the heart of him who has had frequent occasion to test the paltry friendship and gossamer fidelity of mere *Man*.

I married early, and was happy to find in my wife a disposition not uncongenial with my own. Observing my partiality for domestic pets, she lost no opportunity of procuring those of the most agreeable kind. We had birds, gold-fish, a fine dog, rabbits, a small monkey, and *a cat*.

This latter was a remarkably large and beautiful animal, entirely black, and sagacious to an astonishing degree. In speaking of his intelligence, my wife, who at heart was not a little tinctured with superstition, made frequent allusion to the ancient popular notion which regarded all black cats as witches in disguise. Not that she was ever *serious* upon this point, and I mention the matter at all for no better reason than that it happens just now to be remembered.

Pluto – this was the cat's name – was my favourite pet and playmate. I alone fed him, and he attended me wherever I went about the house. It was even with difficulty that I could prevent him from following me through the streets.

Our friendship lasted in this manner for several years, during which my general temperament and character – through the instrumentality of the Fiend Intemperance – had (I blush to confess it) experienced a radical alteration for the worse. I grew, day by day, more moody, more irritable, more regardless of the feelings of others. I suffered myself to use intemperate language to my wife. At length, I even offered her personal violence. My pets of course were made to feel the change in my disposition. I not only neglected, but ill-used them. For Pluto, however, I still retained sufficient regard to restrain me from maltreating him, as I made no scruple of maltreating the rabbits, the monkey, or even the dog, when by accident, or through affection, they came in my way. But my disease grew upon me – for what disease is like Alcohol! – and at length even Pluto, who was now becoming old, and consequently somewhat peevish – even Pluto began to experience the effects of my ill-temper.

One night returning home much intoxicated from one of my haunts about town, I fancied that the cat avoided my presence. I seized him, when, in his fright at my violence, he inflicted a slight wound upon my hand with his teeth. The fury of a demon instantly possessed me. I knew myself no longer. My original soul seemed at once to take its flight from my body, and a more than fiendish malevolence, gin-nurtured, thrilled every fibre of my frame. I took from my waistcoat-pocket a pen-knife, opened it, grasped the poor beast by the throat, and deliberately cut one of its eyes from the socket! I blush, I burn, I shudder, while I pen the damnable atrocity.

When reason returned with the morning – when I had slept off the fumes of the night's debauch – I experienced a sentiment half of horror, half of remorse, for the crime of which I had been guilty, but it was at best a feeble and equivocal feeling, and the soul remained untouched. I again plunged into excess, and soon drowned in wine all memory of the deed.

In the meantime the cat slowly recovered. The socket of the lost eye presented, it is true, a frightful appearance, but he no longer appeared to suffer any pain. He went about the house as usual, but, as might be expected, fled in extreme terror at my approach. I had so much of my old heart left as to be at first grieved by this evident dislike on the part of a creature which had once so loved me. But this feeling soon gave place to irritation. And then came, as if to my final and irrevocable overthrow, the spirit of PERVERSENESS. Of this spirit philosophy takes no account. Yet I am not more sure that my soul lives than I am that perverseness is one of the primitive impulses of the human heart – one of the indivisible primary faculties of sentiments which give direction to the character of Man. Who has not, a hundred times, found himself committing a vile or a silly action for no other reason than because he knows he should *not?* Have we not a perpetual inclination, in the teeth of our best judgment, to violate that which is *Law*, merely because we understand it to be such? This spirit of perverseness, I say, came to my final overthrow. It was this unfathomable longing of the soul *to vex itself* – to offer violence to its own nature – to do wrong for the wrong's sake only – that urged me to continue and finally to consummate the injury I had inflicted upon the unoffending brute. One morning, in cool blood, I slipped a noose about its neck and hung it to the limb of a tree; – hung it with the tears streaming from my eyes, and with the bitterest remorse at my heart; hung it *because* I knew that it had loved me, and *because* I felt it had given me no reason of offence; hung it *because* I knew that in so doing I was committing a sin – a deadly sin that would so jeopardise my immortal soul as to place it, if such a thing were possible, even beyond the reach of the infinite mercy of the Most Merciful and Most Terrible God.

On the night of the day on which this cruel deed was done, I was aroused from sleep by the cry of fire. The curtains of my bed were in flames. The whole house was blazing. It was with great difficulty that my wife, a servant, and myself, made our escape from the conflagration. The destruction was complete. My entire worldly wealth was swallowed up, and I resigned myself thenceforward to despair.

I am above the weakness of seeking to establish a sequence of cause and effect between the disaster and the atrocity. But I am detailing a chain of facts, and wish not to leave even a possible link imperfect. On the day succeeding the fire, I visited the ruins. The walls with one exception had fallen in. This exception was found in a compartment wall, not very thick, which stood about the middle of the house, and against which had rested the head of my bed. The plastering had here in great measure resisted the action of the fire, a fact which I attributed to its having been recently spread. About this wall a dense crowd were collected, and many persons seemed to be examining a particular portion of it with very minute and eager attention. The words 'strange!' 'singular!' and other similar expressions, excited my curiosity. I approached and saw, as if graven in *bas relief* upon the white surface, the figure of a gigantic *cat*. The impression was given with an accuracy truly marvellous. There was a rope about the animal's neck.

When I first beheld this apparition – for I could scarcely regard it as less – my wonder and my terror were extreme. But at length reflection came to my aid. The cat, I remembered, had been hung in a garden adjacent to the house. Upon the alarm of fire this garden had been immediately filled by the crowd, by some one of whom the animal must have been cut from the tree and thrown through an open window into my chamber. This had probably been done with the view of arousing me from sleep. The falling of other walls had compressed the victim of my cruelty into the substance of the freshly-spread plaster; the lime of which, with the flames and the *ammonia* from the carcase, had then accomplished the portraiture as I saw it.

Although I thus readily accounted to my reason, if not altogether to my conscience, for the startling fact just detailed, it did not the less fail to make a deep impression upon my fancy. For months I could not rid myself of the phantasm of the cat, and during this period there came back into my spirit a half-sentiment that seemed, but was not, remorse. I went so far as to regret the loss of the animal, and to look about me among the vile haunts which I now habitually frequented for another pet of the same species, and of somewhat similar appearance, with which to supply its place.

One night as I sat half-stupefied in a den of more than infamy, my attention was suddenly drawn to some black object, reposing upon the head of one of the immense hogsheads of gin or of rum, which constituted the chief furniture of the apartment. I had been looking steadily at the top of this hogshead for some minutes, and what now caused me surprise was the fact that I had not sooner perceived the object thereupon. I approached it, and touched it with my hand. It was a black cat – a very large one – fully as large as Pluto, and closely resembling him in every respect but one. Pluto had not a white hair upon any portion of his body; but this cat had a large, although indefinite splotch of white, covering nearly the whole region of the breast.

Upon my touching him he immediately arose, purred loudly, rubbed against my hand, and appeared delighted with my notice. This, then, was the very creature of which I was in search. I at once offered to purchase it of the landlord; but this person made no claim to it – knew nothing of it – had never seen it before.

I continued my caresses, and when I prepared to go home the animal evinced a disposition to accompany me. I permitted it to do so, occasionally stooping and patting it as I proceeded. When it reached the house it domesticated itself at once, and became immediately a great favourite with my wife.

For my own part, I soon found a dislike to it arising within me. This was just the reverse of what I had anticipated but – I know not how or why it was – its evident fondness for myself rather disgusted and annoyed. By slow degrees these feelings of digust and annoyance rose into the bitterness of hatred. I avoided the creature; a certain sense of shame, and the remembrance of my former deed of cruelty, preventing me from physically abusing it. I did not, for some weeks, strike or otherwise violently ill-use it but gradually – very gradually – I came to look upon it with unutterable loathing, and to flee silently from its odious presence as from the breath of a pestilence.

What added, no doubt, to my hatred of the beast was the discovery, on the morning after I brought it home, that, like Pluto, it also had been deprived of one of its eyes. This circumstance, however, only endeared it to my wife, who, as I have already said, possessed in a high degree that humanity of feeling which had once been my distinguishing trait, and the source of many of my simplest and purest pleasures.

With my aversion to this cat, however, its partiality for myself seemed to increase. It followed my footsteps with a pertinacity which it would be difficult to make the reader comprehend. Whenever I sat, it would crouch beneath my chair or spring upon my knees, covering me with its loathsome caresses. If I arose to walk it would get between my feet and thus nearly throw me down, or fastening its long and sharp claws in my dress, clamber in this manner to my breast. At such times, although I longed to destroy it with a blow, I was yet withheld from so doing, partly by a memory of my former crime, but chiefly – let me confess it at once – by absolute *dread* of the beast.

This dread was not exactly a dread of physical evil – and yet I should be at a loss how otherwise to define it. I am almost ashamed to own – yes, even in this felon's cell, I am almost ashamed to own – that the terror and horror with which the animal inspired me, had been heightened by one of the merest chimeras it would be possible to conceive. My wife had called my attention more than once to the character of the mark of white hair, of which I have spoken, and which constituted the sole visible difference between the strange beast and the one I had destroyed. The reader will remember that this mark, although large, had been originally very indefinite, but by slow degrees – degrees nearly imperceptible, and which for a long time my reason struggled to reject as fanciful – it had at length assumed a rigorous distinction of outline. It was now the representation of an object that I shudder to name – and for this above all I loathed and dreaded, and would have rid myself of the monster *had I dared* – it was now, I say, the image of a hideous – of a ghastly thing – of the GALLOWS! – O, mournful and terrible engine of horror and of crime – of agony and of death!

And now was I indeed wretched beyond the wretchedness of mere humanity. And *a brute beast* – whose fellow I had contemptuously destroyed – *a brute beast* to work out for *me* – for me a man, fashioned in the image of the High God – so much of insufferable woe! Alas! neither by day nor by night knew I the blessing of rest any more! During the former the creature left me no moment alone; and in the latter I started hourly from dreams of unutterable fear, to find the hot breath of *the thing* upon my face, and its vast weight – an incarnate night-mare that I had no power to shake off – incumbent eternally upon my *heart!*

Beneath the pressure of torments such as these, the feeble remnant of the good within me succumbed. Evil thoughts became my sole intimates – the darkest and most evil of thoughts. The moodiness of my usual temper increased to hatred of all things and of all mankind; while from the sudden frequent and ungovernable outbursts of a fury to which I now blindly abandoned myself, my uncomplaining wife, alas! was the most usual and the most patient of sufferers.

One day she accompanied me upon some household errand into the cellar of the old building which our poverty compelled us to inhabit. The cat followed me down the steep stairs, and nearly throwing me headlong, exasperated me to madness. Uplifting an axe, and forgetting in my wrath the childish dread which had hitherto stayed my hand, I aimed a blow at the animal, which of course would have proved instantly fatal had it descended as I wished. But this blow was arrested by the hand of my wife. Goaded by the interference into a rage more than demoniacal, I withdrew my arm from her grasp and buried the axe in her brain. She fell dead upon the spot without a groan.

This hideous murder accomplished, I set myself forthwith and with entire deliberation to the task of concealing the body. I knew that I could not remove it from the house, either by day or by night, without the risk of being observed by the neighbours. Many projects entered my mind. At one period I thought of cutting the corpse into minute fragments and destroying them by fire. At another I resolved to dig a grave for it in the floor of the cellar. Again, I deliberated about casting it in the well in the yard – about packing it in a box, as if merchandise, with the usual arrangements, and so getting a porter to take it from the house. Finally I hit upon what I considered a far better expedient than either of these. I determined to wall it up in the cellar – as the monks of the middle ages are recorded to have walled up their victims.

For a purpose such as this the cellar was well adapted. Its walls were loose constructed and had lately been plastered throughout with a rough plaster, which the dampness of the atmosphere had prevented from hardening. Moreover, in one of the walls was a projection caused by a false chimney or fireplace, that had been filled up and made to resemble the rest of the cellar. I made no doubt that I could readily displace the bricks at this point, insert the corpse, and wall the whole up as before, so that no eye could detect anything suspicious.

And in this calculation I was not deceived. By means of a crowbar I easily dislodged the bricks, and having carefully deposited the body against the inner wall, I propped it in that position, while with little trouble I re-laid the whole structure as it originally stood. Having procured mortar, sand, and hair with every possible precaution, I prepared a plaster which could not be distinguished from the old, and with this I very carefully went over the new brickwork. When I had finished I felt satisfied that all was right. The wall did not present the slightest appearance of having been disturbed. The rubbish on the floor was picked up with the minutest care. I looked around triumphantly, and said to myself – 'Here at last, then, my labour has not been in vain.'

My next step was to look for the beast which had been the cause of so much wretchedness, for I had at length firmly resolved to put it to death. Had I been able to meet with it at the moment there could have been no doubt of its fate, but it appeared that the crafty animal had been alarmed at the violence of my previous anger, and forbore to present itself in my present mood. It is impossible to describe or to imagine the deep, the blissful sense of relief which the absence of the detested creature occasioned in my bosom. It did not make its appearance during the night – and thus for one night at least since its introduction into the house I soundly and tranquilly slept; ay, *slept* even with the burden of murder upon my soul!

The second and the third day passed, and still my tormentor came not. Once again I breathed as a freeman. The monster, in terror, had fled the premises for ever! I should behold it no more! My happiness was supreme! The guilt of my dark deed disturbed me but little. Some few inquiries had been made, but these had been readily answered. Even a search had been instituted – but of course nothing was to be discovered. I looked upon my future felicity as secured.

Upon the fourth day of the assassination, a party of the police came very unexpectedly into the house, and proceeded again to make rigorous investigation of the premises. Secure, however, in the inscrutability of my place of concealment, I felt no embarrassment whatever. The officers bade me accompany them in their search. They left no nook or corner unexplored. At length, for the third or fourth time, they descended into the cellar. I quivered not in a muscle. My heart beat calmly as that of one who slumbers in innocence. I walked the cellar from end to end. I folded my arms upon my bosom, and roamed easily to and fro. The police were thoroughly satisfied, and prepared to depart. The glee at my heart was too strong to be restrained. I burned to say if but one word by way of triumph, and to render doubly sure their assurance of my guiltlessness.

'Gentlemen,' I said at last, as the party ascended the steps, 'I delight to have allayed your suspicions. I wish you all health, and a little more courtesy. By-the-by, gentlemen, this – this is a very well constructed house.' (In the rabid desire to say something easily, I scarcely knew what I uttered at all.) – 'I may say an *excellently* well-constructed house. These walls – are you going, gentlemen? – these walls are solidly put together;' and here, through the mere frenzy of bravado, I rapped heavily with a cane which I held in my hand upon that very portion of the brick-work behind which stood the corpse of the wife of my bosom.

But may God shield and deliver me from the fangs of the arch-fiend! No sooner had the reverberation of my blows sunk into silence than I was answered by a voice from within the tomb! – by a cry, at first muffled and broken, like the sobbing of a child, and then quickly swelling into one long, loud, and continuous scream, utterly anomalous and inhuman – a howl – a wailing shriek, half of horror and half of triumph, such as might have arisen only out of hell, conjointly from the throats of the damned in their agony and of the demons that exult in the damnation.

Of my own thoughts it is folly to speak. Swooning, I staggered to the opposite wall. For one instant the party upon the stairs remained motionless, through extremity of terror and of awe. In the next a dozen stout arms were toiling at the wall. It fell bodily. The corpse, already greatly decayed and clotted with gore, stood erect before the eyes of the spectators. Upon its head, with red extended mouth and solitary eye of fire, sat the hideous beast whose craft had seduced me into murder, and whose informing voice had consigned me to the hangman. I had walled the monster up within the tomb!

From *The Works of Edgar Allan Poe*, 1874

'The Cat With Wings'

You never saw a cat with wings,
I'll bet a dollar – well, I did;
'Twas one of those fantastic things
One runs across in old Madrid.
A walloping big tom it was,
(Maybe of the Angora line,)
With silken ears and velvet paws,
And silver hair, superbly fine.

It sprawled upon a crimson mat,
Yet though crowds came to gaze on it,
It was a supercilious cat,
And didn't seem to mind a bit.
It looked at us with dim disdain,
And indolently seemed to sigh:
'There's not another cat in Spain
One half so marvellous as I.'

Its owner gently stroked its head,
And tickled it with fingers light.
'Ah no, it cannot fly,' he said;
'But see – it has the *wings* all right.'
Then tenderly from off its back
He raised, despite its feline fears,
Appendages that seemed to lack
Vitality – like rabbit's ears.

And then the vision that I had
Of Tabbie soaring through the night,
Quick vanished, and I felt so sad
For that poor pussy's piteous plight.
For though frustration has its stings,
Its mockeries in Hope's despite,
The hell of hells is to have wings
Yet be denied the bliss of flight.

From *More Collected Verse* by Robert W. Service, 1955

Thoreau's Winged Cat

Once I was surprised to see a cat walking along the stony shore of the pond, for they rarely wander so far from home. The surprise was mutual. Nevertheless the most domestic cat, which has lain on a rug all her days, appears quite at home in the woods, and, by her sly and stealthy behavior, proves herself more native there than the regular inhabitants. Once, when berrying, I met with a cat with young kittens in the woods, quite wild, and they all, like their mother, had their backs up and were fiercely spitting at me. A few years before I lived in the woods there was what was called a 'winged cat' in one of the farm-houses in Lincoln nearest the pond, Mr Gilian Baker's. When I called to see her in June, 1842, she was gone a-hunting in the woods, as was her wont, (I am not sure whether it was a male or female, and so use the more common pronoun,) but her mistress told me that she came into the neighborhood a little more than a year before, in April, and was finally taken into their house; that she was of a dark brownish-gray color, with a white spot on her throat, and white feet, and had a large bushy tail like a fox; that in the winter the fur grew thick and flatted out along her sides, forming strips ten or twelve inches long by two and a half wide, and under her chin like a muff, the upper side loose, the under matted like felt, and in the spring these appendages dropped off. They gave me a pair of her 'wings,' which I keep still. There is no appearance of a membrane about them. Some thought it was part flying-squirrel or some other wild animal, which is not impossible, for, according to naturalists, prolific hybrids have been produced by the union of the marten and domestic cat. This would have been the right kind of cat for me to keep, if I had kept any; for why should not a poet's cat be winged as well as his horse?

From *Walden, or, Life in the Woods* by Henry David Thoreau, 1881

'The Cat and the Moon'

The cat went here and there
And the moon spun round like a top,
And the nearest kin of the moon
The creeping cat looked up.
Black Minnaloushe stared at the moon,
For wander and wail as he would
The pure cold light in the sky
Troubled his animal blood.
Minnaloushe runs in the grass
Lifting his delicate feet.
Do you dance, Minnaloushe, do you dance?
When two close kindred meet
What better than call a dance,
Maybe the moon may learn,
Tired of that courtly fashion,
A new dance turn.
Minnaloushe creeps through the grass
From moonlit place to place,
The sacred moon overhead
Has taken a new phase.
Does Minnaloushe know that his pupils
Will pass from change to change,
And that from round to crescent,
From crescent to round they range?
Minnaloushe creeps through the grass
Alone, important and wise,
And lifts to the changing moon
His changing eyes.

From *Later Poems* by W. B. Yeats, 1922

Seven

HATRED

Napoleonic Terror

Ailurophobia is a stronger feeling than hate; it is a most abject kind of fear. Strong men and women are seized with nausea, even faint, in the presence of a tiny kitten, sometimes even an *unseen* kitten. The simplest form of this complaint is asthmatic ailurophobia; in other words people who suffer from asthma or hay-fever find the disease aggravated by the presence of cats. The other form is more serious. I have a friend, otherwise seemingly sane, who exhibits symptoms of the most violent terror at the sight of a kitten four weeks old; an older cat will sometimes throw her into convulsions. This malady is not rare, nor is it limited to women. Scott writes of a gallant Highland chieftain who had been 'seen to change into all the colours of his plaid' when confronted with a cat. Probably the most celebrated ailurophobe in history was Napoleon. According to a popular legend, not long after the battle of Wagram and the second occupation of Vienna by the French, an aide-de-camp of the Corsican, who at the time occupied, together with his suite, the Palace of Schönbrunn, was proceeding to bed at an unusually late hour when, on passing the door of Napoleon's bedroom, he was surprised to hear a most singular noise and repeated calls for assistance from the Emperor. Opening the door hastily, and rushing into the room, he saw the greatest soldier of the age, half undressed, his countenance agitated, beaded drops of perspiration standing on his brow, making frequent and convulsive lunges with his sword through the tapestry that lined the walls, behind which a cat had secreted herself. Madam Junot was aware of this weakness and is reported to have gained an important political advantage over the Little Corporal merely by mentioning a cat at the right moment.

From *The Tiger in the House* by Carl van Vechten, 1921

A Libellous Reference Book

The *domesticus*, or tame cat, is so well known, that it requires no description. It is a useful, but deceitful domestic. Although when young they are playful and gay, they possess at the same time an innate malice and perverse disposition, which increases as they grow up, and which education learns them to conceal, but never to subdue. Constantly bent upon theft and rapine, though in a domestic state, they are full of cunning and dissimulation; they conceal all their designs; seize every opportunity of doing mischief, and then fly from punishment. They easily take on the habits of society, but never its manners; for they have only the appearance of friendship and attachment. This disingenuity of character is betrayed by the obliquity of their movements and the ambiguity of their looks. In a word, the cat is totally destitute of friendship; he thinks and acts for himself alone. He loves ease, searches for the softest and warmest places to repose himself. The cat is likewise extremely amorous; and which is very singular, the female is more ardent than the male: she not only invites, but searches after and calls upon him to satisfy the fury of her desires; and, if the male disdains or flies from her, she pursues, bites, and in a manner compels him. This heat of passion in the females lasts but nine or ten days, and happens twice in the year, namely in the spring and autumn; however, in some it happens thrice or four times in the year. The female goes with young 55 or 58 days, and generally produces four or five at a litter. As the male has an inclination to destroy the young, the female takes care to conceal them from him; and, when she is apprehensive of a discovery, she takes them up in her mouth one by one, and hides them in holes or inaccessible places. When she has nursed a few weeks, she brings them mice, small birds, &c. in order to learn them to eat flesh. But it is worth notice, that these careful and tender mothers sometimes become unnaturally cruel, and devour their own offspring.

The cat is incapable of restraint, and consequently of being educated to any extent. However, we are told, that the Greeks in the island of Cyprus trained this animal to catch and devour serpents, with which that island is greatly infested. This, however, was not the effect of obedience, but of a general taste for slaughter; for he delights in watching, attacking, and destroying all kinds of weak animals indifferently. He has no delicacy of scent, like the dog; he hunts only by the eye: neither does he properly pursue; he only lies in wait, and attacks animals by surprise; and after he has caught them, he sports with and torments them a long time, and at last kills them (when his belly is full), purely to gratify his sanguinary appetite.

The eye of the cat differs greatly from that of most other animals. The pupil is capable of a great degree of contraction and dilation. It is narrow and contracted like a line during the day, round and wide in the dark. It is from this conformation of the eye that the cat sees best in the night, which gives him a great advantage in discovering and seizing his prey.

Although cats live in our houses, they can hardly be called *domestic* animals; they may rather be said to enjoy full liberty; for they never act but according to their own inclination. Besides, the greatest part of them are half wild: they do not know their masters; and frequent only the barns, out-houses, &c. unless when pressed with hunger.

Cats have a natural antipathy at water and cold. They likewise hate bad smells; but they have an affection for certain aromatic smells, and are transported with the root of the valerian.

Cats take about 18 months before they come to their full growth; but they are capable of propagation in 12 months, and retain this faculty all their life, which generally extends to nine or ten years. They eat slowly, and are peculiarly fond of fish. They drink frequently; their sleep is light; and they often assume the appearance of sleeping, when in reality they are meditating mischief. They walk softly, and without making any noise. As their hair is always dry, it easily gives out an electrical fire, which becomes visible when rubbed across in the dark. Their eyes likewise sparkle in the dark like diamonds – The cat, when pleased, purrs, and moves its tail: when angry, it spits, hisses, and strikes with its foot. It washes its face with its forefoot (Linnells says, at the approach of a storm): it always lights on its feet: it is even proverbially tenacious of life.

From *Encyclopaedia Britannica*, 3rd edition, 1787

A Cruel Limerick

There was a Young Person of Smyrna,
Whose Grandmother threatened to burn her;
But she seized on the cat,
And said, 'Granny, burn that!
You incongruous Old Woman of Smyrna!'

From *A Book of Nonsense* by Edward Lear, 1856

Fit for a Queen

In a seventeenth century execution fourteen cats were shut in a cage with a woman who was roasted over a slow fire while the cats in misery and terror clawed her in their own death agonies. When Queen Elizabeth was crowned a feature of the procession was a wicker pope, the interior of which was filled with live cats, who 'squalled in a most hideous manner as soon as they felt the fire.' The culmination of many a religious fête in Germany, France, and England consisted in pitching some wretched puss off a height or into a bonfire. In 1753 certain Frenchmen received a quittance of one hundred *sols parisis* for having furnished during three years all the cats necessary for the fires of the festival of St John.

From *The Tiger in the House* by Carl van Vechten, 1921

'Cat "Tortured and Thrown on Fire"'

A gang of four teenagers and a young man tortured a cat, cutting off its rear legs and tail, and threw it alive on to a fire at a derelict farmhouse, Caerphilly magistrates court heard yesterday.

From the *Daily Telegraph*, 9 July 1992

An Immolation

For the next quarter of an hour we walked in silence. Jane spoke once to ask me again about the butterflies. She seemed less afraid of the canal now and let go of my hand. I wanted to touch her but I could think of no way of doing that without frightening her. I tried to think of a conversation we might have but my mind was blank. The path was beginning to widen out to our right. Round the next bend of canal in an immense space between a factory and a warehouse was the scrap yard. There was black smoke in the sky ahead of us, and as we came round the bend I saw that it was coming from the scrap yard. A group of boys stood round the fire they had built.

They were some kind of gang, they all wore the same blue jackets and cropped hair. As far as I could tell they were preparing to roast a live cat. The smoke hung about them in the still air, behind them the scrapheap towered like a mountain. They had the cat tied up by its neck to a post, the same post the Alsatian dog used to be tied to. The cat's front and back legs were tied together. They were constructing a cage over the fire made up of pieces of wire fencing and as we came past one of them was dragging the cat by the string around its neck towards the fire. I took Jane's hand and walked faster. They were working intently and in silence, and they hardly paused to glance up at us. Jane kept her eyes on the ground. Through her hand I could feel her whole body shaking.

'What were they doing to that cat?'

'I don't know.' I looked back over my shoulder. It was difficult to see what they were doing now because of the black smoke.

From 'Butterflies' in *First Love, Last Rites* by Ian McEwan, 1975

'Ding, Dong, Bell'

Ding, dong, bell,
Pussy's in the well.
Who put her in?
Little Johnny Green.
Who pulled her out?
Little Tommy Stout.
What a naughty boy was that
To try and drown poor pussy cat,
Who never did him any harm,
And killed the mice in his father's barn.

A Scottish Version
Ding dang, bell rang,
Cattie's in the well, man.
Fa' dang her in, man?
Jean and Sandy Din, man.
Fa' took her oot, man?
Me and Willie Cout, man.

A' them that kent her
    When she was alive,
Come to the burialie
    Between four and five.

From *The Oxford Nursery Rhyme Book*, 1955

'Cat Burned in Black Magic Killings'

Detectives have questioned children over the sacrificial killing of a
cat. It is thought they may have been lured into the occult and black
magic rituals. Charred remains of the cat were found on a beach in
Clevedon, Bristol. The animal may have been staked out over an
open fire. In all, the police intend to question eight former and present pupils of Clevedon comprehensive school, aged between 14
and 17. Headmaster Eric Dolling said two sixth formers had already
been interviewed at home in the company of their parents. 'I
believe they have been involved in the fringes of a group of both
youngsters and adults who take part in Satanic activities.'

From the *Daily Mail*, 6 February 1990

Godfrey on the Rotisserie

When Rosie McKechnie opened the front door of 'The Pines' in the
middle of an August afternoon, she thought it was the gasman.
Anyone else would have thought the same. When you get to the
front door, see a shortish figure through the stained-glass panelling,
undo the catch, and immediately hear the word 'Gas', you naturally
think it's the gasman. You don't think about how long it was since
you last had your meter read.

The little man came through the door fast, with his head down,
and butted Mrs McKechnie hard in the left breast. Then he pinioned
her arms to her sides and simply stood there holding on to her . . .

She waited. There was nothing else she could do but wait and see what happened next.

What happened next was that the little man dug in his pocket and pulled out a thick, heavy lino-cutting knife with a retractable blade. It was gunmetal blue, and had a little serrated catch on the top which, when you slid it forward, brought the blade into view. At a sign from the tall man, he walked out of the lounge, down a corridor past a few framed theatre bills, and into the kitchen. He didn't notice Godfrey sitting on the dresser; but Godfrey certainly noticed him.

Godfrey was the McKechnies' large, paunchy, grey-haired tom cat. A big, swaggery, macho cat with firm ideas about territoriality. The sort of cat who would pin females up against the wall and accuse them of being frigid if they wouldn't submit. Even in the feline world, where selfishness and cunning are cardinal virtues, Godfrey was an outstandingly mean cat. Other cats fought shy of him; some of the smaller local dogs had been seen crossing the road to avoid him; not even his owners really liked him. They gave him everything he needed and stayed out of his way as much as possible.

As the little man passed the dresser, he heard a sharp, sibilant hiss. He turned and saw Godfrey. The little man thought he knew his way round cats, and he reached out a hand to tickle Godfrey's chin. Godfrey didn't like his chin being tickled; he didn't really like humans coming near him. As the hand approached, he slashed at it with his right paw.

Godfrey kept his claws in good trim. Three white lines appeared on the back of the man's hand; after a few seconds they seemed to pop, and beads of blood appeared. The man looked at his hand disbelievingly. He stood there and glanced slowly round the kitchen. when his eye fell on the fridge-freezer, he suddenly shot out a hand and grabbed Godfrey by the neck before he could move, walked quickly across the kitchen, pulled open the door of the freezer section, threw the cat in, and slammed the door. He turned, and looked around the kitchen again: bar area, concealed ceiling lighting, stainless steel surfaces, gadgets everywhere; a cooker with an eye-level spit-roaster. He nodded to himself . . .

When Brian got back from London, he thought his wife had burnt the dinner again. A heavy, slow, red-faced man, he stood in the hall puffing from his walk from the station, uncertain whether to go into the kitchen or the lounge first. From the kitchen came a pungent smell of burning, though somehow it wasn't the charred-dinner smell he'd had to get used to over the years; it was something odder, sharper. It smelt as if mattresses were being singed.

From *Duffy* by Dan Kavanagh, 1980

Military Discipline

In a study of the South African Defence Force (SADF), Jacklyn Cock of the University of Witwatersrand records some evidence of a 'brutalisation process involving cruelty to animals'.

I have heard that some SADF special élite training involves soldiers having to carry a puppy around with them for four days – feeding and caring for it. They are then required to kill it with their bare hands. However, I have not been able to locate anyone who actually has had this experience. There have been newspaper reports of gruesome acts of animal cruelty, slaughter, decapitation, and mutilation committed for pleasure by members of the SADF.

'Some national servicemen have claimed that animal cruelty was rife in bases in Namibia and South Africa. Midnight satanic rituals are said to have been held in which drunk soldiers skinned and beheaded cats, drank their blood and chopped off their tails to sell to tribesmen.'

(*Sunday Star* 8.5.1988)

The *Star* newspaper had in its possession a picture of two smiling conscripts holding a decapitated kitten's head in their teeth.'

(*The Star* 9.5.1988)

One soldier spoke of having a pet kitten while he was on a chef's course at a military base in Pretoria. One afternoon he walked into the camp kitchen to find that someone had poured boiling water over his kitten and then set a dog on it:

'He was still alive but in terrible pain . . . I called a private to help me. He chopped the kitten's head off with a spade.

(*Ibid.*)'

[199]

During 1987 this informant witnessed another case of cruelty:

> 'A regimental sergeant-major walked into the kitchen. Three kittens were playing on the floor. He shouted that he wanted them killed. A corporal and private then started kicking them around. I was not the only one who saw what they were doing. There was also a woman sergeant. After they had played their game there were two dead kittens on the floor. The other was alive. They left them there and went to call up one of the black workers to clean up the mess.
>
> *(Ibid.)*'

From *Women and War in South Africa* by Jacklyn Cock, 1992

Neither Sick Nor Sorry

In 1777 a shepherd at Beverley, Yorkshire undertook to eat a live cat on fair day. He was given the biggest black Tom in the neighbourhood, 'not fed for the purpose'; and how he ate it is described in the *Sporting Magazine* of March, 1794. In less than a quarter of an hour he had 'devoured every part'. He was a raw-boned fellow of about forty and seemed perfectly satisfied with his reward of two guineas; for the rest of the afternoon he walked about the fair and was 'neither sick nor sorry'. On March 1, 1788, according to the same source, a wager was agreed between the Duke of Bedford and Lord Barrymore: 'His Lordship betted His Grace £500 to £400 that he produced a man who should eat a live cat, which was performed at the time appointed by a labouring man of Harpenden, near St Albans.'* This was the fifth Duke of Bedford, already mentioned. He and the rapscallion Barrymore were associates of the Prince of Wales. An encomium published in the *Sporting Magazine* in February, 1795, credited the Duke with 'all the nicer sensibilities of the heart ... those amiable qualities that so highly honour human nature.'

*John Lawrence in his *British Field Sports* (1818) refers to the 'devouring of living cats by obscene and loathsome human beasts.' Henry Crowe in *Zoophilos* expresses the view that a cat-eater is capable of cannibalism and murder.

From *All Heaven in a Rage* by E.S. Turner, 1964

Toys for the Boys

Small boys have long held it to be their prerogative to torment cats, tying cans or a string of exploding firecrackers to their tails, installing their paws in walnut shells, or sending them to navigate the horse-pond in a bowl. Booth Tarkington, who may be considered an authority on the adolescent period, writes, 'The suffering of cats is a barometer of the nerve-pressure of boys, and it may be accepted as sufficiently established that Wednesday – after school-hours – is the worst time for cats ... Confirming the effect of Wednesday upon boys in general, it is probable that, if full statistics were available, they would show that cats dread Wednesdays, and that their fear is shared by other animals and would be shared, to an extent by windows, if windows possessed nervous systems. Nor must this probable apprehension on the part of the cats and the like be thought mere superstition. Cats have superstitions, it is true, but certain actions inspired by the sign of a boy with a missile in his hand are better evidence of the workings of logic upon a practical nature than of faith in the supernatural.' Edwin Tenney Brewster tells how boys in default of a proper football played their game through with two living cats bound together with a clothes line. 'The public is sentimental,' he observes. 'It can't bear to have the little things killed. So it drops them into ash-barrels, where they die – in the course of time and not altogether comfortably. It tosses them into cess-pools, and happily the next rain sends water enough to drown them. Specially careful house-wives before consigning kittens to the waste heap have been known to make them into neat bundles, in paper boxes, tied with string. This kindly device protects the helpless creatures from stray dogs and allows them to smother or starve in quiet. A short and easy method in tenement districts is simply to open the window and toss the kittens out. A four-storey drop on to the brick pavement or area spikes is commonly a sufficient hint to an intelligent kitten not to return.' Cats are thrown off church towers with blown bladders attached to their necks, killed by dogs, thrown into barrels with dogs to fight, kicked to death, drowned, turned alive into bakers' ovens and stoves, thrown into lime, their heads crunched under heels, tied together by their tails and hung up. In Spain, in Gautier's day, it was the custom to deprive cats of their ears and their tails, giving them the appearance of 'Japanese chimeras.' In Havana, I have been told, urchins enjoy a merry sport which entails the dipping of puss into a pail of kerosene and a subsequent ignition. Then the comet-like trail of howling fiery fur is released. In 1815, just before the departure of Napoleon for St Helena, a wag perpetrated a joke in the city of Chester. Handbills were distributed which announced that the island was overrun with rats and that 16 shllings would be paid for every full-grown tom cat, 10s. for every full-grown female, 2s. 6d. for every kitten. On the day appointed the city was filled with men, women, and children carrying cats. A riot ensued and the cats escaped. Several hundred were killed and many others drowned while the remainder infested neighbouring houses and barns for many weeks afterwards.

From *The Tiger in the House* by Carl van Vechten, 1921

'Horreo Aluros'

Cats were slower [than dogs] to rise in status. In the Middle Ages they were kept in houses for protection against rats and mice. Only occasionally do they appear as companions and objects of affection, as in the ninth-century poem by an Irish monk about his cat, Pangur Ban, or the fifteenth-century tomb at Old Cleeve, Somerset, which shows a man with his feet resting on a cat, which in turn has its paws resting on a mouse. Many householders deliberately refrained from feeding them, so as to ensure that they had an incentive to hunt. The cat, ruled Topsell in 1607, was 'an unclean and impure beast that liveth only upon vermin and by ravening'. An allergy to cats was common and the dangers of their breath much discussed in the medical books. An early Tudor textbook contains for translation into Latin the simple sentence, 'I hate cats (*horreo aluros sive feles sive cattos*).' It was only in the sixteenth century that Dick Whittington seems to have acquired his cat.

Yet by the early Stuart period there were plenty of authentic cat-lovers, like the third Earl of Southampton, whose portrait commemorating his sojourn in the Tower after Essex's rebellion shows an extremely sleek and alert cat to have been his companion in imprisonment. Archbishop Laud was particularly fond of cats and in the late 1630s was given one of the earliest imported tabbies, then valued at £5 each, but soon to become so common as to supersede the old English cat, which was blue and white. In the same decade the house of the prominent Leeds merchant John Harrison had holes cut in the doors so as to allow cats free passage 'even into the best room of the house', as a later antiquary noted with evident surprise. By the reign of Charles II, according to Defoe, few London families were without them, 'some having several, sometimes five or six in a house'.

It is true that many people still regarded cats as fair game for any sport. On New Year's Day 1638 in Ely Cathedral there was 'a great noise and disturbance near the choir' occasioned by the roasting of a live cat tied to a spit by one William Smyth in the presence of a large and boisterous crowd. A few years later parliamentary troopers used hounds to hunt cats up and down Lichfield Cathedral. During the pope-burning processions of the reign of Charles II it was the practice to stuff the burning effigies with live cats so that their screams might add dramatic effect. At country fairs a popular sport was that of shooting at a cat suspended in a basket. As Alexander Pope remarked in 1713, 'the conceit that a cat has nine lives has cost at least nine lives in ten of the whole race of them.'

From *Man and the Natural World: Changing Attitudes in England 1500–1800*
by Keith Thomas, 1983

A Rare Pleasure

Always there was something to gape at – for the city's festivals, too, all took place in public. The great *loggie*, indeed, which now were added to some of the richer houses (one of the first was that of Francesco's house), were built precisely for this purpose: so that each private festivity could be enjoyed by the whole town. At a wedding the bride and bridegroom walked in procession through the city, attended by their relatives and friends, and sometimes also by trumpeters, mountebanks, and strolling players, to the church steps where the notary was waiting, to read aloud in public the marriage contract . . .

There were also other, more brutal sports, even more pleasing to the crowd. In one of the squares, a pig was enclosed in a wide pen and beaten to death by armed men, as he ran squealing from one to the other, 'among the loud laughter of those present'; in another a live cat was nailed to a post and killed, in spite of her desperate clawing and biting, by men who, with shorn heads and bound hands, drove the life out of her by buffeting her with their heads, 'to the sound of trumpets'.

These, with the accompanying jests and boasts, bleeding backs and broken heads, were rare pleasures.

From *The Merchant of Prato: Daily Life in a Medieval Italian City* by Iris Origo, 1957

To Fling a Cat

Succeeding the cruelties perpetrated on the animal during the Middle Ages, amongst the first signs of improvement in pussy's condition was the publication of an edict in Flanders in 1618 prohibiting the practice of throwing cats from the high tower of Ypres, which had hitherto been a customary performance on the Wednesday of the second week in Lent. The custom of flinging cats into the bonfires kindled at Metz on the festival of St John (held on June 24) lasted longer, and it was not until the middle of the eighteenth century that the wife of the Marshal d'Armentières obtained from her husband an order for the suppression of this act of cruelty. For this ceremony, while it lasted, the magistrates used to assemble with much solemnity in the public square, and place a cage containing cats on a funeral-pile; to this, with great parade, they set fire. The people believed that the frightful cries made by the poor beasts were evidence of the sufferings of an old sorceress, supposed long ago to have been transformed into a cat when she was about to burned.

From *The Cat in History, Legend and Art* by Anne Marks, 1909

'Two Men Jailed over Campaign of Cat Torture'

Two men who preyed on a town's cat population, mutilating and torturing up to 20 pets to death with axes and poles, were each jailed for six months yesterday. Magistrates at Evesham, Hereford and Worcester were told that the cats were lured into a car at night before their limbs were cut off and the animals axed to death.

There were shouts of approval from the packed public gallery as sentence was passed on Philip Nick, 21, a former factory worker, of Kings Road, Evesham, and Richard Middleton, 18, unemployed, of Stoke Prior, Bromsgrove.

They both admitted causing or permitting unnecessary suffering to four cats under the Protection of Animals Act 1911. Nick asked for 16 similar offences to be taken into consideration, and Middleton asked the court to consider five additional offences.

From the *Daily Telegraph*, 2 July 1991

Violent Whimsy

In the late 1730s in a printing shop outside Paris, a handful of young apprentices, for no apparent reason, slaughtered all the neighborhood cats. In fits of laughter they gleefully bashed the heads of cats, snapped the spines of cats, squashed the bodies of cats, twisted cats at the mid-section, and suffocated cats. They even improvised a gallows and hung cats by the neck. They were soon joined in their revelry by the older journeymen printers. The men and boys then gathered the dead and half-dead cats in bags and dumped them in the courtyard, improvised a mock trial, posthumously condemning them to death, and then administered last rites.

When the wife of the print-shop owner returned home to find that her favorite cat, which she had named La Grise, had had its spine crushed with an iron bar, she was hysterical. And when her husband found out what the boys had done, he was aghast. But when he confronted the boys, they pleaded innocent, especially with regard to La Grise. After the master and his wife retired, the lads again dissolved into gales of laughter.

The young men – there were never female apprentices in the printing trades – continued to think that the slaughter of cats was so humorous that they pantomimed the entire event for months to come. More than twenty times they reenacted the role of their triumph. They would pick one from their number to play the cat – the dupe – as they repeated their heroic roles as cat killers. The butt of this joke was called, in a provocative linguistic transformation, the 'goat,' and the game, 'prendre la chèvre' (get the goat), was an unconscious reenactment of one of the most ancient rituals of our species. Find a victim, especially a victim who cannot retaliate, and vent aggression on him or her. The scapegoat, re-formatted in this case into a scapecat, receives the literal brutality, which is then channelled into surrogate forms. The youthful horde is now able to recreate via 'entertainment' a most serious crisis and overcome it.

Why should cats have become goats? Couldn't the apprentices have found more suitable sacrificial victims? And what was the serious crisis? Why should these boys in the eighteenth century have been so distraught as to kill house cats? Why were the reenactments so humorous that they were repeated so often? Why were the apprentices not punished? Their behavior was certainly not something *we* would imitate. Robert Darnton, the historian/anthropologist, attempts a political and economic explanation in *The Great Cat Massacre and Other Episodes in French Cultural History*. Essentially, he argues, the apprentices were caught in a frustrating dilemma to which they had no easy response. They lived in the printing house; they had no rights, no credit, no job security. They could be treated arbitrarily and thus often acted as they were treated. The bourgeois master ran the shop with the meager support and sympathies of the medieval seignior. Nascent capitalism was in many ways far more distressing than the factory system of the nineteenth century.

Instead of the mellow preindustrial shop remembered by Victorian historians, this workplace was closer to a madhouse. Each man knew his job, and, although the jobs were divided, there was no sense of purpose. Young males lived together, worked together, played together. But for what? For the master and the mistress? But they were not a family. For price? But this was piece work. For money? But there was little. For what then?

They didn't know. No one knew. There were no mythologies of work – no work ethic. What the workers did know was that from time to time they felt frustrated, and in these times they would be mischievous, even violent. These explosive potentials are obvious enough to anyone who observes boys at work when the work turns dull, then they seemingly lose concentration and they gang up on some victim. But why should cats be the object of their united attentions and then the subject of their recreative pantomimes? Clearly, eighteenth-century cats were not twentieth-century cats.

With the rise of the bourgeoisie, the domestication of animals continued out of the barnyard into the house. Animals which had had outside jobs herding flocks or cattle or catching mice, were allowed inside to become pets. The apprentices, barely a generation away from living off the land, must have been perplexed by this new social hierarchy, this new rung in the chain of being. As the cats were rising in status, the boys were at greater risk of losing theirs. That the mistress had a favorite cat, a cat which she named and tended while the boys were nameless and unattended, is important, because La Grise will be singled out for special slaughter. As Darnton points out, the boys certainly had every reason to feel jealousy, even hostility, toward animals living under the same roof who were tended and fed better than they. So when they turned their wrath on La Grise, they were doing something we can understand, perhaps even sympathize with, or at least something we can acknowledge that 'other people' could do. Had they killed only this cat, a socioeconomic explanation might suffice. But they killed *all* the neighborhood cats. They captured, tortured, killed, bagged, and then piled up the surrounding cats who had not given offense.

To understand why these unoffending cats were susceptible to such treatment, we need to remember that cats have only recently come into their protected status. In the term made popular by Clifford Geertz, Darnton, and the New Historians, the 'mentalité' of these French boys was based on assumptions no longer extant in Western culture. Cats are no longer goats. In fact, as any trip down the food aisle at the local supermarket or the pet store will prove, cats have become family members. The days of torturing cats by pulling their legs apart while burying a straw mannequin representative of King Carnival at the end of Lent, as was the custom in Burgundy, or of stuffing cats into an effigy of the pope and then burning it to provide sound effects, as was the custom on Guy Fawkes Day in London, are now not only over, not just forgotten, but are almost inconceivable. Morris the cat is a pet. We cannot easily imagine that whenever there was a bonfire celebration, as on the day of St John the Baptist (June 24), Morris was especially susceptible to bagging, suspension, and incineration as a matter of course.

Could the transformation from purr to squeal have been so appealing that cats could be sacrificed for shrieks only? Cats must mimic more than the sounds of human agony. Like other animals in other cultures, cats have a rather particular attraction/revulsion for young males – an experience that is similar to how we linguistically respond to female dogs. The insult is 'son of a bitch' not son of a cow – the veiled insult with cat is 'pussy.' For the French, the semiotics of the word for cat – 'le chat,' 'la chatte,' and 'le minet' – yield a similar concatenation. The difficult, exasperating, contentious, frustrating, yet indomitable cat becomes an object of scornful, sexual reverence. If so, the particular treatment of the mistress's pet cat, La Grise, becomes clear. While much of the young men's aggression is no doubt economic and political, part is surely sexual. Their aggressive action concentrates on the off-limits woman, the master's wife – for the Freudian: the surrogate mother. In killing the cat, in a sense, they have cuckolded the father. Since cuckolding is exactly the kind of human action that calls forth revenge, they had better make sure there can be no retaliation. Thus they choose a victim which will not call forth vengeance. A cat will suffice; so, in fact, will all cats.

Their response now is not so difficult to understand. The cat is, to paraphrase Claude Lévi-Strauss's famous dictum, an animal not to eat, nor just an animal to profane in language like the female dog, but rather an animal to sacrifice. Remember that after the master returns and sees what the apprentices have done to the cats, he turns on his heel and leaves in a huff. The boys fall into fits of laughter. As one young eye-witness, Nicholas Contat, in retrospective third-person narration, recalls:

'Madame to Monsieur: "These wicked men can't kill the masters, so they have killed my pussy . . ." It seems to her that all the workers' blood would not be sufficient to redeem the insult. The poor grise, a pussy without a peer!
'Monsieur and Madame retire, leaving the workers in liberty. The printers delight in the disorder; they are beside themselves with joy.
'What a splendid subject for their laughter, for a *belle copie*! They will amuse themselves with it for a long time. Léveillé will take the leading role and will stage the play at least twenty times. He will mime the master, the mistress, the whole house, heaping ridicule on them all. He will spare nothing in his satire. Among printers, those who excel in this entertainment are called *jobeurs*; they provide *joberie*. (as quoted in Darnton, p. 104)'

While we may understand that their violence was 'a splendid subject for laughter,' the subsequent transposition into ritual is harder to comprehend. One of the original conspirators, Léveillé, now takes to ceremonializing the event. He mimics the action; in printer's jargon he 'prints' a 'copie.' Little does he realize that what he is doing is following an ancient pattern. In much the same way that schoolboys mindlessly reenact a prank by picking on one of their own, usually a weakling, to perform the part of the victim, so these apprentices find a victim to play the part of the goat, the butt, the cat, the pussy. Léveillé is also foreshadowing the future. He contains it in a medium. Essentially, the boys do to the event what printing does to ideas: They fix it, memorialize it. Then they repeat it. During those encores the apprentices and journeymen printers beat their mallets, run the composing sticks across the tops of type cases, shake the presses, and generally make the instruments of their boredom into the instruments of their entertainment. This violent whimsy, however, has an etiology deep in human experience. Recall the Assyrian tablets. Again and again the lion is let loose and again and again the lion is killed.

From *Preposterous Violence: Fables of Aggression in Modern Culture*
by James B. Twitchell, 1989

A Blackguard Sport

This queer letter was, apparently, addressed by the poet Robert Southey to a band of cat-worriers in the Lake District.

Keswick, July 12, 1834

Young Gentlemen,

It has come to the knowledge of the writer that one of your amusements here is to worry cats, – that you buy them from those owners who can be tempted to the sin of selling them for such a purpose, and that you employ boys to steal them for you.

A woman who was asked by her neighbour how she could do so wicked a thing as to sell her cat to you, made answer that she never would have done it, if she could have saved the poor creature; but that if she had not sold it, it would have been stolen by your agents, and therefore she might as well have the half-crown herself.

Neither her poverty nor her will consented; yet she was made to partake in your wickedness because she could not prevent it. She gave up to your barbarity a domestic animal – a fireside companion, with which her children had played, and which she herself had fondled on her lap. You tempted her, and she took the price of its blood.

Are you incapable, young gentlemen, of understanding the injury you have done to this woman in her own conscience, and in the estimation of her neighbours?

Be this as it may, you cannot have been so ill taught as not to know that you are setting an evil example in a place to which you have come for the ostensible object of pursuing your studies in a beautiful country; that your sport is as blackguard as it is brutal; that cruelty is a crime by the laws of God, and theft by the laws also of man; that in employing boys to steal for you, and thus training them up in the way they should not go, you are doing the devil's work; that they commit a punishable offence when serving you in this way, and that you commit one in so employing them.

You are hereby warned to give up these practices. If you persist in them, this letter will be sent to all the provincial newspapers.

From *Selections from the Letters of Robert Southey*, 1856

Throwing Stones at Pussy

Some men, both young and old, think that a cat is a fit subject for torture and cruelty of all kinds; hence they never miss the chance of shying a stone after pussy's retreating figure. Cases, too, are continually cropping up in the police courts, of men having tortured cats to the death with dogs.

Cat skins are considered of some value by the furriers. At a sale not long since in London, there were some three thousand cat skins. Where think you, reader, do these come from? That is a question unfortunately only too easily answered. In almost all large cities there exists a gang of ruffians – you cannot call them by a milder name – who eke out a sort of livelihood by stealing cats by every available means and method. But worse than this remains to be told; it is darkly whispered, and I have some reason to believe it may be but too true, that many of those poor cats are *skinned alive*, in the belief that the living skin thus procured retains the gloss.

In Greenland I have seen young seals flayed alive by the score. That was a sickening sight enough, but skinning alive a poor harmless cat must be many times worse. I wish I could say that it was only the lowest class of ruffians that ill-treat poor cats to the death, but – and I know this for certain – there are men who pass as gentlemen, who night after night set traps for cats that stray into their gardens, and kill them in the cruelest manner; and some of these fellows, too, keep neither poultry, pigeons, nor rabbits, and haven't a flower in their gardens worthy of the name, only *they hate cats*. I know one gentleman (?) who thus traps and kills cats because he has a passion for fur rugs, which he thus indulges on the cheap.

Little boys, and those too, sometimes the sons of respectable parents who ought to have taught them better, are often dreadfully cruel to cats, stoning them wherever found, and setting dogs to worry them to death.

A lady, a friend of mine, once attracted by the heartrending cries of a cat, found two young fiends, with a pretty pussy tied in an apron, gouging its eyes out with a nail!

A common form of cruelty to cats, in some rural districts of England, is that of tying two of them together by the tails and hanging them over a rope or pole to fight to the death.

Such cases as that of cutting cats' tails off for wanton mischief, burning or boiling cats alive, though not unknown, I am happy to say are very rare.

Now, considering how very useful an animal a cat is, I think it is high time the law interfered to protect her from violence and ill-usage.

I should like to see a tax imposed upon all cats, and a home for lost cats, precisely on the same principles as the home for lost and starving dogs, only with this difference, that there should be no reward offered for bringing a cat to the home. Remember this, that a stranger or starving cat will come to anyone who says a kind word to it, so policemen would have no difficulty in catching them.

The revenue from the imposition of even a small tax would be very large, and it would not only help to clear the country of a whole army corps of thieving, prowling, homeless cats, but give to the cats of respectable people a greater value in the eyes of the law, and a greater chance of taking their walks abroad without being molested.

We have a law to protect even our wild birds, why not one for the protection of my friend the harmless, useful cat?

From *The Domestic Cat* by Gordon Stables, 1876

Put to the Sword

In the second part of Don Quixote, *the hero is the victim of a cruel practical joke while he is playing the guitar at his bedroom window one evening.*

Don Quixote had come to this point in his song, which was heard by the Duke and Duchess, Altisidora and almost all the people in the castle, when suddenly, from a balcony which directly overhung his window, a rope was let down with more than a hundred sheep-bells fastened to it and, immediately afterwards, a great sack, full of cats with smaller bells tied to their tails, was flung after it. The jingling of the bells and the squawking of the cats made such a din that even the Duke and Duchess, who had contrived the joke, were aghast, while Don Quixote was dumbfounded with fear. Now two or three of the cats, as fate would have it, got through the window, and as they rushed about the room it was as if a legion of devils had broken in. They knocked over and put out the candles burning there, and ran about trying to find a way of escape. And all the while the rope with the great sheep-bells on it continued to rise and fall, and the majority of the people of the castle, not being in the secret, remained speechless with astonishment. Finally Don Quixote rose to his feet and, drawing his sword, began to make stabs through the window, crying loudly:

'Avaunt, evil enchanters! Avaunt, crew of sorcerers! For I am Don Quixote de la Mancha, against whom your wicked plots are powerless and of no avail.'

Then, turning round upon the cats, who were running about the room, he dealt them many blows. And all of them rushed to the window and jumped out, except one which, finding itself hard pressed by Don Quixote's sword-thrusts, jumped at his face and dug its claws and teeth into his nose, whereupon Don Quixote began to roar his very loudest in pain. Now when the Duke and Duchess heard him, realizing the probable cause, they ran in great haste to his room and, opening the door with the master-key, found the poor knight struggling with all his might to tear the cat from his face. They went in with lights, and when he saw the unequal struggle the Duke ran up to disengage them, although Don Quixote cried out:

'Let no one pull him off! Leave me to deal with this devil, this wizard, this enchanter, hand to hand. For I will teach him myself what it is to deal with Don Quixote de la Mancha.'

But the cat snarled and held on, heedless of his threats. At last, however, the Duke pulled it off and threw it out of the window, Don Quixote coming off with a scratched face and not too whole a nose. But he was much annoyed at not being left to finish the battle he was fighting so stoutly against that perverse enchanter. Then they sent for oil of Hypericum, and that same Altisodora with her whitest of hands put bandages on all his wounds, saying to him in a soft voice, as she bound them up:

'All these misfortunes befall you, flinty-hearted knight, for your sin of hardness and obstinacy. May it please God that your squire Sancho shall forget to whip himself, so that this beloved Dulcinea of yours may never emerge from her enchantment, and you may

[213]

never enjoy her nor come to the bridal bed with her, at least while I, who adore you, am alive.'

To all this Don Quixote gave no word of reply, but heaved a deep sigh, and presently lay down on his bed, after thanking the Duke and Duchess for their kindness, not because he had been in any fear of that cattish and bellish rabble of enchanters, but because he realized their good intentions in coming to his rescue. The noble pair left him to rest and went away concerned at the unfortunate result of their joke, for they had not thought the adventure would have proved so tiresome and costly to Don Quixote. But it kept him confined to his room for five days.

From *The Adventures of Don Quixote* by Miguel de Cervantes Saavedra, 1605,
translated by J. M. Cohen

An Unfriendly Boy

Dostoyevsky's novel The Brothers Karamazov *includes this brief but telling character-sketch of the valet, Smerdyakov.*

He was a young man of about four and twenty, remarkably unsociable and taciturn. Not that he was shy or bashful. On the contrary, he was conceited and seemed to despise everybody.

But we must pause to say a few words about him now. He was brought up by Grigory and Marfa, but the boy grew up 'with no sense of gratitude,' as Grigory expressed it; he was an unfriendly boy, and seemed to look at the world mistrustfully. In his childhood he was very fond of hanging cats, and burying them with great ceremony. He used to dress up in a sheet as though it were a surplice, and sang, and waved some object over the dead cat as though it were a censer. All this he did on the sly, with the greatest secrecy. Grigory caught him once at this diversion and gave him a sound beating. He shrank into a corner and sulked there for a week.

From *The Brothers Karamazov* by Fyodor Dostoyevsky, 1880,
translated by Constance Garnett

Round Up the Usual Suspects

This scene from the novel Baumgartner's Bombay *occurs just after Baumgartner has been found murdered in his flat.*

Two Dobermanns leapt out, held by two policemen who seemed scarcely able to restrain them as they scampered up the stairs. This created instant pandemonium amongst the feline inmates of the flat – they jumped on to cupboards and curtain rods and stood there, arching their backs, spitting and yowling and slashing out with their claws if the dogs approached. Both the Dobermanns and the policemen retreated, apologetically, telling the watchman they would wait outside till the flat had been cleared of these defenders of Baumgartner's realm.

The watchman turned to Farrokh in appeal. How was he to get the cats out of the way? Farrokh stared at him and at the cats, equally helpless. But one of the neighbours ran down and out and returned with two ragged boys with sacks. They earned their living, they claimed, by picking through the dustbins on the streets, and they were quickly persuaded to catch the cats and put them in their sacks and remove them – 'far away', the watchman recovered sufficiently to say, sternly, and Farrokh, tender-hearted, retreated on to the balcony rather than watch. He stood there with his head bent, listening to the furniture falling, the boys shouting, the cats spitting as they dashed from cover to cover. The situation grew worse when the fire brigade arrived: someone had called them on the telephone, thinking that the crowd at Hira Niwas could only mean a fire. Shown into the flat on the third floor, they discovered that all they could do was help in the cat hunt. One cat, cornered on a window-sill, leapt out of the window and fell to its death.

He – it was the lamed Fritzi – missed by inches the bald, perspiring head of the landlord who stepped out of his car and hurried in, moaning and wiping his face. 'Never in all these years,' he groaned as he stumped up the stairs, 'in all these years – in Hira Niwas – has such a thing happened.'

From *Baumgartner's Bombay* by Anita Desai, 1988

'Two Accused over Cat Killed by Bull Terrier'

Two men were arrested yesterday after a cat died when it was allegedly 'fed' to a Staffordshire bull terrier in an alley.

It is alleged they tried to set the dog on police who answered a call from the warden of an old people's home in Montpelier, Bristol.

The 51-year-old warden, who asked not to be named, said the men stroked the tabby cat before grabbing it by the tail and dangling it in front of the dog. At one stage the terrier was hoisted off the ground with its jaws clamped on the cat.

She said: 'One of them pulled the cat off the wall by its tail. The dog started to jump up the wall to get the cat. But they were holding it just out of reach so that it couldn't get it.

'Then they threw the cat in the gutter. It didn't make a sound.'

From the *Daily Telegraph*, 23 May 1991

Just an Animal

'Oh, it's you, Etsuko,' Sachiko said, when I returned to her cottage that evening. Then she laughed and said: 'Don't look so surprised. You didn't expect me to stay here for ever, did you?'

Articles of clothing, blankets, numerous other items lay scattered over the tatami. I made some appropriate reply and sat down where I would not be in the way. On the floor beside me, I noticed two splendid-looking kimonos I had never seen Sachiko wear. I saw also – in the middle of the floor, packed into a cardboard box – her delicate teaset of pale white china.

Sachiko had opened wide the central partitions to allow the last of the daylight to come into the cottage; despite that, a dimness was fast setting in, and the sunset coming across the veranda barely reached the far corner where Mariko sat watching her mother quietly. Near her, two of the kittens were fighting playfully; the little girl was holding a third kitten in her arms.

'I expect Mariko told you,' I said to Sachiko. 'There was a visitor for you earlier. Your cousin was here.'

'Yes. Mariko told me.' Sachiko continued to pack her trunk.

'You're leaving in the morning?'

'Yes,' she said, with a touch of impatience. Then she gave a sigh and looked up at me. 'Yes, Etsuko, we're leaving in the morning.' She folded something away into a corner of her trunk.

'You have so much luggage,' I said, eventually. 'How will you ever carry it all?'

For a little while, Sachiko did not answer. Then, continuing to pack, she said: 'You know perfectly well, Etsuko. We'll put it in the car.'

I remained silent. She took a deep breath, and glanced across the room to where I was sitting.

'Yes, we're leaving Nagasaki, Etsuko. I assure you, I had every intention of coming to say goodbye once all the packing was finished. I wouldn't have left without thanking you, you've been most kind. Incidentally, as regards the loan, it will be returned to you through the post. Please don't worry about that.' She began to pack again.

'Where is it you're going?' I asked.

'Kobe. Everything's decided now, once and for all.'

'Kobe?'

'Yes, Etsuko, Kobe. Then after that, America. Frank has arranged everything. Aren't you pleased for me?' She smiled quickly, then turned away again.

I went on watching her. Mariko, too, was watching her. The kitten in her arms was struggling to join its companions on the tatami, but the little girl continued to hold it firmly. Beside her, in the corner of the room, I saw the vegetable box she had won at the *kuji-biki* stall; Mariko, it appeared, had converted the box into a house for her kittens.

'Incidentally, Etsuko, that pile over there' – Sachiko pointed – 'those items I'll just have to leave behind. I had no idea there was so much. Some of it is of decent enough quality. Please make use of it if you wish. I don't mean any offence, of course. It's merely that some of it is of good quality.'

'But what about your uncle?' I said. 'And your cousin?'

'My uncle?' She gave a shrug. 'It was kind of him to have invited me into his household. But I'm afraid I've made other plans now. You have no idea, Etsuko, how relieved I'll be to leave this place. I trust I've seen the last of such squalor.' Then she looked across to me once more and laughed. 'I can see exactly what you're thinking.

I can assure you, Etsuko, you're quite wrong. He won't let me down this time. He'll be here with the car, first thing tomorrow morning. Aren't you pleased for me?' Sachiko looked around at the luggage strewn over the floor and sighed. Then stepping over a pile of clothes, she knelt beside the box containing the teaset, and began filling it with rolls of wool.

'Have you decided yet?' Mariko said, suddenly.

'We can't talk about it now, Mariko,' said her mother. 'I'm busy now.'

'But you said I could keep them. Don't you remember?'

Sachiko shook the cardboard box gently; the china still rattled. She looked around, found a piece of cloth and began tearing it into strips.

'You said I could keep them,' Mariko said again.

'Mariko, please consider the situation for a moment. How can we possibly take all those creatures with us?'

'But you said I could keep them.'

Sachiko sighed, and for a moment seemed to be considering something. She looked down at the teaset, the pieces of cloth held in her hands.

'You did, Mother,' Mariko said. 'Don't you remember? You said I could.'

Sachiko looked up at her daughter, then over towards the kittens. 'Things are different now,' she said, tiredly. Then a wave of irritation crossed her face, and she flung down the pieces of cloth. 'Mariko, how can you think so much of these creatures? How can we possibly take them with us? No, we'll just have to leave them here.'

'But you said I could keep them.'

Sachiko glared at her daughter for a moment. 'Can't you think of anything else?' she said, lowering her voice almost to a whisper. 'Aren't you old enough yet to see there are other things besides these filthy little animals? You'll just have to grow up a little. You simply can't have these sentimental attachments for ever. These are just ... just *animals* don't you see? Don't you understand that, child? Don't you understand?'

Mariko stared back at her mother.

'If you like, Mariko-San,' I put in, 'I could come and feed them from time to time. Then eventually they'll find homes for themselves. There's no need to worry.'

The little girl turned to me. 'Mother said I could keep the kittens,' she said.

'Stop being so childish,' said Sachiko, sharply. 'You're being deliberately awkward, as you always are. What does it matter about the dirty little creatures?' She rose to her feet and went over to Mariko's corner. The kittens on the tatami scurried back; Sachiko looked down at them, then took a deep breath. Quite calmly, she turned the vegetable box on to its side – so that the wire-grid panels were facing upwards – reached down and dropped the kittens one by one into the box. She then turned to her daughter; Mariko was still clutching the remaining kitten.

'Give me that,' said Sachiko.

Mariko continued to hold the kitten. Sachiko stepped forward and put out her hand. The little girl turned and looked at me.

'This is Atsu,' she said. 'Do you want to see him, Etsuko-San? This is Atsu.'

'Give me that creature, Mariko,' Sachiko said. 'Don't you understand, it's just an animal. Why can't you understand that, Mariko? Are you really too young? It's not your little baby, it's just an animal, just like a rat or a snake. Now give it to me.'

Mariko stared up at her mother. Then slowly, she lowered the kitten and let it drop to the tatami in front of her. The kitten struggled as Sachiko lifted it off the ground. She dropped it into the vegetable box and slid shut the wire grid.

'Stay here,' she said to her daughter, and picked the box up in her arms. Then as she came past, she said to me: 'It's so stupid, these are just animals, what does it matter?'

Mariko rose to her feet and seemed about to follow her mother. Sachiko turned at the entryway and said: 'Do as you're told. Stay here.'

For a few moments, Mariko remained standing at the edge of the tatami, looking at the doorway where her mother had disappeared.

'Wait for your mother here, Mariko-San,' I said to her.

The little girl turned and looked at me. Then the next moment, she had gone.

For a minute or two, I did not move. Then eventually I got to my feet and put on my sandals. From the doorway, I could see Sachiko down by the water, the vegetable box beside her feet; she appeared not to have noticed her daughter standing several yards behind her, just at the point where the ground began to slope down steeply. I left the cottage and made my way to where Mariko was standing.

'Let's go back to the house, Mariko-San,' I said, gently.

The little girl's eyes remained on her mother, her face devoid of any expression. Down in front of us, Sachiko knelt cautiously on the bank, then moved the box a little nearer.

'Let's go inside, Mariko,' I said again, but the little girl continued to ignore me. I left her and walked down the muddy slope to where Sachiko was kneeling. The sunset was coming through the trees on the opposite bank, and the reeds that grew along the water's edge cast long shadows on the muddy ground around us. Sachiko had found some grass to kneel on, but that too was thick with mud.

'Can't we let them loose?' I said, quietly. 'You never know. Someone may want them.'

Sachiko was gazing down into the vegetable box through the wire gauze. She slid open a panel, brought out a kitten and shut the box again. She held the kitten in both hands, looked at it for a few seconds, then glanced up at me. 'It's just an animal, Etsuko,' she said. 'That's all it is.'

She put the kitten into the water and held it there. She remained like that for some moments, staring into the water, both hands beneath the surface. She was wearing a casual summer kimono, and the corners of each sleeve touched the water.

Then for the first time, without taking her hands from the water, Sachiko threw a glance over her shoulder towards her daughter. Instinctively, I followed her glance, and for one brief moment the two of us were both staring back up at Mariko. The little girl was standing at the top of the slope, watching with the same blank expression. On seeing her mother's face turn to her, she moved her head very slightly; then she remained quite still, her hands behind her back.

Sachiko brought her hands out of the water and stared at the kitten she was still holding. She brought it closer to her face and the water ran down her wrists and arms.

'It's still alive,' she said, tiredly. Then she turned to me and said: 'Look at this water, Etsuko. It's so dirty.' With an air of disgust, she dropped the soaked kitten back into the box and shut it. 'How these things struggle,' she muttered, and held up her wrists to show me the scratch-marks. Somehow, Sachiko's hair had also become wet;

one drop, then another fell from a thin strand which hung down one side of her face.

Sachiko adjusted her position then pushed the vegetable box over the edge of the bank; the box rolled and landed in the water. To prevent it floating, Sachiko leaned forward and held it down. The water came almost halfway up the wire-grid. She continued to hold down the box, then finally pushed it with both hands. The box floated a little way into the river, bobbed and sank further. Sachiko got to her feet, and we both of us watched the box. It continued to float, then caught in the current and began moving more swiftly downstream.

Some movement caught my eye and made me turn. Mariko had run several yards down the river's edge, to a spot where the bank jutted out into the water. She stood there watching the box float on, her face still expressionless. The box caught in some reeds, freed itself and continued its journey. Mariko began to run again. She ran on some distance along the bank, then stopped again to watch the box. By this time, only a small corner was visible above the surface.

'This water's so dirty,' Sachiko said. She had been shaking the water off her hands. She squeezed in turn the sleeve-ends of her kimono, then brushed the mud from her knees. 'Let's go back inside, Etsuko. The insects here are becoming intolerable.'

'Shouldn't we go and get Mariko? It will be dark soon.'

Sachiko turned and called her daughter's name. Mariko was now fifty yards or so away, still looking at the water. She did not seem to hear and Sachiko gave a shrug. 'She'll come back in time,' she said. 'Now, I must finish packing before the light goes completely.' She began to walk up the slope towards the cottage.

From *A Pale View of Hills* by Kazuo Ishiguro, 1982

'On Them'

I do not like Them. It is no good asking me why, though I have plenty of reasons. I do not like Them. There would be no particular point in saying I do not like Them if it were not that so many people doted on Them, and when one hears Them praised, it goads one to expressing one's hatred and fear of Them.

I know very well that They can do one harm, and that They have occult powers. All the world has known that for a hundred thousand years, more or less, and every attempt has been made to propitiate Them. James I would drown Their Mistress or burn her, but *They* were spared. Men would mummify Them in Egypt, and worship the mummies; men would carve Them in stone in Cyprus, and Crete and Asia Minor, or (more remarkable still) artists, especially in the Western Empire, would leave Them out altogether; so much was Their influence dreaded. Well, I yield so far as not to print Their name, and only to call Them 'They', but I hate Them, and I'm not afraid to say so.

If you will take a little list of the chief crimes that living beings can commit you will find that They commit them all. And They are cruel; cruelty is even in Their tread and expression. They are hatefully cruel. I saw one of Them catch a mouse the other day (the cat is now out of the bag), and it was a very much more sickening sight, I fancy, than ordinary murder. You may imagine that They catch mice to eat them. It is not so. They catch mice to torture them. And what is worse, They will teach this to Their children – Their children who are naturally innocent and fat, and full of goodness, are deliberately and systematically corrupted by Them; there is diabolism in it.

Other beings (I include mankind) will be gluttonous, but gluttonous spasmodically, or with a method, or shamefacedly, or, in some way or another that qualifies the vice; not so They. They are gluttonous always and upon all occasions, and in every place and for ever. It was only last Vigil of All Fools' Day when, myself fasting, I filled up the saucer seven times with milk and seven times it was emptied, and there went up the most peevish, querulous, vicious complaint and demand for an eighth. They will eat some part of the food of all that are in the house. Now even a child, the most gluttonous one would think of all living creatures, would not do that. It makes a selection, *They* do not. *They* will drink beer. This is not a theory; I know it; I have seen it with my own eyes. They will eat special foods; They will even eat dry bread. Here again I have personal evidence of the fact; They will eat the dog's biscuits, but never upon any occasion will They eat anything that has been poisoned, so utterly lacking are They in simplicity and humility, and so abominably well filled with cunning by whatever demon first brought their race into existence.

They also, alone of all creation, love hateful noises. Some beings indeed (and I count Man among them) cannot help the voice with which they have been endowed, but they know that it is offensive, and are at pains to make it better; others (such as the peacock or the elephant) also know that their cry is unpleasant. They therefore use it sparingly. Others again, the dove, the nightingale, the thrush, know that their voices are very pleasant, and entertain us with them all day and all night long; but They know that Their voices are the most hideous of all the sounds in the world, and, knowing this, They perpetually insist upon thrusting those voices upon us, saying, as it were, 'I am giving myself pain, but I am giving you more pain, and therefore I shall go on.' And They choose for the place where this pain shall be given, exact and elevated situations, very close to our ears. Is there any need for me to point out that in every city they will begin their wicked jar just at the time when its inhabitants must sleep? In London you will not hear it till after midnight; in the county towns it begins at ten; in remote villages as early as nine.

Their Master also protects them. They have a charmed life. I have seen one thrown from a great height into a London street, which when It reached it It walked quietly away with the dignity of the Lost World to which It belonged.

If one had the time one could watch Them day after day, and never see Them do a single kind or good thing, or be moved by a single virtuous impulse. They have no gesture for the expression of admiration, love, reverence or ecstasy. They have but one method of expressing content, and They reserve that for moments of physical repletion. The tail, which is in all other animals the signal for joy or for defence, or for mere usefulness, or for a noble anger, is with Them agitated only to express a sullen discontent.

All that They do is venomous, and all that They think is evil, and when I take mine away (as I mean to do next week – in a basket), I shall first read in a book of statistics what is the wickedest part of London, and I shall leave It there, for I know of no one even among my neighbours quite so vile as to deserve such a gift.

From *On Nothing & Kindred Subjects* by Hilaire Belloc, 1908

None Deeper

From the French poets, Moncrif [in his book *Les Chats*, published in 1727] collects a good many curious tributes to the 'harmless, necessary cat.' I am seized with an ambition to put some fragments of these into English verse. Most of them are highly complimentary. It is true that Ronsard was one of those who could not appreciate a 'matou.' He sang or said:-

There is no man now living anywhere
　Who hates cats with a deeper hate than I;
I hate their eyes, their heads, the way they stare,
　And when I see one come, I turn and fly.

But among the *précieuses* of the seventeenth century there was much more appreciation.

From *Gossip in a Library* by Edmund Gosse, 1891

Hooked on Nicotine

It can scarcely have escaped the notice of thinking men, I think, that the forces of darkness opposed to those of us who like a quiet smoke are gathering momentum daily and starting to throw their weight about more than somewhat. Each morning I read in the papers a long article by another of those doctors who are the spearhead of the movement. Tobacco, they say, hardens the arteries and lowers the temperature of the body extremities, and if you reply that you like your arteries hard and are all for having the temperature of your body extremities lowered, especially in the summer months, they bring up that cat again.

The cat to which I allude is not the cat Poona which I chase at night but the one that has two drops of nicotine placed on its tongue and instantly passes beyond the veil.

'Look,' they say. 'I place two drops of nicotine on the tongue of this cat. Now watch it wilt.'

I can't see the argument. Cats, as Charles Stuart Calverley once observed, may have had their goose cooked by tobacco juice, but, as he went on to point out, we're not as tabbies are. Must we deprive ourselves of all our modest pleasures just because indulgence in them would be harmful to some cat which is probably a perfect stranger?

Take a simple instance such as occurs every Saturday afternoon on the Rugby football field. A scrum is formed, the ball is heeled out, the scrum-half gathers it, and instantaneously two fourteen-stone forwards fling themselves on his person, grinding him into the mud. Are we to abolish Twickenham and Murrayfield because some sorry reasoner tells us that if the scrum-half had been a cat he would have been squashed flatter than a Dover sole? And no use trying to drive into these morons' heads that there is no recorded instance of a team lining up for the kick-off with a cat playing scrum-half. Really, one feels inclined at times to give it all up and not bother to argue . . .

It is pitiful to think that that is how these men spend their lives, placing drops of nicotine on the tongues of cats day in, day out all the year round, except possibly on bank holidays. But if you tell them that, like that Phantom fellow, they have become slaves to a habit, and urge them to summon up their manhood and throw off the shackles, they just stare at you with fishy eyes and mumble that it can't be done. Of course it can be done. If they were to say to themselves, 'I will not start placing nicotine on cats' tongues till after lunch,' they would have made a beginning. After that it would be simple to knock off during the afternoon, and by degrees they would find that they could abstain altogether. The first cat of the day is the hard one to give up. Conquer the impulse for the after-breakfast cat, and the battle is half won.

From Over Seventy by P. G. Wodehouse, 1957

A Discredit to Civilisation

It seems almost too horrible for belief that a creature exquisitely sensitive, daintily fastidious, superlatively clean by choice, capable of reasoning and gifted with emotional faculties of a high type should lead the fugitive, vagabond, and persecuted life which she is allowed to do in our cultivated cities. The only excuse for the apathy of the public is that the details of cat life are unknown to influential persons, of such cat life I mean as is lived in crowded centres. Otherwise the cruel meanness of neglecting to protect a faithful servant merely because he is cheap and tenacious of life would strike them.

It is not by day but by night, it is less in rich and fashionable than in slummy neighbourhoods that the utterly deplorable nature of feline existence can be realized. It is not a tempting invitation I know, but I challenge anybody who has the courage to see for himself or herself what the cat population of a poor district is, and how it lives when it turns out *en masse* after dark. Almost any back street or alley will furnish ample corroboration of what I say, – that the treatment of cats in England is a discredit to a land professedly civilized. As soon as the streets are comparatively empty, and there is a shadowy chance that some vile fragments may be picked up in the gutter without interruption, out steals one phantom-like creature after another from the lurking places where they have hidden all day.

They seem to flit along instead of running, so swift are they to disappear on the least alarm. They are gaunt, famine-stricken, covered, many of them, with sores and wounds. Even this meal of offscourings they pick up in a clandestine and guilty haste. Here and there are the broken limbed or lame, and these seem half crazy from want, owing to being handicapped in the general scrimmage of food. After howling and fighting like fiends, a single conqueror swallows the disgusting offal, from which his soul revolts, while he must eat or perish. He tears in frantic haste the entrails which he has found, lest some other cat, fiercer and stronger than he, should wrest the booty from him; his torn and bleeding ears are pricked to listen for the least sound, though there is now less danger from dogs and stone-throwers than in broad daylight. His shoulder bones are sticking through his skin, his tail is a mere wisp, his eyes glare and seem to occupy half his face. Here you will find a creature who snarls when you go near him, snatching up his prey and vanishing with it like a wild beast into the gloomy shades of some cellar, or through a broken window into a disused and empty house. There you may see 'the poor remains of beauty once admired,' – a Puss who still believes in humanity in spite of all, clings to the legends of her youth, timidly touches your feet, and lifts appealing eyes to yours. She will follow you for half a mile or more if you do but throw a kind word to her.

Even on snowy nights these scenes go on just the same. Perhaps there is some excuse for not believing what one has not seen, especially when it is so much more comfortable and conducive to one's night's rest to be incredulous. I can but say that I have seen and must believe.

I do not think that any words or pictures could overpaint the sorrows of cats in a poor neighbourhood. In one small street alone, in a single poor district of Bristol, no less than three cats were found frozen to death in one night. Of course nobody troubles himself to gather statistics of dead cats; besides, no numbers could fitly express the amount of distress spread through a hundred streets of a thousand towns. If obtainable, these statistics could not indicate, even faintly, the sufferings of shelterless cats before the frost mercifully benumbs those fortunate enough to die.

From *The Cat: Her Place in Society and Treatment* by Edith Carrington, 1896

'A Cat'

She had a name among the children;
But no one loved though someone owned
Her, locked her out of doors at bedtime
And had her kittens duly drowned.

In Spring, nevertheless, this cat
Ate blackbirds, thrushes, nightingales,
And birds of bright voice and plume and flight,
As well as scraps from neighbours' pails.

I loathed and hated her for this;
One speckle on a thrush's breast
Was worth a million such; and yet
She lived long, till God gave her rest.

From *Last Poems* by Edward Thomas, 1918

The Ecclesiastical Cat

As I and my family sat at tea in our parlour, an hour or two after we had taken possession of our lodgings, the door of the room and that of the entrance of the house being open, on account of the fineness of the weather, a poor black cat entered hastily, sat down on the carpet by the table, looked up towards us, and mewed piteously. I never had seen so wretched a looking creature. It was dreadfully attenuated, being little more than skin and bone, and was sorely afflicted with an eruptive malady. And here I may as well relate the history of this cat previous to our arrival which I subsequently learned by bits and snatches. It had belonged to a previous vicar of Llangollen, and had been left behind at his departure. His successor brought with him dogs and cats, who, conceiving that the late vicar's cat had no business at the vicarage, drove it forth to seek another home, which, however, it could not find. Almost all the people of the suburb were dissenters, as indeed were the generality of the people at Llangollen, and knowing the cat to be a church cat, not only would not harbour it, but did all they could to make it miserable; whilst the few who were not dissenters, would not receive it into their houses, either because they had cats of their own, or dogs, or did not want a cat, so that the cat had no home and was dreadfully persecuted by nine-tenths of the suburb. Oh, there never was a cat so persecuted as that poor Church of England animal, and solely on account of the opinions which it was supposed to have imbibed in the house of its late master, for I never could learn that the dissenters of the suburb, nor indeed of Llangollen in general, were in the habit of persecuting other cats; the cat was a Church of England cat, and that was enough: stone it, hang it, drown it! were the cries of almost everybody. If the workmen of the flannel factory, all of whom were Calvinistic Methodists, chanced to get a glimpse of it in the road from the windows of the building, they would sally forth in a body, and with sticks, stones, or for want of other weapons, with clots of horse-dung, of which there was always plenty on the road, would chase it up the high bank or perhaps over the Camlas – the inhabitants of a small street between our house and the factory leading from the road to the river, all of whom were dissenters, if they saw it moving about the perllan, into which their back windows looked, would shriek and hoot at it, and fling anything of no value, which came easily to hand, at the head or body of the ecclesiastical cat. The good woman of the house, who though a very excellent person, was a bitter dissenter, whenever she saw it upon her ground or heard it was there, would make after it, frequently attended by her maid Margaret, and her young son, a boy about nine years of age, both of whom hated the cat, and were always ready to attack it, either alone or in company, and no wonder, the maid being not only a dissenter, but a class teacher, and the boy not only a dissenter, but intended for the dissenting ministry. Where it got its food, and food it sometimes must have got, for even a cat, an animal known to have nine lives, cannot live without food, was only known to itself, as was the place where it lay, for even a cat must lie down sometimes; though a labouring man who occasionally dug in the garden told me he believed that in the springtime it ate freshets, and the woman of the house once said that she believed it sometimes slept in the hedge, which hedge, by the bye, divided our perllan from the vicarage grounds, which were very extensive. Well might the cat having led this kind of life for better than two years look mere skin and bone when it made its appearance in our apartment, and have an eruptive malady, and also a bronchitic cough, for I remember it had both. How it came to make its appearance there is a mystery, for it had never entered the house before, even when there were lodgers; that it should not visit the woman, who was its declared enemy, was natural enough, but why, if it did not visit her other lodgers, did it visit us? Did instinct keep it aloof from them? Did instinct draw it towards us? We gave it some bread-and-butter, and a little tea with milk and sugar. It ate and drank and soon began to purr. The good woman of the house was horrified when on coming in to remove the things she saw the church cat on her carpet. 'What impudence!' she exclaimed, and made towards it, but on our telling her that we did not expect that it should be disturbed, she let it alone. A very remarkable circumstance was, that though the cat had hitherto been in the habit of flying not only from her face, but the very echo of her voice, it now looked her in the face with perfect composure, as much as to say, 'I don't fear you, for I know that I am now safe and with my own people.' It stayed with us two hours and then went away. The next morning it returned. To be short, though it went away every night, it became our own cat, and one of our family. I gave it something which cured it of its eruption, and through good treatment it soon lost its other ailments and began to look sleek and bonny.

We were at first in some perplexity with respect to the disposal of the ecclesiastical cat; it would of course not do to leave it in the garden to the tender mercies of the Calvinistic Methodists of the neighbourhood, more especially those of the flannel manufactory, and my wife and daughter could hardly carry it with them. At length we thought of applying to a young woman of sound church principles who was lately married and lived over the water on the way to the railway station, with whom we were slightly acquainted, to take charge of the animal, and she on the first intimation of our wish willingly acceded to it. So with her poor puss was left along with a trifle for its milk-money, and with her, as we subsquently learned, it continued in peace and comfort till one morning it sprang suddenly from the hearth into the air, gave a mew and died. So much for the ecclesiastical cat.

From *Wild Wales* by George Borrow, 1862

'Ming's Biggest Prey'

Ming was resting comfortably on the foot of his mistress's bunk, when the man picked him up by the back of the neck, stuck him out on the deck and closed the cabin door. Ming's blue eyes widened in shock and brief anger, then nearly closed again because of the brilliant sunlight. It was not the first time Ming had been thrust out of the cabin rudely, and Ming realized that the man did it when his mistress, Elaine, was not looking.

The sailboat now offered no shelter from the sun, but Ming was not yet too warm. He leapt easily to the cabin roof and stepped on the coil of rope just behind the mast. Ming liked the rope coil as a couch, because he could see everything from the height, the cup shape of the rope protected him from strong breezes, and also minimized the swaying and sudden changes of angle of the *White Lark*, since it was more or less the centre point. But just now the sail had been taken down, because Elaine and the man had eaten lunch, and often they had a siesta afterward, during which time, Ming knew, the man didn't like him in the cabin. Lunchtime was all right. In fact, Ming had just lunched on delicious grilled fish and a bit of lobster. Now, lying in a relaxed curve on the coil of rope, Ming opened his mouth in a great yawn, then with his slant eyes almost closed against the strong sunlight, gazed at the beige hills and the white and pink houses and hotels that circled the bay of Acapulco. Between the *White Lark* and the shore where people plashed inaudibly, the sun twinkled on the water's surface like thousands of tiny electric lights going on and off. A water-skier went by, skimming up white spray behind him. Such activity! Ming half dozed, feeling the heat of the sun sink into his fur. Ming was from New York, and he considered Acapulco a great improvement over his environment in the first weeks of his life. He remembered a sunless box with straw on the bottom, three or four other kittens in with him, and a window behind which giant forms paused for a few moments, tried to catch his attention by tapping, then passed on. He did not remember his mother at all. One day a young woman who smelled of something pleasant came into the place and took him away – away from the ugly, frightening smell of dogs, of medicine and parrot dung. Then they went on what Ming now knew was an aeroplane. He was quite used to aeroplanes now and rather liked them. On aeroplanes he sat on Elaine's lap, or slept on her lap, and there were always titbits to eat if he was hungry.

Elaine spent much of the day in a shop in Acapulco, where dresses and slacks and bathing suits hung on all the walls. This place smelled clean and fresh, there were flowers in pots and in boxes out front, and the floor was of cool blue and white tile. Ming had perfect freedom to wander out into the patio behind the shop, or to sleep in his basket in a corner. There was more sunlight in front of the shop, but mischievous boys often tried to grab him if he sat in front, and Ming could never relax there.

Ming liked best lying in the sun with his mistress on one of the long canvas chairs on their terrace at home. What Ming did not like were the people she sometimes invited to their house, people who spent the night, people by the score who stayed up very late eating and drinking, playing the gramophone or the piano – people who separated him from Elaine. People who stepped on his toes, people who sometimes picked him up from behind before he could do anything about it, so that he had to squirm and fight to get free, people who stroked him roughly, people who closed a door somewhere, locking him in. *People!* Ming detested people. In all the world, he liked only Elaine. Elaine loved him and understood him.

Especially this man called Teddie Ming detested now. Teddie was around all the time lately. Ming did not like the way Teddie looked at him, when Elaine was not watching. And sometimes Teddie, when Elaine was not near, muttered something which Ming knew was a threat. Or a command to leave the room. Ming took it calmly. Dignity was to be preserved. Besides, wasn't his mistress on his side? The man was the intruder. When Elaine was watching, the man sometimes pretended a fondness for him, but Ming always moved gracefully but unmistakably in another direction.

Ming's nap was interrupted by the sound of the cabin door opening. He heard Elaine and the man laughing and talking. The big red-orange sun was near the horizon.

'Ming!' Elaine came over to him. 'Aren't you getting *cooked*, darling? I thought you were *in*!'

'So did I!' said Teddie.

Ming purred as he always did when he awakened. She picked him up gently, cradled him in her arms, and took him below into the suddenly cool shade of the cabin. She was talking to the man, and not in a gentle tone. She set Ming down in front of his dish of water, and though he was not thirsty, he drank a little to please her. Ming did feel addled by the heat, and he staggered a little.

Elaine took a wet towel and wiped Ming's face, his ears and his four paws. Then she laid him gently on the bunk that smelled of Elaine's perfume but also of the man whom Ming detested.

Now his mistress and the man were quarrelling, Ming could tell from the tone. Elaine was staying with Ming, sitting on the edge of the bunk. Ming at last heard the splash that meant Teddie had dived into the water. Ming hoped he stayed there, hoped he drowned, hoped he never came back. Elaine wet a bathtowel in the aluminium sink, wrung it out, spread it on the bunk, and lifted Ming on to it. She brought water, and now Ming was thirsty, and drank. She left him to sleep again while she washed and put away the dishes. These were comfortable sounds that Ming liked to hear.

But soon there was another *plash* and *plop*, Teddie's wet feet on the deck, and Ming was awake again.

The tone of quarrelling recommenced. Elaine went up the few steps on to the deck. Ming, tense but with his chin still resting on the moist bathtowel, kept his eyes on the cabin door. It was Teddie's feet that he heard descending. Ming lifted his head slightly, aware that there was no exit behind him, that he was trapped in the cabin. The man paused with a towel in his hands, staring at Ming.

Ming relaxed completely, as he might do preparatory to a yawn, and this caused his eyes to cross. Ming then let his tongue slide a little way out of his mouth. The man started to say something, looked as if he wanted to hurl the wadded towel at Ming, but he wavered, whatever he had been going to say never got out of his mouth, and he threw the towel in the sink, then bent to wash his face. It was not the first time Ming had let his tongue slide out at Teddie. Lots of people laughed when Ming did this, if they were people at a party, for instance, and Ming rather enjoyed that. But Ming sensed that Teddie took it as a hostile gesture of some kind, which was why Ming did it deliberately to Teddie, whereas among other people, it was often an accident when Ming's tongue slid out.

The quarrelling continued. Elaine made coffee. Ming began to feel better, and went on deck again, because the sun had now set. Elaine had started the motor, and they were gliding slowly towards the shore. Ming caught the song of birds, the odd screams, like shrill phrases, of certain birds that cried only at sunset. Ming looked forward to the adobe house on the cliff that was his and his mistress's home. He knew that the reason she did not leave him at home (where he would have been more comfortable) when she went on the boat, was because she was afraid that people might trap him, even kill him. Ming understood. People had tried to grab him from almost under Elaine's eyes. Once he had been suddenly hauled away in a cloth bag, and though fighting as hard as he could, he was not sure he would have been able to get out, if Elaine had not hit the boy herself and grabbed the bag from him.

Ming had intended to jump up on the cabin roof again, but after glancing at it, he decided to save his strength, so he crouched on the warm, gently slopping deck with his feet tucked in, and gazed at the approaching shore. Now he could hear guitar music from the beach. The voices of his mistress and the man had come to a halt. For a few moments, the loudest sound was the *chug-chug-chug* of the boat's motor. Then Ming heard the man's bare feet climbing the cabin steps. Ming did not turn his head to look at him, but his ears twitched back a little, involuntarily. Ming looked at the water just the distance of a short leap in front of him and below him. Strangely, there was no sound from the man behind him. The hair on Ming's neck prickled, and Ming glanced over his right shoulder.

At that instant, the man bent forward and rushed at Ming with his arms outspread.

Ming was on his feet at once, darting straight towards the man, which was the only direction of safety on the rail-less deck, and the man swung his left arm and cuffed Ming in the chest. Ming went flying backwards, claws scraping the deck, but his hind legs went over the edge. Ming clung with his front feet to the sleek wood which gave him little hold, while his hind legs worked to heave him up, worked at the side of the boat which sloped to Ming's disadvantage.

The man advanced to shove a foot against Ming's paws, but Elaine came up the cabin steps just then.

'What's happening? *Ming!*'

Ming's strong hind legs were getting him on to the deck little by little. The man had knelt as if to lend a hand. Elaine had fallen on to her knees also, and had Ming by the back of the neck now.

Ming relaxed, hunched on the deck. His tail was wet.

'He fell overboard!' Teddie said. 'It's true, he's groggy. Just lurched over and fell when the boat gave a dip.'

'It's the sun. Poor *Ming!*' Elaine held the cat against her breast, and carried him into the cabin. 'Teddie – could you steer?'

The man came down into the cabin. Elaine had Ming on the bunk and was talking softly to him. Ming's heart was still beating fast. He was alert against the man at the wheel, even though Elaine was with him. Ming was aware that they had entered the little cove where they always went before getting off the boat.

Here were the friends and allies of Teddie, whom Ming detested by association, although these were merely Mexican boys. Two or three boys in shorts called 'Señor Teddie!' and offered a hand to Elaine to climb on to the dock, took the rope attached to the front of the boat, offered to carry '*Ming! – Ming!*' Ming leapt on to the dock himself and crouched, waiting for Elaine, ready to dart away from any other hand that might reach for him. And there were several brown hands making a rush for him, so that Ming had to keep jumping aside. There were laughs, yelps, stomps of bare feet on wooden boards. But there was also the reassuring voice of Elaine warning them off. Ming knew she was busy carrying off the plastic satchels, locking the cabin door. Teddie with the aid of one of the Mexican boys was stretching the canvas over the cabin now. And

Elaine's sandalled feet were beside Ming. Ming followed her as she walked away. A boy took the things Elaine was carrying, then she picked Ming up.

They got into the big car without a roof that belonged to Teddie, and drove up the winding road towards Elaine's and Ming's house. One of the boys was driving. Now the tone in which Elaine and Teddie were speaking was calmer, softer. The man laughed. Ming sat tensely on his mistress's lap. He could feel her concern for him in the way she stroked him and touched the back of his neck. The man reached out to put his fingers on Ming's back, and Ming gave a low growl that rose and fell and rumbled deep in his throat.

'Well, well,' said the man, pretending to be amused, and took his hand away.

Elaine's voice had stopped in the middle of something she was saying. Ming was tired, and wanted nothing more than to take a nap on the big bed at home. The bed was covered with a red and white striped blanket of thin wool.

Hardly had Ming thought of this, when he found himself in the cool, fragrant atmosphere of his own home, being lowered gently on to the bed with the soft woollen cover. His mistress kissed his cheek, and said something with the word hungry in it. Ming understood, at any rate. He was to tell her when he was hungry.

Ming dozed, and awakened at the sound of voices on the terrace a couple of yards away, past the open glass doors. Now it was dark. Ming could see one end of the table, and could tell from the quality of the light that there were candles on the table. Concha, the servant who slept in the house, was clearing the table. Ming heard her voice, then the voices of Elaine and the man. Ming smelled cigar smoke. Ming jumped to the floor and sat for a moment looking out of the door towards the terrace. He yawned, then arched his back and stretched, and limbered up his muscles by digging his claws into the thick straw carpet. Then he slipped out to the right on the terrace and glided silently down the long stairway of broad stones to the garden below. The garden was like a jungle or a forest. Avocado trees and mango trees grew as high as the terrace itself, there were bougainvillaea against the wall, orchids in the trees, and magnolias and several camellias which Elaine had planted. Ming could hear birds twittering and stirring in their nests. Sometimes he climbed trees to get at their nests, but tonight he was not in the mood, though he was no longer tired. The voices of his mistress and the man disturbed him. His mistress was not a friend of the man's tonight, that was plain.

Concha was probably still in the kitchen, and Ming decided to go in and ask her for something to eat. Concha liked him. One maid who had not liked him had been dismissed by Elaine. Ming thought he fancied barbecued pork. That was what his mistress and the man had eaten tonight. The breeze blew fresh from the ocean, ruffling Ming's fur slightly. Ming felt completely recovered from the awful experience of nearly falling into the sea.

Now the terrace was empty of people. Ming went left, back into the bedroom, and was at once aware of the man's presence, though there was no light on and Ming could not see him. The man was standing by the dressing table, opening a box. Again involuntarily Ming gave a low growl which rose and fell, and Ming remained frozen in the position he had been in when he first became aware of the man, his right front paw extended for the next step. Now his ears were back, he was prepared to spring in any direction, although the man had not seen him.

'*Ssss-st!* Damn you!' the man said in a whisper. He stamped his foot, not very hard, to make the cat go away.

Ming did not move at all. Ming heard the soft rattle of the white necklace which belonged to his mistress. The man put it into his pocket, then moved to Ming's right, out of the door that went into the big living-room. Ming now heard the clink of a bottle against glass, heard liquid being poured. Ming went through the same door and turned left towards the kitchen.

Here he miaowed, and was greeted by Elaine and Concha. Concha had her radio turned on to music.

'Fish? – Pork. He likes pork.' Elaine said, speaking the odd form of words which she used with Concha.

Ming, without much difficulty, conveyed his preference for pork, and got it. He fell to with a good appetite. Concha was exclaiming 'Ah-eee-ee!' as his mistress spoke with her, spoke at length. Then Concha bent to stroke him, and Ming put up with it, still looking down at his plate, until she left off and he could finish his meal. Then Elaine left the kitchen. Concha gave him some of the tinned milk, which he loved, in his now empty saucer, and Ming lapped this up. Then he rubbed himself against her bare leg by way of

[236]

thanks, and went out of the kitchen, made his way cautiously into the living-room en route to the bedroom. But now Elaine and the man were out on the terrace. Ming had just entered the bedroom, when he heard Elaine call:

'Ming? Where are you?'

Ming went to the terrace door and stopped, and sat on the threshold.

Elaine was sitting sideways at the end of the table, and the candlelight was bright on her long fair hair, on the white of her trousers. She slapped her thigh, and Ming jumped on to her lap.

The man said something in a low tone, something not nice.

Elaine replied something in the same tone. But she laughed a little.

Then the telephone rang.

Elaine put Ming down, and went into the living-room towards the telephone.

The man finished what was in his glass, muttered something at Ming, then set the glass on the table. He got up and tried to circle Ming, or to get him towards the edge of the terrace, Ming realized, and Ming also realized that the man was drunk – therefore moving slowly and a little clumsily. The terrace had a parapet about as high as the man's hips, but it was broken by grills in three places, grills with bars wide enough for Ming to pass through, though Ming never did, merely looked through the grills sometimes. It was plain to Ming that the man wanted to drive him through one of the grills, or grab him and toss him over the terrace parapet. There was nothing easier for Ming than to elude him. Then the man picked up a chair and swung it suddenly, catching Ming on the hop. That had been quick, and it hurt. Ming took the nearest exit, which was down the outside steps that led to the garden.

The man started down the steps after him. Without reflecting, Ming dashed back up the few steps he had come, keeping close to the wall which was in shadow. The man hadn't seen him, Ming knew. Ming leapt to the terrace parapet, sat down and licked a paw once to recover and collect himself. His heart beat fast as if he were in the middle of a fight. And hatred ran in his veins. Hatred burned his eyes as he crouched and listened to the man uncertainly climbing the steps below him. The man came into view.

Ming tensed himself for a jump, then jumped as hard as he could, landing with all four feet on the man's right arm near the shoulder. Ming clung to the cloth of the man's white jacket, but they were both falling. The man groaned. Ming hung on. Branches crackled. Ming could not tell up from down. Ming jumped off the man, became aware of direction and of the earth too late, and landed on his side. Almost at the same time, he heard the thud of the man hitting the ground, then of his body rolling a little way, then there was silence. Ming had to breathe fast with his mouth open until his chest stopped hurting. From the direction of the man, he could smell drink, cigar, and the sharp odour that meant fear. But the man was not moving.

Ming could now see quite well. There was even a bit of moonlight. Ming headed for the steps again, had to go a long way through the bush, over stones and sand, to where the steps began. Then he glided up and arrived once more upon the terrace.

Elaine was just coming on to the terrace.

'Teddie?' she called. Then she went back into the bedroom where she turned on a lamp. She went into the kitchen. Ming followed her. Concha had left the light on, but Concha was now in her own room, where the radio played.

Elaine opened the front door.

The man's car was still in the driveway, Ming saw. Now Ming's hip had begun to hurt, or now he had begun to notice it. It caused him to limp a little. Elaine noticed this, touched his back, and asked him what was the matter. Ming only purred.

'Teddie? – Where are you?' Elaine called.

She took a torch and shone it down into the garden, down among the great trunks of the avocado trees, among the orchids and the lavender and pink blossoms of the bougainvillaeas. Ming, safe beside her on the terrace parapet, followed the beam of the torch with his eyes and purred with content. The man was not below here, but below and to the right. Elaine went to the terrace steps and carefully, because there was no rail here, only broad steps, pointed the beam of the light downward. Ming did not bother looking. He sat on the terrace where the steps began.

'Teddie!' she said. '*Teddie!*' Then she ran down the steps.

Ming still did not follow her. He heard her draw in her breath. Then she cried:

'*Concha!*'

Elaine ran back up the steps.

Concha had come out of her room. Elaine spoke to Concha. Then Concha became excited. Elaine went to the telephone, and spoke for a short while, then she and Concha went down the steps together. Ming settled himself with his paws tucked under him on the terrace, which was still faintly warm from the day's sun. A car arrived. Elaine came up the steps, and went and opened the front door. Ming kept out of the way on the terrace, in a shadowy corner, as three or four strange men came out on the terrace and tramped down the steps. There was a great deal of talk below, noises of feet, breaking of bushes, and then the smell of all of them mounted the steps, the smell of tobacco, sweat, and the familiar smell of blood. The man's blood. Ming was pleased, as he was pleased when he killed a bird and created this smell of blood under his own teeth. This was big prey. Ming, unnoticed by any of the others, stood up to his full height as the group passed with the corpse, and inhaled the aroma of his victory with a lifted nose.

Then suddenly the house was empty. Everyone had gone, even Concha. Ming drank a little water from his bowl in the kitchen, then went to his mistress's bed, curled against the slope of the pillows, and fell fast asleep. He was awakened by the *rr-rr-r* of an unfamiliar car. Then the front door opened, and he recognized the step of Elaine and then Concha. Ming stayed where he was. Elaine and Concha talked softly for a few minutes. Then Elaine came into the bedroom. The lamp was still on. Ming watched her slowly open the box on her dressing table, and into it she let fall the white necklace that made a little clatter. Then she closed the box. She began to un-button her shirt, but before she had finished, she flung herself on the bed and stroked Ming's head, lifted his left paw and pressed it gently so that the claws came forth.

'Oh, Ming – Ming,' she said.

Ming recognized the tones of love.

From *The Animal-Lover's Book of Beastly Murder* by Patricia Highsmith, 1975

Old Scumbag

Impervious to pleas and pity,
To tender bribes and winning wiles,
The stratagems of Psycho-Kitty,
Lamb, catnip, scratching post, and smiles,
Charlemagne in his guts and sinews
Detests John still, and John continues
To rave whenever wronged, and flail
His arms around his head, assail
His foe with missiles and invective,
And mutter, 'It's that cat or me,
Liz . . . Lizzie, darling, can't you see
Beyond that mentally defective
Moth-eaten teddy bear to what
A swollen cyst of spite he's got?'

'John, darling, try to understand him.
He's a brave, fine, and useful cat.'
'He'd be more useful if I canned him
For rat food – though I doubt a rat
Could stand the stench – Liz, it's pathetic
That this senescent, enuretic,
Ungrateful flea pad is our pet.
He's had a long life. We should get
Rid of – ' John stops as Liz stares wildly
At his flushed face. She turns to go,
Then, turning back, exclaims, 'You know,
He's always acted pretty mildly
Before you first moved in with me . . .'
'I see.' 'You don't see.' 'Yes I see.

'You cat freaks are, quite simply, crazy.
You'd weep more tears for one lost pet
Than for a flood in Sulawesi.
It serves me right – that's what I get
For thinking I had your affection.
Well, next time, greater circumspection

Is what is called for . . . ' 'Stop it, John –
When you go on and on and on
I love you, but I just can't stand you.
I'm going out to buy some steak
And bread, and take a walk . . . ' 'Well, take
Your anti-nuclear cat to brand you
With Agent Orange – that's a name
More suited to his joyless frame.'

'Good plan. I think I will.' Liz leaves him
To chafe alone against his wrongs.
Suddenly everything aggrieves him:
Cat, house, work, Liz's tuneless songs,
Her tofu-eating, kefir-drinking,
Her 'Darling, what have you been thinking?' –
Quirks that delighted him at first,
Through the months' mill wheels suffer worst
Of all the bills of love discounted –
The bills and coos of dateless love.
Alas, alas, as high above . . .
– To quote – 'As high as we have mounted . . .
(Ah, Wordsworth!) . . . do we sink as low';
And John finds it indeed is so.

These pretty whims that used to rivet
His eyes so fondly on Liz now
Convince him that she's off her pivot.
Why else would she so thwart him? How,
Ignoring clear empirical data
Of felony (which that man-hater,
The miscreant cat, leaves everywhere
From soggy duvet to mauled chair),
Can Liz eschew all objectivity,
All logic, every legal trait,
To justify or mitigate
That scumbag's every vile proclivity?
Could he have known, when first they met,
This amnesty she'd grant her pet?

From *The Golden Gate* by Vikram Seth, 1986

Extremely Provoked

On the whole [Henry James] liked animals, except cats, and owned a succession of dogs, although he was once heard at one of his own tea parties on the lawn at Lamb House to refer to a neighbour's albino Pekingese as 'a positive emetic'. On another occasion, when Henry received some visitors and the conversation flagged, for they were a little shy, one of them praised the canary, which at that time he kept in a cage in the drawing-room. 'Yes, yes,' said the Master, 'the little creature sings his song of adoration each morning with – er – the slightest modicum of encouragement from me'. But he hated cats and would always chase them out of the garden whenever he saw them. He once described to some friends how 'under the extreme provocation of its obscene caterwauling' he had killed one on his lawn. 'The act was followed by nausea and collapse'.

From *Henry James At Home* by H. Montgomery Hyde, 1969

The Scapecat

A memoir of the American writer John Cheever by his daughter

Our family had a cat named Delmore Schwartz, and my father hated him. His descriptions of our household animals and their feelings, as well as his use of voices he attributed to them, were sometimes unusually revealing. His friends and family got letters from the Cheever dogs, complete with hilarious misspellings, describing the family goings-on from their point of view. Other letters almost always mentioned the dogs, whom he loved, or the cats, whom he didn't.

Delmore himself was the unwanted gift of my father's old friend Josie Herbst, who brought him with her when she came for lunch one day in 1960. Josie said the cat was a kitten named Blackie who had been owned by her friend Elizabeth Pollet, the former wife of Delmore Schwartz. My father suspected Josie of lying about the cat's age; he suspected her of unloading an aged, bad-tempered animal on her country friends. The evidence supported him. Blackie the kitten was a large animal with a worn coat and only half a tail. My father made up a past for the cat. Schwartz had locked him in a bathroom for months at a time; he had lost his tail in an accident with a refrigerator door. Blackie was renamed Delmore.

Josie had never made any money, and this kept the edge on her pro-labor 1930s politics. It was the responsibility of the rich to care for the poor, she felt. My father was rich, Delmore was poor. My father accepted this responsibility, but with reluctance. At first, Delmore was used as comic relief. At school in Woodstock, and later at college in Providence, Rhode Island, I got letters from my father about how he had washed the storm windows so well that Delmore had tried to jump through one and folded up like an accordion, or how Delmore had tried to leap from the bathtub to the windowsill and landed in the toilet. Other people's cats caught mice. Delmore sulkily coexisted with the mice and shrews that proliferated in the pantry and the kitchen cupboards. When he did catch a mouse, he was sure to leave it in the bathtub or in one of my father's shoes. Gradually Delmore became a scapegoat as well as a clown. It was Delmore who woke my parents with his angry shrieks at dawn, and who continued to yowl when my father went downstairs, presented him with a breakfast he refused to eat, and finally drop-kicked him out the kitchen door. It was Delmore who left mutilated bird carcasses on the front stairs when the Canfields came over for dinner from Bedford or when the Steegmullers arrived for lunch in their Rolls-Royce. It was Delmore who made a point of relieving himself in the darkest parts of the hallway so that you couldn't see it until you – or a guest – had stepped in it. He even turned up as the sinister black cat in *Bullet Park*. When Hammer's cat comes home smelling of perfume, Hammer follows the scent and the cat into trouble. In 1964, when my father telephoned me at college to say that Delmore was dead, his first words were, 'I want you to know that I didn't have anything to do with it.'

From *Home Before Dark* by Susan Cheever, 1985

President Ceauşescu's Revenge

Dr Theodor Ionescu was the bone surgeon at the Brancovenesc Hospital in Bucharest – as steeped in traditions and as much a part of the city as Bart's in London – who met Ceauşescu when he came to see the earthquake victims in 1977. The hospital treated 30,000 patients a year, handling 50,000 emergency outpatients a year, 200 to 300 emergency patients a day.

But it lay in the path of the Boulevard of Socialist Victory. The doctors in the hospital saw with mounting dismay the demolition of the homes around them, till in 1985 only the hospital stood like an isolated stump in the wasteland.

Dr Ionescu told me: 'One morning, it was a Sunday, without any announcement, he entered the hospital gate. With him was the mayor for this district of Bucharest and his dog, Corbu.' The doctor had heard that Corbu by that time enjoyed the rank of Colonel. 'Of course, there were many Securitate bodyguards around. Inside, there was a discussion about the future of the hospital. While this was going on, Colonel Corbu saw a cat.' The hospital, like many public buildings in Bucharest at the time, was infested with rats, partly because the regime was economising on rat poison. The doctors' response was to resort to nature: the hospital thronged with cats.

'The dog left its master for the cat. The cat skittered off with the dog barking after it. Eventually the dog caught the cat on a doorstep. There was a terrific fight. The dog caught the cat by the neck, but the cat scratched the dog's nose and made it bleed. Ceauşescu's reaction was very violent. He first shouted "Corbu" when it ran away after the cat. Then he started screaming at the bodyguards: "What are you doing standing there? Move!" Three of them ran to split up the dog and cat fighting. Of course, all three of them ended up being scratched to pieces. Corbu came back with blood on its nose. Ceauşescu hit the dog with his fist. It was a moment of despair, because his closest companion had left him for a cat.

'Ceauşescu was very furious. He turned around and left. The bodyguard who looked after the dog picked up Corbu and took him to Elias Hospital.' (This was the one of the best hospitals in Bucharest, the preserve of the party's sick.) 'That afternoon a Securitate car came around, with three bodyguards, to look for the cat. The three Securitate men were very desperate to find the cat because they were afraid they would lose their jobs. So the whole hospital started to look for the cat. All the administration, all the nurses and the porters looked up and down, searched high and low. They caught lots of cats and brought them in front of the three Securitate men and the director of the hospital. But there were so many cats in the hospital. They couldn't find the right one. Cat after cat after cat was caught and shown to them – but it wasn't the right one. At 10.30 that night, having searched all afternoon and most of the evening, they found the right cat. They knew it was the right one because it had a tear on its skin where Corbu had bitten it. The carpenter of the hospital made a special cage. While he was doing so the cat was put in an emergency room and looked after by a special bodyguard. The cat was guarded all night and in the morning she was fed and watered. Usually,' the doctor said, 'we didn't feed the cats. Then the cat went in the special cage to the Institute of Veterinary Medicine. After two weeks we received a note from the Institute of Veterinary Medicine saying the cat had been checked for disease but was all right. In those two weeks Corbu was not allowed to go anywhere near Ceauşescu. But even though the cat was all right, we knew that this fight between the dog and the cat meant the end of the hospital.'

The bulldozers came when Ceauşescu was on a trip to North Korea. In three days they demolished the hospital, its wards, its gardens, its traditions and memories and an exquisite marble staircase. The staircase had been built by the hospital's founder, a nineteenth-century Romanian aristocrat called Grigore Constantin Brancoveanu, who had promoted something of a cultural renaissance in the country in the 1840s. The hospital had an inscription, set in marble, bearing the legend: 'Who endangers this hospital will be cast out from the love of God.'

From *The Life and Evil Times of Nicolae Ceauşescu* by John Sweeney, 1991

A Change of Heart

Part of a letter from Sir Walter Scott to Lord Montagu,
dated 14 March 1822

The greatest advance of age which I have yet found is liking a *cat* an animal I detested & becoming fond of a garden an art which I despised but I suppose the indulgent mother nature has pets and hobby horses suited to her children of all ages.

From *Letters of Sir Walter Scott 1821-1823*

Eight

LOVE

Jeoffry

Christopher Smart's consideration of his cat Jeoffry is, like Jeoffry himself, a wild but loving mixture of gravity and waggery. The poem in which it appears, Jubilate Agno, *was written in about 1760 while poor mad Smart was in Bedlam, but not discovered and published until 1939.*

For I will consider my Cat Jeoffry.

For he is the servant of the Living God duly and daily serving him.

For at the first glance of the glory of God in the East he worships in his way.

For is this done by wreathing his body seven times round with elegant quickness.

For then he leaps up to catch the musk, which is the blessing of God upon his prayer.

For he rolls upon prank to work it on.

For having done duty and received blessing he begins to consider himself.

For this he performs in ten degrees.

For first he looks upon his fore-paws to see if they are clean.

For secondly he kicks up behind to clear away there.

For thirdly he works it upon stretch with the fore paws extended.

For fourthly he sharpens his paws by wood.

For fifthly he washes himself.

For Sixthly he rolls upon wash.

For Seventhly he fleas himself, that he may not be interrupted upon the beat.

For Eighthly he rubs himself against a post.

For Ninthly he looks up for his instructions.

For Tenthly he goes in quest of food.

For having consider'd God and himself he will consider his neighbour.

For if he meets another cat he will kiss her in kindness.

For when he takes his prey he plays with it to give it chance.

For one mouse in seven escapes by his dallying.

For when his day's work is done his business more properly begins.

For he keeps the Lord's watch in the night against the adversary.

For he counteracts the powers of darkness by his electrical skin and glaring eyes.

For he counteracts the Devil, who is death, by brisking about the life.

For in his morning orisons he loves the sun and the sun loves him.

For he is of the tribe of Tiger.

For the Cherub Cat is a term of the Angel Tiger.

For he has the subtlety and hissing of a serpent, which is goodness he suppresses.

For he will not do destruction, if he is well-fed, neither will he spit without provocation.

For he purrs in thankfulness, when God tells him he's a good Cat.

For he is an instrument for the children to learn benevolence upon.

For every house is incompleat without him and a blessing is lacking in the spirit.

For the Lord commanded Moses concerning the cats at the departure of the Children of Israel from Egypt.

For every family had one cat at least in the bag.

For the English Cats are the best in Europe.

For he is the cleanest in the use of his fore-paws of any quadrupede.

For the dexterity of his defence is an instance of the love of God to him exceedingly.

For he is the quickest to his mark of any creature.

For he is tenacious of his point.

For he is a mixture of gravity and waggery.

For he knows that God is his Saviour.

For there is nothing sweeter than his peace when at rest.

For there is nothing brisker than his life when in motion.

For he is of the Lord's poor and so indeed is he called by benevolence perpetually – Poor Jeoffry! poor Jeoffry! the rat has bit thy throat.

For I bless the name of the Lord Jesus that Jeoffry is better.

For the divine spirit comes about his body to sustain it in compleat cat.

For his tongue is exceeding pure so that it has in purity what it
      wants in musick.
For he is docile and can learn certain things.
For he can set up with gravity which is patience upon
      approbation.
For he can fetch and carry, which is patience in employment.
For he can jump over a stick which is patience upon proof
      positive.
For he can spraggle upon waggle at the word of command.
For he can jump from an eminence into his master's bosom.
For he can catch the cork and toss it again.
For he is hated by the hypocrite and miser.
For the former is affraid of detection.
For the latter refuses the charge.
For he camels his back to bear the first notion of business.
For he is good to think on, if a man would express himself neatly.
For he made a great figure in Egypt for his signal services.
For he killed the Ichneumon-rat very pernicious by land.
For his ears are so acute that they sting again.
For from this proceeds the passing quickness of his attention.
For by stroaking of him I have found out electricity.
For I perceived God's light about him both wax and fire.
For the Electrical fire is the spiritual substance, which God sends
      from heaven to sustain the bodies both of man and beast.
For God has blessed him in the variety of his movements.
For, tho he cannot fly, he is an excellent clamberer.
For his motions upon the face of the earth are more than any
      other quadrupede.
For he can tread to all the measures upon the musick.
For he can swim for life.
For he can creep.

From *The Poetical Works of Christopher Smart*, 1980

Jubilate Matteo'

For I rejoice in my cat Matty.

For his coat is variegated in black and brown, with white undersides.

For in every way his whiskers are marvellous.

For he resists the Devil and is completely neuter.

For he sleeps and washes himself and walks warily in the ways of Putney.

For he is at home in the whole district of SW 15.

For in this district the great Yorkshire Murderer ate his last meal before he entered into captivity.

For in the Book of Crime there is no name like John Reginald Halliday Christie.

For Yorkshire indeed excels in all things, as Geoffrey Boycott is the best Batsman.

For the Yorkshire Ripper and the Hull Arsonist have their horns exalted in glory.

For Yorkshire is therefore acknowledged the greatest County.

For Hull was once of the company, that is now of Humberside.

For Sir Leonard Hutton once scored 364 runs in a Test Match.

For Fred Trueman too is a flagrant glory to Yorkshire.

For my cat wanders in the ways of the angels of Yorkshire.

For in his soul God has shown him a remarkable vision of Putney.

For he has also trodden in the paths of the newly fashionable.

For those who live in Gwendolen Avenue cry 'Drop dead, darling!'

For in Cambalt Road and Dealtry Road where the Vet lives there are professional people.

For Erpingham Road and Danemere Street and Dryburgh Road include the intelligentsia.

For in Clarendon Drive the British Broadcasting Corporation is rampant.

For the glory of God has deserted the simple.

For the old who gossiped in Bangalore Road are unknown to the dayspring.

For there is a shortage of the old people who adorned the novels
      of William Trevor.
For in the knowledge of this I cling to the old folk ways of
      Gwalior Road and Olivette Street.
For I rejoice in my cat, who has the true spirit of Putney.

From *Collected Poems 1980-1990* by Gavin Ewart, 1991

'Jeoffrey'

For I will consider my master Christopher
For he also is the servant of the living God
For he yowls at all hours singing psalms
For he is of the house of Asaph the chief musician
For all poets are of the royal household of David
For deprived of ink and paper he scrawls verses on the door of his
      prison with a key
For he prays naked in the rain – but I do not accompany him in this
For I have too much concern for my fur which is the robe of honour
      the Lord has given me
For he has no passion for clean linen, and is lousy
For he could seek better instruction from me in these matters
For maybe he spares his lice out of charity
For the Lord created them from the dust of the earth
For the Lord created Adam from the red clay
For man and louse are brothers before the mercy seat
For he is called Smart for he smarts from the whips of his keepers
For he is called Christopher for he also is a bearer of Christ
Let Smart, house of Smart, rejoice with poor Jeoffrey, his good cat

For the cherub cat is a term of the angel tiger.

From *Cats' Parnassus* by John Heath-Stubbs, 1987

Mr Rich's Busy Pets

*An account of the first meeting between the great eighteenth-century
actress Peg Woffington and the theatre manager John Rich,
'the father of English pantomime'.*

To the residence of John Rich, situated in the then highly fashionable quarter of Bloomsbury Square, the Woffington betook herself,
and demanded an interview with the eccentric manager; but, as she
refused to give her name, she found this was no easy matter to
obtain. According to John Galt, she paid no less than nineteen visits
before she was admitted. At last she told the servant to say Miss
Woffington desired to speak with Mr Rich; when the man returned
with a thousand civil speeches and apologies, and informing her
that his master would see her at once, showed her into his private
apartment. Entering the room, she found the manager lounging on
a sofa, a book in one hand, a china cup, from which he occasionally
sipped tea, in another, whilst around him were seven and twenty
cats, engaged in the various occupations of staring at him, licking
his tea-cup, eating the toast from his mouth, walking round his
shoulders, and frisking about him with the freedom of long-stand-
ing pets.

From *The Life and Adventures of Peg Woffington* by J. Fitzgerald Molloy, 1887

Worshipping Ginger

Though my mother could never teach me to read, she taught me
hymns and poetry by rote, which incited me to write rhymes on my
own account. I had many favourites among cats, dogs and birds, my
mother's reprobation and the servants' nuisance; but I turned them
all to account and wove them into stories, to which I tried to give as
much personal interest as old Mother Hubbard bestowed on her
dog.

The head favourite of my menagerie was a magnificent and very
intelligent cat, 'Ginger,' by name, from the colour of her coat,
which though almost orange was very much admired. She was the

last of a race of cats sacred in the traditions of the Music Hall. Pat Brennan,

'The sad historian of the ruined towers,'

held them in the greatest reverence mingled with superstitious awe. Brennan was a good Catholic, but rather given to exaggeration, which rendered his testimony to matters of fact proverbially questionable; and it became a bye word among unbelieving neighbours when any one told a wonderful story, to ask, 'Do you know Brennan? Well, then, enough said!' After this, there was nothing left for the disconcerted narrator but to walk away. One of his stories was – that the monastic cats had *stings* in their tails, which after their death were preserved by the monks for purposes of flagellation, or by the nuns – Brennan was not sure which!

Ginger was as much the object of my idolatry as if she had had a temple and I had been a worshipper in ancient Egypt; but, like other dieties, she was reprobated by those who were not of my faith.

I made her up a nice little cell, under the beaufet, as side-boards were then called in Ireland – a sort of alcove cut out of the wall of our parlour where the best glass and the family 'bit of plate' – a silver tankard – with the crest of the Hills upon it (a dove with an olive branch in its mouth), which commanded great respect in our family.

Ginger's sly attempt to hide herself from my mother, to whom she had that antipathy which animals so often betray to particular individuals, were a source of great amusement to my little sister and myself; but when she chose the retreat of the beaufet as the scene of her *accouchement*, our fear lest it should come to my mother's knowledge, was as great as if we had been concealing a moral turpitude.

It was a good and pious custom of my mother's to hear us our prayers every night; when Molly tapped at the parlour door at nine o'clock, we knelt at my mother's feet, our four little hands clasped in her's, and our eyes turned to her with looks of love, as they repeated that simple and beautiful invocation, the Lord's Prayer; to this was always added the supplication, 'Lighten our darkness we beseech Thee;' after which we were accustomed to recite a prayer of our affectionate suggestion, calling a blessing on the heads of all we knew and loved, which ran thus, 'God bless papa, mamma, my dear sister, and Molly, and Betty, and Joe, and James, and all our good friends.' One night, however, before my mother could pronounce her solemn 'amen,' a soft muttered 'purr' issued from the cupboard, my heart echoed the appeal, and I added, 'God bless Ginger the cat!' Wasn't my mother shocked! She shook both my shoulders and said, 'What do you mean by that, you stupid child?'

'May I not say, "Bless Ginger?"' I asked humbly.

'Certainly *not*,' said my mother emphatically.

'Why, mamma?'

'Because Ginger is not a Christian.'

'*Why* is not Ginger a Christian?'

'Why? because Ginger is only an animal.'

'Am I a Christian, mamma, or an animal?'

'I will not answer any more foolish questions tonight. Molly, take these children to bed, and do teach Sydney not to ask those silly questions.'

So we were sent off in disgrace, but not before I had given Ginger a wink, whose bright eyes acknowledged the salute through the half-open door.

The result of this was that I tried my hand at a poem.

The jingle of rhyme was familiar to my ear through my mother's constant recitation of verses, from the sublime Universal Prayer of Pope to the nursery rhyme of Little Jack Horner; whilst my father's dramatic citations, which had descended even to the servants, had furnished me with the tags of plays from Shakespeare to O'Keefe; so that 'I lisped in numbers' though the numbers never came.

Here is my first attempt:

> My dear pussy cat,
> Were I a mouse or rat,
>   Sure I never would run off from you,
> You're so funny and gay,
> With your tail when you play,
>   And no song is so sweet as your 'mew;'
> But pray keep in your press,
> And don't make a mess,
>   When you share with your kittens our posset;
> For mamma can't abide you,

And I cannot hide you,
Except you keep close in your closet!

I tagged these doggrels together while lying awake half the night, and as soon as I could get a hearing in the morning I recited them to the kitchen, and no elocution ever pronounced in *that* kitchen (although it was dedicated to Melpomene, whose image shone on an orchestra that had been converted into a dresser, the whole apartment being the remains of the fantastic Ridotto, though now being converted to culinary purposes in the same floor as our dining-room), no elocution had ever excited more applause. James undertook to write it down, and Molly corrected the press. It was served up at breakfast to my father, and it not only procured me his rapturous praise but my mother's forgiveness.

My father took me to Moira House; made me recite my poem, to which he had taught me to add appropriate emphasis and action, to which my own tendency to grimace added considerable comicality. The Countess of Moira laughed heartily at the 'infant Muse' as my father called me, and ordered the housekeeper to send up a large plate of bread and jam, the earliest recompense of my literary labours.

From *Lady Morgan's Memoirs* by Sydney, Lady Morgan, 1862

An Emergency

*Matthew Arnold's love of animals is recalled by his niece,
the novelist Mrs Humphry Ward*

His visits to Russell Square, and our expeditions to Cobham where he lived, in the pretty cottage beside the Mole, are marked in memory with a very white stone. The only drawback to the Cobham visits were the 'dear, dear boys'! – i.e. the dachshunds, Max and Geist, who, however adorable in themselves, had no taste for visitors and no intention of letting such intruding creatures interfere with their possession of their master. One would go down to Cobham, eager to talk to 'Uncle Matt' about a book or an article – covetous at any rate of *some* talk with him undisturbed. And it would all end in a breathless chase after Max, through field after field where the little wretch was harrying either sheep or cows, with the dear poet, hoarse with shouting, at his heels. The dogs were always *in the party*, talked to, caressed, or scolded exactly like spoilt children; and the cat of the house was almost equally dear. Once, at Harrow, the then ruling cat – a tom – broke his leg, and the house was in lamentation. The vet was called in, and hurt him horribly. Then Uncle Matt ran up to town, met Professor Huxley at the Athenaeum, and anxiously consulted him. 'I'll go down with you,' said Huxley. The two travelled back instanter to Harrow, and while Uncle Matt held the cat, Huxley – who had begun life, let it be remembered, as Surgeon to the *Rattlesnake*! – examined him, the two black heads together. There is a rumour that Charles Kingsley was included in the consultation. Finally the limb was put in splints, and left to nature. All went well.

From *A Writer's Recollections* by Mrs Humphry Ward, 1918

Noble Pleasures

It is the misfortune of cats, that they are generally brought into contrast with dogs, whose fidelity, attachment, and sagacity are so often subjects of admiration. But it is obviously unfair to bring into comparison animals differently constituted, and dissimilar both in their pretensions and capabilities. Mankind, in such estimates, are apt, besides, to be influenced by selfish motives, and to applaud those qualities only which minister to their own interest, importance, or gratification. The character of the dog, for example, however admirable in our own eyes, would, *if viewed in a universal spirit*, be open to impeachment. His attachment and fidelity are certainly very gratifying, so far as *we* are concerned; but it cannot be denied, that he is *a traitor to his own order*, and a terror, not to speak of a disgrace, to all his four-footed connexions. He abandons his kind, and becomes the willing slave and fawning parasite of man – ready to wage war with every creature, his own tribe not excepted. There is no indignity, whether of lash or kick, from the hands of his master, to which he will object, and no paltry office, not even that of turnspit, too humiliating for him to fulfil. He will go crouching

[257]

through the fields to point out poor partridges for destruction, and condescend to watch wood-yards with a chain about his neck, as if he had a standing interest in fir deals and splinters! Look if the cat will so far forget her natural dignity, or outrage any of her inherent propensities, for the gratification of man. *She* is connected with royalty, the head of her family being the lion, the king of the forest – and she therefore appropriately leads a luxurious life, having a proper aristocratic indifference to every thing which does not minister to her own pleasure. It must be from her relationship that the adage has arisen, 'A cat may look at a king.'

Like the rest of the nobility, she is much given to hunting, birding, and fishing, but hates all other sorts of exertion. When not engaged in the chase after 'mice and such small deer,' she loiters by the fireside, on chair or sofa, humming a tune, in falsetto voice, or feeling with her paw the length of her whiskers.

From Interesting Anecdotes of the Animal Kingdom by Thomas Brown, 1834

Uncommonly Tender

Soon after she came back to Haworth [in January 1844], in a letter to one of the household in which she had been staying, there occurs this passage: – 'Our poor little cat has been ill two days, and is just dead. It is piteous to see even an animal lying lifeless. Emily is sorry.' These few words relate to points in the characters of the two sisters, which I must dwell upon a little. Charlotte was more than commonly tender in her treatment of all dumb creatures, and they, with that fine instinct so often noticed, were invariably attracted towards her. The deep and exaggerated consciousness of her personal defects – the constitutional absence of hope, which made her slow to trust in human affection, and consequently slow to respond to any manifestation of it – made her manner shy and constrained to men and women, and even to children. We have seen something of this trembling distrust of her own capability of inspiring affection, in the grateful surprise she expresses at the regret felt by her Belgian pupils at her departure. But not merely were her actions kind, her words and tones were ever gentle and caressing, towards animals; and she quickly noticed the least want of care or tenderness on the part of others towards any poor brute creature.

From *The Life of Charlotte Brontë* by Mrs Gaskell, 1857

Ruled by a Tabby

A memoir of the artist Philip Wilson Steer

'Old Pussy Steer', irreverently so-called in our household, had affinities with those pets, susceptible as he was no less to 'magic kindlings' of the senses than to chilly outer airs, and disposed to somnolence when at peace. The sleek, comfortable aloofness of the cats appealed to him, and their dignity, though he may not have imputed the condescension of the proud uncanny creatures to their Egyptian godhead. The reigning tom-cat, accordingly, was a third important member of the household, and Miss Hamilton has furnished a chronicle of the dynasty.

Steer enjoyed the quiet companionship of a cat and used to say that he liked them because they were not sycophants and provided their own boots. He made friends with strolling cats along the streets in Chelsea, talking to them in a special voice. As a child he had his special pussies, the 'Duchess', a tortoiseshell, and her daughter, the 'Countess'. His first attempt to handle oils at an early age was a portrait of the sleeping 'Duchess', and in letters while he was studying abroad were inquiries for his 'Mr Pop'.

It was not until he settled down at Cheyne Walk that he was able to keep a cat of his own in London. In *Hydrangeas* the girl on the sofa is playing with the first Mr Thomas, a black-and-white kitten, much beloved. After its death in 1906 a magnificent tabby was brought up from the country by his niece. This beautiful and sagacious creature ruled Steer for eighteen years. There never was such a cat! He could do no wrong and on the only occasion when he made a hole in his manners by jumping up on a mantelpiece and breaking a Sèvres vase he was forgiven.

When Steer began preparations for his annual outing this cat would become restive and distressed and afterwards mourn his absence, but upon the master's return after three months he was treated with hauteur for days. 'So you left me, did you? – Well then you can get on with it!' A chair was kept for him opposite Steer's. The great creature would leap noiselessly upon the table and contemplate anyone who sat in it with an expression of revolted patience till Steer would say, 'I am afraid you are sitting in Mr Thomas's chair.' I had become the excited possessor of a dubious Monticelli and had taken it round one sunny morning for my uncle's verdict. As he sat contemplating it, in walked the cat and sitting down before the picture, yawned at it. 'Well,' laughed Steer, 'that's all old Thomas thinks of it and I believe he is right!'

He was heartbroken when the great tabby died of influenza in 1924. His last cat died just before the 'blitz'; a powerful striped tabby who hunted seagulls on the mud banks opposite the house. Once when Steer was seriously ill, Tonks with his medically trained mind was horrified to find the cat asleep on the end of Steer's bed, so he shoo'd it out of the room and shut the door. It came in again through another door, and Steer would not have it put out a second time.

An anonymous band-box was once handed in at '109' containing a kitten. Steer guessed that some of the Slade students had sent it to console him for a pet that had died; this touched and pleased him immensely. He was indifferent to dogs, though there was always one of uncertain breed on guard at Cheyne Walk, but they lived downstairs under the care of Mrs Raynes and later of 'Flo'. They were always procured from the milkman, as Mrs Raynes's theory was that only a milkman could supply them.

There was a fresh grievance for the pussy when Steer added to his summer absences visits in the Isle of Wight along with Gray at Easter-time to Dorothy, second wife and widow of Hugh Hammersley. That lady had precisely the qualities of hospitable care without fuss and of easy understanding to make her guest happy and by an exception in his correspondence they became familiarly 'Dot' or 'Dotto' and 'Phil' to one another. In the punctual 'Collins' which did justice to her kindness and her provision in particular for the return journey he writes:

16.4.31

The dog was demonstrative but the cat treated me somewhat coldly but condescended to sleep at the foot of my bed.

[260]

Ron [Ronald Gray] and I arrived home safely on Friday after a delightful visit and I very much enjoyed the peaceful time you provided, which is exactly my idea of a holiday and I think on the whole we were very lucky in the weather as to day here it is dull and raining. To insure a good crossing I retired to the cabin and lay down before the boat started, which much amused Ronny, but I was taking no risks and consequently enjoyed the delicious hard boiled eggs and brown bread and butter which you had so thoughtfully provided, when we got into the train.

On arriving home I found the household struggling with a floor cloth which they had divided down the middle with the economical idea of turning the sides to the centre. I also got a warm welcome from the dog and even, strange to say, from the cat, who I think must have missed the siesta he is sometimes accustomed to take on my knee in the afternoon.

20.4.33

I found my home still standing and all well but was sorry to hear that my dear old cat took my absence to heart and roamed about the house and would not take his food as usual. However all is well now I have returned, but it is depressing to think of the same thing happening when I go away for the summer!

Steer painted the great 'Mr Thomas' as a kitten, playing with the girl's hat in *The Muslin Dress*.

From *Life, Work and Setting of Philip Wilson Steer* by D. S. MacColl, 1945

'Cats and Women'

When I say 'I like cats'
I don't count the ones that look like Zsa Zsa Gabor,
the big fluffy Persians with bad-tempered faces
or most of the cats that win prizes at Cat Shows.
The cats I like are almost always tabbies,
ginger cats or tortoiseshells – or black and white.
Pure black cats too, that were once persecuted
because they were associated with witches . . .

When I say 'I like women'
I don't mean models or Elizabeth Taylor
or any professional beauties in real fur coats
or any of the ones that are in love with themselves.
The women I like don't have elaborate hairstyles
and they're certainly not dyed blondes.
What's more, they're shaped like women
and not like coathangers or stick insects.

From Collected Poems 1980-1990 by Gavin Ewart, 1991

Flattery

It is needless to spend any time over her loving nature to man, how she flattereth by rubbing her skin against one's legs, how she whurleth with her voice, having as many tunes at turnes, for she hath one voice to beg and to complain, another to testify her delight and pleasure, another among her own kind by flattering, by hissing, by puffing, by spitting, in so much that some have thought that they have a peculiar intelligible language among themselves. Therefore how she playeth, leapeth, looketh, catcheth, tosseth with her foot, riseth up to strings held over her head, sometimes creeping, sometimes lying on the back, playing with foot, apprehending greedily anything save the hand of a man, with divers such gestical actions, it is needless to stand upon; in so much as Collins was wont to say, that being free from his studies and more urgent weighty affairs, he was not ashamed to play and sport himself with his cat, and verily it may be called an idle man's pastime.

From The History of Four-Footed Beasts by Edward Topsell, 1658

'Keats and Cats'

An essay by Robert Gittings

The title is not merely for euphony, nor is this a philological essay. It is true that Keats's west-country father possibly sometimes wrote and quite probably often pronounced his name 'Kates', and that in parts of Dorset, curiously close to the spot where Keats last touched English soil on his journey to die in Italy, this version of the name was often spelt with an initial C; but we are dealing with creatures as much as with letters.

Five cats, or groups of cats, can be distinguished in the life of the poet. I shall discuss their general significance and the light it throws on Keats's biography, as well as considering them – the cats – historically and individually; for, like all their kind, they were supremely individual. There is no doubt about the personality displayed by the subject of Keats's splendid exercise in the Miltonic sonnet-form, *To Mrs Reynolds's Cat*.

> Cat! who has past thy Grand Climacteric,
> How many mice and Rats has in thy days
> Destroy'd? – how many tit bits stolen? Gaze
> With those bright languid segments green and prick
> Those velvet ears – but pr'ythee do not stick
> Thy latent talons in me – and upraise
> Thy gentle mew – and tell me all thy frays
> Of Fish and Mice, and Rats and tender chick.
> Nay look not down, nor lick thy dainty wrists –
> For all the weezy Asthma – and for all
> The tail's tip is nicked off – and though the fists
> Of many a Maid have given thee many a maul,
> Still is that fur as soft as when the lists
> In youth thou enter'dst on glass bottled wall.

This poem, dated 16 January 1818 in the fair copy in Keats's hand in the Buffalo and Erie Counnty Public Library, shows Keats devoting all his recent reading in Milton to a noble end. Having been rebuked in the previous summer by his Oxford friend, Benjamin Bailey, for crtiticizing Milton without reading him, Keats had been giving himself a deliberate course of Milton in preparation for his own epic,

Hyperion. By this January he had got deep enough for a parody of Milton, for that is what this poem is. Its opening, 'Cat!' echoes many sonnet-openings by Milton – *Lawrence, Cyriack, Fairfax, Vane*, and *Cromwell*. Its inversions – 'segments green' – , its sonorous phrases – 'Grand Climacteric' – and its triumphant heroic ending exactly catch Milton's manner. Yet, though printed in *The Comic Annual* nine years after Keats's death, it is not merely a comic poem. A portrait emerges, drawn with affection. Keats feels for this battered ten-year-old mog – I take 'Grand Climacteric' to be nine years or so, on the assumption that 1 Cat-year=7 human – much as Rupert Brooke described his own poetic feeling about the greasy old tramp; this portrait of the cat, wheezily purring and 'making bread' with its latent talons on the poet's lap, may uncover a deep truth about Keats's life. From adolescence onward, Keats had never had a real home of his own, and he himself recognized this orphaned state as a misfortune. He was the perpetual visitor to other people's houses, the person on whom the family cat, after a cautious survey, jumps up and settles down by the fireside.

Hence Keats's biography can be mapped in what may be termed Cat-phases, periods of calm and home-seeking by other people's hearts alternating with the restless fever of personal turmoil and travel. Mrs Reynolds's cat initiates the first recorded instance of these phases, in a house in Little Britain, the home of George Reynolds, the writing-master of Christ's Hospital and father of the poet's friend John Hamilton Reynolds. It sets off a whole cluster of cat images, allusions and phrases in Keats's letters, at a time of great mental activity when he was writing 'many songs & Sonnets'. A week later, he wrote of his friend James Rice, who never allowed ill-health to interfere with his enjoyment of life, that 'he always comes on his Legs like a Cat'. On 14 February, he copies with approval an extract from the manuscript lent to him by the author, Horace Smith, of *Nehemiah Muggs*, a Hudibras-like satire on Methodists:

> Or is it that a heated brain
> When it is rubbed against the grain,
> Like a Cat's back though black as charcoal
> Will in the gloom appear to sparkle.

On 13 March from Teignmouth, where he had gone to nurse his younger brother Tom, he wrote light-heartedly to Bailey:

So you must not stare if in any future letter I endeavour to prove
that Appollo as he had a cat gut string to his Lyre used a cats' paw as
a Pecten –

while on 8 April he notes as a certain sign of the coming Spring that
'Cats are becoming more vociferous'. Nor were these merely in-
cidental prose remarks. On 25 March, in a long verse-epistle to
John Hamilton Reynolds, he begins with a catalogue of 'Things all
disjointed', such as:

Two witch's eyes above a cherub's mouth

and to these he adds:

Old Socrates a tying his cravat;
And Hazlitt playing with Miss Edgworth's cat;

Maria Edgeworth, we know, was a cat-lover; the restless Hazlitt,
we can infer from this line, was not.

Keats himself now enters a restless and disturbed period, during
which there is no room in his life for cats, and very little for poetry
either. His other brother George decided to marry and to emigrate
to North America; Keats, at this prospect of a further break-up in
the family circle, decided to see George off at Liverpool, and proceed north on a walking-tour of the Lakes and Scotland with his
Hampstead friend Charles Brown. On his return, he was plunged
into almost continuous nursing of his brother Tom, who died on 1
December 1818. These events gave him no time for cats; but when
Charles Brown invited the bereaved poet to share his part of Wentworth Place, Hampstead, next door to their mutual friends, Mr and
Mrs Charles Dilke, the familiar domestic influence was soon at
work again, with the result that may be seen in Keats's letter of 3
January 1819 to his brother and sister-in-law:

Mrs Dilke has two Cats – a Mother and a Daughter – now the
Mother is a tabby and the daughter a black and white like the
spotted child – Now it appears ominous to me for the doors of both
houses are opened frequently – so that there is a complete thorough
fare for both Cats (there being no board up to the contrary) they
may one and several of them come into my room ad libitum. But no
– the Tabby only comes – whether from sympathy from ann the
maid or me I can not tell – or whether Brown has left behind him

[265]

any atmosphere spirit of Maidenhood I can not tell. The Cat is not an old Maid herself – her daughter is a proof of it – I have questioned her – I have look'd at the lines of her paw – I have felt her pulse – to no purpose – why should the *old* Cat come to me? I ask myself – and myself has not a word to answer.

There is a distinct air of mystery, felt by Keats himself, about the situation he describes; we can only make a guess at its cause in the recesses of his unconscious mind. The clue might be found in the repeated presence next door of Mrs Brawne and her daughter Fanny. Keats twice mentions having a tiff with Fanny at this time, but he was evidently strongly attracted by her, and he found her mother 'a very nice woman'. Is there an overtone in 'Why should the *old* Cat come to me?' in this recital of mother and daughter? These are deep psychological waters indeed.

There is nothing fanciful or introvert about Keats's next encounter with a cat in the following month of February 1819. He was then at the height of his powers, having just written *The Eve of St Agnes* and the beautiful fragment *The Eve of St Mark*, which incidentally contains a picture, worked on a tapestry screen, of a 'silken-furr'd Angora cat'. This new cat, though anonymous, provides perhaps the most famous tribute to the poet's character. It is first mentioned eleven years later in a letter from George Keats to Charles Dilke. Citing Keats's alliance of ready sympathy with manly qualities, George wrote:

You will remember the tale of his fight with a scoundrel in Livery in a blind Alley at hampstead about cruelty to a cat –

This statement by George, who had his brother's gift of oracular utterance without his genius, remained unconfirmed until 1845, when Joseph Severn, providing notes for Monckton Milnes's biography of Keats, added to them, with characteristic casualness, the afterthought:

His fighting with the butcher.

Were the 'scoundrel in Livery' and this butcher the same? A year later, Charles Cowden Clarke gave the answer:

[266]

When I last saw him (March 1819) he was in fine health and spirits; and he told me that he had, not long before our meeting had an encounter with a fellow who was tormenting a kitten, or puppy, and who was big enough to have eaten him: that they fought for nearly an hour; and that his opponent was led home. He used to be pointed out as 'the little fellow who licked the butcher-boy'.

The interpolation 'or puppy' can be discounted. Clarke often elsewhere gets the main story right, but adds details that prove to be inaccurate. The point of the story as an indication of Keats's character was quite missed by Leigh Hunt when he wrote in his biography (1850):

He once chastized a butcher, who had been insolent, by a regular stand-up fight.

'Who had been insolent' – personal insult had little or no effect on Keats. When insulted at the theatre in Teignmouth, he took no notice. What moved him was injury done to the weak and helpless. George Keats had first mentioned the cat as an illustration of John's general character:

John was open, prodigal, and had no power of calculation whatever. John's eyes moistened, and his lips quivered at the relation of any tale of generosity, of benevolence or noble daring, or at sights of loveliness or distress – he had no fears of self thro interference in the quarrels of others; he would at all hazzards, without calculating his power to defend, or his reward for the deed, defend the oppressed and distressed with heart and soul, with hand and purse.

Yet soon after this noble incident, life was to enter into one of its restless phases for Keats. It is perhaps a portent of this that early in April 1819, the Dilkes and their comforting cats left Wentworth Place for Westminster. Their place was taken by Fanny Brawne and her mother, whose dog, Carlo, is described by Keats at a later date as a somewhat overbearing character. However, one should not insist slavishly on any cat-versus-dog theme in Keats's life, particularly as cats were still in his mind when on May 1st he used them to make a joke to his sister Fanny about the wife of her unlikeable guardian, Abbey, in his verses for her, *Two or Three:*

Two or three Cats
And two or three mice
Two or three sprats
At a very great price –
Two or three sandies
And two or three tabbies
Two or three dandies –
And two Mrs – mum!

It is worth remembering that these verses, with their persistent cat-theme, were perhaps written on the same day as the *Ode to a Nightingale*. Now restless and catless days were to ensue. Brown had let his part of Wentworth Place for the summer. Keats was in money difficulties. The summer was spent in rootless lodgings in the Isle of Wight and Winchester, writing for money. Autumn was a time of growing illness and love-difficulties. His calmest port of call was 3 Romney Street, Westminster, where he often dined with Mrs Wylie, George's mother-in-law. His descriptions of her household are more cheerful than the general tenor of his letters at this time, and some possible cause may be indicated by a letter to George's wife of 28 January 1820, after he had been helping her mother to pack some parcels to America for her:

> Thinking you might want a Ratcatcher I put your mother's old quaker-colour'd Cat into the top of your bonnet – she's wi' kitten, so you may expect to find a whole family – I hope the family will not grow too large for its lodging.

This cheerful fancy contrasts with the purposeless uncreative life Keats felt himself to be leading as disease overtook him. Even his poetic judgement seemed impaired in the long and generally unsuccessful comic poem, *The Cap and Bells*, with which he occupied his days, though there is a flash of relief here. In stanza xxxv, l. 315, Keats permitted one of his characters to utter the threat:

> or I will kill your Cat.

It is clear what inroads disease had made on the poet's judgement; but not so much that he did not retrieve such an error of taste by substituting a lame but quite innocuous half-line in the manuscript, shortly before his fatal illness made itself finally manifest.

This brief cat's-eye view of Keats's biography is, of course, a partial one, but it contains, I think, a truth. Keats was an essentially home-loving and domestic person, deprived at an early age. He found himself the perpetual visitor in other people's houses, and though he seemed to have no hope of a settled home for himself – 'god forbid we should what people call, *settle*' he wrote to Fanny Brawne – he appreciated the amenities of a household and was appreciated by them. To the chief of these amenities, cats, he paid tribute in poetry and prose, and they paid him the compliment of their evident attention.

Five cats or groups of cats were numbered at the beginning of this essay, and I must not be thought to have forgotten the last. Joseph Severn, who sailed with Keats to Italy, wrote to their 'oak friend' Haslam on 17 September 1820, the day he and Keats boarded the *Maria Crowther* in London Docks, 'We were soon reconsiled to every thing about, from the Captain down to his Cat', and though both Keats and Severn afterwards criticized the Captain, there is no word of criticism of the cat. Unfortunately Severn's journal of the voyage, except for one brief sheet now in the Keats-Shelley House at Rome, seems to have disappeared: a great loss, not the least because we might have learnt from it whether the hardship of the poet's last voyage was softened by the helpful presence of one of those gentler influences upon his life and work.

From *Essays and Studies*, 1962

Infinite Variety

An account of the childhood of Margaret Mitchell,
the author of Gone With The Wind

The girl had other passions. She adored all animals and kept a regular menagerie. Besides horses and ponies in the stable out back, and a cow in the vacant field, the family zoo included dogs, ducks, turtles, and, at one time, even two alligators. She may or may not have played with dolls, but 'an infinite variety of cats' allowed her every opportunity for playing house and mother. Cat tales run through every account of her childhood, and afterward she recalled her 'long suffering' mother's toleration of her pets. The animals thronged the house and yard and charmed her when all else failed. When teary at a portrait session, the three-year-old lit up when the photographer produced a tiny kitten. 'On this occasion she was led to believe it was the cat's picture that was desired, not hers, and she was delighted to assist.' In the tall pine tree in the sideyard where she and Stephens had built a treehouse, she rigged up a wicker elevator for hauling Piedy's progeny up to her perch – much to the animals' annoyance, according to Stephens. After Piedy died, Hypatia and Lowpatia joined the household. The latter won fame for a special trick: 'Margaret taught him to stand up and salute with his right paw beside his ear. When he performed this in a proper military manner, he was rewarded by being fed cantaloup, his favorite delicacy.'

From *Southern Daughter: The Life of Margaret Mitchell*
by Darden Asbury Pyron, 1991

A Feline Opiate

Every visitor to Hanover Terrace [Sir Edmund Gosse's house] will remember Caruso; he figured at meals on a chair beside Gosse, and was always to be found in his vicinity when he was reading or at work in his library. Like Bayle's friend, Mlle Dupuy, who attributed her skill in playing the harp to 'the critical taste' of her favourite cat, Gosse seemed to draw some opiate quality for his nerves from the very proximity of Caruso, and his predecessors and successors. The serenity and majestic indifference, the padded paws and noiseless step, the green eyes set in jet black fur with their grave regard, seemed to communicate calm and subdue agitation. Even Gosse's conversation would assume a more intimate and serene quality if it was accompanied by the purring of Caruso or in later years of his successor Buchanan. In his essay on cats Gosse, quoting Paradis de Moncrif, relates the story of 'Mahomet who, being consulted one day on a point of piety, preferred to cut off his sleeve on which his favourite pussy was asleep, rather than wake her violently by rising.' Modern sartorial conditions would frustrate any such operation, but it was a gesture with which Gosse would have sympathised. He would deprecate interruptions which involved readjustments in his cat's scheme of inertia. In his household there was none of the outrageous tyranny exercised by favourite dogs, but the rights of a constitutional sovereignty were assigned to the cat, and his sway accepted within legitimate limits. Occasionally there was protest, as is evident from a letter written in 1915 to John Drinkwater, who was ill at the time and who owned a cat named Punch. 'I hope you will take the greatest possible care of yourself, and obey Dr Punch, whose expressed view I know to be that you should stay in bed and make warm corners in the coverlid for him to fold his paws into. There I envy you, for instead of seeing that pansy face smile and purr up at me, I have to endure the fierce contempt and sneering malice of Caruso, without any question the most ungenerous cat in Christendom. There is no doubt that he is a German at heart, and he rules us on the system of "frightfulness." There is a theory that the atrocious soul of Nietzsche has entered into him.' But Caruso was only one in a line of succession, which was never suffered to lapse or to know a vacant throne. Théophile Gautier divided his affection between cats and the singular choice of white rats; Gosse favoured no other species of domestic animal, but like Chateaubriand and Victor Hugo, like Baudelaire and Sainte-Beuve, gave his undivided preference to cats.

From *The Life and Letters of Sir Edmund Gosse* by the Hon. Evan Charteris, KC, 1931

The Pets of Gentlemen

*When H. P. Lovecraft was a boy, he was devastated by
the disappearance of his black cat, Nigger-Man.*

What a boy he was! I watched him grow from a tiny black handful to one of the most fascinating & understanding creatures I've ever seen. He used to talk in a genuine language of varied intonations – a special tone for every different meaning. There was even a special 'prrr'p' for the smell of roast chestnuts, on which he doted. He used to play ball with me – kicking a large rubber sphere back at me from half across the room with all four feet as he lay on the floor.

And on summer evenings in the twilight he would prove his kinship to the elfin things of shadow by racing across the lawn on nameless errands, darting into the blackness of the shrubbery now & then, & occasionally leaping at me from ambush & then bounding away again into invisibility before I could catch him.

Lovecraft, who achieved some fame as a writer of 'weird tales', never kept another pet. However,

he made friends with all the neighbourhood cats wherever he lived and got them in the habit of calling on him by keeping catnip mice for them to play with. He lavishly praised their beauty, grace, self-sufficiency, and other supposed aristocratic qualities: 'Dogs, then, are peasants and the pets of peasants, cats are gentlemen and the pets of gentlemen.' When he visited [a friend,] and a kitten went to sleep in his lap, he sat up all night rather than disturb the animal.

In 1934 he wrote a verse on the death of one of the 'neighbourhood cats', a much-loved kitten named Sam Perkins:

The ancient garden seems at night
A deeper gloom to bear,
As if some silent shadow's blight
Were hov'ring in the air.

With hidden griefs the grasses sway,
Unable quite to word them –
Remembering from yesterday
The little paws that stirred them.

From *Lovecraft: A Biography* by L. Sprague de Camp, 1976

'The Happy Cat'

The cat's asleep, I whisper *kitten*
Till he stirs a little and begins to purr –
He doesn't wake. Today out on the limb
(The limb he thinks he can't climb down from)

He mewed until I heard him in the house.
I climbed up to get him down: he mewed.
What he says and what he sees are limited.
My own response is even more constricted.
I think, 'It's lucky; what you have is too.'
What do you have except – well, me?
I joke about it but it's not a joke:
The house and I are all he remembers.
Next month how will he guess that it is winter
And not just entropy, the universe
Plunging at last into its cold decline?
I cannot think of him without a pang.
Poor rumpled thing, why don't you see
That you have no more, really, than a man?
Men aren't happy: why are you?

From *The Complete Poems* by Randall Jarrell, 1971

Antonia White's Fur Bundle

If ever Mother was out when I was at home, I used to take the opportunity to play the piano, since there was no fear of disturbing her. I had not been able to resist buying a piano score of *The Consul* [an opera by Gian Carlo Menotti] and was dying to see if any of the arias that had been haunting me had easy accompaniments. I had found one I could sight-read, and was beginning to learn it, when Sue came in and sat beside me. We were in full throat in the middle of Magda's lilting aria 'Yes, yes, yesterday' when Mother burst into the room. She had mistaken the date of the meeting and made the journey to Roehampton in vain. Seeing us two sisters happily singing together was apparently more than she could bear.

She grabbed Domina, the over-fed cat who had never been out of doors – except for the time she fell out of the window – and set off down the stairs with Domina under her arm, murmuring, 'No one cares about me except the poor puss-cat.'

The flat door slammed behind her. We were sure she would come straight back, but she didn't. We went to look out of the window, just in time to see her small figure disappearing down

Harrington Gardens with the fur bundle struggling in her arms. We looked at each other aghast: Was this serious? Might she be heading for the river as in the Tom days?

We telephoned the Glossops. 'Now don't you worry, Lynnie!' Silas reassured me. 'Tony isn't going to harm herself. She'll come home as soon as she realises what a damn fool she's being. The best thing is for you and Sue to come straight over and we'll have dinner as planned.'

Relieved that we need not worry, Sue went to run herself a bath and get changed, and I went back to playing the piano. Suddenly I heard footsteps on the stairs and called Sue. Mother walked past us looking demented. Her arms were bloody from scratches but she was reassuring the petrified cat she loved only it in the world. I plucked up all my courage to ask, 'But Mother, what's the matter?' She seemed not to hear and went over to a cupboard and began ferreting around until she found a cat-basket. She shoved the protesting Domina into it and set off downstairs again, ignoring my second question, 'Where are you going, Mother?'

As she was about to go out of the flat door something made Mother look up suddenly. She turned round, and rushed back upstairs. She went straight to the bathroom which was above the stairs. We followed. The room was flooded and water was pouring over the edge of the bath-tub. As she turned off the taps, she bellowed, 'Susan, *your* doing I presume!'

The old Antonia was back in full force. The three of us spent the next ten minutes mopping up the bathroom floor while Domina yowled furiously from inside the basket. Then Antonia liberated her ally, made herself a cup of tea and went up to her work-room and shut the door without addressing a further word to us.

From *Nothing to Forgive: A Daughter's Life of Antonia White*
by Lyndall P. Hopkinson, 1988

'Addition and Subtraction'

In our world, where there are more and more faces, more and more alike, it is difficult for an individual to reinforce the originality of the self and to become convinced of its inimitable uniqueness.

There are two methods for cultivating the uniqueness of the self: the method of *addition* and the method of *subtraction*. Agnes subtracts from her self everything that is exterior and borrowed, in order to come closer to her sheer essence (even with the risk that zero lurks at the bottom of the subtraction). Laura's method is precisely the opposite: in order to make her self ever more visible, perceivable, seizable, sizeable, she keeps adding to it more and more attributes and she attempts to identify herself with them (with the risk that the essence of the self may be buried by the additional attributes).

Let's take her cat as an example. After her divorce, Laura remained alone in a large apartment and felt lonely. She longed for a pet to share her solitude. First she thought of a dog, but soon realized that a dog needed the kind of care she would be unable to provide. And so she got a cat. It was a big Siamese cat, beautiful and wicked. As she lived with the cat and regaled her friends with stories about it, the animal that she had picked more or less by accident, without any special conviction (after all, her first choice was a dog!), took on an ever growing significance: she began to lavish praise on her pet and forced everyone to admire it. She saw in the cat a superb independence, pride, freedom of action and constancy of charm (so different from human charm, which is always spoiled by moments of clumsiness and unattractiveness); in the cat, she saw her paradigm; in the cat, she saw herself.

It is not at all important whether Laura's nature resembled that of a cat or not, the important thing is that she made the cat part of her coat of arms and that the cat (love for the cat, apologies for the cat) became one of the attributes of her self. From the beginning, many of her lovers were irritated by this egocentric and evil animal, which would spit and scratch for no apparent reason, and so the cat became an acid test of Laura's power; as if she wanted to tell everyone: you can have me, but the way I really am, and that includes the cat. The cat became the image of her soul, and a lover had to accept her soul if he wished to have her body.

The method of addition is quite charming if it involves adding to the self such things as a cat, a dog, roast pork, love of the sea or of cold showers. But the matter becomes less idyllic if a person decides to add love for communism, for the homeland, for Mussolini, for Roman Catholicism or atheism, for fascism or anti-fascism.

In both cases the method remains exactly the same: a person stubbornly defending the superiority of cats over other animals is doing basically the same thing as one who maintains that Mussolini was the sole saviour of Italy: he is proud of this attribute of the self and he tries to make this attribute (a cat or Mussolini) acknowledged and loved by everyone.

Here is that strange paradox to which all people cultivating the self by way of the addition method are subject: they use addition in order to create a unique, inimitable self, yet because they automatically become propagandists for the added attributes, they are actually doing everything in their power to make as many others as possible similar to themselves; as a result, their uniqueness (so painfully gained) quickly begins to disappear.

We may ask ourselves why a person who loves a cat (or Mussolini) is not satisfied to keep his love to himself, and wants to force it on others. Let us seek the answer by recalling the young woman in the sauna, who belligerently asserted that she loved cold showers. She thereby managed to differentiate herself at once from one half of the human race, namely the half that prefers hot showers. Unfortunately, that other half now resembled her all the more. Alas, how sad! Many people, few ideas, so how are we to differentiate ourselves from each other? The young woman knew only one way of overcoming the disadvantage of her similarity to that enormous throng devoted to cold showers: she had to proclaim her credo 'I adore cold showers!' as soon as she appeared in the door of the sauna and to proclaim it with such fervour as to make the millions of other women who also enjoy cold showers seem like imitations of herself. Let me put it another way: a mere (simple and innocent) love for showers can become an attribute of the self only on condition that we let the world know we are ready to fight for it.

The one who chooses as an attribute of the self a love for Mussolini becomes a political warrior, while the partisan of cats, music or antique furniture bestows gifts on his surroundings.

From *Immortality* by Milan Kundera, translated by Peter Kussi, 1991

A Leak in the Loft

*While hiding from the Nazis in the secret annexe of her family's
house in Amsterdam, Anne Frank found great consolation
in the company of her cat, Mouschi.*

Wednesday, 10th May, 1944

Dear Kitty,

We were sitting in the attic doing some French yesterday afternoon when I suddenly heard water pattering down behind me. I asked Peter what it could be, but he didn't even reply, simply tore up to the loft, where the source of the disaster was, and pushed Mouschi, who, because of the wet earth box, had sat down beside it, roughly back to the right place. A great din and disturbance followed, and Mouschi, who had finished by that time, dashed downstairs.

Mouschi, seeking the convenience of something similar to his box, had chosen some wood shavings. The pool had trickled down from the loft into the attic immediately and, unfortunately, landed just beside and in the barrel of potatoes. The ceiling was dripping, and as the attic floor is not free from holes either, several yellow drips came through the ceiling into the dining-room between a pile of stockings and some books, which were lying on the table. I was doubled up with laughter, it really was a scream. There was Mouschi crouching under a chair, Peter with water, bleaching powder and floorcloth, and Van Danan trying to soothe everyone. The calamity was soon over, but it's a well known fact that cats' puddles positively stink. The potatoes proved this only too clearly and also the wood shavings, that Daddy collected in a bucket to be burned. Poor Mouschi! How were you to know that peat is unobtainable?

Yours, Anne

From *The Diary of Anne Frank*, 1947
translated by B. M. Moyaart-Doubleday

Ecstatic Mania

The composer Peter Warlock, whose real name was Philip Heseltine, was a man of wild, unbridled appetites – not the least of which was his passion for cats, as his biographer records.

The most important members of the household at Eynsford, both in status and number, were cats – cats masculine, feminine, and neuter: cats young, old, and middle-aged: cats of all sizes, breeds, and colours. Cats had always been one of the ruling passions of his life, and it was one that grew in intensity as the years went on until it almost became a mania with him. It was not confined to individual specimens but extended to the entire species. The Small Cat House in the Zoo was one of his favourite haunts, and every year he attended the Cat Show at the Crystal Palace with an almost religious fervour, exhorting others to go and do likewise. 'You must go to the cat show at the Crystal Palace to-morrow,' he wrote me once, 'which is the last day. I spent an ecstatic couple of hours there to-day. Such lovely mogs you can't imagine – including the best cat in the world, surely – an immense short-haired grey; also the heaviest cat in England which, though physically stoneless, weighs, by a curious chance, two stones.'

He had a special vocabulary for defining the various grades of feline excellence, beginning with 'pussum' and culminating in MOG – the supreme cat, the Platonic cat, the cat in the mind of God, the Great One of the Night of Time. His conception of the ideal cat underwent several changes at different periods; the authentic mog at the time when I first knew him was a gigantic black, and as we see from this letter it was later a short-haired grey. But in the last years the supreme object of his adoration was that exceptional rarity known as the 'self-red', of which, indeed, only a few specimens exist. In his consuming ambition to possess a specimen himself he followed up clues to their existence all over the country. I have known him to journey to the other end of London with the sole purpose of seeing one of which he had heard, and to leap off a bus going at full speed, into the middle of the crowded traffic, at the sight of a reddish-hued cat which we had passed, in order to ascertain whether it was of the authentic variety for which he was seeking. Truly, Moby Dick, the White Whale of Herman Melville, was not pursued with greater ardour and tenacity by Captain Ahab than the Great Mog, the Red Cat, was by Philip. In the end he succeeded in finding it, but, as with Captain Ahab, it was indeed the end; the self-red survived his master, but not for long.

On settling at Eynsford Philip threw off every vestige of the restraint that had hitherto governed these proclivities, and both through acquisition and the normal processes of nature the feline population increased by leaps and bounds. On one occasion I remember him waking up one morning to find a litter of newly born kittens on his chest – an event which he declared to be a highly auspicious omen.

It is related of Antonio Sacchini, an Italian composer of the eighteenth century, that he was unable to write music unless surrounded by cats and mistresses, and Peter Warlock must surely have possessed some secret affinity to this 'graceful, elegant and judicious composer', as Burney calls him, for in addition to the vast number of cats on the premises there was always a steady and abundant supply of the latter commodity also.

Warlock committed suicide in December 1930, aged 36. The last thing he did before gassing himself was to put out the cat, as a neighbour testified at the inquest.

The Coroner. You looked into the yard and saw a kitten? – Yes, I did not know they had a cat. I heard the little thing crying. Apparently Mr Warlock had put some food out. The poor little thing was terrified.

You suggested that he might have let the cat out? – Yes, he must have thought about the cat.

If Mr Heseltine took his own life, you could not throw any light on it? – Nothing at all.

From *Peter Warlock: A Memoir of Philip Heseltine* by Cecil Gray, 1934

A Final Request

In the mornings, nowadays, George Harvey Bone was awakened by a fluffy white cat belonging to the hotel. At about seven o'clock he would hear a little cry – petulant rather than appealing – outside his door, and he would blunder out of bed in the darkness and open the door. He would blunder back into bed and hear no more.

Then there would be a sudden springy soft weight on his body, and the cat would begin to manoeuvre near his head. Sleepy as he was, he could put out his hand and stroke its fur.

After a while this motion seemed to generate an electrical disturbance within the animal – an aeroplane-like throbbing, slowly growing in volume and drawing nearer – the purring of the cat in his ear. The purring, this surrender of its being to a rhythmic and externally audible throbbing, in its turn seemed to induce in the cat a sort of frenzy, a frenzy manifesting itself mainly in its front paws, which, in an agony of restless pleasure, stretched and relaxed, the right paw stretching while the left relaxed, and the other way about, in eager alternation. George called this 'playing the piano'. He did not know the name of the cat so he called it 'Pussy'. 'Don't make such a noise, Pussy,' the big drinking man would gently murmur in the darkness. 'And stop playing the piano.' But the cat would not stop until a place had been found under the bedclothes near George's head: then it would go to sleep, and George would attempt to do the same.

But usually it would be too late, and in a few moments he would be wide awake, grinding out the problems of his life, delving into the night before to see where he had got to exactly, where he had left off. This morning he knew, because of the sickness in his heart, and the giddiness in his head, that he had got drunk, but he couldn't at first remember how or where . . .

Disappointed in love, drunk and desolate, Bone murders two friends who have betrayed him and then travels to Maidenhead in search of salvation. Failing to find it, he decides to kill himself.

He went into the High Street and asked a policeman where he might find rooms, and the policeman directed him to a mean street where he found an 'apartments' sign and got a room with a gas-ring on the top floor front after giving up his last ten shillings as deposit. He had now only one and sevenpence left. He slept on the bed in his shirt till two o'clock in the afternoon, missing the cat. 'I'd have brought you here, pussy,' he whispered to the sheets, 'if only I'd known it was no good.'

He went out and had coffee and a bun at 'The Olde Tea Shoppe' in the High Street, which cost him fivepence. He then bought a packet of writing paper and envelopes from Smith's, a pencil and five newspapers. They were all about the sinking of the *Athenia*. He was sorry for everybody. Then he took a long walk along the river, returning at about six, and having a cup of tea at the same place. Then, completely penniless, he went back to his room and slept until it was dark.

Then he rose and lit the gas, and sat down in its dim light to write a note. As he wrote it, he drank, with the aid of a toothglass and water-bottle, the remains of his bottle of whisky, which was still three-quarters full. He wrote:

Dear Sir
   I am taking my life, as coming to Maidenhead was not of any use. I thought it would be all right if I came here, but I am wrong. No doubt you will have found my friends by now. I left all in order with nothing disturbed. This will help you. I am so tired I cannot write clearly. I realize I am not well. I feel in a dream.
   Please order that they look after my white cat which I left behind. He belongs to the hotel, but I gave him milk nightly and it was my custom to let him into the room in the morning. I do not know its name. I know that I have done wrong, but I am not well. I do not really know what I am doing. I thought I was right, but now I am wrong about Maidenhead, I may be wrong. Please remember my cat.

Yours faithfully
                                        George Harvey Bone.

He put this in an envelope and addressed it to 'THE CORONER, MAIDENHEAD'.

Then he got the newspapers and stuffed the crevices in the door and windows with them, as well as he could. Then he put out the gas and crawled down in the darkness and turned on the gas-ring.

He pulled it near to his face, and it made a dreadful roaring noise, and it smelt acrid and choking. But he was so full of whisky and tiredness he felt he could stand it – he didn't mind.

Before his eyes, great coloured whorls of whisky and gas spread out and closed in again, and spread out and closed. Then he began to go down a dark tunnel – then he began to go up a dark shaft. He realized he was having an operation. He was under gas.

He was under chloroform. It was like that time, years and years ago, when he was a little boy before he went to school, when he had that operation for adenoids, and his sister Ellen was allowed in to hold his hand . . .

He put out his hand to see if Ellen's hand was still there. Yes, he felt it there – amidst all the whorls and tunnels and shafts. 'All right,' she said, as she said in those old days. 'It's all right. Don't be frightened, George. It's all right.'

He died in the early morning, and because of the interest then prevailing in the war, was given very little publicity by the press. Indeed only one newspaper, a sensational picture daily, gave the matter any space or prominence – bringing out (his crude epitaph) the headlines:

SLAYS TWO
FOUND GASSED
THINKS OF CAT

From *Hangover Square* by Patrick Hamilton, 1941

Caressed With a Glove

Part of a letter from Maria Edgeworth to Lucy Edgeworth

12 January, 1822

After this cat's departure Agnes took to heart a kitten, who was very fond of her. This kitten, the first night she slept in her room, on wakening in the morning looked up from the hearth at Agnes, who was lying awake, but with her eyes half-shut, and marked all pussy's motions; after looking some instants, puss jumped up on the bed, crept softly forward and put her paw, with its glove on, upon one of Miss Baillie's eyelids and pushed it gently up. Miss Baillie looked at her fixedly, and Puss, as if satisfied that her eyes were *there* and safe, went back to her station on the hearth and never troubled herself more about the matter.

From *Behold, This Dreamer!*, edited by Walter de la Mare, 1939

Desdemona's Preference

In old family portraits, the ladies are painted with birds or animals as the accessories of the picture. Such playthings were, in fact, the great resources of our female ancestors, whose uneducated minds, and unsocial position (when there were neither books nor assemblies) threw them upon dogs, monkeys, parrots, and cats, as a refuge from *ennui*. Fondness for animals arises out of the idleness of barbarism, as the tolerance of the various nuisances they occasion does from its coarseness. It is not, however, the less true, that the playful kitten, with its pretty little tigerish gambles, is infinitely more amusing than half the people one is obliged to live with in the world.

I have observed, that all domestic animals are more amiable and intelligent on the continent, than with us: it may be they are better treated; for nothing tames like kindness. The fine breed of Angola cats, so common in the South of Italy, is a proof of the assertion; they are much caressed and attended to, and are as intelligent and as attachable as dogs. The first day we had the honour of dining at the palace of the Archbishop of Taranto, at Naples, he said to me, 'You must pardon my passion for cats (*la mia passione gattesca*), but I never exclude them from my dining-room, and you will find they make excellent company.'

Between the first and second course, the door opened, and several enormously large and beautiful cats were introduced, by the names of Pantalone, Desdemona, Otello, and other dramatic *cognomina*. They took their places on chairs near the table, and were as silent, as quiet, as motionless and as well behaved, as the most *bon ton* table in London could require. On the bishop requesting one of the chaplains to help the Signora Desdemona to something, the butler stept up to his lordship and observed, 'Desdemona will prefer waiting for the roasts.' After dinner they were sent to walk on the terrace, and I had the honour of assisting at their *coucher*, for which a number of comfortable cushions were prepared in the bishop's dressing-room. The Archbishop of Taranto, so well known through Italy as the author of many clever works, has also produced one on cats, full of ingenuity and pleasantry.

On my return from Naples, and during our second happy residence in Milan (the remembrance of which is now clouded and embittered by the horrible fate of those superior beings, who were the cause of that return and that residence), I happened to mention my observation on the sensible character of the animals of the South of Italy, and of the *douceur* and intelligence of the archbishop's beautiful Desdemona; when the young and gifted author of 'Francesca da Rimini' (who now lies buried in his living tomb – an Austrian *carcere duro*), related to me the story of a '*passione gattesca,*' which had recently occurred in a neighbouring village, perfectly illustrative of my hypothesis – here it is: –

Il Gatto del Cimitero

THE CAT OF THE CEMETERY.

A beautiful peasant girl of the village of Monte-orsano, in the Brianza, had obtained a sort of melancholy celebrity by an infliction, which frequently struck her down to the earth, in the midst of the village festival, or church ceremony, where her beauty and piety were the boast and the edification of her village friends. Every physician in Lombardy, every saint in the calendar, had been applied to, on behalf of *Clementina*; and vows and offerings had been made in vain, to cure, what was incurable, a confirmed epilepsy. If the saints, however, were negligent, Clementina had one friend, whose vigilance never slumbered. It was her cat; which not only shared her bed and her *polenta*, but followed her in her walks and devotions, from the vineyard to the altar.

The first time that *Mina* saw her young mistress fall in a fit, and wound herself against a tomb in the village cemetery, she exhibited the most extraordinary emotion. She soon acquired the habit, from a frequent recurrence of the infirmity, of watching its approach; and at last seemed to have obtained such a knowledge of the change of countenance and colour, which preceded the attack, that she was wont, on the first symptom, to run to the parents of Clementina, and, by dragging their clothes, scratching at their persons or mewing in the most melancholy manner, ('*Miagolando in tuono mesto ed affannoso,*') she succeeded in awakening their attention, and trotted out before them, mewing them on to the spot, where her young mistress lay lifeless. Mina at last obtained such confidence for her warnings, that, on the first cry of the faithful cat, the friends of Clementina flew to her assistance before she incurred any injury from her sudden fall.

At fifteen, the malady of the beautiful Clementina brought her to the tomb. Her cat walked after her bier, on which she was exposed, (as is the custom in Italy), and covered with flowers. During the funeral service, she sat at the head of the bier, gazing with an intent look on the lifeless features of her young mistress; and when the grave was filling, she made a vain endeavour to jump in, but was withheld by the bystanders, who carried home this chief mourner after the melancholy ceremony. Mina, however, was seen the next morning stretched upon the new made grave, which she continued to visit daily, until she visited it for the last time, a few months after her friend's death; when she was found dead upon the green mound that covered her remains.

The celebrity of the '*Gatto del Cimitero,*' has not yet passed away from the village of Monte-orsano. I dedicate this little history of the faithful *Mina*, to my young friend *Ina*; whose '*passione gattesca,*' entitles her to the distinction. Kindness to animals is but a form of sensibility, and in youth is always the harbinger of higher and deeper-seated feelings. It should not be confounded with the misplaced instinct of maternity in childless old maids, or the capricious fondness of adults for the brute creation, which is unaccompanied by any touch of kindness for their biped dependants, or any manifestation of sympathy for human misfortune.

From The Book of the Boudoir by Lady Morgan, 1829

Searching For Tiger

The painter Gwen John was one of the most dedicated ailurophiles of modern times. In June 1906, finding Paris 'intolerably stuffy', she wrapped her cat, Tiger, in a shawl and took her on a visit to Meudon, where Gwen John's lover, Auguste Rodin, owned a villa. It was a disastrous outing.

She found a 'room' among the bushes outside the fence, unpacked her cat and her sketch-book and started to draw the villa. Tiger was ecstatic. 'It was a pleasure to see the little figure in the country,' she told Rodin, 'beaming with happiness, her tail straight as she ran.' Soon a woman came into the garden, followed by two dogs, and sat on the bench. She was elderly and dressed in grey, and Gwen John felt sure she was Rose Beuret, the peasant woman who had shared Rodin's life and borne him a son, but had never been his wife. To

Gwen John she was a friend for while Rodin was at Meudon with the thorny Rose no other woman dared approach him.

When darkness fell Gwen took the tram home. To her horror, when it stopped at St Cloud, Tiger shot from her shawl and out through the door. Some 'red dogs' in the street gave chase and soon the cat had disappeared. Frantically Gwen John ran up and down the village calling her name. She asked everyone she saw, 'Have you seen my cat?' Some of them laughed at her, imitating her pronunciation and several men offered her an arm and said *they* would find her a cat if she would come this way. Three evil-looking girls sitting outside a house with their 'mother' started pretending to see the cat when it wasn't there, and the old woman who called Gwen John a *poupée* turned out to be the owner of the local brothel.

Between the houses and the river there was a piece of waste ground. Frantic to get away from the jeering prostitutes and their patrons, Gwen John wandered there among the clumps of nettles and piles of rubbish. The ground was rough and several times she stumbled into holes. Sometimes she thought she heard the distant cry of a cat, but it was always too far away. She decided to spend what was left of the night on the ground.

For nine days Gwen John went native. 'I am living like Robinson Crusoe under a tree,' she told Rodin. She laid an elaborate grid of meat parcels over the whole area each night and lay down to wait. Her dreams were punctuated by the squeaks of rats and toads, for 'only loathsome creatures inhabit this place'. She woke stiff each morning and found the grass drenched. The meat parcels would be gone, but she knew it was not Tiger who had taken them, for she would have 'unwrapped the paper, not torn it'.

Then she launched a campaign of which a general might have been proud. She offered a reward of twenty francs for the finder of the cat (the money to be paid by Rodin) and she asked Rodin to send her a permit to search every garden in St Cloud and Meudon. This searching of gardens was not popular. One wealthy widow by the river at St Cloud refused to open her premises to a hatless young woman (Gwen John afterwards insisted she was wearing a *small* hat) and promised to investigate the garden herself. Gwen came back that night uninvited and searched it. Once when trespassing at night she was chased by a big dog. Playing for time she threw it the parcel of meat she was carrying and flung herself over the garden fence only to find herself suspended by her skirt on the far side. By undoing the skirt she managed to release herself, but was left standing in the street naked from the waist down.

After six days she lost hope. The men of St Cloud had taxed their brains for original ways for a cat to die and were gratified by the English lady's reactions to their suggestions. *La chatte* might be shut in a house, she might have died of hunger, or boredom, might have been eaten by a dog, a rabbit or a tramp, she might have eaten a frog, she might have gone down a railway tunnel or down a well. She might even have swum the Seine and got to Boulogne.

Gwen John was by now dishevelled and desperate. She went into Paris to keep a modelling engagement with Constance Lloyd, an old friend from the Slade, but turned white and had to stop after an hour. Worse still, there was an unkind letter from Rodin waiting. He had been angry with her for losing the cat and was angrier with her for sleeping out. After reading the letter she knew that Rodin no longer loved her because she was a stupid person who could not even take care of a cat. 'All is finished for me,' she wrote to him. 'I would like to live longer but I will not be pretty and happy for you without my cat.'

She walked that night by the Seine and sat on the high parapet of the Pont d'Alma. The black water sparkled under the lights of the barges. Suddenly she looked round and saw a crowd behind her. Too embarrassed to move, she looked back at the water and hoped they'd go away. 'Why are you sitting there, young woman?' someone called.

'She's a foreigner.'

'Yes, English.'

'Are you alone in Paris?'

Still Gwen John did not reply.

'Poor thing.'

Now she saw a hand beside her on the parapet. It was a *gendarme*. 'Keen on fishing?' Everyone laughed and Gwen John at last found the courage to escape.

Her room looked forlorn after six days' neglect. Tiger was no longer curled on the wicker chair. She began to prepare the room for death. She did not want Rodin to find anything out of order when she was gone. She dusted and polished and changed the flowers. Perhaps she thought of the death scene in the last chapter of *The Idiot*. And then a message came from Meudon. A cat that looked white from the front and tabby from the side had been seen near the Villa des Brillants.

Gwen John took the train to Val Fleuri and hurried up the hill to her 'room' among the bushes. Secretly she had always thought Tiger would return to the place where they had spent the day together. Once more she arranged meat on paper plates among the surrounding bushes. A kind peasant woman living with her husband and child near Rodin's villa said, 'As sure as I carry this pot you will see your cat in eight days.' She insisted on making up a bed for Gwen John in her garden but once she was asleep Gwen John slipped away to sleep in her 'room'. The grass rustled, the owls hooted and the mice 'played the flute and the piccolo'. For three days and nights she lay in the undergrowth, naked by day, and turned brown. And then before dawn on the morning of 17 July Tiger came. Gwen John had just risen, stiff from the wet ground, to take a look at a Greek torso. When she returned to the 'room' a white figure was standing there with big unhappy eyes. It was Tiger. In a moment the cat was purring in her owner's arms. Gwen John ran to the peasant's house to proclaim the good news and get food for the famished animal. But it was still only four a.m. and he and his wife were asleep. By climbing on to an outhouse roof Gwen John could see them in bed through the bedroom window. There was nothing to do but settle down once more and wait. The exhausted cat lay quietly across her stomach. When the peasants woke she broke the news. 'How happy we are, Mademoiselle,' they cried. 'How beautiful the little *chatte* is,' although in fact, as Gwen John remarked, she was not beautiful at all but thin and dirty.

From *Gwen John 1876-1939* by Susan Chitty, 1981

Cat Overboard (1)

The 18. day we abode still at anker, looking for a gale to returne backe, but it was contrary: and the 19. we set saile, but the currant having more force then the winde, we were driven backe, insomuch, that the ship being under saile, we cast the sounding lead, and (nothwithstanding the wind) it remained before the shippe, there we hadde muddie ground at fifteen fadome. The same day about 4. of the clocke, wee set saile againe, and sayled West alongst the coast with a fresh side-winde. It chanced by fortune, that the shippes Cat lept into the Sea, which being downe, kept her selfe very valuantly above water, notwithstanding the great waves, still swimming, but which the master knowing, he caused the Skiffe with half a dosen men to goe towards her and fetch her againe, when she was almost halfe a mile from the shippe, and all this while the shippe lay on staies. I hardly believe they would have made such haste and meanes if one of the company had bene in the like perill. They made the more haste because it was the patrons cat. This I have written onely to note the estimation that cats are in, among the Italiana, for generally they esteem their cattes, as in England we esteeme a good Spaniell. The same night about tenne of the clocke the winde calmed, and because none of the shippe knewe where we were, we let fall an anker about 6 mile from the place we were at before, and there wee had muddie ground at twelve fadome.

From *The Principal Navigations, Voyages, Traffiques and Discoveries
of the English Nation* by Richard Hakluyt, 1589

Cat Overboard (2)

Thursday, July 11 [1754]

This gale continued till towards noon; when the east end of the island bore but little ahead of us. The captain swaggered and declared he would keep the sea; but the wind got the better of him, so that about three he gave up the victory, and making a sudden tack stood in for the shore, passed by Spithead and Portsmouth, and came to an anchor at a place called Ryde on the island.

A most tragical incident fell out this day at sea. While the ship was under sail, but making as will appear no great way, a kitten, one of four of the feline inhabitants of the cabin, fell from the window into the water: an alarm was immediately given to the captain, who was then upon deck, and received it with the utmost concern and many bitter oaths. He immediately gave orders to the steersman in favour of the poor thing, as he called it; the sails were instantly slackened, and all hands, as the phrase is, employed to recover the poor animal. I was, I own, extremely surprised at all this; less indeed at the captain's extreme tenderness than at his conceiving any possibility of success; for if puss had had nine thousand instead of nine lives, I concluded they had been all lost. The boatswain, however, had more sanguine hopes, for, having stripped himself of his jacket, breeches, and shirt, he leaped boldly into the water, and to my great astonishment in a few minutes returned to the ship, bearing the motionless animal in his mouth. Nor was this, I observed, a matter of such great difficulty as it appeared to my ignorance, and possibly may seem to that of my fresh-water reader. The kitten was now exposed to air and sun on the deck, where its life, of which it retained no symptoms, was despaired of by all.

The captain's humanity, if I may so call it, did not so totally destroy his philosophy as to make him yield himself up to affliction on this melancholy occasion. Having felt his loss like a man, he resolved to shew he could bear it like one; and, having declared he had rather have lost a cask of rum or brandy, betook himself to threshing at backgammon with the Portuguese friar, in which innocent amusement they had passed about two-thirds of their time.

But as I have, perhaps, a little too wantonly endeavoured to raise the tender passions of my readers in this narrative, I should think myself unpardonable if I concluded it without giving them the satisfaction of hearing that the kitten at last recovered, to the great joy of the good captain, but to the great disappointment of some of the sailors, who asserted that the drowning a cat was the very surest way of raising a favourable wind; a supposition of which, though we have heard several plausible accounts, we will not presume to assign the true original reason.

However, as Fielding reported later that month, the good captain's joy was short-lived.

The captain ... even extended his humanity, if I may so call it, to animals, and even his cats and kittens had large shares in his affections. An instance of which we saw this evening, when the cat, which had shewn it could not be drowned, was found suffocated under a feather-bed in the cabin. I will not endeavour to describe his lamentations with more prolixity than barely by saying they were grievous, and seemed to have some mixture of the Irish howl in them.

From The Journal of a Voyage to Lisbon by Henry Fielding, 1755

Cat Overboard (3)

'Where have they all come from?' said Titty, as another of those long timbers rocked past them. A squared end, orange with the wetness of the wood, lifted clear of the water and dropped into the smooth back of a wave.

'Deck cargo from a timber-ship,' said John. 'Norwegian probably, like the one we saw in the harbour. Jim says they roll like anything, and it was awfully rough in the night.

'First one side and then the other,' said Titty, 'and then a wave would come washing along and a whole lot of logs would be floating in the sea.'

Susan was steering. John had made his rope fast with a bowline round his middle and was rummaging in the locker for the little brass handle of the reefing gear.

'There's a whole lot more,' said Titty.

'There's something that isn't a log,' cried Roger. 'It's a box. Bother. I wish she'd keep still for a moment.' He was trying to look through the binoculars and finding it very difficult, as the *Goblin* rose and fell, not to lose sight of the thing, whatever it was, that kept showing on the top of a wave ahead of them, disappearing in the trough and then showing once more.

'It's not a box,' he said at last. 'It's a sort of cage.'

They came nearer and nearer to it, steering to leave it twenty or thirty yards to port. 'Don't go too near,' said John. He did not mean the *Goblin* to bump even into a biscuit box, if he could help it, and this thing looked a good deal bigger than a biscuit box.

'It's a chicken coop,' cried Titty. 'How lovely. Don't you remember the poem about the pirates, after they'd scuppered the ship? . . . "And hear the drowning folks lament the absent chicken coop." It's the absent chicken coop that ought to have been there and wasn't.'

And then a graver thought struck her. 'What's happened to the chickens? Eaten or drowned? I wonder which they'd mind most.'

'They'd be eaten either way,' said Roger. 'If they were drowned some shark or other would be glad to gobble them up.'

'But at least they'd be allowed to keep their feathers,' said Titty.

'Hi!' spluttered Roger, trying to keep the binoculars steady. 'There's something on it . . . There is . . . Do go a little nearer. Oh I say. It's a dead kitten . . .'

'Oh . . .'

'Drowned.'

All four of them could see it now, as the chicken coop lifted and fell among the waves. It was no more than a scrap of wet fur plastered flat on the wooden slats. It drifted by perhaps a dozen yards away. They could see the head of the kitten, the fur on it sticking close to the skull, the slip of wet body, the hind legs stretched out as if they had no bones, the tail like a bit of wet string. They tried to look away from it, but their eyes came back to it in spite of themselves. Even John, who had found his handle and was in a hurry to go forward and get the sail unreefed, stopped to watch it.

'How awful,' said Titty.

'It must have been washed off with all those logs,' said John. 'Perhaps the same big wave . . .'

'Asleep,' said Titty, 'and then in the water and just clinging on till it was drowned.'

John and Susan knew well enough how easily they, too, might have found themselves struggling in the water in the dark.

The chicken coop, with that soaking wisp of fur on it, was already astern of them when Roger suddenly shouted, 'It's alive!'

'It can't be.'

'I saw its pink mouth.'

And then, as the chicken coop lurched away astern, all four of them saw that pink mouth open again, just a little, as if the kitten, too weak to shout, were whispering a cry for help they could not hear.

'We must save it,' cried Titty.

John was already hauling in the mainsheet.

'*When there's a man overboard always jibe.*' He could see the printed sentence as he had read it in the book on how to sail. Gosh, he was glad the sail was still reefed and easy to handle, and that the wind had fallen light. 'Now then, Susan, bring her round. No . . . No . . . To port . . . Come on . . . Round with her . . . I'll look after that backstay. Don't lose sight of it, Roger . . . Look out for the boom coming over . . . It's coming . . . Now . . .'

The boom swung over as the *Goblin* turned sharp on her heel and headed back, close-hauled into the wind. Frantically John made his backstay fast, let go one jib sheet, flung himself across the cockpit and hardened in the other.

'Where is it now? You haven't lost it . . .'

'Over there . . . It's a long way off . . . There . . . There . . .'

'We'll have to tack . . .'

'Can you manage it?' said Susan.

'We can't leave it to drown,' cried Titty.

'We won't,' said John.

It is none too easy to pick up small things at sea unless you have had a lot of practice. John had had none. Susan gave up the tiller to him, and he clenched his teeth together, and looked at that bobbing chicken coop and then up at the burgee at the masthead. No, they couldn't do better than this without going on the other tack.

'It's going farther away,' said Roger.

'Much farther,' said Titty. 'Oh, John!'

'Ready about,' said John, and the jib flapped and the boom swung across, and Titty and Susan threw themselves on the sheets. The *Goblin* was off again, this time coming nearer and nearer to the kitten and its raft.

'How are we going to get hold of it?' said Susan.

'Boathook?' said Roger.

'Have it ready,' said John. 'No. Don't. I'll go right alongside.'

'You're going to pass in front of it,' said Titty.

'No I'm not,' said John.

'Hang on, Pussy!' shouted Titty, almost climbing up on the cabin roof.

'We'll knock it off if we bump the coop,' said Susan.

'I know,' said John. 'Give me your shoulder to hang on to.' He half stood on the seat in the swaying cockpit, steadying himself with a grip on Susan, who shouted to him not to go overboard. He was bringing the *Goblin* straight up into the wind, heading towards the chicken coop, just as if he were Jim Brading, bringing her up to her mooring buoy. He had to stand on the seat to be able to see the coop which was now close ahead.

'There it is . . . Now . . . Now . . . ' gasped Titty

The chicken coop touched the *Goblin*'s side, and there was a groan of terror from somebody. But it was only a touch. The next moment the coop was floating past the side of the cabin. John let go the tiller.

'Hang on to my feet,' he cried. In another second it would be too late. He flung himself half out of the cockpit, reaching down across the side deck. The chicken coop lifted towards him. He grabbed the little cold wisp of wet fur. The kitten, with the last of its strength, hung on to the slats of the coop. One hand was not enough. John let go of the boat, to be able to use both. The next moment the chicken coop rolled slowly over and fell astern, and John hung there, more than half over the side, with the dripping kitten in his hands.

Titty and Susan hung on to his legs and hauled. Roger lugged at the rope that was tied round John's middle. John wriggled desperately, and, inch by inch, was pulled back into the cockpit.

He gave the kitten to Susan, and, a good deal out of breath, took the tiller once more, glanced up at the burgee, looked round to see that they were in no danger of running into a log, and then kept his eyes on the compass.

Susan sat down with the wet little wisp of fur on her lap, shielded by her hands.

'He's nearly frozen,' she said.

The kitten lay perfectly still, too weak to move.

'He can't have swallowed much water,' said Titty, who was kneeling on the cockpit floor. 'He hasn't got a stomach at all.'

'Probably starving,' said Roger.

'What do they do to people who are nearly drowned?' said Titty.

'Dry clothes and brandy,' said Susan. 'We've got no brandy.'

'We can dry his fur,' said Titty. 'And what about Jim Brading's aunt's rum? . . . This *is* a medicinal purpose . . . '

'We'll take him down into the cabin and get him warm,' said Susan. 'You go down first, Titty, and I'll pass him to you.'

'I'm going to get the rum,' said Roger, and was half-way down the steps in a moment.

Titty followed and waited at the bottom, while Susan carefully reached down and put the shipwrecked kitten in her hands. She was just going down herself when John stopped her.

'You can see it's no good trying to go back. Not until the wind changes. I'm heading her as near the wind as she'll go, and the best she'll do is south of west. On the other tack she'd be going much too far north, and to go back we want to head about north-west by west. It's no good going right up the North Sea. It's far better to go on as we were going and get somewhere.'

'All right,' said Susan. 'I say, do you think it will be good for the kitten to give him rum?'

'See if it'll lick a drop off the end of your finger,' said John. 'And try it with the condensed milk. But look here, Susan, give me a hand to get back on the course. If you'll take the tiller, I can manage the rest . . . And I *must* let those reefs out. We ought not to waste a minute. I was just going to do it when we sighted the kitten. If you'll take the tiller till I've done it, I'll be all right by myself. Those logs are easy enough to see . . .'

Susan called down the companion to Titty. 'Wrap him up, first in one bit of towel and then in another, to get the wet out of his fur. I'll be down in a minute . . .'

In the cabin, Titty was sitting on the lee bunk with the kitten in her lap, tenderly mopping it with a towel. She tried to warm it by putting her hands round its empty little stomach. Roger had got the store-cupboard open and was hunting for that small flat bottle. Suddenly the *Goblin* heeled over on the other side, and Titty had to shift across, while Roger as nearly as possible dropped the bottle on the cabin floor in grabbing for something to steady himself.

'What's happened now?'

'It's all right,' said Roger. 'It's only that they've turned round again. We're going on.'

'Do tell Susan to hurry up. I believe he's going to die after all.'

'Susan,' Roger shouted up through the companion. 'Buck up. Titty says it's lost eight of its lives already.'

'Coming,' said Susan. 'I say, John, I must. The kitten may really be dying.'

'Go on down,' said John. 'But do be as quick as you can. I can't get the reefs out till you come back.' He took the tiller once more, while Susan hurried down into the cabin.

The kitten lay between Titty's hands.

'He's still alive,' she said. 'Look. You can see a fluttering inside him. Stick to it, Pussy. You're quite safe.'

[295]

Susan, with trembling fingers, was pulling the cork out of the flat bottle. 'Rum. For Medicinal Purposes Only.' She read the label written by Jim's aunt. She pressed the mouth of the bottle against her finger and turned the bottle upside down and back again. A transparent golden drop stayed on her finger-tip. Tenderly, kneeling on the cabin floor, she pushed her finger into a corner of the kitten's mouth. She got another drop from the bottle and worked it into the kitten's mouth in the same way. The kitten gave a feeble splutter.

'Get a tin of milk,' said Susan. 'Spike two holes in the top of it. Go on. Use the spike of your knife.' She scrambled up and got a spoon and a saucer out of the cupboard under the stove. She took a drop of water from the tap. Then, when Roger had spiked the milk-can with the marline spike on his scout knife, she poured some milk into the water and stirred it up.

'Now then, Pussy,' she said, and dipped the kitten's mouth into the saucer.

The kitten spluttered again.

'He'll get it up his nose,' said Titty. 'You'll choke him.'

But a thin pink tongue slipped out and in again like a tiny pink handkerchief. Susan took milk on her finger and smeared it on the kitten's mouth. Again that little tongue slipped in and out. The kitten opened its eyes and instantly closed them again. It opened its mouth and . . .

'Did you hear him?' said Titty.

'John,' shouted Roger up the companion. 'It's mewed.'

'Salt water in his eyes,' said Susan, and soaked her handkerchief in fresh water from the tap and gently wiped the kitten's face. Titty dipped her finger in the milk and the kitten licked her finger clean with a rough little tongue.

'He's going to recover,' said Susan. She pushed the saucer under the kitten's chin. A lurch of the *Goblin* spilt some of the milk on Titty, who did not even think of wiping it off. The kitten's tongue shot out almost eagerly and began to lap.

'We mustn't let him have too much at once,' said Susan. 'Take another towel and go on drying him. I've got to go up to help John.' Titty and Roger were left alone with the kitten.

From *We Didn't Mean to Go to Sea*, by Arthur Ransome, 1937

Unhooked

Henrietta Dodgson, Lewis Carroll's youngest sister, recalls her brother's kindness to animals.

When away from home he saw a kitten in the street with a fish-hook in its mouth. Knowing what suffering this would cause, he carried the kitten to the house of a medical man for relief. 'Your own cat, I suppose?' said the doctor, but any knowledge of it was disclaimed. Happily the removal of the hook was no difficult matter. Lewis Carroll held the kitten, and I think the doctor was able to snip off the barbed end, so that the hook came easily out. Payment having been declined, Lewis Carroll took the kitten back to where he had found it.

From *The Lewis Carroll Picture Book*, 1899

A Freudian Analysis

In her *Journal*, a documentary gold mine for historians of analysis, Lou [Andreas-Salomé] faithfully records the proceedings of the analytic meetings she attended in Vienna, as well as her responses to papers and her impressions of participants. She quickly grew close to Freud, often walking home with him after meetings or going to the Ronacher Café, where discussion extended into the night. On several occasions she was a guest at his home. Although their conversations probed her childhood and covered analytic terrain, Lou never underwent anything approaching a formal analysis with Freud or anyone else. Given the resolutely intellectual thrust of both Lou's *Journal* and her memoir, it is not always easy to glean what specific interpretations Freud might have made. None the less, her *Journal* entry of 2 February 1913 gives us a tantalizing glimpse into what may have been a key moment in her analysis. On that Sunday, Freud spoke to her about his life. What she notes as perhaps 'most personal of all' was his charming account of the 'narcissistic cat'.

The cat, so the story goes, had come in through an open window, arousing mixed feelings in Freud, especially when it climbed down from the sofa on which it had made itself comfortable and began to inspect in passing the antique objects which he had placed for the time being on the floor. But when the cat proceeded to make known its archaeological satisfaction by purring and with its lithe grace did not cause the slightest damage, Freud's heart melted and he ordered milk for it. From then on the cat claimed its rights daily to take a place on the sofa, inspect the antiques, and get its bowl of milk. However, despite Freud's increasing affection and admiration, the cat paid him not a bit of attention and coldly turned its green eyes with their slanting pupils toward him as toward any other object. When for an instant he wanted more of the cat than its egoistic-narcissistic purring, he had to put his foot down from his comfortable chaise and court its attention with the ingenious enticement of his shoe-toe. Finally, after this unequal relationship had lasted a long time without change, one day he found the cat feverish and gasping on the sofa. And although it was most painstakingly treated ... it succumbed to pneumonia, leaving naught of itself behind but a symbolic picture of all the peaceful and playful charm of true egoism.

Lou makes no comment on this story, leaving it to hang enticingly in the text and moving on to what is certainly related material: Freud's query to her about why she had become so deeply involved in psychoanalysis. Her immediate answer to the question is hardly relevant. What is important is the intervention: it is almost as if Freud is asking her to reflect on her similarity to the cat and asking her what she, Lou, so like the cat in her narcissistic feline distance and self-containment, wants from him. Is psychoanalysis simply the gift of a sustaining bowl of milk and a purring exploratory stroll through the archaeological depths?

From *Freud's Women* by Lisa Appignanesi and John Forrester, 1992

Waltzing Chattie

Chattie jumped up on the window-sill, with her usual stealthy *aplomb*, and rubbed herself against the girl's face.

'Oh, Chattie!' cried Rose, throwing her arms around the cat, 'if Catherine'll *only* marry Mr Elsmere, my dear, and be happy ever afterwards, and set me free to live my own life a bit, I'll be *so* good, you won't know me, Chattie. And you shall have a new collar, my beauty, and cream till you die of it!'

And springing up she dragged in the cat, and snatching a scarlet anemone from a bunch on the table, stood opposite Chattie, who stood slowly waving her magnificent tail from side to side, and glaring as though it were not at all to her taste to be hustled and bustled in this way.

'Now, Chattie, listen! Will she?'

A leaf of the flower dropped on Chattie's nose.

'Won't she? Will she? Won't she? Will – Tiresome flower, why did Nature give it such a beggarly few petals? If I'd had a daisy it would have all come right. Come, Chattie, waltz; and let's forget this wicked world!'

And, snatching up her violin, the girl broke into a Strauss waltz, dancing to it the while, her cotton skirts flying, her pretty feet twinkling, till her eyes glowed, and her cheeks blazed with a double intoxication – the intoxication of movement, and the intoxication of sound – the cat meanwhile following her with little mincing perplexed steps as though not knowing what to make of her.

'Rose, you madcap!' cried Agnes, opening the door.

'Not at all, my dear,' said Rose calmly, stopping to take breath. 'Excellent practice and uncommonly difficult. Try if you can do it, and see!'

From *Robert Elsmere* by Mrs Humphry Ward, 1888

Disorderly Conduct

There was an old man on the Border,
Who lived in the utmost disorder;
He danced with the cat,
And made tea in his hat,
Which vexed all the folks on the Border.

From More Nonsense by Edward Lear, 1889

A Tabby Among the Nawabs

Connop Thirlwall, Bishop of St David's, describes a reception given by the Duchess of Argyll at the India Office in May 1869

It was a very splendid scene. The centre of the quadrangle, where the ball was given to the Sultan last year, was occupied by some regimental band. The company circulated in the surrounding galleries. It was the only gathering of the kind where something was to be seen beside people's faces. On the second floor is the museum, composed of all the treasures of Indian products and industry formerly lodged at the India House, Leadenhall Street, and increased by many later additions. One curiosity I remember to have seen very long ago – a figure of the size of life, of a tiger with a man under him. When you turn a handle the tiger's paw strikes the man, who utters a moan. This was a toy of Tippoo Sahib's, and represented an Englishman in the position in which he would have liked to see every one of the race.

The scene was animated by the presence of several Indian potentates – Nawabs or something – moving about in gorgeous oriental costume. (Also by a dear little cat, who glided through the throng with perfect composure, though not an Indian, or even a Persian, but a simple English tabby.)

From Letters to a Friend by Connop Thirlwall, Late Lord Bishop of St David's edited by
the Very Revd Arthur P. Stanley, 1861

Intervention from the Floor

In July 1874, a debate in the House of Commons on the Public Worship Regulation Bill was enlivened by a feline interjection. The incident was punctiliously recorded in The Times's *Parliamentary Report the following day.*

The right hon. gentleman was at this moment startled by a burst of laughter from the crowded House, caused by the appearance of a large grey tabby cat, which, after descending the Opposition gangway, proceeded leisurely to cross the floor. Being frightened by the noise, the cat made a sudden spring from the floor over the shoulder of the members sitting on the front Ministerial bench below the gangway, and, amid shouts of laughter, bounded over the heads of members on the back benches until it reached a side door, when it vanished. This sudden apparition, the cat's still more sudden disappearance, and the astonishment of the members who found it vaulting so close to their faces and beards, almost convulsed the House.

The Times, 10 July 1874

Without a Dog-Collar

I have only once seen a pussy in church. It was not a parish church, but the chapel of one of the great London hospitals. The congregation was assembled and was awaiting the entrance of the chaplain, when a young pussy of an age somewhere between cat and kitten solemnly marched, with tail erect, up the middle gangway. Without hesitation, and as if fulfilling a usual duty, he made for the reading-desk, entered it, and for an instant was lost to view. But a moment later head and shoulders appeared above the desk, and a small wise face looked round with an air of quiet assurance and professional unconcern. I quite expected to see the little paws reverently folded, and to hear a tiny voice say: 'Let us purr'!

From *Home and Garden* by Gertrude Jekyll, 1900

Idiotic, Indefensible Love

In Geoffrey Household's thriller Rogue Male, *the unnamed hero is a fugitive who hides from his pursuers in a burrow at the edge of a field. During his weeks of* de facto *captivity he has only one companion – a cat, whom he names Asmodeus.*

I observed him first as two ears and two eyes apparently attached to a black branch. When I moved my head, the ears vanished, and when I stood up the rest of him had vanished. I put out some scraps of bully beef behind the branch, and an hour later they too had vanished.

One morning when I had just gone to bed, and was lying with my head out of the burrow chewing biscuits, he slunk on to my platform and watched me, tail gripping the ground, head savage and expectant. He was a thin and powerful tom-cat, black, but with many of his hairs ending in a streak of silver, like a smooth-headed Mediterranean beauty just turning grey. I don't think that in his case it is age, but a freak of colouring inherited from some silver ancestor. I threw him a biscuit; he was out of sight while it was still in the air. It had gone, of course, when I woke up, and so had half a tin of bully beef.

He began to consider me as a curious show for his leisure hours, sitting motionless at a safe distance of ten feet. In a few more days he would snatch food from my hand, hissing and bristling if I dared advance the hand to touch him. It was then that I named him Asmodeus for he could make himself appear the very spirit of hatred, and malignity.

I won his friendship with a pheasant's head, attached to the end of a string. I have noticed that what cats most appreciate in a human being is not the ability to produce food – which they take for granted – but his or her entertainment value. Asmodeus took to his toy enthusiastically. In another week he permitted me to stroke him, producing a raucous purr, but, in order to save his face, pretending to be asleep. Soon afterwards he started a habit of sleeping in the burrow with me during the day, and hunting while I worked at night. But bully beef was the meat he preferred; no doubt it gave him the maximum nourishment for the minimum effort . . .

Space I have none. The inner chamber is a tumbled morass of wet earth which I am compelled to use as a latrine. I am confined to my original excavation, the size of three large dog-kennels, where I lie on or inside my sleeping-bag. I cannot extend it. The noise of working would be audible in the lane.

I spend a part of each day wedged in the enlarged chimney, with my head out of the top; but that is more for change of position than for fresh air. The domed, prolific bush is so thick and so shadowed by its companions and by the hedge that I can be sure it is day only when the sun is in the east. The lifeless centre seems full of gases, unsatisfying in themselves and carrying in suspension the brown dust and debris that fall from above and the soot from my fires that has accumulated on the under side of the leaves.

Asmodeus, as always, is my comfort. It is seldom that one can give to and receive from an animal close, silent, and continuous attention. We live in the same space, in the same way, and on the same food, except that Asmodeus has no use for oatmeal, nor I for field-mice. During the hours while he sits cleaning himself, and I motionless in my dirt, there is, I believe, some slight thought trans-ference between us. I cannot 'order' or even 'hope' that he should perform a given act, but back and forth between us go thoughts of fear and disconnected dreams of action. I should call these dreams madness, did I not know they came from him and that his mind is, by our human standards, mad.

Asmodeus is eventually killed by one of the pursuers
when he ventures out of the burrow.

Taking Asmodeus' head in my hand, I drew his remains into the den. Poor old boy, he had been shot at close quarters full in the chest. It was my fault. People who sat quietly in the lane were, in his only experience, friendly and had bully beef. He had been shot as he confidently sat up to watch them.

I was choking with sorrow and rage. Yes, I know – or one side of me knows – that it was the idiotic, indefensible love of an Anglo-Saxon for his animal. But Asmodeus' affection had been of so much harder price than that of a creature which one has fed and brought up from birth. Our companionship had a stern quality, as of the deep love between two people who have met in middle age, each looking back to an utterly unshared and independent life.

From *Rogue Male* by Geoffrey Household, 1939

'A Portrait with a Cat'

A little girl looks at a book with a picture of a cat
Who wears a fluffy collar and has a green velvet frock.
Her lips, very red, are half opened in a sweet reverie,
This takes place in 1910 or 1912, the painting bears no date.
It was painted by Marjorie C. Murphy, an American
Born in 1888, like my mother, more or less.
I contemplate the painting in Grinnell, Iowa,
At the end of the century. That cat with his collar
Where is he? And the girl? Am I going to meet her,
One of those mummies with rouge, tapping with their canes?
But this face: a tiny pug nose, round cheeks,
Moves me so, quite like a face that I, suddenly awake
In the middle of the night, saw by my side on a pillow.
The cat is not here, he is in the book, the book in the painting.
No girl, and yet she is here, before me
And has never been lost. Our true encounter
Is in the zones of childhood. Amazement called love,
A thought of touching, a cat in velvet.

From *The Collected Poems 1931-1987* by Czeslaw Milosz, 1988

The Master's Cat

Charles Dickens had dogs galore in his lifetime, but few cats. One of his daughters, Mamie, left this memoir of the cats who succeeded in penetrating the novelist's defences.

On account of our birds, cats were not allowed in the house; but from a friend in London I received a present of a white kitten – Williamina – and she and her numerous offspring had a happy home at 'Gad's Hill.' She became a favorite with all the household, and showed particular devotion to my father. I remember on one occasion when she had presented us with a family of kittens, she selected a corner of father's study for their home. She brought them one by one from the kitchen and deposited them in her chosen corner. My father called to me to remove them, saying that he could not allow the kittens to remain in his room. I did so, but Williamina brought them back again, one by one. Again they were removed. The third time, instead of putting them in the corner, she placed them all, and herself beside them, at my father's feet, and gave him such an imploring glance that he could resist no longer, and they were allowed to remain. As the kittens grew older they became more and more frolicsome, swarming up the curtains, playing about on the writing table and scampering behind the book shelves. But they were never complained of and lived happily in the study until the time came for finding them other homes. One of these kittens was kept, who, as he was quite deaf, was left unnamed, and became known by the servants as 'the master's cat,' because of his devotion to my father. He was always with him, and used to follow him about the garden like a dog, and sit with him while he wrote. One evening we were all, except father, going to a ball, and when we started, left 'the master' and his cat in the drawing-room together. 'The master' was reading at a small table, on which a lighted candle was placed. Suddenly the candle went out. My father, who was much interested in his book, relighted the candle, stroked the cat, who was looking at him pathetically he noticed, and continued his reading. A few minutes later, as the light became dim, he looked up just in time to see puss deliberately put out the candle with his paw, and then look appealingly toward him. This second and unmistakable hint was not disregarded, and puss was given the petting he craved. Father was full of this anecdote when all met at breakfast the next morning.

From *My Father As I Recall Him* by Mamie Dickens, 1897

Gurgles of Endearment

George Rose, the hero of Fr. Rolfe's novel Hadrian the Seventh, *has a little yellow cat, Flavio, who is described as 'the only living creature to whom he ever spoke with affection as well as with politeness'.*

He rose and went to the window. The yellow cat deliberately stretched himself, yawned, and followed; and proceeded to carry out a wonderful scheme of feints and ambuscades in regard to a ping-pong ball which was kept for his proper diversion. The man looked on almost lovingly. Flavio at length captured the ball, took it between his forepaws, and posed with all the majesty of a lion of Trafalgar Square. Anon he uttered a little low gurgle of endearment, fixing the great eloquent mystery of amber and black and velvet eyes, tardy, grave, upon his human friend. No notice was vouchsafed. Flavio got up; and gently rubbed his head against the nearest hand.

'My boy!' the man murmured; and he lifted the little cat on to his shoulder.

From *Hadrian the Seventh* by Fr. Rolfe, 1904

Cosseted and Cherished

When Delia, the cat belonging to Walter Stonehouse, Rector of Darfield, Yorkshire, died in the mid seventeenth century he buried her in his garden and wrote a Latin verse epitaph. In the eighteenth century the domestic cat established itself as a creature to be cosseted and cherished for its companionship. The antiquary William Stukeley was deeply affected by the death of his cat, Tit, 'an uncommon creature and of all I ever knew the most sensible, most loving and indeed with many other engaging qualities'. He grieved for her 'exceedingly', believing that she had 'sense so far superior to her kind' and 'such incontestable ways of testifying her love to her master and mistress'. English cats, like English dogs, thought Christopher Smart, were the best in Europe. It is likely that the cat gained in popularity as standards of domestic cleanliness rose. In 1809 William Bingley thought that it was because of the animals' cleanliness and elegance that some people were 'passionately fond of cats'. But he also noted that they exhibited 'many pleasing traits of character' and were 'susceptible of considerable educational attainments'. In the mid nineteenth century the cats'-meat man interviewed by Henry Mayhew told him that in London there was at least one cat for every ten people; and that they were twice as numerous as dogs. The first cat show was in 1871.

From *Man and the Natural World: Changing Attitudes in England 1500–1800*
by Keith Thomas, 1983

I see that up to here I have never described Tam at work. I expect to be stigmatised as feeble-minded for ascribing the ability to write a book to the presence of a cat. The conviction may well be a super-stition or a fetish; but if I start to name the writers since the beginnings of literature who have been dependent on cats, this will turn into a catalogue. My present cat, in passing, is satisfactory. He spends the entire day on a couch beside me where my working material is laid out in a succession of folders and boxes. He chooses a spot in the middle of this and goes into the admirable trance which to an ordinary person is a cat asleep, but to an ailurophile means the essence of concentration and also of relaxation. The sight of such a cat soothes and stretches the mind and the nerves. I think it is also the difference between dry desolation in one's solitude and the sense that there can be a living creature who wants nothing more than to share it in total silence and grace.

But Tam involved himself even more in what I was doing. He was with me every moment of the day and the night. When I went from one place to another, in the house or out of doors when I was in the country, Tam walked ahead of me. In the mornings when I went to my study to work, Tam – like my present cat – was already at the door. Tam then leapt on to my desk, always with the trill by which he announced himself. He took his place on top of the pile of manuscript at my right. There he stayed all day, most of the time asleep, sometimes watching me from an eye closed to the merest slit. Tam always knew when I was coming to the end of a page, just before I was ready to remove the sheet of paper from the type-writer. He would then stand up, stretch, arch his back, say something to me, and move aside so that I could put the page on the pile of manuscript; then he would settle on the manuscript again and wait for the next page, asleep unless you knew the nature of his awareness.

At dinner, when I was alone or with intimates, Tam always sat on the corner of the table at my right hand. He would poise himself as close to the edge of the table as he could without falling off, his front paws hidden beneath his frill. He never begged. He purred from the beginning to the end of the meal, which seemed to me a generous tribute to other people's good appetite. I always kept a titbit for him on my plate but he pretended with grave courtesy not to notice it until I took the morsel in my fingers and offered it to him. Even then he did not move or disturb the symmetry of the table to which he had contributed. He ate his treat daintily and looked for nothing more. He paid no attention to anybody else; to him that would have been a breach of manners.

From *Too Strong for Fantasy* by Marcia Davenport, 1968

Bows and Curtseys

Part of Elizabeth Barrett Browning's 'Paraphrases on Heine',
written in Rome in 1860

My child, we were two children,
Small, merry by childhood's law;
We used to crawl to the hen-house
And hide ourselves in the straw.

We crowed like cocks, and whenever
The passers near us drew –
Cock-a-doodle! they thought
'Twas a real cock that crew.

The boxes about our courtyard
We carpeted to our mind,
And lived there both together –
Kept house in a noble kind.

The neighbour's old cat often
Came to pay us a visit;
We made her a bow and curtsey,
Each with a compliment in it.

After her health we asked,
Our care and regard to evince –
(We have made the very same speeches
To many an old cat since).

From *The Poetical Works of Elizabeth Barrett Browning*, 1904

A Very Fine Cat Indeed

I never shall forget the indulgence with which he [Dr Johnson] treated Hodge, his cat: for whom he himself used to go out and buy oysters, lest the servants having that trouble should take a dislike to the poor creature. I am, unluckily, one of those who have an antipathy to a cat, so that I am uneasy when in the room with one; and I own, I frequently suffered a good deal from the presence of this same Hodge. I recollect him one day scrambling up Dr Johnson's breast, apparently with much satisfaction, while my friend smiling and half-whistling, rubbed down his back, and pulled him by the tail; and when I observed he was a fine cat, saying, 'Why yes, Sir, but I have had cats whom I liked better than this'; and then as if perceiving Hodge to be out of countenance, adding, 'but he is a very fine cat, a very fine cat indeed.'

This reminds me of the ludicrous account which he gave Mr Langton, of the despicable state of a young Gentleman of good family. 'Sir, when I heard of him last, he was running about town shooting cats.' And then in a sort of kindly reverie, he bethought himself of his own favourite cat, and said, 'But Hodge shan't be shot; no, no, Hodge shall not be shot.'

From *The Life of Samuel Johnson LL D* by James Boswell, 1799

'To a Cat'

I

Stately, kindly, lordly friend,
    Condescend
Here to sit by me, and turn
Glorious eyes that smile and burn,
Golden eyes, love's lustrous meed,
On the golden page I read.

All your wondrous wealth of hair,
    Dark and fair,
Silken-shaggy, soft and bright
As the clouds and beams of night,
Pays my reverent hand's caress
Back with friendlier gentleness.

Dogs may fawn on all and some
    As they come;
You, a friend of loftier mind,
Answer friends alone in kind.
Just your foot upon my hand
Softly bids it understand.

Morning round this silent sweet
    Garden-seat
Sheds its wealth of gathering light,
Thrills the gradual clouds with might,
Changes woodland, orchard, heath,
Lawn, and garden there beneath.

Fair and dim they gleamed below:
    Now they glow
Deep as even your sunbright eyes,
Fair as even the wakening skies.
Can it not or can it be
Now that you give thanks to see?

May not you rejoice as I,
    Seeing the sky
Change to heaven revealed, and bid
Earth reveal the heaven it hid
All night long from stars and moon,
Now the sun sets all in tune?

What within you wakes with day
    Who can say?
All too little may we tell,
Friends who like each other well,

What might haply, if we might,
Bid us read our lives aright.

II

Wild on woodland ways your sires
    Flashed like fires;
Fair as flame and fierce and fleet
As with wings on wingless feet
Shone and sprang your mother, free,
Bright and brave as wind or sea.

Free and proud and glad as they,
    Here to-day
Rests or roams their radiant child,
    Vanquished not, but reconciled,
Free from curb of aught above
Save the lovely curb of love.

Love through dreams of souls divine
    Fain would shine
Round a dawn whose light and song
Then should right our mutual song
Speak, and seal the love-lit law
Sweet Assisi's seer foresaw.

Dreams were theirs; yet haply may
    Dawn a day
When such friends and fellows born,
Seeing our earth as fair at morn,
May for wiser love's sake see
More of heaven's deep heart than we.

From *The Complete Works of Algernon Charles Swinburne*
edited by Sir Edmund Gosse and Thomas James Wise, 1925

Donnish Salutes

This story about the Cambridge philosopher Jack McTaggart, quoted in his biography, is attributed to 'one of his many women friends'.

The last time Jack stayed in Winchester with us was in March 1913, and I remember vividly a walk we took, just he and I. His talk was fascinating, but I can't recall it, though three piquant little incidents remain. Delighting in his habit of greeting every cat he passed by a salutation, I wickedly started the walk by leading him through a network of back streets in the old town which I knew to be infested with cats. Sure enough, he gave every one a faint acknowledgment with his right hand, as a master passing down College Street would have acknowledged the boys' salutes. We didn't mention cats. Later on our walk led us over grassy downs where the larks were shouting that March morning. I remarked 'Aren't the larks glorious?' 'Larks, larks!' he exclaimed, peering about on the ground as if I had warned him against rabbit holes, or said the thyme was out! But his enchanting vagueness and absence of mind reached a climax as we returned down a country road. We passed the most striking-looking man I have seen in Europe. Immensely tall, erect, with flashing black eyes but snowy hair, thin as a death mask, in rags of theatrical raggedness, and striding along at a great rate, he was a figure after whom people would naturally turn to gaze. Directly he had passed I asked Jack what he made of him. 'I never saw anyone' he said.

On the same subject, the biographer quotes another of McTaggart's women friends, Miss Stawell:

I was laughing at him for the way he spoilt Pushkin: 'Why,' I said, 'I believe if there was only one cosy chair in the room you would give it to Pushkin and take the floor yourself'. 'Of course I would,' he said, 'it would be only fair. I could think about the Absolute and I don't believe Pushkin can.'

From *J. McT. E. McTaggart* by G. Lowes Dickinson, 1931

Nine

FELLOW-CREATURES

'Sonnet: Cat Cruelty'

Our cat brings a mouse to the window and drops it.
It hobbles a few feet. One leg is injured.
The cat in an excess of delicate energy
dribbles it like a forward. From now on
there is only one tortuous path for it to follow,
only one destination, and that one a dark one.
The cat mouths it and walks off.
They know how to maim and not to kill.

Cat Inquisition. Extraordinary questions.
From those claws – only the dark destination.
Urbain Grandier. Such things certainly
would go near to make a man hate Life.
For lunch I am eating a savoury stew;
the small bones crunch in my mouth with disgust.

From *The Collected Ewart 1933-1980* by Gavin Ewart, 1980

Pangur Bán

This famous poem, about a monk and his pet cat, was written
in the eighth century on a copy of St Paul's Epistles by a student of
the monastery of Carinthia.

I and my white Pangur
Have each his special art:
His mind is set on hunting mice,
Mine is upon my special craft.

I love to rest – better than any fame! –
With close study at my little book;
White Pangur does not envy me:
He loves his childish play.

When in our house we two are all alone –
A tale without tedium!
We have – sport never-ending!
Something to exercise our wit.

At times by feats of derring-do
A mouse sticks in his net,
While into my net there drops
A difficult problem of hard meaning.

He points his full shining eye
Against the fence of the wall:
I point my clear though feeble eye
Against the keenness of science.

He rejoices with quick leaps
When in his sharp claw sticks a mouse:
I too rejoice when I have grasped
A problem difficult and dearly loved.

Though we are thus at all times,
Neither hinders the other,
Each of us pleased with his own art
Amuses himself alone.

He is a master of the work
Which every day he does:
While I am at my own work
To bring difficulty to clearness.

From *Ancient Irish Poetry*, edited by Kuno Meyer, 1913

One Mouse, More or Less

Sophia says that just before I came home, Min caught a mouse, and was playing with it in the yard. It had got away from her once or twice and she had caught it again, and now it was stealing off again, as she was complacently watching it with her paws tucked under her, when her friend, Riorden's stout cock, stepped up inquisitively, looked down at it with one eye, turning its head, then picked it up by the tail, gave it two or three whacks on the ground, and giving it a dexterous toss in the air, caught it in its open mouth, and it went, head foremost and alive, down its capacious throat in the twinkling of an eye, never again to be seen in this world; Min all the while, with paws comfortably tucked under her, looking on unconcerned. What matters it one mouse, more or less, to her? The cock walked off amid the currant-bushes, stretched his neck up and gulped once or twice, and the deed was accomplished. Then he crowed lustily in celebration of the exploit. It might be set down among the *Gesta gallorum*. There were several human witnesses. It is a question whether Min ever understood where that mouse went to. She sits composedly sentinel, with paws tucked under her, a good part of her days at present, by some ridiculous little hole, the possible entry of a mouse.

From *Autumn* by Henry David Thoreau, 1884

The Rat's Strong Foe

I have (and long shall have) a white great nimble cat,
A king upon a mouse, a strong foe to a rat,
Fine eares, long tail he hath, with Lion's curbed clawe,
Which oft he lifteth up, and stayes his lifted pawe,
Deepe musing to himselfe, which after-mewing showes,
Till with lickt beard, his eye of fire espie his foes.

From *Arcadia* by Sir Philip Sidney, 1598

Smale Wilde Bestes

The catte hatte *mureligus* and *musio* and hatte also *catus*. And hath that name *mureligus* for he is enemy to mys and to rattes, and communliche ycleped *catus* and hath that name of ravenyng, for he ravyssheth mys and rattes. Other he hath that name *catus* of *catat* that is 'for to see', for he seeth so sharpliche that he overcometh derknesse of the night by schynyng of the light of his yhen. And the name *catus* cometh of grew and is to menynge 'sly and witty', as Ysidorus seith *libro xii.*

And is a beste of uncerteyn here and colour. For som catte is whyte, som reed, and som blak, and som scowed and splenked in the feet and the face and in the eeren, and is most yliche to the lepard. And hath a gret mouth and sawe teeth and scharpe and longe tonge and pliaunt, thynne, and sotile. And lapeth therwith whanne he drynketh as othere bestes doon that haven the nether lip schorter than the over, for bycause of vneuenesse of lippes suche bestes souken nought in drykynge but lapeth and likketh, as Aristotil seith and Plinius also. And he is a ful leccherous beste in southe, swyfte, plaunte, and mery. And lepeth [and] reseth on alle thyng that is tofore him and is yladde by a strawe and pleyeth therwith. And is a wel hevy beste in eelde and ful slepy. And lith sliliche in awayte for mys and is ware where they ben more by smelle than by sight. And hunteth and reseth on hem in privey place. And whanne he taketh a mous he pleyeth therwith and eteth him after the pleye. And is as it were wylde and goth about in tyme of generacioun. Among cattes in tyme of love is hard fightynge for wyves, and oon craccheth and rendeth the other grevousliche with bytyng and with clawes. And he maketh a reweliche noyse and horrible whan oon profreth to fighte with another. And is a cruel beste whanne he is wilde and waonyeth in wodes and hunteth thanne smale wilde bestes, as conynges and hares. And falleth on his owne feet whanne he falleth out of highe place and is unnethe yhurte whanne he is ythrowe doun of an high place. His drytte stynketh ful foule and therfore he hydeth it under erthe and gadereth therupon coverynge with feet and clawes. And whanne he hat a fayre skynne he is as it were prowde therof and goth faste aboute; and whanne his skynne is ybrende thanne he abydeth at home. And is ofte for his fayre skynne ytake of the skynnere and yslayne and yhulde.

From *De Proprietatibus Rerum* by Bartholomaeus Anglicus, translated by John Trevisa, c.1495.

A Vision of a Rat

Focus found the atmosphere lowering and asked to be let out of the front door.

'Well, be careful,' warned Aunt Irene. 'Some awful person might make you into a muff. Don't leave the garden.'

Normally Focus wouldn't have dreamed of leaving the garden. He would sit under the magnolia daring its blossom to compete with his beauty, and watching the birds, but he was no different from anyone else when it came to being ordered about. He didn't like it.

As soon as Aunt Irene closed the door Focus stepped on to the pavement and gazed round warily. He was perfectly sensible of the dangers inherent in being so attractive, and was taking no risks. Aunt Irene had a very sinister sepia-tinted photograph of one of her relations on a snowy railway station wearing a hat which looked to Focus as though it might well be related to him.

There was no one in the street, so he went for a little walk towards the church waving his tail, and there, sitting on a garden wall was that rat. Major Mason saw it too, only he didn't believe it. He was out for a constitutional, because he was determined to become very healthy now that he had given up drinking, and this rat vision struck him as most unfair. He knew it must be a hallucination because that dopey-looking cat was taking no notice of it at all. Poor Major Mason couldn't know that Focus was merely going to some lengths to maintain his dignity, having been had before.

Major and cat passed each other looking steadily ahead while the rat smirked. Focus went home and tapped on the dining-room window, and the Major went down to the river to breathe in some refreshing effluent.

From *The 27th Kingdom* by Alice Thomas Ellis, 1982

'You'd Take The Entire Universe to Bed With You'

You'd take the entire universe to bed with you,
I think, just out of boredom, you lecherous, idle shrew!
You need, to keep your teeth sound, exercise your jaws,

Daily, for dinner, some new heart between your paws!
Your eyes, all lighted up like shops, like public fairs,
How insolent they are! – as if their power were theirs
Indeed! – this borrowed power, this Beauty, you direct
And use, whose law, however, you do not suspect.

Unwholesome instrument for health, O deaf machine
And blind, fecund in tortures! – how is it you have not seen,
You drinker of the world's blood, your mirrored loveliness
Blench and recoil? how is it you feel no shame? confess:
Has never, then, this evil's very magnitude
Caused you to stagger? – you, who think yourself so shrewd
In evil? – seeing how Nature, patient and abstruse –
O Woman, Queen of Sins, Vile Animal, – has made use
Of you, to mould a genius? – employed you all this time?

O muddy grandeur! – ignominy ironic and sublime!

From *Flowers of Evil* by Charles Baudelaire, 1857
translated by Edna St Vincent Millay

Low Opinion

CAT. *n.f.* [*katz*, Teuton, *chat*, Fr.] A domestick animal that catches mice, commonly reckoned by naturalists the lowest order of the leonine species.

From *A Dictionary of the English Language* by Samuel Johnson, 1755

Le Patron Mange Ici

Once upon a time there was a village shop. The name over the window was 'Ginger and Pickles.'

It was a little small shop just the right size for Dolls – Lucinda and Jane Doll-cook always bought their groceries at Ginger and Pickles.

The counter inside was a convenient height for rabbits. Ginger and Pickles sold red spotty pocket-handkerchiefs at a penny three farthings.

They also sold sugar, and snuff and galoshes.

In fact, although it was such a small shop it sold nearly everything – except a few things that you want in a hurry – like bootlaces, hair-pins and mutton chops.

Ginger and Pickles were the people who kept the shop. Ginger was a yellow tom-cat, and Pickles was a terrier.

The rabbits were always a little bit afraid of Pickles.

The shop was also patronized by mice – only the mice were rather afraid of Ginger.

Ginger usually requested Pickles to serve them, because he said it made his mouth water.

'I cannot bear,' said he, 'to see them going out at the door carrying their little parcels.'

From The Tale of Ginger and Pickles by Beatrix Potter, 1909

'Red Slippers'

A wicked cat, grown old and gray,
That she was a shoemaker chose to say,
And put before her window a board
Where slippers for young maidens were stored;
While some were of morocco made,
Others of satin were there display'd;
Of velvet some, with edges of gold,
And figured strings, all gay to behold.
But fairest of all exposed to view
Was a pair of slippers of scarlet hue;
They gave full many a lass delight
With their gorgeous colours and splendour bright.

A young and snow-white noble mouse
Who chanced to pass the shoemaker's house
First turn'd to look, and then stood still,
And then peep'd over the window sill.
At length she said: 'Good day, mother cat;
You've pretty red slippers, I grant you that

If they're not dear, I'm ready to buy,
So tell me the price, if it's not too high.'

'My good young lady,' the cat replied,
'Pray do me the favor to step inside,
And honor my house, I venture to pray,
With your gracious presence. Allow me to say
That the fairest maidens come shopping to me,
And duchesses too, of high degree.
The slippers I'm willing full cheap to sell,
Yet let us see if they'll fit you well.
Pray step inside, and take a seat' –
Thus the wily cat did falsely entreat,
And the poor white thing in her ignorance then
Fell plump in the snare in that murderous den.
The little mouse sat down on a chair,
And lifted her small leg up in the air,
In order to try how the red shoes fitted,
A picture of innocent calm to be pitied.
When sudden the wicked cat seized her fast,
Her murderous talons around her cast,
And bit right off her poor little head.
'My dear white creature,' the cat then said,
'My sweet little mouse, you're as dead as a rat.
The scarlet red slippers that served me so pat
I'll kindly place on the top of your tomb,
And when is heard, on the last day of doom,
The sound of the trump, O mouse so white,
From out of your grave you'll come to light,
Like all the rest, and then you'll be able
To wear your red slippers.' Here ends my fable.

MORAL

Ye little white mice, take care where you go,
And don't be seduced by worldly show;
I counsel you sooner barefooted to walk,
Than buy slippers of cats, however they talk.

From *The Poems of Heine*, translated by E. A. Bowring, 1861

A Cat's Example

For three whole days I and my cat
Have come up here, and patiently sat –
    We sit and wait on silent Time;
He for a mouse that scratched close by,
At a hole where he sets his eye –
    And I for some music and rhyme.

Is this the Poet's secret, that
He waits in patience, like this cat,
    To start a dream from under cover?
A cat's example, too, in love,
With Passion's every trick and move,
    Would burn up any human lover.

From *W. H. Davies: Selected Poems*, 1985

'A Very Sexy Drug'

On the afternoon of the American Cancer Society's Great American Smokeout, almost everyone in Lucky Strike, a restaurant in SoHo without a no-smoking section, was smoking. Jimmie Durham, an artist and sculptor who has done a painting of poppies with what appears to be a cigarette burn in it, smoked half a pack of Camels without remorse. When he was asked what he thought was the most fun about smoking, Mr Durham said, 'I think just the narcotic. It keeps me on an even keel. When I quit smoking, I have too much energy. What is the very most fun is to quit for three weeks and then smoke a cigarette. You get a beautiful rush' . . .

Jimmie Durham laughed, and smoked some more, and talked about his dead cat. 'I used to have a cat that would sit and think when I was sitting and working. I took him to Mexico, and he became a scorpion addict. He wanted every one. He liked to play with scorpions. And he liked for them to sting him. I got stung by a baby one in Mexico, just on the finger, and it was very, very painful. But it was a very sexy drug.' Mr Durham was eating an omelette and pale

[322]

French fries. He lit another Camel with his violet lighter. A young man at a table nearby had been lighting each new Marlboro off the previous one. Mr Durham had given his smoking a forty-five-second rest. He went on, 'You could watch him. He'd have a scorpion hanging from his nose by the stinger and stuck on his paw, like this, and then he would shake around and shiver and look for another scorpion. He liked the excitement of being stung. But it had an accumulative effect.'

From the New Yorker, 7 December 1992

'Of Food Which Has Been Alive'

A large part of the bodies which have had life will pass into the bodies of other animals, that is the houses no longer inhabited will pass piece-meal through those which are inhabited, ministering to their needs and bearing away with them what is waste; that is to say, the life of man is made by things which he eats, and these carry with them that part of man which is dead.

The rat was being besieged in its little dwelling by the weasel which with continual vigilance was awaiting its destruction, and through a tiny chink was considering its great danger. Meanwhile the cat came and suddenly seized hold of the weasel and forthwith devoured it. Whereupon the rat, profoundly grateful to its deity, having offered up some of its hazel-nuts in sacrifice to Jove, came out of its hole in order to repossess itself of the lately lost liberty, and was instantly deprived of this and of life by the cruel claws and teeth of the cat.

From The Notebooks of Leonardo da Vinci (1452-1519)
edited by Irma A. Richter, 1952

'To My Child Carlino'

Carlino is Charles Savage Landor, the son of Walter Savage Landor.

> Carlino! What art thou about, my boy? . . .
> Does Cincirillo follow thee about?

Inverting one swart foot suspensively,
And wagging his dread jaw, at every chirp
Of bird above him in the olive-branch?
Frighten him then away! 'twas he who slew
Our pigeons, our white pigeons, peacock-tailed,
That fear'd not you and me . . . alas, nor him!
I flattened his striped sides along my knee,
And reasoned with him on his bloody mind,
Till he looked blandly, and half-closed his eyes
To ponder on my lecture in the shade.
I doubt his memory much, his heart a little
And in some minor matters (may I say it?)
Could wish him rather sager. But from thee
God hold back wisdom yet for many years!

From *The Pentameron* by Walter Savage Landor, 1837

Cat Meets Lion

*In the autumn of 1931 the writer Marcia Davenport was depressed after
the suicide of a friend.*

Early in November my daughter reminded me that I had promised
to take her to the annual Empire Cat Club show, which then used
to be in Madison Square Garden. I had forgotten about it. We
walked slowly through the aisles lined with cages occupied by
glorious cats. Normally I would have been in ecstasies but as it was,
I felt no pleasure. We were ready to leave and were passing the last
cage in the last aisle, when something caught my skirt and I
stopped to disentangle it. I looked down into the face of a very
young red Persian kitten, who had thrust his paw through the bars
of his cage and caught my skirt with his claws. The little face en-
treated me; I heard the kitten purring as I bent down. It rubbed
itself against my fingers as I put them through the bars. I found
myself in tears. The ice fell away from where it was lodged inside
me.

'Is this kitten for sale?' I asked the woman who was sitting there.
It was, she said; the price was ten dollars. I ought to have been

suspicious, either that the kitten was not a good one or that the woman had some discreditable reason for wanting to get rid of it. Ten dollars was a ridiculous price for a good long-haired kitten. But none of that mattered, then or later. The kitten had elected me. That is the way real cat-human relationships are formed. I found a shoe-box in back of the cages somewhere, we punched holes in it, I paid the woman and took the kitten home. Not until I was in the taxi did I remember that Russell [Davenport, her husband] for two years had refused to have a cat in the house, my first attempt – to induce a country cat to live with propriety in the city – having been a failure. I took the kitten in its box to Russell's room where he was in bed with one of the recurrent stomach ailments that were more often an escape-hatch than an affliction. Without a word I put the box on the bed, loosening the lid. The kitten sprang out. Visibly Russell fell apart as I had done. Nobody could have resisted that kitten. It was Russell who named him Tamerlane the King of Persia. And Tam for sixteen years thereafter was the companion of every instant of my life except when I was in Europe.

I soon learned why the woman had asked only ten dollars. Tam had every ailment that a kitten can have. He had fleas. He had worms. He had ringworm which of course I caught, and which cost ten times the price I had paid for Tam, to cure. He had dreadful in-testinal troubles requiring care such as one would give an infant. He had rickets so badly that at one time he could not stand up at all. Two veterinarians advised me to put him down, saying that such a kitten was not worth raising, but all I did was weep and look for someone who would understand why I had to keep him. That someone was Dr Raymond Garbutt, who understood cats and the aberrations of what I call cat-people, with intuition only explained by the fact that he was a cat-person himself, a gentle, deliberate man who did not need the language of words in which to com-municate with animals.

We won the battle, after months of the most difficult nursing. When he was a year old Tam began to bloom. He was spectacu-larly beautiful, a big sixteen-pound cat with wonderful eyes of deep topaz and a coral-coloured nose. If it is ever claimed that a cat does not feel, nor in his eyes show emotion, that person can never have known a Tam. He had a glorious coat and great thick plodding forepaws on which he used to proceed into a room with the self-assurance of royalty. Like most beautiful animals he had a keen sense of vanity and of his own importance and knew exactly how to show himself off to best advantage, taking a pose in the centre medallion of a Persian rug, or choosing a piece of furniture upholstered in soft blue or green, the colours most flattering to him. But all that was like the vanity of a pretty woman. It was his character for which I loved him. He was attached to me as people mistakenly think only a dog can be attached. They can never have known the devotion of a cat. Dr Garbutt used to say that Tam's extraordinary devotion was developed through the struggle to save his life, which he sensed he owed to me. I do not know.

In 1939 the Davenports spent the summer in Connecticut, in a rented house called Great Marsh. It was there that Tam acquired an unwelcome feline colleague.

My birthday came along shortly after we moved to Great Marsh and Russell was late that day coming out from town. He had driven in in his horrible old black Chrysler instead of taking the train. When I heard it come snarling in from the highroad I glanced out of the window of my room where I was changing my dress. Russell had driven down to the barn instead of stopping at the front door. I wondered what he was doing there. It was out of sight of the house. There was a long delay. Then I saw him walking slowly across the lawn. He was holding what looked like a long rope and on the other end of it – 'Damn!' I said aloud. I thought of the arrival of the cows in Vermont. In the dusk I could not see what he was leading but it looked big and tawny in colour. I thought he had bought a Great Dane. I was ready to kill him.

Then my cat Tam who was crouched beneath my hand on the window-sill suddenly began to swell like a blowfish. His spine went up, his claws came out, and he let out a noise that was both a hiss and a yowl. His eyes were sharper than mine. Russell had a lion on the end of a long chain. She was a cub three months old – my birthday present. She was enchanting. I named her Kitty. She was a perfect kitten in maximum. She played with strings and balls and bouncy toys; she rolled over and waved her huge paws when she was happy; she cried when she was lonely; she purred with a noise like a large electric motor. Her affection and enthusiasm were a little dangerous since she had no idea of her own strength – she weighed about sixty pounds – and she would fling herself at me, asking to play, or wrap her paws around my ankles. Stockings went at the rate of dozens a week, and lion scratches, even those from love-pats, can be toxic unlike those of felis domesticus. I settled for strong denim overalls, a long-sleeved jacket, and gloves when I went out to play with my pet. Tam was miserable. When Kitty was not in her loose-box in the barn she was tethered by her chain to a long wire between two trees, and Tam remained in my room, yowling with jealousy on the window sill.

At first sight Kitty petrified most people, including the ice-man, who asked me, 'Is that there what I think that is?' Her favourite treat and toy on hot days was a lump of ice. She had sprung on to the first piece of ice when it slid off the back of the truck, and thereafter she bounded joyfully on her tether to greet the ice-man whenever he came. I assured him that Kitty was harmless but soon the local game warden came round. He could not make up his mind what he was supposed to do about Kitty. I offered to take out a licence for her. He hadn't thought of that. In fact, there was no such thing, and no precedent for this situation. Was there a law applicable to Kitty? Well, not exactly. He stood watching Kitty who was amiably playing with a spray of rambler roses. He pushed his hat to the back of his head and said, 'Aw, shucks, it can stay.'

From *Too Strong For Fantasy* by Marcia Davenport, 1968

'Esther's Tomcat'

Daylong this tomcat lies stretched flat
As an old rough mat, no mouth and no eyes,
Continual wars and wives are what
Have tattered his ears and battered his head.

Like a bundle of old rope and iron
Sleeps till blue dusk. Then reappear
His eyes, green as ringstones: he yawns wide red,
Fangs fine as a lady's needle and bright.

A tomcat sprang at a mounted knight,
Locked round his neck like a trap of hooks
While the knight rode fighting its clawing and bite.
After hundreds of years the stain's there

On the stone where he fell, dead of the tom:
That was at Barnborough. The tomcat still
Grallochs odd dogs on the quiet,
Will take the head clean off your simple pullet,

Is unkillable. From the dog's fury,
From gunshot fired point-blank he brings
His skin whole, and whole
From owlish moons of bekittenings

Among ashcans. He leaps and lightly
Walks upon sleep, his mind on the moon.
Nightly over the round world of men,
Over the roofs go his eyes and outcry.

From *Selected Poems 1957-1981* by Ted Hughes, 1982

A Horrid Dog

Parts of two letters from Connop Thirlwall, Bishop of St David's,
to his friend Miss Johnes

Abergwili Palace, 1 Oct., 1866

I should have accepted your kind offer with pleasure and gratitude
if I had been catless, especially as I am particularly fond of *good* tortoiseshell cats, which are very rare. I once had one which was a
perfect beauty, and no less amiable than beautiful. The lovely creature came to an untimely end, killed by a horrid big black dog
(abetted, I am afraid, by one of my own, who should have known
better) who came into the house one Sunday while we were all at
church. But I do not venture to introduce a second cat into the

family without the express consent of the one now reigning, which I do not expect him to give; and I remember many years ago receiving a kitten from Aberglasney, which was destroyed by an elder cat of that day; and, as a general rule, I believe that cats do not get on well together unless they are members of the same family . . .

Abergwili Palace, 7 June, 1871

No friend of an Angola kitten would bring it within reach of my Lion, who is a lamb when unprovoked, but would not bear the sight of a rival. The house, now so quiet, would become a scene of swearing, cattering and wauling . . .

From *Letters To a Friend by Connop Thirlwall, Late Lord Bishop of St David's*,
edited by the Very Revd Arthur P. Stanley, 1861

Investigating a Rabbit Warren

I took the opportunity of repairing to the widow's cottage, where I found her in some anxiety about her cat, which had been absent all day. I comforted her with as many anecdotes of that animal's roving propensities as I could recollect.'I'm feared o' th' gamekeepers,' said she, 'that's all 'at I think on. If th' young gentlemen had been at home, I should a' thought they'd been setting their dogs at her, an' worried her, poor thing, as they did *many* a poor thing's cat; but I haven't that to be feared on now.' Nancy's eyes were better, but still far from well: she had been trying to make a Sunday shirt for her son, but told me she could only bear to do a little bit at it now and then, so that it progressed but slowly, though the poor lad wanted it sadly. So I proposed to help her a little, after I had read to her, for I had plenty of time that evening, and need not return till dusk. She thankfully accepted the offer.

'An' you'll be a bit o' company for me too, miss,' said she; 'I like as I feel lonesome without my cat.' But when I had finished reading, and done the half of a seam, with Nancy's capacious brass thimble fitted on to my finger by means of a roll of paper, I was disturbed by the entrance of Mr Weston, with the identical cat in his arms. I now saw that he could smile, and very pleasantly too.

'I've done you a piece of good service, Nancy,' he began: then seeing me, he acknowledged my presence by a slight bow. I should have been invisible to Hatfield, or any other gentleman of those parts. 'I've delivered your cat,' he continued, 'from the hands, or rather the gun, of Mr Murray's gamekeeper.'

'God bless you, sir!' cried the grateful old woman, ready to weep for joy as she received her favourite from his arms.

'Take care of it,' said he, 'and don't let it go near the rabbit warren, for the gamekeeper swears he'll shoot it if he sees it there again: he would have done so to-day, if I had not been in time to stop him. – I believe it is raining, Miss Grey,' added he, more quietly, observing that I had put aside my work, and was preparing to depart. 'Don't let me disturb you – I shan't stay two minutes.'

'You'll *both* stay while this shower gets owered,' said Nancy, as she stirred the fire, and placed another chair beside it; 'what! there's room for all.'

'I can see better here, thank you, Nancy,' replied I, taking my work to the window, where she had the goodness to suffer me to remain unmolested, while she got a brush to remove the cat's hairs from Mr Weston's coat, carefully wiped the rain from his hat, and gave the cat its supper, busily talking all the time: now thanking her clerical friend for what he had done; now wondering how the cat had found out the warren; and now lamenting the probable consequences of such a discovery. He listened with a quiet, good-natured smile, and at length took a seat in compliance with her pressing invitations, but repeated that he did not mean to stay.

'I have another place to go to,' said he, 'and I see' (glancing at the book on the table) 'some one else has been reading to you.'

'Yes, sir; Miss Grey has been as kind as read me a chapter; an' now she's helping me with a shirt for our Bill – but I'm feared she'll be cold there. Won't you come to th' fire, miss?'

'No, thank you, Nancy, I'm quite warm. I must go as soon as this shower is over.'

'Oh, miss! You said you could stop while dusk!' cried the provoking old woman, and Mr Weston seized his hat.

'Nay, sir,' exclaimed she, 'pray don't go now, while it rains so fast.'

'But it strikes me I'm keeping your visitor away from the fire.'

'No, you're not, Mr Weston,' replied I, hoping there was no harm in a falsehood of that description.

'No, sure!' cried Nancy. 'What, there's lots o' room!'

'Miss Grey,' said he, half-jestingly, as if he felt it necessary to change the present subject, whether he had anything particular to say or not, 'I wish you would make my peace with the squire when you see him. He was by when I rescued Nancy's cat, and did not quite approve of the deed. I told him I thought he might better spare all his rabbits than she her cat, for which audacious assertion he treated me to some rather ungentlemanly language; and I fear I retorted a trifle too warmly.'

'Oh, lawful sir! I hope you didn't fall out wi' th' maister for sake o' my cat! he cannot bide answering again – can th' maister.'

'Oh! it's no matter, Nancy: I don't care about it, really; I said nothing *very* uncivil; and I suppose Mr Murray is accustomed to use rather strong language when he's heated.'

From Agnes Grey by Anne Brontë, 1847

'Dogs, Cats, Books, and the Average Man'

A letter to the editor of The Yellow Book from 'The Yellow Dwarf'.

Sir,

I hope you will not suspect me of making a bid for his affection, when I remark that the Average Man loves the Obvious. By consequence (for, like all unthinking creatures, the duffer's logical), by consequence, his attitude towards the Subtle, the Elusive, when not an attitude of mere torpid indifference, is an attitude of positive distrust and dislike.

Of this ignoble fact, pretty nearly everything – from the popularity of beer and skittles, to the popularity of Mr Hall Caine's novels; from the general's distaste for caviare, to the general's neglect of Mr Henry James's tales – pretty nearly everything is a reminder. But, to go no further afield, for the moment, than his own hearthrug, may I ask you to consider a little the relative positions occupied in the Average Man's regard by the Dog and the Cat?

The Average Man ostentatiously loves the Dog.

The Average Man, when he is not torpidly indifferent to that princely animal, positively distrusts and dislikes the Cat.

I have used the epithet 'princely' with intention, in speaking of the near relative of the King of Beasts. The Cat is a Princess of the Blood. Yes, my dear, always a Princess, though the Average Man, with his unerring instinct for the malappropriate word, sometimes names her Thomas. The Cat is always a Princess, because everything nice in this world, everything fine, sensitive, distinguished, everything beautiful, everything worth while, is of essence Feminine, though it may be male by the accident of sex; – and that's as true as gospel, let Mr W. E. Henley's lusty young disciples shout their loudest in celebration of the Virile. – The Cat is a Princess.

The Dog, on the contrary, is not even a gentleman. Far otherwise: His admirers may do what they will to forget it, the circumstance remains, writ large in every Natural History, that the Dog is sprung from quite the meanest family of the Quadrupeds. That coward thief the wolf is his bastard brother; the carrion hyena is his cousin-german. And in his person, as in his character, bears he not an hundred marks of his base descent? In his rough coat (contrast it with the silken mantle of the Cat); in his harsh, monotonous voice (contrast it with the flexible organ of the Cat, her versatile mewings, chirrupings, and purrings, and their innumerable shades and modulations); in the stiff-jointed clumsiness of his movements (compare them to the inexpressible grace and suppleness of the Cat's); briefly, in the all-pervading plebeian commonness that hangs about him like an atmosphere (compare it to the high-bred reserve and dignity that invest the Cat). The wolf's brother, is the Dog not himself a coward? Watch him when, emulating the ruffian who insults an unprotected lady, he puts a Cat to flight in the streets: watch him when the lady halts and turns. Faugh, the craven! with his wild show of savagery so long as there is not the slightest danger – and his sudden chopfallen drawing back when the lady halts and turns! The hyena's cousin, is he not himself of carrion an impassioned amateur? At Constantinople he serves ('tis a labour of love; he receives no stipend) he serves as Public Scavenger, swallowing with greed the ordures cast by the Turk. Scripture tells us to what he returneth: who has failed to observe that he returneth not to his own alone? And the other day, strolling upon the sands by the illimitable sea, I came upon a friend and her pet terrier. She was holding the little beggar by the scruff of his neck, and giving him repeated sousing in a pool. I stood a pleased spectator of this exercise, for the terrier kicked and spluttered and appeared to be unhappy. 'He found a decaying jelly-fish below there, and rolled in it,' my friend pathetically explained. I should like to see the Cat who could be induced to roll in a decaying jelly-fish. The Cat's fastidiousness, her meticulous cleanliness, the time and the pains she bestows upon her toilet, and her almost morbid delicacy about certain more private errands, are among the material indications of her patrician nature. It were needless to allude to the vile habits and impudicity of the Dog.

Have you ever met a Dog who wasn't a bounder? Have you ever met a Dog who wasn't a bully, a sycophant, and a snob? Have you ever met a Cat who was? Have you ever met a Cat who would half frighten a timid little girl to death, by rushing at her and barking? Have you ever met a Cat who, left alone with a visitor in your drawing-room, would truculently growl and show her teeth, as often as that visitor ventured to stir in his chair? Have you ever met a Cat who would snarl and snap at the servants, Master's back being turned? Have you ever met a Cat who would cringe to you and fawn to you, and kiss the hand that smote her?

Conscious of her high lineage, the Cat understands and accepts the responsibilities that attach to it. She knows what she owes to herself, to her rank, to the Royal Idea. Therefore, it is you who must be the courtier. The Dog, poor-spirited toady, will study your eye to divine your mood, and slavishly adapt his own mood and his behaviour to it. Not so the Cat. As between you and her, it is you who must do the toadying. A guest in the house, never a dependant, she remembers always the courtesy and the consideration that are her due. You must respect her pleasure. Is it her pleasure to slumber, and do you disturb her: note the disdainful melancholy with which she silently comments your rudeness. Is it her pleasure to be grave: tempt her to frolic, you will tempt in vain. It is her pleasure to be cold: nothing in human possibility can win a caress from her. Is it her pleasure to be rid of your presence: only the physical influence of a closed door will persuade her to remain in the room with you. It is you who must be the courtier, and wait upon her desire.

But then!

When, in her own good time, she chooses to unbend, how graciously, how entrancingly, she does it! Oh, the thousand wonderful lovelinesses and surpises of her play! The wit, the humour, the imagination, that inform it! Her ruses, her false leads, her sudden triumphs, her feigned despairs! And the topazes and emeralds that sparkle in her eyes; the satiny lustre of her apparel; the delicious sinuousities of her body! And her parenthetic interruptions of the game: to stride in regal progress round the apartment, flourishing her tail like a banner: or coquettishly to throw herself in some enravishing posture at length upon the carpet at your feet: or (if she loves you) to leap upon your shoulder, and press her cheek to yours, and murmur rapturous assurances of her passion! To be loved by a Princess! Whosoever, from the Marquis de Carabas down, has been loved by a Cat, has savoured that felicity. My own particular treasure of a Cat, at this particular moment is lying wreathed about my neck, watching my pen as it moves along the paper, and purring approbation of my views. But when, from time to time, I chance to use a word that doesn't strike her altogether as the fittest, she reaches down her little velvet paw, and dabs it out. I should like to see the Dog who could do that.

But – the Cat is subtle, the Cat is elusive, the Cat is not to be read at a glance, the Cat is not a simple equation. And so the Average Man, gross mutton-devouring, money-grubbing mechanism that he is, when he doesn't just torpidly tolerate her, distrusts her and dislikes her. A great soul, misappreciated, misunderstood, she sits neglected in his chimney-corner; and the fatuous idgit never guesses how she scorns him.

But – the Dog is obvious. Any fool can grasp the meaning of the Dog. And the Average Man, accordingly, recreant for once to the snobbism which is his religion, hugs the hyena's cousin to his bosom.

What of it?

Only this: that in the Average Man's sentimental attitude towards the Dog and the Cat, we have a formula, a symbol, for his sentimental attitude towards many things, especially for his sentimental attitude towards Books.

Some books, in their uncouthness, their awkwardness, their boisterousness, in their violation of the decencies of art, in their low truckling to the tastes of the purchaser, in their commonness, their vulgarity, in their total lack of suppleness and distinction, are the very Dogs of Bookland. The Average Man loves 'em. Such as they are, they're obvious.

And other books, by reason of their beauties and their virtues, their graces and refinements; because they are considered finished; because they are delicate, distinguished, aristocratic; because their touch is light, their movement deft and fleet; because they proceed by omission, by implication and suggestion; because they employ the *demi-mot* and the *nuance*; because, in fine, they are Subtle – other books are the Cats of Bookland. And the Average Man hates them or ignores them.

From *The Yellow Book*, Volume X, July 1896

A Dog's Advantages

Pussy can sit by the fire and sing,
  Pussy can climb a tree,
Or play with a silly old cork and string
  To 'muse herself, not me.
But I like *Binkie* my dog, because
  He knows how to behave;
So, *Binkie*'s the same as the First Friend was,
  And I am the Man in the Cave!

Pussy will play Man Friday till
  It's time to wet her paw
And make her walk on the window-sill
  (For the footprint Crusoe saw);
Then she fluffles her tail and mews,
  And scratches and won't attend.
But *Binkie* will play whatever I choose,
  And he is my true First Friend!

Pussy will rub my knees with her head
  Pretending she loves me hard;
But the very minute I go to my bed
  Pussy runs out in the yard,
And there she stays till the morning-light;
  So I know it is only pretend;
But *Binkie*, he snores at my feet all night,
  And he is my Firstest Friend!

From *Just So Stories* by Rudyard Kipling, 1902

'The Cat that Walked by Himself'

Hear and attend and listen; for this befell and behappened and became and was, O my Best Beloved, when the Tame animals were wild. The Dog was wild, and the Horse was wild, and the Cow was wild, and the Sheep was wild, and the Pig was wild – as wild as wild could be – and they walked in the Wet Wild Woods by their wild lones. But the wildest of all the wild animals was the Cat. He walked by himself, and all places were alike to him.

Of course the Man was wild too. He was dreadfully wild. He didn't even begin to be tame till he met the Woman, and she told him that she did not like living in his wild ways. She picked out a nice dry Cave, instead of a heap of wet leaves, to lie down in; and she strewed clean sand on the floor; and she lit a nice fire of wood at the back of the Cave; and she hung a dried wild-horse skin, tail-down, across the opening of the Cave; and she said, 'Wipe your feet, dear, when you come in, and now we'll keep house.'

That night, Best Beloved, they ate wild sheep roasted on the hot stones, and flavoured with wild garlic and wild pepper; and wild duck stuffed with wild rice and wild fenugreek and wild coriander; and marrow-bones of wild oxen; and wild cherries, and wild grenadillas. Then the Man went to sleep in front of the fire ever so happy; but the Woman sat up, combing her hair. She took the bone of the shoulder of mutton – the big flat blade-bone – and she looked at the wonderful marks on it, and she threw more wood on the fire, and she made a Magic. She made the First Singing Magic in the world.

Out in the Wet Wild Woods all the wild animals gathered together where they could see the light of the fire a long way off, and they wondered what it meant.

Then Wild Horse stamped with his wild foot and said, 'O my Friends and O my Enemies, why have the Man and the Woman made that great light in that great Cave, and what harm will it do us?'

Wild Dog lifted up his wild nose and smelled the smell of the roast mutton, and said, 'I will go up and see and look, and say; for I think it is good. Cat, come with me.'

'Nenni!' said the Cat. 'I am the Cat who walks by himself, and all places are alike to me. I will not come.'

'Then we can never be friends again,' said Wild Dog, and he trotted off to the Cave. But when he had gone a little way the Cat said to himself, 'All places are alike to me. Why should I not go too and see and look and come away at my own liking?' So he slipped after Wild Dog softly, very softly, and hid himself where he could hear everything.

When Wild Dog reached the mouth of the Cave he lifted up the dried horse-skin with his nose and sniffed the beautiful smell of the roast mutton, and the Woman, looking at the blade-bone, heard him, and laughed, and said, 'Here comes the first. Wild Thing out of the Wild Woods, what do you want?'

Wild Dog said, 'O my Enemy and Wife of my Enemy, what is this that smells so good in the Wild Woods?'

Then the Woman picked up a roasted mutton-bone and threw it to Wild Dog, and said, 'Wild Thing out of the Wild Woods, taste and try.' Wild Dog gnawed the bone, and it was more delicious than anything he had ever tasted, and he said, 'O my Enemy and Wife of my Enemy, give me another.'

The Woman said, 'Wild Thing out of the Wild Woods, help my Man to hunt through the day and guard this Cave at night, and I will give you as many roast bones as you need.'

'Ah!' said the Cat, listening. 'This is a very wise Woman, but she is not so wise as I am.'

Wild Dog crawled into the Cave and laid his head on the Woman's lap, and said, 'O my Friend and Wife of my Friend, I will help your Man to hunt through the day, and at night I will guard your Cave.'

'Ah!' said the Cat, listening. 'That is a very foolish Dog.' And he went back through the Wet Wild Woods waving his wild tail, and walking by his wild lone. But he never told anybody.

When the Man waked up he said, 'What is Wild Dog doing here?' And the Woman said, 'His name is not Wild Dog any more, but the First Friend, because he will be our friend for always and always and always. Take him with you when you go hunting.'

Next night the Woman cut great green armfuls of fresh grass from the water-meadows, and dried it before the fire, so that it smelt like new-mown hay, and she sat at the mouth of the Cave and plaited a halter out of horse-hide, and she looked at the shoulder-of-mutton bone – at the big broad blade-bone – and she made a Magic. She made the Second Singing Magic in the world.

Out in the Wild Woods all the wild animals wondered what had happened to Wild Dog, and at last Wild Horse stamped with his foot and said, 'I will go and see and say why Wild Dog has not returned. Cat, come with me.'

'Nenni!' said the Cat. 'I am the Cat who walks by himself, and all places are alike to me. I will not come.' But all the same he followed Wild Horse softly, very softly, and hid himself where he could hear everything.

When the Woman heard Wild Horse tripping and stumbling on his long mane, she laughed and said, 'Here comes the second. Wild Thing out of the Wild Woods, what do you want?'

Wild Horse said, 'O my Enemy and Wife of my Enemy, where is Wild Dog?'

The Woman laughed, and picked up the blade-bone and looked at it, and said, 'Wild Thing out of the Wild Woods, you did not come here for Wild Dog, but for the sake of this good grass.'

And Wild Horse, tripping and stumbling on his long mane, said, 'That is true; give it me to eat.'

The Woman said, 'Wild Thing out of the Wild Woods, bend your wild head and wear what I give you, and you shall eat the wonderful grass three times a day.'

'Ah!' said the Cat, listening. 'This is a clever Woman, but she is not so clever as I am.'

Wild Horse bent his wild head, and the Woman slipped the plaited-hide halter over it, and Wild Horse breathed on the Woman's feet and said, 'O my Mistress, and Wife of my Master, I will be your servant for the sake of the wonderful grass.'

'Ah!' said the Cat, listening. 'That is a very foolish Horse.' And he went back through the Wet Wild Woods, waving his wild tail and walking by his wild lone. But he never told anybody.

When the Man and the Dog came back from hunting, the Man said, 'What is Wild Horse doing here?' And the Woman said, 'His name is not Wild Horse any more, but the First Servant, because he will carry us from place to place for always and always and always. Ride on his back when you go hunting.'

Next day, holding her wild head high that her wild horns should not catch in the wild trees, Wild Cow came up to the Cave, and the Cat followed, and hid himself just the same as before; and everything happened just the same as before; and the Cat said the same things as before; and when Wild Cow had promised to give her milk to the Woman every day in exchange for the wonderful grass, the Cat went back through the Wet Wild Woods waving his wild tail and walking by his wild lone, just the same as before. And he never told anybody. And when the Man and the Horse and the Dog came home from hunting and asked the same questions same as before, the Woman said, 'Her name is not Wild Cow any more, but the Giver of Good Food. She will give us the warm white milk for always and always and always, and I will take care of her while you and the First Friend and the First Servant go hunting.'

Next day the Cat waited to see if any other Wild Thing would go up to the Cave, but no one moved in the Wet Wild Woods, so the Cat walked there by himself; and he saw the Woman milking the Cow, and he saw the light of the fire in the Cave, and he smelt the smell of the warm white milk.

Cat said, 'O my Enemy and Wife of my Enemy, where did Wild Cow go?'

The Woman laughed and said, 'Wild Thing out of the Wild Woods, go back to the Woods again, for I have braided up my hair, and I have put away the magic blade-bone, and we have no more need of either friends or servants in our Cave.'

Cat said, 'I am not a friend, and I am not a servant. I am the Cat who walks by himself, and I wish to come into your Cave.'

Woman said, 'Then why did you not come with First Friend on the first night?'

Cat grew very angry and said, 'Has Wild Dog told tales of me?'

The the Woman laughed and said, 'You are the Cat who walks by himself, and all places are alike to you. You are neither a friend nor a servant. You have said it yourself. Go away and walk by yourself in all places alike.'

Then Cat pretended to be sorry and said, 'Must I never come into the Cave? Must I never sit by the warm fire? Must I never drink the warm white milk? You are very wise and very beautiful. You should not be cruel even to a Cat.'

Woman said, 'I knew I was wise, but I did not know I was beautiful. So I will make a bargain with you. If ever I say one word in your praise, you may come into the Cave.'

'And if you say two words in my praise?' said the Cat.

'I never shall,' said the Woman, 'but if I say two words in your praise, you may sit by the fire in the Cave.'

[339]

'And if you say three words?' said the Cat.

'I never shall,' said the Woman, 'but if I say three words in your praise, you may drink the warm white milk three times a day for always and always and always.'

Then the Cat arched his back and said, 'Now let the Curtain at the mouth of the Cave, and the Fire at the back of the Cave, and the Milk-pots that stand beside the Fire, remember what my Enemy and the Wife of my Enemy has said.' And he went away through the Wet Wild Woods waving his wild tail and walking by his wild lone.

That night when the Man and the Horse and the Dog came home from hunting, the Woman did not tell them of the bargain that she had made with the Cat, because she was afraid that they might not like it.

Cat went far and far away and hid himself in the Wet Wild Woods by his wild lone for a long time till the Woman forgot all about him. Only the Bat – the little upside-down Bat – that hung inside the Cave knew where Cat hid; and every evening Bat would fly to Cat with news of what was happening.

One evening Bat said, 'There is a Baby in the Cave. He is new and pink and fat and small, and the Woman is very fond of him.'

'Ah,' said the Cat, listening. 'But what is the Baby fond of?'

'He is fond of things that are soft and tickle,' said the Bat. 'He is fond of warm things to hold in his arms when he goes to sleep. He is fond of being played with. He is fond of all those things.'

'Ah,' said the Cat, listening. 'Then my time has come.'

Next night Cat walked through the Wet Wild Woods and hid very near the Cave till morning-time, and Man and Dog and Horse went hunting. The Woman was busy cooking that morning, and the Baby cried and interrupted. So she carried him outside the Cave and gave him a handful of pebbles to play with. But still the Baby cried.

Then the Cat put out his paddy paw and patted the Baby on the cheek, and it cooed, and the Cat rubbed against its fat knees and tickled it under its fat chin with his tail. And the Baby laughed; and the Woman heard him and smiled.

Then the Bat – the little upside-down Bat – that hung in the mouth of the Cave said, 'O my Hostess and Wife of my Host and Mother of my Host's Son, a Wild Thing from the Wild Woods is most beautifully playing with your Baby.'

'A blessing on that Wild Thing whoever he may be,' said the Woman, straightening her back, 'for I was a busy woman this morning and he has done me a service.'

That very minute and second, Best Beloved, the dried horse-skin Curtain that was stretched tail-down at the mouth of the Cave fell down – *woosh*! – because it remembered the bargain she had made with the Cat; and when the Woman went to pick it up – lo and behold! – the Cat was sitting quite comfy inside the Cave.

'O my Enemy and Wife of my Enemy and Mother of my Enemy,' said the Cat, 'it is I: for you have spoken a word in my praise, and now I can sit within the Cave for always and always and always. But still I am the Cat who walks by himself, and all places are alike to me.'

The Woman was very angry, and shut her lips tight and took up her spinning-wheel and began to spin.

But the Baby cried because the Cat had gone away, and the Woman could not hush it, for it struggled and kicked and grew black in the face.

'O my Enemy and Wife of my Enemy and Mother of my Enemy,' said the Cat, 'take a strand of the thread that you are spinning and tie it to your spindle-whorl and drag it along the floor, and I will show you a Magic that shall make your Baby laugh as loudly as he is now crying.'

'I will do so,' said the Woman, 'because I am at my wits' end; but I will not thank you for it.'

She tied the thread to the little clay spindle-whorl and drew it across the floor, and the Cat ran after it and patted it with his paws and rolled head over heels, and tossed it backward over his shoulder and chased it between his hind legs and pretended to lose it, and pounced down upon it again, till the Baby laughed as loudly as it had been crying, and scrambled after the Cat and frolicked all over the Cave till it grew tired and settled down to sleep with the Cat in its arms.

'Now,' said Cat, 'I will sing the Baby a song that shall keep him asleep for an hour.' And he began to purr, loud and low, low and loud, till the Baby fell fast asleep. The Woman smiled as she looked down upon the two of them, and said, 'That was wonderfully done. No question but you are very clever, O Cat.'

That very minute and second, Best Beloved, the smoke of the

Fire at the back of the Cave came down in clouds from the roof – *puff!* – because it remembered the bargain she had made with the Cat; and when it had cleared away – low and behold! – the Cat was sitting quite comfy close to the fire.

'O my Enemy and Wife of my Enemy and Mother of my Enemy,' said the Cat, 'it is I: for you have spoken a second word in my praise, and now I can sit by the warm fire at the back of the Cave for always and always and always. But still I am the Cat who walks by himself, and all places are alike to me.'

Then the Woman was very very angry, and let down her hair and put more wood on the fire and brought out the broad blade-bone of the shoulder of mutton and began to make a Magic that should prevent her from saying a third word in praise of the Cat. It was not a Singing Magic, Best Beloved, it was a Still Magic; and by and by the Cave grew so still that a little wee-wee mouse crept out of a corner and ran across the floor.

'O my Enemy and Wife of my Enemy and Mother of my Enemy,' said the Cat, 'is that little mouse part of your Magic?'

'Ouh! Chee! No indeed!' said the Woman, and she dropped the blade-bone and jumped upon the footstool in front of the fire and braided up her hair very quick for fear that the mouse should run up it.

'Ah,' said the Cat, watching. 'Then the mouse will do me no harm if I eat it?'

'No,' said the Woman, braiding up her hair, 'eat it quickly and I will ever be grateful to you.'

Cat made one jump and caught the little mouse, and the Woman said, 'A hundred thanks. Even the First Friend is not quick enough to catch little mice as you have done. You must be very wise.'

That very minute and second, O Best Beloved, the Milk-pot that stood by the fire cracked in two pieces – *ffft!* – because it remembered the bargain she had made with the Cat; and when the Woman jumped down from the footstool – lo and behold! – the Cat was lapping up the warm white milk that lay in one of the broken pieces.

'O my Enemy and Wife of my Enemy and Mother of my Enemy,' said the Cat, 'it is I: for you have spoken three words in my praise, and now I can drink the warm white milk three times a day for always and always and always. But *still* I am the Cat who walks by himself, and all places are alike to me.'

Then the Woman laughed and set the Cat a bowl of the warm white milk and said, 'O Cat, you are as clever as a man, but remember that your bargain was not made with the Man or the Dog, and I do not know what they will do when they come home.'

'What is that to me?' said the Cat. 'If I have my place in the Cave by the fire and my warm white milk three times a day I do not care what the Man or the Dog can do.'

That evening when the Man and the Dog came into the Cave, the Woman told them all the story of the bargain, while the Cat sat by the fire and smiled. Then the Man said, 'Yes, but he has not made a bargain with *me* or with all proper Men after me.' Then he took off his two leather boots and he took up his little stone axe (that makes three) and he fetched a piece of wood and a hatchet (that is five altogether), and he set them out in a row and he said, 'Now we will make *our* bargain. If you do not catch mice when you are in the Cave for always and always and always, I will throw these five things at you whenever I see you, and so shall all proper Men do after me.'

'Ah!' said the Woman, listening. 'This is a very clever Cat, but he is not so clever as my Man.'

The Cat counted the five things (and they looked very knobby) and he said, 'I will catch mice when I am in the Cave for always and always and always; but *still* I am the Cat who walks by himself, and all places are alike to me.'

'Not when I am near,' said the Man. 'If you had not said that last I would have put all these things away for always and always and always; but now I am going to throw my two boots and my little stone axe (that makes three) at you whenever I meet you. And so shall all proper Men do after me!'

Then the Dog said, 'Wait a minute. He has not made a bargain with *me* or with all proper Dogs after me.' And he showed his teeth and said, 'If you are not kind to the Baby while I am in the Cave for always and always and always, I will hunt you till I catch you, and when I catch you I will bite you. And so shall all proper Dogs do after me.'

'Ah!' said the Woman, listening. 'This is a very clever Cat, but he is not so clever as the Dog.'

Cat counted the Dog's teeth (and they looked very pointed) and he said, 'I will be kind to the Baby while I am in the Cave, as long as he does not pull my tail too hard, for always and always and always. But *still* I am the Cat who walks by himself, and all places are alike to me.'

'Not when I am near,' said the Dog. 'If you had not said that last I would have shut my mouth for always and always and always; but *now* I am going to hunt you up a tree whenever I meet you. And so shall all proper Dogs do after me.'

Then the Man threw his two boots and his little stone axe (that makes three) at the Cat, and the Cat ran out of the Cave and the Dog chased him up a tree; and from that day to this, Best Beloved, three proper Men out of five will always throw things at a Cat whenever they meet him, and all proper Dogs will chase him up a tree. But the Cat keeps his side of the bargain too. He will kill mice, and he will be kind to Babies when he is in the house, just as long as they do not pull his tail too hard. But when he has done that, and between times, and when the moon gets up and night comes, he is the Cat that walks by himself, and all places are alike to him. Then he goes out to the Wet Wild Woods or up the Wet Wild Trees or on the Wet Wild Roofs, waving his wild tail and walking by his wild lone.

From *Just So Stories* by Rudyard Kipling, 1902

'Getting The Bird'

A blackbird darted past, a worm dangling from its beak.

'Winsome little creatures, birds,' said Kuching, who was in one of his rare sentimental moods. 'They sing madrigals, I am told.'

Sunshine made a mental note of the expression. Mad regals: sung by birds.

'Thoughtful of them, learning to fly, and leaving firmer terra to us. A great pity they don't observe the rule more rigorously.'

'Perhaps they would, if worms flew.' Sunshine's facetious intrusion went unheeded.

A sorrowful look came over Kuching's face, and he lowered his head. 'Once, when I was a green youth, I was – to some extent – responsible for the demise of one of them. I make no excuses. I happened to yawn, and an incompetent young bird fell plump into my mouth. The shock was such that I closed my mouth instinctively. I have regretted the incident ever since. Indeed, I regretted it right away – my mouth was full of feathers and small bones . . .' He drew himself up. 'But it is vain to repine. What's done is done. The little bird might well have grown up to be unhappy . . . And no doubt its tummy was crammed with innocent worms and grubs.'

'It would be nice to fly,' Sunshine uttered under his breath, but not quietly enough to escape Kuching's notice. 'I wish I could fly, just once.' How impressed Sirikit would be as he soared overhead, flapping his tail! That would show how right she was when she called him 'different'. Or was it 'diffident' she had said?

'Bird thou never wert. Nor will be.' Kuching ended the conversation abruptly. He had recalled an old dream in which he turned into a bird of some sort, and was chased by huge cats, more like pumas, and he couldn't get his wings to work properly. When he woke up, he was shaking all over.

From *The Way of The Cat* by D. J. Enright, 1992

'The Cat and the Canary'

A friend told me she knew an old lady, still living, who possessed a cat and a canary, both of which she was very fond. They both inhabited the dining-room, and so far were well accustomed to each others' society. The lady was aghast one afternoon, on opening the door, to see the room full of feathers; the bird cage was empty. Where was the bird? Alas! the cat crouched beneath the stand, guilt too evident. Condign punishment was administered with many exhortations. How much did the cat understand? She slunk away, not to appear for many days and nights. When at last she did appear she laid at the feet of her mistress a fluffy little canary, quite unharmed. The lady picked it up; it spread its wings and preened its plumage. She recognised the bird; it was a favourite of a friend living a few doors off. The cat also knew that bird, and had hovered about all those days and nights, watching for the opportunity to catch it, an offering to bring, in kind, to make good its guilty deed. Was this remorse?

Animals in close contact with human beings seem to catch some of their feelings.

From *Strange But True: Anecdotes of Cats, Dogs and Birds*
by Beatrice Braithwaite-Batty, 1931

'A Bird and Cat Catastrophe'

Sir, –
Here is the story of a cat and a bird. Two young ladies dwelt to-gether, – one the owner of a canary, which she petted and played with; the other was the mistress of a beautiful cat, which was nursed and patted and petted also. They were a happy and united family. The owner of the cat went abroad for a time, and pussy grew sad and melancholy, and at last became jealous of the bird, which was daily petted as usual, while she was sadly neglected. Pussy could not, and would not, stand this treatment; her jealousy grew day by day till at last, in a fit of rage, she made a dash at the little bird and tore him limb from limb. Then seized by remorse she fled, but the owner of the bird was frantic, and she beat the cat and mourned for her bird; and the owner of the cat when she heard of the catastrophe shed sad tears, not, indeed, because the bird was dead, but because her pussy had been beaten; and so the peace of that happy family was destroyed for a time. Pussy, overwhelmed with remorse at the crime she had committed, was found the next day curled up and asleep in the little bird's cage. Now, the problem for psychologists required to be solved is, why did that cat go into that cage? The only solution that suggests itself to the persons con-cerned is, that by going there she thought she might regain the favour of the mistress whose happiness she had so ruthlessly des-troyed, by taking the place of the bird, and so, perhaps, in due time, be changed into a little petted bird herself. –

I am, Sir, &c.,

Catalonia

From *The Spectator*, 19 October 1895

'The Owl and the Pussy-cat'

The Owl and the Pussy-cat went to sea
  In a beautiful pea-green boat,
They took some honey, and plenty of money,
  Wrapped up in a five-pound note.
The Owl looked up to the stars above,
  And sang to a small guitar,
'O lovely Pussy! O Pussy, my love,
  What a beautiful Pussy you are,
      You are,
      You are!
  What a beautiful Pussy you are!'

Pussy said to the Owl, 'You elegant fowl!
  How charmingly sweet you sing!
O let us be married! too long we have tarried:
  But what shall we do for a ring?'
They sailed away, for a year and a day,
  To the land where the Bong-tree grows;
And there in a wood a Piggy-wig stood,
  With a ring at the end of his nose,
      His nose,
      His nose,
  With a ring at the end of his nose.

'Dear Pig, are you willing to sell for one shilling
  Your ring?' Said the Piggy, 'I will.'
So they took it away, and were married next day
  By the Turkey who lives on the hill.
They dined on mince, and slices of quince,
  Which they ate with a runcible spoon;
And hand in hand, on the edge of the sand,
  They danced by the light of the moon,
      The moon,
      The moon,
  They danced by the light of the moon.

From *Nonsense Songs* by Edward Lear, 1872

'Le Hibou et la Poussiquette'

A free translation of 'The Owl and the Pussy-cat' into French,
by Francis Steegmuller

Hibou et Minou allèrent à la mer
Dans une barque peinte en jaune-canari;
Ils prirent du miel roux et beaucoup de sous
Enroulés dans une lettre de crédit.
Le hibou contemplait les astres du ciel,
Et chantait, en grattant sa guitare,

'O Minou chérie, ô Minou ma belle,
O Poussiquette, comme tu es rare,
    Es rare,
    Es rare!
O Poussiquette, comme tu es rare!'

Au chanteur dit la chatte, 'Noble sieur à deux pattes,
Votre voix est d'une telle élégance!
Voulez-vous, cher Hibou, devenir mon époux?
Mais que faire pour trouver une alliance?'
Ils voguèrent, fous d'amour, une année et un jour;
Puis, au pays où le bong fleurit beau,
Un cochon de lait surgit d'une forêt,
Une bague accrochée au museau,
    Museau,
    Museau,
Une bague accrochée au museau.

'Cochon, veux-tu bien nous vendre pour un rien
Ta bague?' Le cochon consentit.
Donc ils prirent le machin, et le lendemain matin
Le dindon sur le mont les unit.
Ils firent un repas de maigre et de gras,
Se servant d'une cuillère peu commune;
Et là sur la plage, le nouveau ménage
Dansa au clair de la lune,
    La lune,
    La lune,
Dansa au clair de la lune.

From *Le Hibou et La Poussiquette* by Francis Steegmuller, 1961

Murdering For Fun

May is chiefly remarkable for being the only month in which one does not like cats. June, too, perhaps; but, after that, one does not mind if the garden is full of cats. One likes to have a wild beast whose movements, lazy as those of Satan, will terrify the childish birds out of the gooseberry bushes and the raspberries and straw-berries. He will not, we know, have much chance of catching them as late as that. They will be as cunning as he, and the robin will wind his alarum-clock, the starling in the plum-tree will cry out like a hysterical drake, and the blackbird will make as much noise as a farmyard. The cat can but blink at the clamour of such a host of cunning sentinels and, pretending that he had come out only to take the air, return majestically to his dinner of leavings in the kitchen. In May and June, however, one does not wish the birds to be fright-ened. One would like one's garden to be an Alsatia for all their wings and all their songs. There is no hope of this in a garden full of cats. Even a Tetrazzini would cease to be able to produce her best trills if, every time she opened her mouth, a tiger padded in her direction down a path of currant bushes. There are, it may be admitted, heroic exceptions. The chaffinch sits in the plum and blusters out his music, cat or no cat. To be sure, he only sings, a flush of all the colours, in order to distract our attention. He is not an artist but a watchman. If you look into the buddleia-tree beside him, you will see his hen moving about in silence, creeping, danc-ing, fluttering, as she gorges herself with insects. She is a fly-catcher at this season, leaping into the air and pirouetting as she seizes her prey and returns to the bough. She is restless and is not content with the spoil of a single tree. She flings herself gracefully, like a ballet-dancer, into the plum, and takes up a caterpillar in her beak. She does not eat it at once, but stands still, eyeing you as though waiting your applause, and her husband, sitting on the top-most spray, goes on singing his version of *The Roast Beef of Old England*. She does not even now eat the caterpillar, but hurries along the paths of the branches with the obvious purpose of finding a tasty insect to eat along with it. It may be that there are insects that play the part of mustard or Worcestershire sauce in the chaf-finch world. What a meal she is making in any case before she hurries back to her nest! It seems that among the chaffinches the male is the more spiritual of the sexes. But then he has so little to do compared with the female. He is still in that state of savagery in which the male dresses finely and idles.

The thrush cannot maintain the same indifference to cats. He is the most nervous of parents, and spends half his time calling on his children to be careful. The young thrush hopping about on the lawn knows nothing of cats and refuses to believe that they are dangerous. He is not afraid even of human beings. His parent becomes argumentative to the point of tears, but the young one stays where he is and looks at you with a sideways jerk of his head as much as to say: 'Listen to the old 'un.' You, too, begin to be alarmed at such boldness. You know, like the pitiful parent, that the world is a very dangerous place, and that your neighbour's cat goes about like a roaring lion seeking whom he may devour. It has been contended by some men of science that all birds are born fearless after the manner of the young thrush, and that fear is a lesson that has to be taught to each new generation by the more experienced parents. Fear, they say, is not an inherited instinct, but a racial tradition that has to be communicated like the morality of civilized people. The young thrush on the lawn is certainly a witness on behalf of this theory. He hops towards you instead of away from you. He moves his gaping beak as though he were trying to say something. If there were no cats in the world, you would encourage his confidences, but you feel that, much as you would like to make friends with him, you must, for his own sake, give him his first lesson in fear. You try to give yourself the appearance of a grim giant: it has no effect on him. You make a quick movement to chase him away: he runs a few yards and then stops and looks round at you as though you were playing a game. It is too much to expect of you that you will actually throw stones at a bird for its good, and so you give up his education as a bad job. Alas, in two days, your worst fears are justified. His dead body is found, torn and ruffled, among the bushes. Some cat has murdered him – murdered him, evidently, not in hunger, but just for fun. Two indignant children, one gold, one brown, discover the dead body and bring in the tale. They prepare the funeral rites of one whose only sin was his innocence. This is not the first burial in the garden. There is already a cemetery marked with half-a-dozen crosses and heaped with flowers under the pear-tree on the south wall. Here is where the mouse was buried; here where the starling; and here the rabbit's skull. They all lie there under the earth in boxes, as you and I will lie, expecting the Last Trump. The robins are not kinder to the 'friendless bodies of unburied men' than are children to the bodies of mice and birds. Here the ghost of no creature haunts reproaching us with the absence of a tomb, as the dead sailor washed up on an alien shore reproaches us so often in the pages of *The Greek Anthology*. There is a procession to the grave and all due ceremony. There is even a funeral service. Over the starling, perhaps, it lacked something in appropriateness. The buriers meant well, however. Their favourite in verse at the time was *Lars Porsena of Clusium*, and they gave the starling the best they knew – gave it to him from beginning to end. What he made of it, there is no telling: he is, it is said, an impressionable bird, though something of a satirist. Someone, overhearing them, recommended a briefer and more fitting service for the future. The young thrush had the benefit of the advice. He was laid to his last rest with the recitation of that noblest of valedictories: 'Fear no more the heat o' the sun,' over his tomb. He is now gone where there is no cat or parent to disturb. The priests who buried him declare that he has been turned into a golden nightingale, and that there must be no noise or romping in the garden for three days, as not till then will he have arrived safely at the Appleiades. That is the name they give to the Pleiades – the seven golden islands whither pass the souls of dead mice and birds and dolls and where Scarlatti lives and where you, too, may expect to go if you please them. Even the black cat will probably go there – one's own black cat. But not the neighbour's cat – the reddish-brown one – thief, murderer and beast. It is the neighbour's cat that makes one believe there is a hell.

From *The Pleasures of Ignorance* by Robert Lynd, 1930

Greedy for Caged Birds

Mrs Flyte in Bleak House *had a large collection of*
'larks, linnets and goldfinches'. Her downstairs neighbour, Krook,
had a fierce grey cat, Lady Jane.

The birds began to stir and cheep.

'I cannot admit the air freely,' said the little old lady; the room
was close, and would have been the better for it; 'because the cat
you saw downstairs – called Lady Jane – is greedy for their lives.
She crouches on the parapet outside for hours and hours. I have
discovered,' whispering mysteriously, 'that her natural cruelty is
sharpened by a jealous fear of their regaining their liberty. In consequence of the judgment I expect being shortly given. She is sly
and full of malice. I half believe, sometimes, that she is no cat, but
the wolf of the old saying. It is so very difficult to keep her from the
door.'

From *Bleak House* by Charles Dickens, 1853

'Phyllyp Sparowe'

Part of a poem by John Skelton which was probably written in 1505.
Skelton, described by Erasmus as a 'light and glory' of English literature,
died in 1529. What became of Gyb the cat is not recorded.

Pla ce bo,
　　Who is there, who?
Di le xi,
　　Dame Margery,
Fa, re, my, my.
　　Wherfore and why, why?
For the sowle of Philip Sparowe,
That was late slayn at Carowe,
Among the Nones Blake.
For that swete soules sake,
And for all sparowes soules
Set in our bede rolles,
Pater noster qui,

With an *Ave Mari*,
And with the corner of a Crede,
The more shal be your mede.

  When I remembre agayn
How mi Philyp was slayn,
Never halfe the payne
Was betwene you twayne,
Pyramus and Thesbe,
As then befell to me:
I wept and I wayled,
The tearys downe hayled;
But nothynge it avayled
To call Phylyp agayne,
Whom Gyb our cat hath slayne.
  Gyb, I saye, our cat,
Worrowyd her on that
Which I loved best.
It can not be exprest
My sorowfull hevynesse,
But all without redresse;
For within that stounde,
Halfe slumbrynge, in a sounde
I fell downe to the grounde . . .

  That vengeaunce I aske and crye,
By way of exclamacyon,
On all the hole nacyon
Of cattes wylde and tame –
God send them sorowe and shame!
That cat specyally,
That slew so cruelly
My lytell prety sparowe
That I brought up at Carowe!
  O cat of carlyshe kynde,
The fynde was in thy mynde
Whan thou my byrde untwynde!
I wold thou haddest ben blynde!
The leopardes savage,
The lyons in theyr rage,

Myght catche the in theyr pawes,
And gnawe the in theyr jawes!
The serpents of Lybany
Myght stynge the venymously!
The dragones with their tonges
Might poyson thy lyver and longes!
The mantycors of the montaynes
Myght fede them on thy braynes!
    Melancates, that hounde
That plucked Acteon to the grounde,
Gave hym his mortall wounde –
Chaunged to a dere
(The story doth appere)
Was chaunged to an harte:
So thou, foule cat that thou arte,
The selfe-same hounde
Myght the confounde,
That his owne lorde bote
Myght byte asondre thy throte!
    Of Inde the gredy grypes
Myght tere out all thy trypes!
Of Arcady the beares
Might plucke away thyne eares!
The wylde wolfe Lycaon
Byte asondre thy backe bone!
Of Ethna the brennynge hyll
That day and night brenneth styl,
Set in thy tayle a blase
That all the world may gase
And wonder upon the,
From Occyan the great se
Unto the Iles of Orchady,
From Tyllbery fery
To the playne of Salysbery!
So trayterously my byrde to kyll
That never ought the evyll wyll!

From *Phyllyp Sparowe* by John Skelton (?1460-1529)

'Ex-Pigeon Takes a Plucky Third in Race'

A ginger tom ruined the triumph of a racing pigeon called Billy Blue in a 500-mile cross-Channel race.

No sooner had Billy Blue flopped exhausted on to his owner's roof in Crookes, Sheffield, after flying for 25 hours through howling winds and torrential rain, than the cat snatched him up and carried him off.

Billy's owner, Patrick Lees, 55, told yesterday how he dashed up to his roof at 6.55 am to retrieve the bird.

'It was a nightmare,' he said. 'This bloody ginger tom popped up and got him. It was all so quick. There was nothing I could do. I shed a tear because he was one of my favourite birds. He was four years old and I had raised him.'

Mr Lees, who has been trying to win the Central Marking Race for 40 years, said his bird's time was 30 minutes better than the pigeon eventually given first place after 1,000 set off from Royan in south-west France to lofts in Yorkshire, Derbyshire and Nottinghamshire.

'He would have been a champion if it hadn't been for that blooming cat,' he said. 'I'm sick to death of the animal. It has had eleven of my pigeons over the last year or so but I have never managed to get near it.'

From the Daily Telegraph, 8 July 1992

The Trial of Mysouff

Alexandre Dumas was woken one morning by his servant, Michel, with the news that his monkeys had escaped from their cage and the birds in his aviary had all been eaten by the cat, Mysouff.

We left Mysouff gloating over the mangled remains of his feathered victims, and his capture presented little difficulty. By merely shutting the door of the aviary we had the culprit at the disposition of justice.

The only question was to decide his fate. Michel voted to shoot him straight away. I opposed such a step, which seemed too violent altogether.

I proposed to wait for the coming Sunday and have Mysouff brought to trial before the friends who always visited me on that day.

In addition to the regular weekly habitués of the house, we could invite others specially for the occasion. This was accordingly done, and judgment postponed till the fateful Sunday.

Meantime Mysouff remained a prisoner on the very scene of his crime. Michel removed the last vestiges of the dead birds on which he was feeding without a touch of compunction. He was put on a diet of bread and water, Michel constituting himself his gaoler.

When Sunday came, both the ordinary weekly habitués and the specially invited guests having turned up in force, the necessary quorum for a jury was more than provided.

Michel was nominated Procureur-Général, and Nogent Saint-Laurent official Counsel for the Defence.

I am bound to say the minds of the jury were manifestly predisposed against the prisoner, and that after the Public Prosecutor's speech, a sentence of death seemed a practical certainty.

But the clever advocate to whom poor Mysouff's defence had been entrusted, taking the accusation in the most serious way and calling all his eloquence into play, insisted on the animal's innocent intentions contrasted with the mischievousness of the monkeys, on the absence of initiation on the part of the four-footed as compared with two-handed vertebrates. He demonstrated how, closely approximating to men as they did, the latter were bound to be full of criminal promptings. He showed Mysouff incapable by himself of meditating such a crime. He showed him sleeping the sleep of the just; then suddenly awakened from his harmless slumbers by the odious apes that had long been watching the aviary intent on committing murder. He described Mysouff, still only half awake, stretching his paws, purring softly the while, opening his little pink mouth and showing his pretty tongue; listening, and shaking his ears, – a plain sign that he rejected the odious proposal his tempters dared to make; at first refusing all participation in the foul deed (the speaker asserted positively that his client had begun by refusing); then, young and easily led astray, demoralised moreover by the cook, who instead of giving him his innocent bread and milk and bowl of broth according to orders, had excited his carnivorous appetite by feeding him on scraps of meat, the remains of bullocks' hearts and mutton bones; gradually degenerating more from weakness of character and feebleness to resist temptation than from actual greediness and cruelty; following, even now only part awake, with half-shut eyes and staggering steps, the wretched apes, the true instigators of the crime. Then he took the accused in his arms, displayed his paws, drew attention to their shape and form, appealed to the anatomists, calling upon them to say if, with such paws, an animal could open a locked aviary. Finally he borrowed from Michel himself his famous *Dictionary of Natural History*; he opened it at the article 'Cat,' – *domestic cat, brindled cat*; he demonstrated that Mysouff, albeit not of the brindled sort, was not a whit less interesting for having a white coat – the token of his innocence. Then, to wind up, he struck a resounding blow on the book.

'Cat!' he exclaimed vehemently, 'cat! . . . yes, I will read you what Buffon, the great Buffon, who always wrote in lace ruffles, what he wrote on the knees of Mother Nature, concerning the cat –

'The cat,' M. de Buffon tells us, 'is but a faithless domestic pet, one we only keep out of necessity, to keep down other household enemies even more annoying, and which we cannot otherwise get rid of . . . ; true,' continues the illustrious Naturalist, 'true, the cat, and still more the kitten, has pretty ways, it has at the same time an inborn love of mischief, a treacherous disposition, a natural perversity, which age only increases and training only succeeds in partially concealing.'

'Well,' pursued the orator, after concluding this description of his client, 'what need I say more? . . . Did Mysouff, I ask you, did poor Mysouff present himself here with a false certificate of character signed, it may be, by Lacépède or Geoffroy Saint-Hilaire, to weigh in the balance against Buffon's indictment? – No, he scorned to do so. – It was the cook herself who went and fetched him from M. Acoyer's, who hunted him out from behind a heap of firewood where he had taken refuge, who then invented a fictitious tale to enlist her master's sympathies of how she had found the creature mewing piteously in the cellar. Was any attempt made to give him an idea of the wickedness he was guilty of in killing these unfortunate birds, these poor little creatures, – greatly to be pitied, of course, yet which, when all is said and done, – the quails in particular, – were liable to be sacrificed at any moment to satisfy man's hunger, and now find themselves happily delivered from the agonies of terror they must daily have experienced every time they saw

[357]

the cook come near their cage? . . . In a word, gentlemen, I appeal to your sense of fairness; we have invented a new word to excuse crime among ourselves, as featherless bipeds, endowed with free will, to wit *monomania*; when, thanks to the word, we have saved the lives of the greatest criminals, shall we not admit that the unfortunate and interesting Mysouff yielded not merely to his natural instincts but also to extraneous suggestions? . . . I have done, gentlemen. I claim for my client the benefit of extenuating circumstances.'

Shouts of enthusiasm greeted this flight of eloquence, which was purely extempore. The jury gave their verdict whilst still under the impression of the great advocate's address, and Mysouff was declared guilty of complicity in the assassination of the doves and quails, also of the wrynecks, widow-birds, Indian sparrows, and other rare birds, but with extenuating circumstances. He was merely condemned to five years of incarceration with the apes.

From *My Pets* by Alexandre Dumas, 1867, translated by Alfred Allinson

A Daring Rescue

West Humble, 30 June 1866

My dearest Mother – Your long double letter and anecdotes deserved a speedier answer . . . In return for your anecdotes I must tell you one about Lucy [his daughter]. She was on the lawn with Flu and Mrs Slade when the cat jumped out of the bushes with a bird in her mouth. Mrs Slade called out, 'Oh, that horrid cat has got a bird'; but, as she herself says, for a thousand birds she should not have ventured to interfere. Lucy sprang on the cat, seized it by the throat, made it drop the bird, pushed it away, and stroked and smoothed the bird for a minute or two till it flew off quite happy. The charming thing is, she had not a notion of doing anything remarkable, and is troubled about having given the cat a violent push from her, and says, 'I couldn't help giving the cat a slap, but I hope I didn't hurt it, because you know, mamma, it was its nature to kill birds.'

From *Letters of Matthew Arnold 1848-1888*, edited by George W. E. Russell, 1895

Irreconcilable Affections

The mice were encouraged by [Jeremy] Bentham to play about in his work-shop. I remember, when one got among his papers, that he exclaimed, 'Ho! ho! here's a mouse at work; why won't he come into my lap? – but then I should be stroking him when I ought to be writing legislation, and that would not do.'

'I have been catching fish,' he said one day; 'I have caught a carp. I shall hang him up, – feed him with bread and milk. He shall be my tame puss, and shall play about on the floor. But I have a new tame puss. I will make Roebuck my puss for his article on Canada; and many a mouse shall he catch.'

One day while we were at dinner, mice had got, as they frequently did, into the drawers of the dinner-table, and were making no small noise. 'O you rascals' exclaimed Bentham: 'there's an uproar among you. I'll tell puss of you;' and then added: 'I became once very intimate with a colony of mice. They used to run up my legs, and eat crumbs from my lap. I love everything that has four legs: so did George Wilson. We were fond of mice, and fond of cats; but it was difficult to reconcile the two affections.

'From my youth I was fond of cats – as I still am. I was once playing with one in my grandmother's room. I had heard the story of cats having nine lives, and being sure of falling on their legs; and I threw the cat out of the window on the grass-plot. When it fell, it turned towards me, looked in my face and mewed. "Poor thing!" I said, "thou art reproaching me with my unkindness." I have a distinct recollection of all these things.'

From *The Works of Jeremy Bentham* by John Bowring, 1843

Foster Parent

Selborne, May 9, 1776

Dear Sir,

> . . . *admôrunt ubera tigres.*

We have remarked in a former letter how much incongruous

animals, in a lonely state, may be attached to each other from a spirit of sociality; in this it may not be amiss to recount a different motive which has been known to create as strange a fondness.

My friend had a little helpless leveret brought to him, which the servants fed with milk in a spoon, and about the same time his cat kittened and the young were dispatched and buried. The hare was soon lost, and supposed to be gone the way of most foundlings, to be killed by some dog or cat. However, in about a fortnight, as the master was sitting in his garden in the dusk of the evening, he observed his cat, with tail erect, trotting towards him, and calling with little short inward notes of complacency, such as they use towards their kittens, and something gamboling after, which proved to be the leveret that the cat had supported with her milk and continued to support with great affection. Thus was a graminivorous animal nurtured by a carnivorous and predaceous one!

Why so cruel and sanguinary a beast as a cat, of the ferocious genus of *Feles*, the *murium leo*, as Linnaeus calls it, should be affected with any tenderness towards an animal which is its natural prey, is not so easy to determine.

This strange affection probably was occasioned by that *desiderium*, those tender maternal feelings, which the loss of her kittens had awakened in her breast; and by the complacency and ease she derived to herself from the procuring her teats to be drawn, which were too much distended with milk, till, from habit, she became as much delighted with this foundling as if it had been her real offspring.

This incident is no bad solution of that strange circumstance which grave historians as well as the poets assert, of exposed children being sometimes nurtured by female wild beasts that probably had lost their young. For it is not one whit more marvellous that Romulus and Remus, in their infant state, should be nursed by a she-wolf, than that a poor little sucking leveret should be fostered and cherished by a bloody grimalkin.

From *The Natural History and Antiquities of Selborne* by the Revd Gilbert White, 1789

Strained Relations

White House, Jan. 2, 1908.

Dear Archie,

Mother continues much attached to Scamp, who is certainly a cunning little dog. He is very affectionate, but so exceedingly busy when we are out on the grounds, that we only catch glimpses of him zigzagging at full speed from one end of the place to the other. The kitchen cat and he have strained relations but have not yet come to open hostility.

White House, Jan. 27, 1908.

Dear Archie,

Scamp is really a cunning little dog, but he takes such an extremely keen interest in hunting, and is so active, that when he is out on the grounds with us we merely catch glimpses of him as he flashes by. The other night after the Judicial Reception when we went up-stairs to supper the kitchen cat suddenly appeared parading down the hall with great friendliness, and was forthwith exiled to her proper home again.

From *Theodore Roosevelt's Letters to his Children*
edited by Joseph Bucklin Bishop, 1919

Unusual Attachments

There are few animals who have a stronger attachment for their young than the cat; and she has frequently been known to transfer her affections to other young animals, and to nurture them with much assiduity. She is also capable of attaching herself to animals, that are supposed to be naturally opposed to her, and with whose nurture she had nothing to do. In illustration of these positions, we are enabled to present the reader with a variety of anecdotes.

A cat, belonging to a person in Taunton, having lost her kittens, transferred her affections to two ducklings which were kept in the yard adjoining. She led them out every day to feed, seemed quite pleased to see them eat, returned with them to their usual nest, and evinced as much attachment for them as she could have shown to her lost young ones.

A lady had a tame bird, which she was in the habit of letting out of its cage every day. One morning, as it was picking crumbs of bread off the carpet, her cat, who always before showed great kindness for the bird, seized it on a sudden, and jumped with it in her mouth upon the table. The lady was much alarmed for the safety of her favourite, but, on turning about, instantly discovered the cause. The door had been left open, and a strange cat had just come into the room. After turning it out, her own cat came down from her place of safety, and dropped the bird, without doing it the smallest injury.

A man one day saw, in a hay field, in the parish of Storrington, Surrey, a cat and a hare at play together; and he was gratified with the sight for more than ten minutes, when the timid animal, on being alarmed at his nearer approach, ran into a thicket of fern, and was followed by the cat.

A gentleman who lived in the neighbourhood of Portsmouth, had a cat, which kittened four or five days after a hen had brought out a brood of chickens. As he did not wish to keep more than one cat at a time, the kittens were all drowned, and the same day the cat and one chicken went amissing. Diligent search was immediately made in every place that could be thought of, both in and and out of the house, but to no purpose; it was then concluded that some mischance had befallen both. Four days afterwards, however, the servant having occasion to go into an unfrequented part of the cellar, discovered, to his great astonishment, the cat lying in one corner, with the chicken hugged close to her body, and one paw laid over it as if to preserve it from injury. The cat and adopted chicken were brought into a closet in the kitchen, where they continued some days, the cat treating the chicken in every respect as a kitten. Whenever the chicken left the cat to eat, she appeared very uneasy, but, on its return, she received it with the affection of a mother, pressed it to her body, purred, and seemed perfectly happy. If the chicken was carried to the hen, it immediately returned to the cat. The chicken was by some accident killed, and the cat would not eat for several days afterwards, being inconsolable for its loss.

From *Interesting Anecdotes of the Animal Kingdom* by Thomas Brown, 1834

All Bark and No Bite

The original title of Jerome K. Jerome's best-known book was Three Men
in a Boat – To Say Nothing of the Dog. *The dog in question,
Montmorency, was not a cat-lover.*

We got up tolerably early on the Monday morning at Marlow, and
went for a bathe before breakfast; and, coming back, Montmorency
made an awful ass of himself. The only subject on which Montmorency and I have any serious difference of opinion is cats. I like cats;
Montmorency does not.

When I meet a cat, I say, 'Poor Pussy!' and stoop down and
tickle the side of its head; and the cat sticks up its tail in a rigid, cast-
iron manner, arches its back, and wipes its nose up against my
trousers; and all is gentleness and peace. When Montmorency
meets a cat, the whole street knows about it; and there is enough
bad language wasted in ten seconds to last an ordinary respectable
man all his life, with care.

I do not blame the dog (contenting myself, as a rule, with merely
clouting his head or throwing stones at him), because I take it that
it is his nature. Fox-terriers are born with about four times as much
original sin in them as other dogs are, and it will take years and
years of patient effort on the part of us Christians to bring about
any appreciable reformation in the rowdiness of the fox-terrier
nature . . .

Such is the nature of fox-terriers; and, therefore, I do not blame
Montmorency for his tendency to row with cats; but he wished he
had not given way to it that morning.

We were, as I have said, returning from a dip, and half-way up
the High Street a cat darted out from one of the houses in front of
us, and began to trot across the road. Montmorency gave a cry of
joy – the cry of a stern warrior who sees his enemy given over to
his hands – the sort of cry Cromwell might have uttered when the
Scots came down the hill – and flew after his prey.

His victim was a large black tom. I never saw a larger cat, nor a
more disreputable-looking cat. It had lost half its tail, one of its
ears, and a fairly appreciable proportion of its nose. It was a long,
sinewy-looking animal. It had a calm, contented air about it.

Montmorency went for that poor cat at the rate of twenty miles an hour; but the cat did not hurry up – did not seem to have grasped the idea that its life was in danger. It trotted quietly on until its would-be assassin was within a yard of it, and then it turned round and sat down in the middle of the road, and looked at Montmorency with a gentle, inquiring expression, that said:

'Yes! You want me?'

Montmorency does not lack pluck; but there was something about the look of that cat that might have chilled the heart of the boldest dog. He stopped abruptly, and looked back at Tom.

Neither spoke; but the conversation that one could imagine was clearly as follows:

THE CAT: 'Can I do anything for you?'

MONTMORENCY: 'No – no, thanks.'

THE CAT: 'Don't you mind speaking if you really want anything, you know.'

MONTMORENCY (*backing down the High Street*): 'Oh, no – not at all – certainly – don't you trouble. I – I am afraid I've made a mistake. I thought I knew you. Sorry I disturbed you.'

THE CAT: 'Not at all – quite a pleasure. Sure you don't want anything, now?'

MONTMORENCY (*still backing*): 'Not at all, thanks – not at all – very kind of you. Good morning.'

THE CAT: 'Good morning.'

Then the cat rose, and continued his trot; and Montmorency, fitting what he calls his tail carefully into its groove, came back to us, and took up an unimportant position in the rear.

To this day, if you say the word 'Cats!' to Montmorency, he will visibly shrink and look up piteously at you, as if to say:

'Please don't.'

From *Three Men in a Boat* by Jerome K. Jerome, 1889

Dutch Courage

Mouse, after drinking a drop of Monbazillac: 'Now where is that bloody cat?'

From *Geoffrey Madan's Notebooks*, edited by J. A. Gere and John Sparrow, 1981

Ten

DEATH

'The Death of a Cat'

I

Since then, those months ago, these rooms miss something,
A link, a spark, and the street down there reproves
My negligence, particularly the gap
For the new block which, though the pile of timber
Is cleared on which he was laid to die, remains
A gap, a catch in the throat, a missing number.

You were away when I lost him, he had been absent
Six nights, two dead, which I had not learnt until
You returned and asked and found how he had come back
To a closed door having scoured the void of Athens
For who knows what and at length, more than unwell
Came back and less than himself, his life in tatters.

Since when I dislike that gap in the street and that obdurate
Dumb door of iron and glass and I resent
This bland blank room like a doctor's consulting room
With its too many exits, all of glass and frosted,
Through which he lurked and fizzed, a warm retort,
Found room for his bag of capers, his bubbling flasket.

For he was our puck, our miniature lar, he fluttered
Our dovecot of visiting cards, he flicked them askew,
The joker among them who made a full house. As you said,
He was a fine cat. Though how strange to have, as you said later,
Such a personal sense of loss. And looking aside
You said, but unconvincingly: What does it matter?

II

To begin with he was a beautiful object:
Blue crisp fur with a white collar,
Paws of white velvet, springs of steel,
A Pharaoh's profile, a Krishna's grace,
Tail like a questionmark at a masthead
And eyes dug out of a mine, not the dark
Clouded tarns of a dog's, but cat's eyes –

Light in a rock crystal, light distilled
Before his time and ours, before cats were tame.

To continue, he was alive and young,
A dancer, incurably male, a clown,
With his gags, his mudras, his entrechats,
His triple bends and his double takes,
Firm as a Rameses in African wonderstone,
Fluid as Krishna chasing the milkmaids,
Who hid under carpets and nibbled at olives,
Attacker of ankles, nonesuch of nonsense,
Indolent, impudent, cat catalytic.

To continue further: if not a person
More than a cipher, if not affectionate
More than indifferent, if not volitive
More than automaton, if not self-conscious
More than mere conscious, if not useful
More than a parasite, if allegorical
More than heraldic, if man-conditioned
More than a gadget, if perhaps a symbol
More than a symbol, if somewhat a proxy
More than a stand-in – was what he was!
A self-contained life, was what he must be
And is not now: more than an object.

And is not now. Spreadeagled on coverlets –
Those are the coverlets, bouncing on chairbacks –
These are the chairs, pirouetting and sidestepping,
Feinting and jabbing, breaking a picture frame –
Here is the picture, tartar and sybarite,
One minute quicksilver, next minute butterballs,
Precise as a fencer, lax as an odalisque,
And in his eyes the light from the mines
One minute flickering, steady the next,
Lulled to a glow or blown to a blaze,
But always the light that was locked in the stone
Before his time and ours; at best semi-precious
All stones of that kind yet, if not precious,
Are more than stones, beautiful objects
But more than objects. While there is light in them.

Canyons of angry sound, catastrophe, cataclysm,
Smells and sounds in cataracts, cat-Athens,
Not, not the Athens we know, each whisker buzzing
Like a whole Radar station, typhoons of grapeshot,
Crossfire from every roof of ultra-violet arrows
And in every gutter landmines, infra-red,
A massed barrage of too many things unknown
On too many too quick senses (cossetted senses
Of one as spoilt as Pangur Ban, Old Foss
Or My Cat Jeoffrey), all the drab and daily
Things to him deadly, all the blunt things sharp,
The paving stones a sword dance. Chanting hawkers
Whose street cries consecrate their loaves and fishes
And huge black chessmen carved out of old priests
And steatopygous boys, they all were Gogs and Magogs
With seven-league battering boots and hair-on-ending voices
Through which he had to dodge. And all the wheels
Of all the jeeps, trucks, trams, motor-bicycles, buses, sports cars,
Caught in his brain and ravelled out his being
To one high horrible twang of breaking catgut,
A swastika of lightning. Such was Athens
To this one indoors cat, searching for what
He could not grasp through what he could not bear,
Dragged to and fro by unseen breakers, broken
At last by something sudden; then dragged back
By his own obstinate instinct, a long dark thread
Like Ariadne's ball of wool in the labyrinth
Not now what he had played with as a kitten
But spun from his own catsoul, which he followed
Now that the minotaur of machines and men
Had gored him, followed it slowly, slowly, until
It snapped a few yards short of a closed door,
Of home, and he lay on his side like a fish on the pavement
While the ball of wool rolled back and down the hill,
His purpose gone, only his pain remaining
Which, even if purpose is too human a word,
Was not too human a pain for a dying cat.

Out of proportion? Why, almost certainly.
You and I, darling, knew no better
Than to feel worse for it. As one feels worse
When a tree is cut down, an ear-ring lost,
A week-end ended, a child at nurse
Weaned. Which are also out of proportion.

Sentimentality? Yes, it is possible;
You and I, darling, are not above knowing
The tears of the semi-, less precious things,
A pathetic fallacy perhaps, as the man
Who gave his marble victory wings
Was the dupe – who knows – of sentimentality.

Not really classic. The Greek Anthology
Laments its pets (like you and me, darling),
Even its grasshoppers; dead dogs bark
On the roads of Hades where poets hung
Their tiny lanterns to ease the dark.
Those poets were late though. Not really classical.

Yet more than an object? Why, most certainly.
You and I, darling, know that sonatas
Are more than sound and that green grass
Is more than grass or green, which is why
Each of our moments as they pass
Is of some moment; more than an object.

So this is an epitaph, not for calamitous
Loss but for loss; this was a person
In a small way who had touched our lives
With a whisk of delight, like a snatch of a tune
From which one whole day's mood derives.
For you and me, darling, this is an epitaph.

From *The Collected Poems of Louis MacNeice*, 1966

'An Unusual Cat Poem'

My cat is dead
But I have decided not to make a big tragedy out of it.

From *Serious Concerns* by Wendy Cope, 1992

'Lines on the Death of a College Cat'

The Junior Fellow's vows were said;
Among his co-mates and their Head
   His place was fairly set.
Of welcome from friends old and new
Full dues he had, and more than due;
   What could be lacking yet?

One said, 'The Senior Fellow's vote!'
The Senior Fellow, black of coat,
   Save where his front was white,
Arose and sniffed the stranger's shoes
With critic nose, as ancients use
   To judge mankind aright.

I – for 'twas I who tell the tale –
Conscious of fortune's trembling scale,
   Awaited the decree;
But Tom had judged: 'He loves our race,'
And, as to his ancestral place,
   He leapt upon my knee.

Thenceforth in common-room and hall
A *verus socius* known to all
   I came and went and sat,
Far from cross fate's or envy's reach;
For none a title could impeach
   Accepted by the cat.

While statutes changed, and freshmen came,
His gait, his wisdom were the same,
    His age no more than mellow;
Yet nothing mortal may defy
The march of *Anno Domini,*
    Not e'en the Senior Fellow.

Beneath our linden shade he lies;
Mere eld hath softly closed his eyes
    With late and honoured end.
He seems, while catless we confer,
To join with faint Elysian purr,
    A tutelary friend.

From *Leading Cases Done Into English, and Other Diversions*
by Sir Frederick Pollock, Bart., 1892

Poisoned

*The novelist George Moore, preparing to move from London to Dublin,
bids farewell to his housekeeper, Jane.*

Your life is all pleasure and glory, but I shall have to look round for
another place, I heard her say, as she pulled at the straps of my
portmanteau, and her resentment against me increased when I put a
sovereign into her hand. She cooked me excellent dinners, making
life infinitely agreeable to me; a present of five pounds was certainly her due, and a sovereign was more than enough for the
porter, whom I suspected of poisoning my cat – a large, grey, and
affectionate animal upon whom Jane, without the aid of a doctor,
had impressed the virtue of chastity so successfully that he never
sought the she, but remained at home, a quiet, sober animal that did
not drink milk, only water, and who, when thrown up to the ceiling, refrained from turning round, content to curl himself into a
ball, convinced that my hands would receive him – an animal to
whom I was so much attached that I had decided to bring him with
me in a basket; but a few weeks before my departure he died of a
stoppage in his entrails, brought about probably by a morsel of
sponge fried in grease – a detestable and cruel way of poisoning

cats often practised by porters. It was pitiful to watch the poor animal go to his pan and try to relieve himself, but he never succeeded in passing anything, and after the third day refused to try any more. We had recourse to a dose of castor oil, but it did not move him and after consultation we resolved to give an enema if he would allow us. The poor animal allowed us to do our will; he seemed to know that we were trying to help him, and received my caresses and my words with kindly looks while Jane administered the enema, saying that she didn't mind if the whole courtyard saw her do it, all she cared for was to save Jim's life. But the enema did not help him, and after it he neither ate nor drank, but lay down stoically to die. Death did not come to him for a long while; it seemed as if he would never drop off, and at last, unable to bear the sight of his sufferings any longer, Jane held his head in a pail of water, and after a few gasps the trial of life was over. It may have been that he died of the fur that he licked away, collecting in a ball in his entrails, and that there is not cause for me to regret the sovereign given to the porter when the great van drove up to my door to take away the bedroom and kitchen furniture.

From *Salve* by George Moore, 1912

A Sudden Seizure

Cats sometimes behave like dogs. The writer possessed an animal that used to come to his whistle just as a terrier would, and in the night time, when dogs and pedestrians were not about, used to accompany him in his walks in May Fair

This cat was not formed like others of its species. It was a tabby, with rather longish hair and with a thick tail, which was not more than six inches long. How the remainder was lost was a question; but from its extreme irritability when its tip was touched, a butcher-boy's chopper was suspected. The cat was odd in other ways; when her master was at his desk writing, she would always select a small piece of writing paper on which she sat down, no doubt putting herself on a literary footing with him. Her diet was also extraordinary; she would eat pickles and drink brandy-and-water. One day she rose suddenly and sprang up the chimney, a fire burning in the grate all the time. A couple of hundred years ago the writer would without doubt have been burned as a wizard for keeping a familiar. The cat when she found the top of the register too hot for her feet came down, a little blacker than when she went up. One day, however, poor puss suddenly rushed round the room in a circle for a few seconds, and then fell down dead. This finale explained many of her peculiarities when alive. She suffered from epileptic fits, and these always affect the brain in a singular manner, and no doubt accounted for the depraved nature of her appetite.

From Fruit Between the Leaves by Andrew Wynter, 1875

Qualities of Mercy

And now, in concluding, may I suggest that there is 'a time to kill, and a time to heal,' and that when a favourite cat is really ill, in pain, or has met with a serious accident, it is often both wise and merciful to drown or shoot the poor animal effectually, and without delay. Drowning, as I have before observed, is, perhaps, the simplest and the least painful of the ordinary methods of destruction. Shooting must be resorted to with care and forethought, and no possibility allowed of the cat escaping but only wounded. Poison is at all times to be avoided.

From The Cat: Its Natural History, Domestic Varieties, Management and Treatment by
Philip M. Rule, 1887

Sleep Without Waking

Before going on to speak of the training of youthful pussy, there is one subject which deserves a word or two at least – namely, the humane destruction of cats, when such destruction becomes necessary.

Kittens, at least, people have often to get rid of, or the whole world would be peopled with cats, and that would hardly do. Although I am no advocate for the rash and hasty condemnation of the sickest cat that ever is, still, I must confess that, at times, to destroy a cat is to be merciful to it.

Never give kittens poison, it is cruel in the extreme; you might chloroform them to death, but one doesn't like to waste much time in taking life, if merely a kitten's; the pail is always handy, and the poor wee things don't really suffer much if you do it properly. Always sink them, and keep the pail for three hours, after which bury them at once. I'll give you an example of the wrong way of doing things. Miss M—n, who lived not a stone's throw from where I now write, and who is an old maid (and may a merciful Providence keep her so!), was changing her residence last month, and at the last moment thought she couldn't be bothered with more than one of her kittens – little Persian beauties, whom she had let live a whole month – so one was snatched from its mother's arms, and pitched carelessly into a pail of water. She never heeded its cries, nor the mother's piteous appeal to save her offspring; so presently kitty was dead, to all appearance, and the bucket was emptied over the wall into an adjoining field. This was at eleven o'clock in the morning, and late that evening some boys, in passing, were attracted to the spot by plaintive mews, and there they found the kitten crawling in the grass, with sadly swollen body and inflamed mouth. The boys drowned and buried it, being more humane than old maid M—n.

If necessity, then, compels you to part by death with an old cat, and probably an old friend and favourite, I do not advise you to have her drowned. It is cruel in many ways; there is the catching of her, the putting of her into the sack with the stone, and the march to the waterside, the cat knowing all the while what is going to happen, and that her mistress ordered her death. Do not drown her. If there is any one you can really trust, that you are sure knows the difference between a gun and a washing-stick, by all means have her shot. It is over in a moment. The next best plan is to administer morphia. Don't grudge her a good dose – five or even ten grains. Cats are wonderfully tenacious of life, but they can't stand that. Make the morphia into a pill, with a little of the extract of liquorice, and force it down the throat. Pussy will sleep the sleep that knows no waking, and you will have the satisfaction of knowing she did not suffer.

From *The Domestic Cat* by Gordon Stables, 1876

The Throbbing Impulse

Drowning is a very painful and lingering death for a grown-up cat, poisoning is dreadful, though swift. In chloroform we find an ideal death for her, one which she deserves and which no false sentiment rooted in self-love ought to make us delay when it is right that she should die. Death from chloroform is not dying, but falling asleep. Perhaps puss feels a little puzzled, a little frightened, perchance some preternatural instinct whispers that the strange scent is deadly and means adieu to this life for evermore; but that it all. The best and easiest way to administer chloroform is undoubtedly under a bell glass, the size of which must, of course, be adapted to that of the cat. A small one will do for new-born kittens, while a glass some fourteen or sixteen inches in diameter will cover any cat easily.

A sponge or bit of cotton wool on a saucer can easily be pushed under the edge without letting the cat out, and the chloroform poured on this. Care must be taken now that no air gets in round the rim. If done out of doors, the glass may be pressed tightly into the loose earth; if indoors, a cloth can be thrown over the glass and fitted well in close to the edge. The glass must be held firmly for some minutes till Pussy sinks into a profound slumber. She will never wake again, unless any fresh air finds its way into her lungs. She must be left where she is for a time. Twenty minutes ought to be amply sufficient, if one ounce and a half of pure chloroform be used; less will do for new-born kittens under a small glass. The body can be put under water after twenty minutes to make sure, if desired; in this way the air will be prevented from reaching her and effecting a revival. Some people prefer a tin box in which the cat is placed, but I have not found this plan so successful or easy. If a box is used, a sheet of wadding should be placed across the open sides before putting on the cover to make it air tight. Others tie a sponge-bag holding the chloroform on cotton wool over the cat's head, holding her on the lap till she sleeps. This is not so good a plan because air gets in round the edge of the bag and prolongs the scene, not to mention that the struggles of Pussy on one's knee seem to add an item of needless distress.

When at last you lift the cloth which has shrouded her last moments from your sight, the body under the bell glass will look as if she were taking her usual rest, you can hardly believe that she will not purr when you stroke her, nor lift those loving eyes to yours again. All her pains are over, and that innocent little soul 'free'd by the throbbing impulse we call death', is enjoying itself somewhere else.

From *The Cat: Her Place in Society and Treatment* by Edith Carrington, 1896

'Feline Mourners'

Sir,

Knowing your regard for animals – even for the despised cat – I send you two cognate anecdotes, and ask you or your readers if they can throw any light on the matter of the expression of grief by animals. I had a favourite Angora cat, who died after a week of suffering, the result of an accident. During his illness, his mother, a fine old cat of the ordinary sort, was often with him; but she was not present at the time of his death. He died late in the evening, and was taken into the cellar, to await his burial the next day. When he was brought up, stiff and cold, in a box, his mother was taken to see him; she gave one look, uttered a shriek, and ran way.

On relating this circumstance to a lady, she told me that there was a pet cat in her family, who was very fond of this lady's mother. When the latter was in her last illness, the cat was continually with her, lying on the bed. The lady died, and the cat was, of course, not again admitted to the room, though presenting herself again and again at the door. When the coffin was being carried downstairs, the cat happened to appear, and, on seeing it, uttered a shriek. In both these cases, the sound made was entirely unlike those made by cats under any circumstances unless it be the cry made when in sudden pain. In the latter case, the most remarkable part remains to be told. The cat went to the funeral, and then disappeared for many days. But after that, she repeatedly attended funerals in the same cemetery, walking before the clergyman, her master.

I am, Sir, &c.,

A Lover of the Despised

From *The Spectator*, 1 September 1883

A Strange Monster

April 20 [1644] when comming to Orleans, and lying at the White-Crosse (where I found Mr John Nicholas, eldest sonne to Mr Secretary) there kitten'd a Cat on my bed, which left on it a Young one having 6 Eares, eight leggs, two bodys from the navil downewards, & two tayles: which strange Monster, I found dead; but warme by me in the Morning when I awaked.

From *The Diary of John Evelyn*, edited by E.S. de Beer, 1985

Epitaph for a Duchess's Cat

Mme Deshoulières wrote a whole series of songs and couplets about her cat, Grisette. In a letter to her husband, referring to the attentions she herself receives from admirers, she adds: –

> 'Deshoulières cares not for the smart
>   Her bright eyes cause, disdainful hussy,
> But, like a mouse, her idle heart
>   Is captured by a pussy.'

Much better than these is the sonnet on the cat of the Duchess of Lesdiguières, with its admirable line: –

> 'Chatte pour tout le monde, et pour les chats tigresse.'

A fugitive epistle by Scarron, delightfully turned, is too long to be quoted here, nor can I pause to cite the rondeau which the Duchess of Maine addressed to her favourite. But she supplemented it as follows: –

> 'My pretty puss, my solace and delight,
> To celebrate thy loveliness aright
> I ought to call to life the bard who sung
> Of Lesbia's sparrow with so sweet a tongue;

[377]

But 'tis in vain to summon here to me
So famous a dead personage as he,
And you must take contentedly to-day
This poor rondeau that Cupid wafts your way.'

When this cat died the Duchess was too much affected to write its epitaph herself, and accordingly it was done for her, in the following style, by La Mothe le Vayer, the author of the *Dialogues*: –

'Puss passer-by, within this simple tomb
    Lies one whose life fell Atropos hath shred;
The happiest cat on earth hath heard her doom,
    And sleeps for ever in a marble bed.
Alas! what long delicious days I've seen!
    O cats of Egypt, my illustrious sires,
You who on altars, bound with garlands green,
    Have melted hearts, and kindled fond desires, –
Hymns in your praise were paid, and offerings too,
    But I'm not jealous of those rights divine,
Since Ludovisa loved me, close and true,
    Your ancient glory was less proud than mine.
To live a simple pussy by her side
Was nobler far than to be deified.'

From *Gossip in a Library* by Edmund Gosse, 1891

RIP Malaysia

This album is dedicated to Malaysia, my late cat, who waited 'til I'd finished singing before losing a battle with a car in England's green and pleasant land. May the great litter box in the sky have room for us all.

From the sleeve notes of Dusty Springfield's LP *Reputation*, 1990

Hemingway's Tears

As I came down from the tower after sunning on February 20 [1953], I found our cat Willie hunching himself forward along the terrace, all tilted to starboard. Willie was smiling and purring and his gray-and-black striped coat looked still shiny from his morning lick-bath. But his right forepaw was doubled under. He was crawling on the knee. Then I saw with horror that his back hip was broken, a bit of bone protruding through the fur. 'Willie, Willie, wait,' I moaned, stroking his head. He was heading for the Cat House, our cats' sanctum. I ran to Ernest in his room and panted, 'Something terrible has happened to Willie. He's all broken apart.' Ernest came back unbelieving from wherever he was in his manuscript. We went out and there was Willie near the Cat House door, purring, no blood showing. Tears were making rivulets down my cheeks as Ernest examined him.

'You think he's hurt internally? Could we make splints for him?'

'Don't handle him. Don't let him see you cry. Splints no good.'

'A plaster cast?' René had joined us, and Roberto.

'Get me the .22,' Ernest said.

'No. No. No. Why can't we try a plaster cast? Why can't we get a vet? Why does this have to be so quick?' I was blubbering.

'He's too smashed up. He'll begin to feel it soon.'

I ran to my refuge, my bed.

The happenings of that day gave us no chance to try to assimilate our grief. While René held Willie gently in his arms and Ernest shot him in the head, a Cadillac stopped at the front steps, having ignored the signs on the gate, and a young man and his white-coated attendant emerged. Before anybody could stop them they were inside the house, the attendant saying their clinic for the mentally deranged had given them permission to come to Cuba to visit Ernest, as I heard it through the door as I dressed for lunch. The young man spoke cruel phrases – 'An interesting time to arrive . . . Hemingway crying because he has shot a cat . . . He loves cats . . . so he shoots them.' I waited for the sounds of a shot and a body collapsing but heard only conversation and the front screen door announcing their departure.

When the boys had been children, Willie had been Patrick's and Gregory's favourite cat and had elected himself a non-cat people's chum except when the lure of bird hunting overtook him. To strangers he presented a conservative banker's mien, aloof and businesslike. But with friends he allowed himself to be picked up, cradled, his stomach stroked, or he would dance across the floor chasing a wiggling string, or lying on a table in the lamplight would nuzzle into a pal's hair, teasing, pretending to eat it. Remembering Willie, Ernest and I held each other close for a long time that night.

From *How It Was* by Mary Welsh Hemingway, 1977

Buying the Farm

After splitting up with his girlfriend, Jimmy Zoole, the narrator of James Kirkwood's P.S. Your Cat is Dead!, *catches a burglar in his apartment on New Year's Eve. He knocks him about a bit, ties him up and then sits down to dinner.*

He continued to watch me while I ate. After a while, he sighed. 'Mean. Jesus – *mean!* I never saw nothin' like you for mean. I hadda aunt once used to say, "Mean as cat's meat." Well, that fits you, you're fuckin' mean as cat's meat. Eatin' in front of a person. I didn't eat since last night. I'm fuckin' hungry.' When I didn't reply, he added: 'And speakin' of cat's meat – I'm glad your *fuckin' cat's dead!* Serves you right.'

I looked up from my food. 'My – what?'

I saw it strike him. 'Ahh! Oh, oh, Jesus, yeah – !' He broke off laughing. 'That's right, you didn't *know* – your fuckin' cat's bought the farm! Hee . . .' He howled with delight.

I stood up, all I could do was look at him.

His laugh turned to a cough. When he was coughed out, he said, with pure glee in his voice: 'That's *right*, youse didn't know!'

I stepped toward him. 'What do you mean, my cat's dead?'

He flinched. 'Wait, I'll tell you! Right after I got here, the ball-breaker [Zoole's girlfriend] flew in. My gun fell out of my pocket when I dropped from the skylight. My mistake was puttin' it down when I was collecting the goodies together. I was standing right next to the bed when I heard the key in the lock so I quick ducked underneath. She was only here a couple of minutes when the phone rang. The cat hospital and – '

'The *cat* hospital?'

He shrugged. 'Cat hospital, animal hospital . . . Whatever. Oh man, she was upset when she heard. She right away called some guy – Fred, she called him – said the cat had died and maybe they should change their plans on accounta how much you likes the cat, plus the combination her goin' off for New Year's. But she listens to a lot of blah-blah-blah on the other end and says yeah, he's right, she'll meet him in half an hour.'

I said nothing. What could I say? I could hardly believe it, yet I knew from the way he'd told it he hadn't made it up.

My cat was dead. Bobby Seale was dead. Jesus, the results were still coming in.

'Yeah,' Vito sighed, 'I kept waitin' for her to drop it on you. Hmn ... if you treated your cat the way you treat people, it's probably a good thing. See, what I mean is – I'm *hungry!*'

I turned and walked away from him. For a moment I thought of phoning the vet's but I knew it was true.

'I'm goddam hungry!' he shouted. I wanted him to be quiet. I was suddenly tired of him, weary of hearing his voice. I also could not absorb this latest.

DON'T TAUNT THE WRETCHED!

He laughed again, to my ears a moronic sort of laugh. He had a habit of diverting his laughter to a high keening 'Hee ... ' sound. By doing this he was able to keep the laughter from lodging in his throat and bringing on a fit of coughing.

'Hee ... !' once more and I knew he was laughing about the cat. I let him laugh himself out. When he finished he was quiet for a short spell, until he shouted once more: 'Goddamnit, I'm hungry, even in jail they feed you!'

His persistence got to me, that together with his total joy in delivering the news about Bobby Seale. 'Let's see if we can't find something for you!'

He cocked his head as I walked to the refrigerator. 'You mean it?'

'Sure I mean it.' I took out a bowl of lime jello with bananas that had overstayed its time. I walked back to him. 'Here ... ' I upended the bowl, thumping the top and dumping the congealed mass on top of his head.

'Jesus! Oh, *Jesus!*'

I scooped the rest that clung to the bowl out with my hand and pressed it on to his forehead. 'There, take it all!'

Much later, when burglar and burglee have calmed down, Jimmy Zoole looks round his kitchen:

I noticed Bobby Seale's water and food dishes on the floor.

My heart took on weight. I'd momentarily forgotten. I found a large shopping bag and put his two dishes in it, also three cans of catfood and a box of catnip. I wandered around the room collecting all his things, his red scratching post, three rubber balls, and an old sock of mine tied into a knot with catnip inside. I even found a book on the care and training of cats I'd bought when I first adopted him. He'd never learned any tricks, but he had enough of his own. God, I loved that scroungy cat!

From *P.S. Your Cat Is Dead!* by James Kirkwood, 1972

'In Memory of My Cat, Domino: 1951–66'

Rising at dawn to pee, I thought I saw you
Curved in a chair, with head raised to look at me,
As you did at such hours. But the next moment,
More used to the gloom, there was only a jar
And a face-cloth. Time enough, nonetheless,
For love's responsibilities to return
To me. The unique character of the dead
Is the source of our sense of mourning and loss;
So, back in bed, I avoided calling up
What I know is intact in my mind, your life,
Entirely possessed as it was by my care.

I could conceive you not as dead but merely
Gone before me to a world that sends to us
Decreasing intimations of its beings –
No doubt because they find us in the end
Pathetic, worthy, but of small importance.

So long had we been together it never
Occurred to me I might fall somewhat behind.
Even when, familiar fur in my hands,
The sickly wave of barbiturate rose up,
I thought it was I who was journeying on –
But looking back there is only emptiness,

Your dusty medicaments and my portrait
Taken with you: sad mode of life you've outpaced.

From *New and Collected Poems, 1934–84* by Roy Fuller, 1985

A Sudden Plague

In 1934, while living at Frankfort Manor in Norfolk, the novelist Sylvia Townsend Warner wrote a satirical roman à clef. *She insisted to her publisher, Chatto & Windus, that her authorship be concealed under a pseudonym.*

Such scruples proved unnecessary when the novel was rejected by Chatto & Windus in the spring, the first such blow Sylvia had ever received, and one which she took with remarkable grace, writing to Harold Raymond [of Chatto], 'don't let us be hurt, either of us, over what is only a traffic. I have the greatest esteem for my butcher, whose fillet steak is all I could desire; but when I thought there were too many lights [. . .] in the cats-meat, I told him so without flinching. Nor did he, from what I saw, flinch much either. I should hate to think I had less philosophy than my butcher has . . .'

A week later a much worse blow fell at Frankfort Manor in the shape of a sudden, inexplicable and deathly plague among the cats. It affected cats, dogs and squirrels first, and the local people feared it might spread to the cattle, as had a plague sixty years before. Meep, who was in kit, was removed to Winterton, but the two grey cats died, as did at least two of the rough cats, and the rats, who were unaffected by the disease, began to take over the outbuildings. The plague struck quickly and was as quickly gone. Meep's grey kittens returned to Frankfort Manor and helped alleviate the gloomy atmosphere which had prevailed during that unhappy week in March. Sylvia, working in the rich soil of the lovely garden, listening to Valentine [Ackland, her lover] whistling contentedly nearby and hanging the grey kittens in trellised pink roses to be out of the way, felt it 'impossible to know greater happiness'.

From *Sylvia Townsend Warner: A Biography* by Claire Harman, 1989

Mortal Monotony

The strained atmosphere at Max Gate [home of Thomas Hardy and
his first wife, Emma] can hardly have been alleviated by the monotonous run of casualties to the household cats. Three had been
killed on the railway in 1901, doubtless another reason for Emma's
depression in that year; now in 1904 yet another suffered the same
fate, prompting Hardy to the composition of one of the finest
animal poems in the English language, 'Last Words to a Dumb
Friend'.

From *The First Mrs Thomas Hardy* by Denys Kay-Robinson, 1979

'Last Words to a Dumb Friend'

Pet was never mourned as you,
Purrer of the spotless hue,
Plumy tail, and wistful gaze,
While you humoured our queer ways,
Or outshrilled your morning call
Up the stairs and through the hall –
Foot suspended in its fall –
While, expectant, you would stand
Arched, to meet the stroking hand;
Till your way you chose to wend
Yonder, to your tragic end.

Never another pet for me!
Let your place all vacant be;
Better blankness day by day
Than companion torn away.
Better bid his memory fade,
Better blot each mark he made,
Selfishly escape distress
By contrived forgetfulness,
Than preserve his prints to make
Every morn and eve an ache.

From the chair whereon he sat

Sweep his fur, nor wince thereat;
Rake his little pathways out
Mid the bushes roundabout;
Smooth away his talons' mark
From the claw-worn pine-tree bark,
Where he climbed as dusk enbrowned
Waiting us who loitered round.

Strange it is this speechless thing,
Subject to our mastering,
Subject for his life and food
To our gift, and time, and mood;
Timid pensioner of us Powers,
His existence ruled by ours,
Should – by crossing at a breath
Into safe and shielded death,
By the merely taking hence
Of his insignificance –
Loom as largened to the sense,
Shape as part, above man's will,
Of the Imperturbable.

As a prisoner, flight debarred,
Exercising in a yard,
Still retain I, troubled, shaken,
Mean estate, by him forsaken;
And this home, which scarcely took
Impress from his little look,
By his faring to the Dim,
Grows all eloquent of him.

Housemate, I can think you still
Bounding to the window-sill,
Over which I vaguely see,
Your small mound beneath the tree,
Showing in the autumn shade
That you moulder where you played.

From *The Collected Poems of Thomas Hardy*, 1930

On the Road

I'm driving down a country road at night in a rainstorm, going to somebody's house to watch *Cheers*, can barely make out the road ahead, when I see it off to my right, twitching horribly. I don't know what it is yet but immediately I feel like being sick; it's an animal, smashed up on the road, still alive, a cat, probably, and I think: at least I'll stop, at least I won't drive past. And then what? Kill it? Drive it somewhere while it's still alive? Pick up a dying animal with my bare hands and put it on the seat next to me, have it twitch and pulsate in agony as I drive along? I can't imagine bringing myself to do any of this.

But I skid to a halt on the muddy bank at the side of the road, press the footbrake down, clutch up, stalling the car, marginally out of control already, thinking of the absolute horror of what I will now definitely be doing in just a few moments – standing over the mutilated body of an animal, watching it suffer, with nobody there to tell me what to do, no formal code of behaviour to comply with. And the noises. It will probably be making terrible, ugly noises. I feel very sick, almost ready to retch.

I open the door and the wind and rain belt into me and another car is coming in the other direction, towards where the thing is. The other car stops. I jog up the road, crouching low against the rain. Now I can hear the noises as I come up to the car and I can hear the panicky noises, loud, screaming almost. It's a cat, but I can't yet see it. A window winds down; a woman with a tiny baby strapped to her. A man is driving. I open the negotiations.

'Look, I'm going to get a vet. I can drive and get a vet. I know where the vet is. You get the cat off the road. That's all you have to do.'

The noises are loud, agonised; you can hear the real pain, the real anguish.

'But we've got a small baby.'

'Yes. I can see that. But all you have to do is get the cat off the road. Then I'll come back with the vet. The vet's up the road there. I know where the vet is.'

I am raving. The woman is two feet away, but I am shouting as if she were in the far distance, halfway across the fields.

She looks at me. 'Okay. I'll do it.'

But before I run back to my car I feel that I must look over the bonnet, that this is somehow part of the deal. The sight is so repulsive that it racks me with panic; the cat, a tortoiseshell, is broken, parts of it crushed, other parts moving with a jerky, weird supernatural energy, one front paw clawing the air and vibrating, the head swivelling, whipping round in the rain. I run back, trying to think of the car, the U-turn I will make, the muddy bank. Not the cat.

Now the woman is standing in the middle of the road flagging me down.

I pull up, wind down the window.

'I'd better not move it. I might damage the spine.'

My move. 'Block the road with your car. Stay there and wave the other drivers past.'

She agrees. I set off again, driving through the rain. If the vet is in, I'm saved. This thing will be over in five minutes.

Nobody answers the bell. The lights are on inside. I run around the house, hitting windows, shouting. Then I ring the bell again. For a long time. Then I run round the house again, hitting windows again. Of course: people leave lights on in their houses to *pretend* they're in. Then I face up to the terrible fact: now I have to do it on my own.

But I run down the drive of the house opposite, press on the bell, hammer on the glass of the door with my fist. A dog barks inside the house. I press the bell again. The dog barks. For a long time nothing. I press the bell again. Then a light comes on and the door opens, held on a chain. A woman, frightened, and two large dogs.

'I have to use your phone. Let me in. It's urgent. There's . . . a cat. In the road. I mean, dying. I need to call the vet. So just let me in and I'll just, I'll, call. On your phone.'

She really doesn't want to, but I am shouting: the force of my shouting is enough to make her open the door. I take a step inside and begin to close the door. 'No! Don't close the door. Stay there.' She brings the telephone towards me on a little table, stretching the wire; the rain is pouring into the house.

'But the rain . . .'

'No! Stay there!' She is certainly frightened, beginning to be angry. I dial the number of the vet and have to wait while my call is diverted. The rain is now beginning to soak the woman's carpet.

She stands, cowering, at the back of the hall. A man answers. The vet. I ask him, right out, if he'll come and pick up the cat. 'No, I can't. I'm 15 miles away. You can bring the cat to me.' My last shot. 'But I might damage the spine if I pick it up.'

'Just use a coat or something. Put your jacket under it and pick it up.' The vet is calm, practical, by necessity thrifty with his compassion. He gives me slow, detailed directions – I must drive to the coast, turn west along the coast, drive through a town, turn back inland and at a particular confusing roundabout ... that's when it starts getting complicated. The woman, who now believes I have not come to rob her, hands me a pen.

I run back out into the drive, terrified. I must now handle the cat, touch the body, drive 15 miles through the rain with the cat twitching and screaming, and now, I realise, possibly bleeding, in my car.

'Hello.' It's a man with a beard. 'It's our cat. We've taken her in. She's dying. There's nothing we can do. Her eyes are glazed. She can't move properly. She's . . .'

I give the man directions – the coast road, the town, the confusing roundabout – and shake his hand. I feel supremely happy, lightheaded with joy.

He trudges off towards horror, anguish, sadness, recrimination, the bewildered tears of his family. I get back in my car and drive off. When I arrive, *Cheers* has already started; I've never laughed so much in my life.

From 'A Brief Encounter with Death Along the Road to *Cheers*' by William Leith,
Independent on Sunday, 17 November 1991

A Life Saved

Part of a letter from Connop Thirlwall, Bishop of St David's, to his friend Miss Johnes

Abergwili Palace, 26 Jan., 1867

I am glad that you were able to take part in the festivities of A— without being knocked up by them. Sometimes I believe an extraordinary exertion is a cure for weakness. Some years ago I had a cat who was reduced to the very last stage of inanition and debility. As a last chance I sent her into Carmarthen in a basket for medical advice. On the way she took fright at something or other, jumped out of the basket, and scampered some distance before she was caught. That effort and shock saved her life. From that moment, without any other perceptible cause, she began to recover, and lived many years after.

From *Letters to a Friend by Connop Thirlwall, Late Lord Bishop of St David's* edited by the Very Revd Arthur P. Stanley, 1861

Loss of Foss

Villa Tennyson, San Remo, 29 November 1887

My dear Lord Aberdare,

I have been wanting to know how your hand is now – if quite recovered, or still giving trouble? But I am little able now a days to write albeit I have a great deal of writing to get through.

For, whoever has known me for 30 years has known that for all that time my Cat Foss has been part of my solitary life.

Foss is dead: & I am glad to say did not suffer at all – having become quite paralyzed on all one side of him. So he was placed in a box yesterday, & buried deep below the Figtree at the end of the Orange walk & tomorrow there will be a stone placed giving the date of his death & his age (31 years,) – (of which 30 were passed in my house.)

'Qui sotto è sepolto il mio buon
Gatto Foss. Era 30 anni in casa
mia, e morì il 26 Novembre
1887, di età 31 anni.'

[Here lies buried my good cat Foss. He was 30 years in my house, and died on 26 November 1887, at the age of 31 years.]

All those friends who have known my life will understand that I grieve over this loss. As for myself I am much as usual, only suffering from a very bad fall I had on Novr. 5th – having risen, the Lamp having gone out, & the matches misplaced, so that I could not find them.

The effects of this fall have lasted several days – but now – THANK GOD THURSDAY 29th are beginning to cause less worry. Salvatore has the stone for Foss, & the Inscription, & I suppose in a day or two all will be as before, except the memory of my poor friend Foss . . .

Let me know before long how your hand is now. I have lost many friends latterly, among these, Harvie Farquhar, brother of Mrs George Clive.

My love to all of you. Yours affectionately

Edward Lear

From *Edward Lear: Selected Letters*, edited by Vivien Noakes, 1988

'A 14-Year Old Convalescent Cat in the Winter'

I want him to have another living summer,
to lie in the sun and enjoy the *douceur de vivre* –
because the sun, like golden rum in a rummer,
is what makes an idle cat *un tout petit peu ivre* –

I want him to lie stretched out, contented,
revelling in the heat, his fur all dry and warm,
an Old Age Pensioner, retired, resented
by no one, and happinesses in a beelike swarm

to settle on him – postponed for another season
that last fated hateful journey to the vet
from which there is no return (and age the reason),
which must soon come – as I cannot forget.

From *Collected Poems 1980–1990* by Gavin Ewart

The Most Perfect Life

That summer passed all too quickly. Charles was content to lie at ease in the sun and except for the flies, which we both hated, I think it was the happiest time of his life. We had been at Copyhold Farm for a year, and there were no signs of another move; not even preparations for an annual family holiday. The suitcases and trunks were all buried away. Sometimes I went to London for the day but I think he could tell from the family conversation that I was expected to return in a short time. Food was plentiful, and much to his liking. Best of all, he could count on day after day of undisturbed routine.

But in the bright sunlight I could see that he was ageing fast. He had a grey look about him and his movements, though still graceful, were more deliberate. He walked slowly across the grass, and slept more than ever. He was still ready to play and I could always tempt him. But he was no longer a young cat.

These were physical signs. In other ways he was the same affectionate and intelligent cat, always responsive to my mood. He was a cat of acute perceptions. He knew at once when I was melancholy or depressed and had his own ways of comforting me. If I were in a bad temper he was silent and unobtrusive, waiting for my evil mood to pass. When I was cheerful and ready for play, so was he. There were days when I had to stay in bed, and then he rarely left me. Not even the glowing sun outside could lure him from my room.

His devotion when he knew that something was amiss with me moved me deeply. I was intermittently ill during the summer and in the autumn I had to remain in bed for about a fortnight. During that time Charles never left me except to go out on his lawful occasions, or to eat; and he was never away for long. My doctor smiled indulgently when he saw Charles lying on my bed.

I had for some time been dreading, on Charles's account, the coming winter; and I think I must have had a premonition of his death, for my wife will bear witness that I spoke several times of his not surviving the winter which was fast approaching. I believe that Charles too knew that his end was near, for he seemed to want to stay with me all the time. At night, when I slept badly, he did his best to comfort me, licking my hand to show his sympathy, and lying as close to me as he could.

When I was up and about again a sudden spell of cold weather descended on us. There was an official ban on central heating that autumn and Edna considerately made room in the linen cupboard for the cats. Both Charles and Rissa spent much of their time there. No doubt they wondered when we were going to make the pipes and radiators hot again, but they enjoyed the freedom of the linen cupboard until it was possible to use the central heating, luxuriously occupying the shelf that had been reserved for them.

One morning early in December I knew there was something wrong with Charles. He followed me into the bathroom, which he had not done for a long time, and sat under the hot towel rail while I had my bath. When I spoke to him he looked up at me with sadness in his eyes, and only the faintest sound came from him. I looked at him more closely. When I saw that his breathing was irregular I telephoned Addis in Newbury.

When Mr Kefford came he found that Charles's temperature was slightly above normal. There were indications of bronchitis and tonsillitis. Charles must be kept indoors, he said, out of draughts, and he would send a bottle of friar's balsam and some pills from Newbury.

The next day Charles seemed no worse, although he would not eat. That did not surprise me, for even slight indisposition always put him off his food. In the night, when I was lying awake, I heard a faint squeaking noise which sounded like mice in the wainscot. Charles heard it too and jumped off the bed to investigate. It was a good sign. The following morning there was a definite improvement. Charles drank a little milk, ate a few morsels of rabbit and seemed much more cheerful. When Mr Kefford arrived and took his temperature he purred. That may have been because he liked his new doctor, who dealt so gently with him when his ear had had to be treated and who now handled him with expert kindness.

The temperature was down to normal. 'Give the pills a chance,' said Kefford, 'but his breathing is not laboured now, so don't bother with the friar's balsam.'

Giving pills to Charles was something I always hated, for in my anxiety not to hurt or frighten him I usually made a mess of the job. It looks so simple when you see a skilled veterinary surgeon put a pill on a cat's tongue, gently close the mouth on it and stroke the throat downwards to assist the passage of the pill. When I tried it the pill somehow found its way to the side of or under the tongue, and would be spat out as soon as Charles could conveniently get rid of it. But I persevered, and although Charles resisted my clumsy efforts I think he knew I was trying to cure him.

The next day Charles again refused all food. His breathing was no longer irregular but he sat quietly on my bed or in one of his favourite corners. Except for his loss of appetite there seemed little wrong with him, and I was not unduly alarmed. That night he jumped on my bed as usual, and slept peacefully.

He was still rather subdued the next day but he drank some water. To outward appearances he was recovering. That afternoon the sun was shining and I went out for a walk. When I came back, it was to hear that Charles had seemed distressed, and had been lying stretched out on the landing.

I went up at once. He was then sitting in his favourite corner, by the hot-water pipe at the back of the chest of drawers from which he had so often watched the martins darting in and out of their nest. He purred when I stroked him. If he was really ill he was making no fuss or complaint. An hour later I carried him downstairs to give him his pill, and then I saw that he was worse. He lay listlessly in my arms, and the lightness of him frightened me. He seemed to have lost weight very suddenly.

I put him gently down on a cushion in front of the fire and he began to cough silently, his tongue hanging out. I hurried to get a kettle of boiling water for the friar's balsam. When I returned a few minutes later he was behind the curtains of the french windows. I picked him up and he lay still in my arms, his jaw sagging. As gently as I could I put him in his basket, which I had put on a chair over the steaming kettle. He rose feebly to his feet, turned round twice, and laid down as if to sleep. But I knew it was no ordinary sleep. My little cat was dead.

'When the day comes for Bunny or Coney to break my heart again,' Eleanor Farjeon wrote to me, 'I shall tell myself this – for more than nine years I have been able to give to a living thing I love the most perfect life possible for a cat to have. It is something that, with all our hearts and wills, we cannot do for our children, whose growing-up and discovery of life is beyond all our longing to keep them happy. You can tell yourself that for nearly thirteen years all Charles's needs of love and care and comfort were perfectly filled by you . . .'

From *Charles: The Story of a Friendship* by Michael Joseph, 1943

'The King of the Cats is Dead'

The light on his thigh was like
a waterfall in Iceland, and his hair
was the tidal rip between two rocks,
his claws retracted sat in softness
deeper than the ancient moss of Blarney,
his claws extended were the coulter
of the gods and a raw March wind
was in his merely agricultural yawn.
Between his back legs was a catapult
of fecundity and he was riggish
as a red-haired man. The girls
of our nation felt him brush their legs
when they were bored with telling rosaries –
at night he clawed their brains in their
coffined beds and his walnut mind
wrinkled on their scalps. His holidays
were upside down in water and then
his face was like the sun: his smell
was in the peat smoke and even his midden
was a harmony of honey. When he stalked
his momentary mice the land shook
as though Atlantic waves were bowling
at the western walls. But his eyes
were the greatest thing about him.
They burned low and red so that drunks
saw them like two stars above a hedge,
they held the look of last eyes
in a drowning man, they were the sight
the rebel angels saw the first morning
of expulsion. And he is dead – a voice
from the centre of the earth told of his death
by treachery, that he lies in a hole
of infamy, his kidneys and his liver
torn from his body.

Therefore tell
the men and horses of the market-place,
the swallows laying twigs, the salmon
on the ladder that nothing is
as it has been
time is explored
and all is known, the portents
are of brief and brutal things, since
all must hear the words of desolation,
The King of the Cats is Dead
and it
is only Monday in the world.

From *Collected Poems* by Peter Porter, 1983

ACKNOWLEDGEMENTS

For permission to reprint copyright material the publishers gratefully acknowledge the following:

DIGBY ANDERSON: 'The Essential Ingredient' from 'Imperative Cooking' in *The Spectator*, 31 August 1991, by permission of *The Spectator*;

LISA APPIGNANESI and JOHN FORRESTER: 'A Freudian Analysis' from *Freud's Women*, (Weidenfeld & Nicolson, 1992) by permission of Weidenfeld & Nicolson Ltd;

WILLIAM BALDWIN: 'A Noise and a Wawling' from *Beware The Cat*, edited by William A. Ringler, Jnr. and Michael Flachmann, (Huntington Library Publications, 1988) by permission of the Henry E. Huntington Library;

HILAIRE BELLOC: 'On Them' from *On Nothing to Kindred Subjects*, (Methuen, 1908) by permission of the Peters Fraser & Dunlop Group Ltd;

CONNIE BENSLEY: 'The Covetous Cat' in *The Spectator*, 16 May 1992, and to be published *Choosing to be a Swan* (Bloodaxe, 1994) by permission of Connie Bensley;

EDMUND BLUNDEN: 'Uninvited Guests' from *Thomas Hardy*, (Macmillan, 1941) by permission of the Peters Fraser & Dunlop Group Ltd;

MIKHAIL BULGAKOV: 'A Glass of Vodka' from *The Master and Margarita*, (Picador, 1989) by permission of Dasha Shenkman Associates;

KAREL CAPEK: 'Magical Whistling' and 'From the Laws of the Cats' from *Intimate Things*, translated by Dora Round, (George Allen & Unwin, 1935) by permission of George Allen & Unwin, now Unwin Hyman, an imprint of Harper Collins Publishers Limited;

MIGUEL DE CERVANTES SAAVEDRA: 'Put to the Sword' from *The Adventures of Don Quixote*, translated by J. M. Cohen, (Penguin Classics, 1950) translation copyright © J. M. Cohen, 1950 by permission of Penguin Books Ltd;

THE HON. EVAN CHARTERIS, K.C.: 'A Feline Opiate' from *The Life and Letters of Sir Edward Gosse*, (Heinemann, 1931) by permission of William Heinemann Ltd, part of Reed International Books;

SUSAN CHEEVER: 'The Scapecat' from *Home Before Dark*, (Weidenfeld & Nicolson, 1985) by permission of Weidenfeld & Nicolson Ltd;

SUSAN CHITTY: Extracts from *Gwen John 1876-1939*, (Hodder & Stoughton,

E. S. de Beer, (Clarendon Press, 1985) by permission of Oxford University Press;

<small>GAVIN EWART</small>: 'Sonnet: Cat Logic' and 'Sonnet: Cat Cruelty' from *The Collected Ewart 1933-1980*, (Hutchinson, 1980); and 'A 14-Year-Old Convalescent Cat in the Winter', 'Jubilate Matteo' and 'Cats and Women' from *Collected Poems 1980-1990*, (Hutchinson, 1991) by permission of Random House UK Limited;

<small>ANNE FRANK</small>: 'A Leak in The Loft' from *The Diary of Anne Frank*, translated by B. M. Moyaart-Doubleday, (Pan Books, 1954) by permission of Valentine Mitchell, Esq.;

<small>ROY FULLER</small>: 'Mr Macmillan's Cat' and 'In Memory of My Cat' from *Collected Poems 1934-84*, (Secker & Warburg, 1985) by permission of Martin Secker & Warburg Ltd, part of Reed International Books;

<small>DAVID GARNETT</small>: 'Give me your Voice', extract from letter to T. H. White, 18 October 1958, from *The White-Garnett Letters*, edited by David Garnett, (Jonathan Cape, 1968) by permission of A. P. Watt Ltd on behalf of The Executors of the Estate of David Garnett;

<small>MARTIN GILBERT</small>: 'Milk with the Prime Minister', from *Winston S. Churchill: Road to Victory 1941-1945*, (Heinemann, 1986) © 1986 C. & T. Publications Ltd, by permission of Curtis Brown Group Ltd, London, on behalf of C. & T. Publications Ltd;

<small>ROBERT GITTINGS</small>: 'Keats and Cats' from *Essays and Studies*, (John Murray for The English Association, 1962) by permission of The English Association;

<small>ROBERT GRAVES</small>: 'Cat Goddesses' from *Collected Poems*, (Cassell, 1975) by permission of A. P. Watt Ltd on behalf of the Robert Graves Copyright Trust;

<small>CECIL GRAY</small>: 'Ecstatic Mania' from *Peter Warlock: A Memoir of Philip Heseltine*, (Jonathan Cape, 1934) by permission of A. P. Watt Ltd on behalf of The Executors of the Estate of the late Cecil Gray;

<small>PETER HAINING</small>: 'Stage Fright' from *Superstitions*, (Sidgwick & Jackson, 1979) by permission of Pan Macmillan Ltd;

<small>PATRICK HAMILTON</small>: 'A Final Request' from *Hangover Square*, (Constable, 1941) by permission of Constable and Company Limited;

<small>CLAIRE HARMAN</small>: 'A Sudden Plague' from *Sylvia Townsend Warner: A Biography* (Chatto & Windus, 1989) by permission of A. M. Heath & Co. Ltd;

<small>JOHN HEATH-STUBBS</small>: 'Jeoffrey' from *Cat's Parnassus*, (Hearing Eye, 1987) by permission of David Higham Associates;

<small>MARY WELSH HEMINGWAY</small>: 'The Importance of Sibilants', 'Melons and Chop Suey' and 'Hemingway's Tears' from *How It Was*, (Weidenfeld & Nicolson, 1977) by permission of Weidenfeld & Nicolson Ltd;

<small>PATRICIA HIGHSMITH</small>: 'Ming's Biggest Prey' from *The Animal-Lover's Book of*

T. H. WHITE: 'Boiled Alive' from *The Once and Future King*, (Collins, 1958) by permission of David Higham Associates Limited;

A. N. WILSON: 'A Kitten's Recollections' from *Stray*, copyright © 1987 A. N. Wilson, (Walker Books, 1987) by permission of Walker Books Limited and Orchard Books, New York;

P. G. WODEHOUSE: 'Hooked on Nicotine' from *Over Seventy*, (Herbert Jenkins, 1957) by permission of Random House UK Limited and A. P. Watt Ltd. on behalf of The Trustees of the Wodehouse Estate;

ZOLAR: 'In Sickness and in Health' from *Zolar's Encyclopaedia of Omens, Signs and Superstitions*, (Simon & Schuster, London, 1989) by permission of Simon & Schuster Limited.

Chatto and Windus apologize for any errors or omissions in the above list and would be grateful to be notified of any corrections that should be incorporated in any future edition or reprint of this volume.

INDEX

Kittenhood   Voices   Death   Names   V

Names   Eating   Hatred   Fellow-creature

Magic   Love   Names   Eating

Wisdom

Love   Death   Kittenhood   Hatre

Fellow-creatures   Magic   Love

Names

Death   Kittenhood   Eating   V.

Magic   Names

Love   Voices   Fellow-creatures

Eating   Wisdom   Love   Death

Hatred   Names

Kittenhood   Voices   Fellow-creatures

Love   Death   Eating   Wisdom

Hatred   Kittenhood   Love

Magic

Names   Fellow-creatures   Hatred

Voices   Love   Wisdom   Kittenhood